IFIP Advances in Information and Communication Technolo

IFIP – The International Federation for Information Processing

IFIP was founded in 1960 under the auspices of UNESCO, following the First World Computer Congress held in Paris the previous year. An umbrella organization for societies working in information processing, IFIP's aim is two-fold: to support information processing within its member countries and to encourage technology transfer to developing nations. As its mission statement clearly states,

> *IFIP's mission is to be the leading, truly international, apolitical organization which encourages and assists in the development, exploitation and application of information technology for the benefit of all people.*

IFIP is a non-profitmaking organization, run almost solely by 2500 volunteers. It operates through a number of technical committees, which organize events and publications. IFIP's events range from an international congress to local seminars, but the most important are:

- The IFIP World Computer Congress, held every second year;
- Open conferences;
- Working conferences.

The flagship event is the IFIP World Computer Congress, at which both invited and contributed papers are presented. Contributed papers are rigorously refereed and the rejection rate is high.

As with the Congress, participation in the open conferences is open to all and papers may be invited or submitted. Again, submitted papers are stringently refereed.

The working conferences are structured differently. They are usually run by a working group and attendance is small and by invitation only. Their purpose is to create an atmosphere conducive to innovation and development. Refereeing is less rigorous and papers are subjected to extensive group discussion.

Publications arising from IFIP events vary. The papers presented at the IFIP World Computer Congress and at open conferences are published as conference proceedings, while the results of the working conferences are often published as collections of selected and edited papers.

Any national society whose primary activity is in information may apply to become a full member of IFIP, although full membership is restricted to one society per country. Full members are entitled to vote at the annual General Assembly, National societies preferring a less committed involvement may apply for associate or corresponding membership. Associate members enjoy the same benefits as full members, but without voting rights. Corresponding members are not represented in IFIP bodies. Affiliated membership is open to non-national societies, and individual and honorary membership schemes are also offered.

Wojciech Cellary Elsa Estevez (Eds.)

Software Services for e-World

10th IFIP WG 6.11 Conference
on e-Business, e-Services, and e-Society, I3E 2010
Buenos Aires, Argentina, November 3-5, 2010
Proceedings

Volume Editors

Wojciech Cellary
Poznan University of Economics
Department of Information Technology
Mansfelda 4, 60-854 Poznan, Poland
E-mail: cellary@kti.ue.poznan.pl

Elsa Estevez
The United Nations University
International Institute for Software Technology (UNU-IIST)
Casa Silva Mendes, Est. do Engenheiro Trigo No. 4, P.O. Box 3058
Macao SAR, China
E-mail: elsa@iist.unu.edu

CR Subject Classification (1998): J.1, C.2, H.4, H.3, K.6.5, D.2

ISSN 1868-4238
ISBN-10 3-642-42363-9 Springer Berlin Heidelberg New York
ISBN-13 978-3-642-42363-5 Springer Berlin Heidelberg New York

springer.com

Softcover re-print of the Hardcover 1st edition 2010

Typesetting: Camera-ready by author, data conversion by Scientific Publishing Services, Chennai, India
Printed on acid-free paper 219/3180

Preface

I3E 2010 marked the 10th anniversary of the IFIP Conference on e-Business, e-Services, and e-Society, continuing a tradition that was invented in 1998 during the International Conference on Trends in Electronic Commerce, TrEC 1998, in Hamburg (Germany). Three years later the inaugural I3E 2001 conference was held in Zurich (Switzerland). Since then I3E has made its journey through the world: 2002 Lisbon (Portugal), 2003 Sao Paulo (Brazil), 2004 Toulouse (France), 2005 Poznan (Poland), 2006 Turku (Finland), 2007 Wuhan (China), 2008 Tokyo (Japan), and 2009 Nancy (France).

I3E 2010 took place in Buenos Aires (Argentina) November 3–5, 2010. Known as "The Pearl" of South America, Buenos Aires is a cosmopolitan, colorful, and vibrant city, surprising its visitors with a vast variety of cultural and artistic performances, European architecture, and the passion for tango, coffee places, and football discussions. A cultural reference in Latin America, the city hosts 140 museums, 300 theaters, and 27 public libraries including the National Library. It is also the main educational center in Argentina and home of renowned universities including the University of Buenos Aires, created in 1821. Besides location, the timing of I3E 2010 is also significant—it coincided with the 200th anniversary celebration of the first local government in Argentina.

I3E 2010 provided a forum for researchers and practitioners to present their latest findings in e-business, e-services, and e-society. The submitted contributions addressed challenging issues of Web services and service-oriented architecture, e-transformation of business processes, measuring and assessment of e-services, new e-services for society, social networks, virtual organizations, semantics, trust, and security.

The 56 papers submitted for consideration for publication originated from 30 countries from all over the world: Argentina, Australia, Austria, Brazil, China, Estonia, Finland, France, Germany, Greece, India, Japan, Republic of Korea, Macao SAR, Malaysia, Mexico, New Zealand, Norway, Pakistan, Poland, Portugal, Spain, Sweden, Switzerland, Thailand, United Arab Emirates, UK, USA, Uruguay, and Vietnam.

After a thorough reviewing process, 28 papers were selected for presentation and publication in the proceedings—the acceptance rate was 50%. We are pleased that these proceedings are included in the IFIP AICT series (*IFIP Advances in Information and Communication Technology*) published by Springer and indexed by SCOPUS and ISI Web of Science.

This conference was made possible through the efforts of many people. We wish to thank everyone involved, including those who worked diligently behind the scenes and without formal recognition.

First, we would like to thank IPIP Working Group 6.11 for constant support of the I3E series of conferences and for selecting Buenos Aires to hold the 10th anniversary I3E 2010 conference. We also wish to express our most sincere thanks to the local organizer of I3E 2010, the Argentinean Society of Informatics (SADIO) and its collaborators, whose efforts and enthusiasm made the conference possible. We are most grateful to the key sponsor—National Information Technology Promotion Agency (NIPA), Republic of Korea, and sponsors—International Development Research Centre, Canada (IRDC), and Agencia Nacional de Promoción Científica y Tecnológica (Argentina), whose contributions greatly facilitated the organization of the conference.

We wish to acknowledge the efforts of the whole conference team: General Chair – Ricardo Bruzzi (SADIO), Publication Chair Jacek Chmielewski (Poznan University of Economics, Poland), and Local Organization Chairs Jose Carllini (SADIO), Alejandra Villa (SADIO), and Pablo Villareal (Universidad Tecnológica Nacional, Santa Fe, Argentina). We thank Michal Florczak for new Web design and Ignacio Marcovecchio and Rilwan Basanya for technical support.

We would like to thank the Program Committee members and reviewers for a very rigorous and outstanding reviewing process.

We wish to thank Yanchun Zhang (Victoria University, Australia), Anthony Cresswell (University at Albany, USA), Wim Van Grembergen (University of Antwerp, Belgium), and Winfried Lamersdorf (Hamburg University, Germany) for graciously accepting our invitations to serve as keynote speakers.

We also thank to Pontificia Universidad Catolica Argentina for providing the venues for the conference.

Finally, we thank the attendees for their participation in I3E 2010. We hope they enjoyed the conference and grew professionally and personally.

Wojciech Cellary
Elsa Estevez

Organization

General Chair	Ricardo Bruzzi, Argentina
Program Chairs	Wojciech Cellary, Poland Elsa Estevez, Macao SAR, China
Publication Chair	Jacek Chmielewski, Poland
Steering Committee	Wojciech Cellary, Poland Winfried Lamersdorf, Germany Reima Suomi, Finland
Organization Chair	Pablo Villarreal, Argentina
Financial Chair	Jose Carllinni, Argentina
Registration Chair	Alejandra Villa, Argentina

Program Committee

Antonio Abelém, Brazil
Esma Aimeur, Canada
Joao Paulo Almeida, Brazil
Hernán Astudillo, Chile
Evandro Baccarin, Brazil
Khalid Benali, France
Salima Benbernou, France
Djamal Benslimane, France
Sami Bhiri, Ireland
Markus Bick, Germany
Melanie Bicking, Germany
Omar Boucelma, France
Regis Cabral, Sweden
Gérôme Canals, France
Alejandra Cechich, Argentina
François Charoy, France
Jen-Yao Chung, USA
Bruno Defude, France
Dirk Deschoolmeester, Belgium
Alicia Diaz, Argentina
Toumani Farouk, France
Marie-Christine Fauvet, France
Jesus Favela, Mexico
Fernand Feltz, Luxembourg
Pablo Fillottrani, Argentina
Simone Fischer-Huebner, Sweden
Raúl García-Castro, Spain
Claude Godart, France
Americo Nobre Goncalves Ferreira Amorim, Brazil
Ruediger Grimm, Germany
Adam Grzech, Poland
Adnene Guabtni, Australia
Mohand-Said Hacid, France
Birgit Hofreiter, Austria
Tomasz Janowski, Macao SAR
Marijn Janssen, The Netherlands
Carlos Kamienski, Brazil
Atsushi Kanai, Japan
Ranjan Kini, USA
Dimitri Konstantas, Switzerland
Irene Krebs, Germany
Dennis Kundisch, Germany
Winfried Lamersdorf, Germany
Alain Leger, France
Hongxiu Li, Finland
Heiko Ludwig, USA
Jose Machado, Portugal

Tiziana Margaria, Germany
Hidenori Nakazato, Japan
Jose Neves, Portugal
Andreas Oberweis, Germany
Harri Oinas-Kukkonen, Finland
Boissier Olivier, France
Makoto Oya, Japan
Hervé Panetto, France
Spyridon Papastergiou, Greece
Olivier Perrin, France
Florence Sedes, France
Santosh Shrivastava, UK
Zhaohao Sun, China
Reima Vesa Suomi, Finland
Herve Verjus, France
Jörn von Lucke, Germany
Gottfried Vossen, Germany
Hans Weigand, The Netherlands
Mathias Weske, Germany
Hiroshi Yoshiura, Japan
Hans-Dieter-Zimmermann, Switzerland
Steffen Zimmermann, Austria

Organizing Institution

Key Sponsoring Institution

Sponsoring Institution

Supporting Institutions

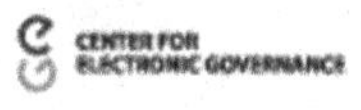

Table of Contents

Abstracts of Keynote Speeches

e-Health: Data Integration, Data Mining, and Knowledge Management in Health Informatics ... 1
Yanchun Zhang

The Public Value of Government ICT Investments: Foundations and Applications ... 2
Anthony Cresswell

From IT Governance to Enterprise Governance of IT: A Journey for Creating Business Value Out of IT ... 3
Wim Van Grembergen

Actual Paradigms of Distributed Software Development: Services and Self Organization ... 4
Winfried Lamersdorf

Session 1: Web Services and SOA

Middleware for the Autonomous Web Services (AWS) ... 5
Makoto Oya, Masaki Ito, and Taisuke Kimura

Dynamic Resources Allocation for Delivery of Personalized Services ... 17
Adam Grzech, Paweł Świątek, and Piotr Rygielski

Mobile Interfaces for Building Control Surveyors ... 29
Jacek Chmielewski, Krzysztof Walczak, and Wojciech Wiza

Session 2: e-Transformation and Business Processes

An Agent-Based B2B Collaboration Platform for Executing Collaborative Business Processes ... 40
Edgar Tello-Leal, Omar Chiotti, and Pablo D. Villarreal

Compound Web Service for Supply Processes Monitoring to Anticipate Disruptive Event ... 51
Erica Fernández, Enrique Salomone, and Omar Chiotti

Bridging the Gaps between eTransforming SMEs and SME - ICT Providers ... 61
Ana Hol and Athula Ginige

Session 3: Measuring and Assessment

Measuring Accumulated Revelations of Private Information by Multiple Media 70
Komei Kamiyama, Tran Hong Ngoc, Isao Echizen, and Hiroshi Yoshiura

A Methodology to Assess the Benefits of Smart Order Routing 81
Bartholomäus Ende, Peter Gomber, Marco Lutat, and Moritz C. Weber

Ontology-Based Evaluation of ISO 27001 93
Danijel Milicevic and Matthias Goeken

Session 4: e-Services for Society

The Importance of Confirming Citizens' Expectations in e-Government 103
Daniel Belanche, Luis V. Casaló, and Carlos Flavián

E-Democracy and Network Externalities – The Case of Websites of Finnish Members of Parliament 112
Reima Suomi

Educateca: A Web 2.0 Approach to e-Learning with SCORM 118
Rebeca P. Díaz Redondo, Ana Fernández Vilas, and Jose J. Pazos Arias

Session 5: Specifications and Semantics

Achieving Meaning Understanding in E-Marketplace through Document Sense Disambiguation 127
Jingzhi Guo and Guangyi Xiao

Automatically Detecting Opportunities for Web Service Descriptions Improvement 139
Juan Manuel Rodriguez, Marco Crasso, Alejandro Zunino, and Marcelo Campo

Exploiting the Social Capital of Folksonomies for Web Page Classification 151
Daniela Godoy and Analía Amandi

Session 6: Social Networks and Virtual Organizations

Guidelines to Transform Industry Clusters in Virtual Organization Breeding Environments – A Case Study 161
Fabiano Baldo and Ricardo J. Rabelo

A Research Framework on Social Networking Sites Usage: Critical Review and Theoretical Extension 173
Kathy Ning Shen and Mohamed Khalifa

A Digital Platform for Marketing Communications in the Mobile and Social Media Space 182
Otto Petrovic

Session 7: e-Services

Reusing Geographic E-Services: A Case Study in the Marine Ecological Domain 193
Patricia Pernich, Agustina Buccella, Alejandra Cechich, Maria del Socorro Doldan, and Enrique Morsan

Ontology-Based Process for Recommending Health WebSites 205
Edelweis Rohrer, Regina Motz, and Alicia Díaz

A Morphological Box for Handling Temporal Data in B2C Systems 215
Gerhard F. Knolmayer and Alessandro Borean

Session 8: Trust and Security

Trust and Privacy Enabled Service Composition Using Social Experience 226
Shahab Mokarizadeh, Nima Dokoohaki, Mihhail Matskin, and Peep Küngas

Trust and Compliance Management Models in Emerging Outsourcing Environments 237
Aljosa Pasic, Juan Bareño, Beatriz Gallego-Nicasio, Rubén Torres, and Daniel Fernandez

Security Architecture of Smart Metering Systems 249
Natasa Zivic and Christoph Ruland

Session 9: ICT Utilization

IT Alignment in the 3PL Industry: A Comparative Study 260
Kwok Hung Lau

Against All Odds - A Story of a Successful Mobile System Acceptance among a Tough Crowd 272
Jonna Järveläinen and Annukka Vahtera

Critical Success Factors of Open Markets on the Internet in Terms of Buyers 282
Sung Ho Ha and Luo Tao Liu

Service Oriented Approach for Autonomous Exception Management in Supply Chains 292
Armando Guarnaschelli, Omar Chiotti, and Enrique Salomone

Author Index 305

e-Health: Data Integration, Data Mining, and Knowledge Management in Health Informatics

Yanchun Zhang

Centre for Applied Informatics & School of Engineering and Science
Victoria University, Australia
yanchun.zhang@vu.edu.au

Abstract of a Keynote Speech. In last few decades, with the advent of database systems and networking technologies, a huge volume of health data and valuable medical knowledge have been electronically available, accessible and processible, especially over the virtual cyberspace – the Web, even from a remote corner in the world. Nowadays the wide deployment of Hospital Information Management Systems (HIMS) and Web based clinical or medical systems, for example, the Medical Director, a generic GP clinical system, have made it possible to record, disseminate and implement the health information and clinical practices easily and globally. And health care and medical service is becoming more data-intensive and evidence-based since electronic health records are used to track individuals' and communities' health information (particularly changes). These substantially motivate and advance the emergence and the progress of data-centric health data and knowledge management research and practice, for example, *Health Informatics*.

In this presentation, we will introduce several case studies and research projects to address the challenges encountered in health service. These include data exchange and health service Integration in health information systems, health information visualisation, data mining and data analyse for patient care management. We will then introduce a framework of data integration, knowledge management and user behaviour modelling for complementing and improving existing health care and service systems.

W. Cellary and E. Estevez (Eds.): I3E 2010, IFIP AICT 341, p. 1, 2010.

The Public Value of Government ICT Investments: Foundations and Applications

Anthony Cresswell

Center for Technology in Government
University at Albany, USA
tcresswell@ctg.albany.edu

Abstract of a Keynote Speech. This paper discusses the concept of public value in relation to government ICT investment from three perspectives -- theory foundations, assessment methods, and an application example. The discussion of theory foundations combines attention to the roots of the concept of public value in political philosophy and public administration. The origins of the concept of public value are discussed in terms of foundational ideas in political and moral philosophy about the nature of the good society: utilitarianism and the social contract. The concern with public value, or utility, in early Western moral and political philosophy is central to the two major schools of thought, utilitarian and social contractarian. The social order that produces the greatest good or utility for the greatest number is preferred in the utilitarian perspective. The contractarian view holds that a good society should be based on shared principles and arrangements that avoid the potential evils of unconstrained greed. Though these two views political and moral philosophy differ, they weave similar connections among the basic concept of value, individual interests, societal interests, and institutional forms. These concepts and connections are basic to the public value framework .

The framework links value to the workings of government in terms of individual and group interests in relation to government policies and programs. this view is reflected in recent thinking in public administration, particularly in the public value program described by Moore (1995). In Moore's terms, "value is rooted in the desires and perceptions of individuals—not necessarily in physical transformations, and not abstractions called societies." (p. 52) Moore includes both public sector production, i.e., "things of value to particular clients and beneficiaries," and "establishing and operating an institution that meets citizens' (and their representatives') desires for properly ordered and productive public institutions." (Moore, 1995:53)

These foundational ideas then form the basis for an assessment method and framework designed to operationalize and provide useful data about the public value outcomes of government investment decisions. The paper presents a description of the assessment framework, followed by an example of how the method applies to a specific ICT investment in a government human service program. A discussion of the implications of the public value framework for investment and performance assessment concludes the paper.

W. Cellary and E. Estevez (Eds.): I3E 2010, IFIP AICT 341, p. 2, 2010.

From IT Governance to Enterprise Governance of IT: A Journey for Creating Business Value Out of IT

Wim Van Grembergen

University of Antwerp (UA)
University of Antwerp Management School (UAMS)
IT Alignment and Governance (ITAG) Research Institute
wim.vangrembergen@ua.ac.be

Abstract of a Keynote Speech. IT governance is one of those concepts that suddenly emerged and became an important issue in IT. In academic and professional literature, articles mentioningIT governance in the title began to emerge during the late 1990s. In the context of the leading academic HICSS conference, it was defined as the organizational capacity exercised by the board, executive management and IT management, to control the formulation and implementation of IT strategy and in this way ensure the fusion of business and IT.

After the emergence of the IT governance concepts, the notion received a lot of attention. However, due to the focus on "IT" in the naming, the IT governance discussion mainly remained a discussion within IT. Many IT governance implementations are still mainly an issue "within IT", while one would expect that the business would and should take a leading role here as well.

It is clear that business value from IT investments cannot only be realized through its use of IT capabilities. For example, there will be no business value created when IT delivers a new customer relationship management (CRM) application on time, on budget, and to specification if the business has not made the necessary changes to the business model, business processes, organizational structures, people competencies, and the reward system required to effectively integrate the new IT system into its business operations. IT-enabled investments should therefore always be treated as business programs, composed of a collection of business and IT projects delivering all the capabilities required to create and sustain business value.

This discussion clarifies the need for the business to take ownership of, and be accountable for, governing the use of IT in creating value from IT-enabled business investments. It also implies a crucial shift in the minds of the business and IT, moving away from managing IT as a "cost" toward managing IT as an "asset" to create business value. Acknowledging the prime accountability of the business in value creation initiated a shift in the definition of IT governance, focusing on the business involvement, toward "enterprise governance of IT" (instead of IT governance).

W. Cellary and E. Estevez (Eds.): I3E 2010, IFIP AICT 341, p. 3, 2010.

Actual Paradigms of Distributed Software Development: Services and Self Organization

Winfried Lamersdorf

Distributed Systems (VSIS), Informatics Department
University of Hamburg, Germany
Winfried.Lamersdorf@informatik.uni-hamburg.de

Abstract of a Keynote Speech. State-of-the-art development of distributed software systems is, among other software development techniques, fundamentally based on the paradigm of distributed "software services". Such services may already exist or may be newly developed for specific application purposes. They are able to interact – also in open and heterogeneous distributed software environments – based on standardised interfaces and inter-connection protocols as, e.g., provided by related "Web Services" standards.

On the application side, a service-based software development paradigm reflects directly modern (e.g. business) scenarios which are increasingly structured as sets of distributed co-operating entities. Such applications often involve many and heterogeneous services from various sources – both internally as well as from external sources. Based on such elementary services, "business procedures" implement more complex business semantics by composing services – even in dynamically changing environments – according to predefined (functional as well as non-functional) application needs.

If, finally, such service become more "independent" and act "autonomously" in order to achieve given (abstract) goals and characteristics, services as well as business procedures may increasingly become "self-organised" according to another actual distributed software paradigm.

Based on such an approach, the EU Network of Excellence on "Software Services and Systems" (S-Cube) coordinates and conducts European research in the area of service-oriented development of distributed software and applications. It aims at establishing agile and holistic service engineering and adaptation principles, techniques and methods to foster innovation for preparing new service technologies integration by establish a unified and multidisciplinary research community.

W. Cellary and E. Estevez (Eds.): I3E 2010, IFIP AICT 341, p. 4, 2010.

Middleware for the Autonomous Web Services (AWS)

Makoto Oya, Masaki Ito, and Taisuke Kimura

Shonan Institute of Technology, 1-1-25, Tsujido Nishi-Kaigan, Fujisawa, 251-8511, Japan

Abstract. The purpose of the Autonomous Web Services (AWS) is to enable business transaction exchange in the Internet between systems having different business process models, by dynamically harmonizing them when the systems encounter. Based on the principles and the basic methods proposed in the previous researches such as [3], we succeeded in development of the experimental implementation of the AWS middleware. The AWS middleware consists of three software layers - the dynamic model harmonization layer, the application framework layer, and the messaging layer. This paper mentions the development principles, operation concepts, proposed specifications, detailed algorithms and test results of the AWS middleware that we developed. This success of implementation demonstrates the AWS's theoretical properness and its availability to real world applications, as well as the applicability of the improved model harmonization algorithm proposed in this paper.

Keywords: Web Services, autonomy, business process model, e-commerce.

1 Introduction

The Web services is a well matured technology and widely used as the infrastructure for business transaction exchange between systems over the Internet. In the present Web services, it is prerequisite that a global business process model across relevant systems, like BPEL [6], is precisely defined in advance, and each system is built conforming to the global business process model (Fig.1 (a)). Therefore, a voluntarily and freely built system cannot participate in the concerning service. This prerequisite is very strong and not appropriate for ordinary business transactions except large scale or fixed form transactions. The Autonomous Web Services (AWS), whose concept was defined in [3], does not assume the existence of a predefined global business process model. It dynamically harmonizes (i.e. adjusts each other) business process models in individual systems when the systems encountered in the Internet (Fig.1 (b)). The AWS aims to realize that systems independently built and having different business models can freely exchange business transactions.

The AWS's theoretical backbone is the Dynamic Model Harmonization (DMH), proposed in [1][2], and systematized in [3]. In addition, the AWS's core technologies include the application framework based on model driven execution and the messaging mechanism as their infrastructure. Based on these preceding research results, we succeeded in development of the experimental implementation of the AWS middleware

W. Cellary and E. Estevez (Eds.): I3E 2010, IFIP AICT 341, pp. 5–16, 2010.

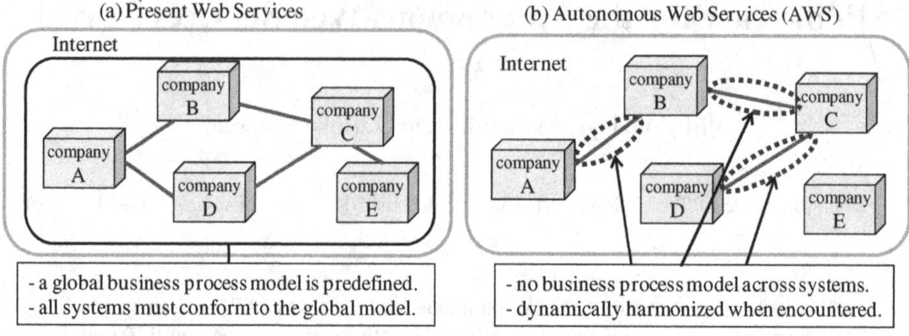

Fig. 1. Present Web Services and the Autonomous Web Services (AWS)

The purpose of the AWS middleware is to execute the AWS's complex mechanism hiding the implementation details from applications. It enables application developers easy to develop AWS applications only by coding business logics corresponding to input/output operations.

The structure of this paper is: Section 2 surveys the core technologies of the AWS in the previous works. It also contains a newly improved DMH algorithm. Section 3 is the main part of this paper and explains the development principle, operation concepts, specifications and detailed algorithm of the AWS middleware that we developed. Section 4 provides brief discussions and conclusions.

2 Essences of the Autonomous Web Services (AWS)

This section surveys the theoretical background and principles of the AWS. It also proposes the improved DMH algorithm.

2.1 Dynamic Model Harmonization (DMH)

The core principle of the AWS is the DMH (Dynamic Model Harmonization) (Fig.2). Systems export own business process models (BPMs). A BPM is a description of possible flow of input and output message sequences. An example is "ask estimation, and receive the estimation results, then, order, and receive its acceptance". The BPMs of both systems are exchanged when the systems encounter over the Internet. By the DMH algorithm, the original BPM is modified adjusting with the opponent's BPM. Then, the business transaction exchange starts using the modified BPM (called the harmonized BPM). In this way, business conversation between systems having different BPMs is executed with best efforts.

BPM is formally defined as BPM = (O, B), where:

- O is a set of *operations op*, where *op* = (*pattern*, *format*), a *pattern* specifies 'output' or 'input', and a *format* specifies a format of message, and

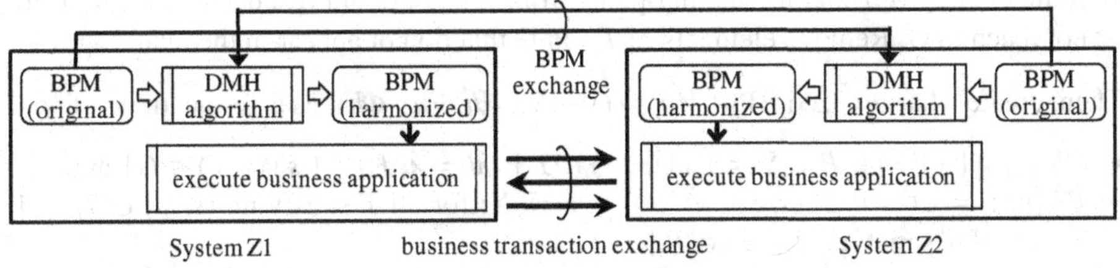

Fig. 2. Overview of the Dynamic Model Harmonization

- A *behavior B* is, in general, represented as a finite state machine, namely: $B = (S, \lambda, F, \Phi)$, where S is a set of states, λ ($\in S$) is a starting status, F ($\subset S$) is a set of final states, and Φ is a transition function.

Note that O corresponds to "interface" or "portType" in WSDL [8], and *pattern* corresponds to the MEP (message exchange pattern) though restricted 'input only' and 'output only'.

As discussed in [3], we assume a three-valued matching function t_match(f, g) is given from the outer environment, where f is an output and g is an input format, and

t_match(f, g) = true (if all instances of f match to g), or
false (if some instance of f does not match to g), or
undefined (if cannot determine either true or false).

Variety of implementation of t_match() is possible. A trivial one is: true if $f = g$ and false if $f \neq g$ when both f and g are in a same name space, and undefined when f and g are in different name spaces. This trivial t_match() is used at testing the middleware in this research. Implementation of t_match() is out of scope of this paper but another interesting research theme. Solutions applying ontology or semantic web have been proposed [2][5][4]. At the same time, it is valuable to report that the DMH properly harmonizes BPMs even in cases when such a simple t_match() is applied.

In this paper, we limit a behavior B is a non-deterministic automaton, as the previous studies did. Under this limitation, Φ is restricted as $S \times O \rightarrow S$. We introduced the following DMH algorithm improved from the previous researches [1][3].

Let an original BPM of the own system be M and a BPM received from the opponent system be M', where $M = (O, (S, \lambda, F, \Phi))$ and $M' = (O', (S', \lambda', F', \Phi'))$. First, create $N = (P, (T, \mu, G, \Gamma))$ in the following steps:

- $P = \{ (o, o') \mid o \in O$ and $o' \in O'$ and o_match(o, o') $\neq$ false$\}$, where o_match(o, o') is t_match(fo, fo') if o is output and o' is input, and t_match(fo', fo) if o is input and o' is output, and false if both o and o' are input or output. (fo and fo' are formats of o and o' respectively.)
- $T = S \times S'$, $\mu = (\lambda, \lambda')$, $G = F \times F'$.
- $\Gamma((s, s'), (o, o')) = \Phi(s, o) \times \Phi'(s', o')$, where $(s, s') \in T$ and $(o, o') \in P$.

- Remove all $\tau \in T$ and its relating paths from Γ that are not reachable from μ or do not reach to G. Remove elements of T and G that do not appear in the resulting Γ.

Then, create a harmonized BPM $Mh = (Oh, (Sh, \lambda h, Fh, \Phi h))$ as a "projection" of N:

- $Oh = \{ o \mid (o, o') \in P \}$, $Sh = (s \mid (s, s') \in T \}$, $\lambda h = \lambda$, $Fh = \{ s \mid (s, s') \in G\}$ and
- $\Phi h(s, o) = \cup^{X} \cup^{Y} \Gamma((s, s'), (o, o'))$ [where X: for all s' satisfying $(s, s') \in T$, and Y: for all o' satisfying $(o, o') \in P$.]

2.2 Model Driven Application Execution

As a consequence of BPM modification, the control flow of the application program must also be modified. The second problem is how to handle this situation. The following solution has been proposed in [3]:

- A user develops an application program as a set of process units (called AP segments) corresponding to each input/output operation.
- The AWS middleware successively transits a status of the harmonized BPM, and invokes an AP segment corresponding to an input/output operation at the current status. (see Fig.3)

2.3 Messaging Mechanism with VL Session

The third problem is on infrastructure to perform message exchange over the Internet/Web. It is well known that peer-to-peer asynchronous messaging is most appropriate for business message exchange. Many studies have been done and the protocol for Web services has already been standardized [9]. In addition to these well-known technologies, [3] has pointed out the necessity to manage very long sessions (VL sessions) and endurable queues. Fig.3 illustrates information flow from the DMH to peer-to-peer message sending/receiving through a VL session.

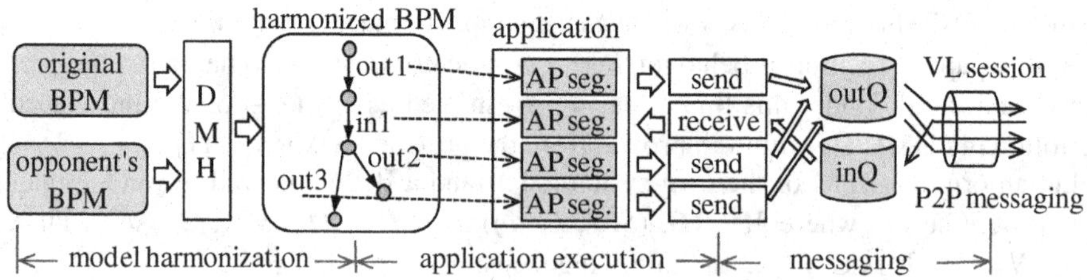

Fig. 3. DMH, Application Execution, and Messaging

3 AWS Middleware

This is the main part of this paper, explaining the development principles, operation concepts, specifications and detailed algorithms of the AWS middleware that we developed.

The purpose of the AWS middleware is to execute the AWS's complex mechanisms such as BPM modification, application flow modification and message sending/receiving protocol, and to hide such AWS's implementation details from application programs. Thus, an application developer can easily develop an AWS application that performs a series of transaction exchange in the AWS's way, only by describing a BPM and coding business logics corresponding to input/output operations. The AWS middleware consists of three software layers, the model harmonization layer, the application framework layer, and the messaging layer, which respectively correspond to the three phases in Fig.3.

3.1 Model Harmonization Layer

As Fig.3 shows, the role of the model harmonization layer is to get an original BPM description and an opponent's BPM description, execute the DMH algorithm, and generate a harmonized BPM. The harmonized BPM is passed to the application framework layer as a Java object, not as an external description. The issues on implementing the model harmonization layer were (a) a format of BPM description, (b) implementation of the DMH algorithm, and (c) a specification of a BPM object passed to the application framework layer. (b) was realized by implementing the algorithm in 2.1. The solutions to (a) and (c) are mentioned below in this section.

3.1.1 BPM Description

We adopted XML encoding to describe a BPM, considering consistency with other Web technologies. BPM is formally defined as (O, B). O is a set of operations, which corresponds to a portType or an interface in WSDL. We introduce BPM description syntax for O simplifying the WSDL syntax. As for a behavior B, two types of description are considered - (i) in a state transition table form, (ii) in a regular expression form. (i) is a simple way and has a merit relationship between AP segments and an application control flow is simplified, but has a demerit a description tends to be long. On the other hand, (ii) realizes a short description and easy to understand, but has a problem timings of AP segment invocation are not explicit and may have difficulty in programming AP segment codes. Therefore, we adopted both types of description. Users can choose either convenient description type depending on the application. Fig.4 shows an example of BPM description in two types.

3.1.2 BPM Object

A BPMS is internally represented by a Java object. Several methods are prepared to a BPM object for access in the framework layer. Important are init() to reset the current status to the initial status, getNextOps() to return an array of possible next operations when transits from the current status, and transit(*op*) to transit to the next status from the current status after executing an operation *op*. getNextOps() simply returns a set of next possible operations and does not causes state transition. When more than two operations are next possible, a desired operation can be selected by setNextOperations()

(a) State transition table type description

```
<BPModel>
  ..operations description, same as (b)..
<behavior>
<states>
  <state no="0">
   <next operation=" AskEstim">1</next>
  </state>
  <state no="1">
   <next operation ="RecEstim">2</next>
  </state>
  <state no="2">
   <next operation= ="Order">3</next>
   <next operation="Cancel">4</next>
  </state>
  <state no="3">
   <next operation= ="RecAccept">4</next>
  </state>
  <state no="4"></state>
 </states>
 <first>0</first>
 <last>4</last>
</behavior>
</BPModel>
```

(b) Regular expression type description

```
<BPModel>
<operations>
  <operation name="AskEstim" format="Est01">
    <pattern>output</pattern> </operation>
  <operation name="RecEstim" format="Rep01">
   <pattern>input</pattern></operation>
  .....
</operations>
<behavior>
  <atom operation="AskEstim"/>
  <atom operation="RecEstim"/>
  <choice>
    <sequence>
      <atom operation="Order"/>
      <atom operation="RecAccept"/>
    </sequence>
    <atom operation="Cancel"/>
  </choice>
</behavior>
</BPModel>
```

Fig. 4. Two Types of BPM Description

by the AP segment. Note that a special operation 'term' is returned when the current status is final. Fig.5 shows an example of status transitions by transit() and operation sequences returned by getNextOps().

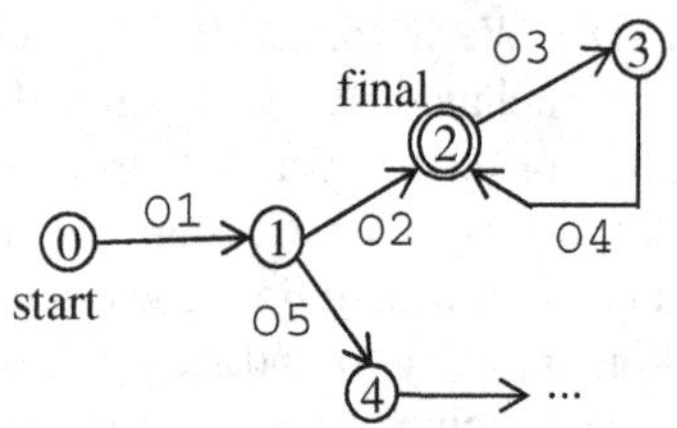

transition	state	NextOps
init()	0	O1
transit(O1)	1	O2, O5
transit(O2)	2	O3, 'term'
transit(O3)	3	O4
transit(O4)	2	O3, 'term'
transit('term')	-	-

Fig. 5. Example of State Transition and Next Possible Operations

3.2 Application Framework Layer

The application framework layer controls the application execution flow driven by the harmonized BPM object, and performs the message input/output and the format translation in place of the application program. At the same time, it hides the AWS's underlining complex mechanism from application programs. This section mentions what functions are prepared for application developers and how these functions are realized inside the framework.

3.2.1 Functions Prepared for Application Development

The body of the application framework layer is a class AWSFramework. A developer creates an application class inheriting AWSFramework. Section 2.2 explains an application is created as a set of AP segments. We implemented an AP segment as a Java method (called an AP method). To develop an application, a developer codes Java methods in an application class corresponding to each operation in the original BPM. Fig.6 is an example of application. This class contains three AP methods, apOrder(), apResponse() and apPay(). Only by writing such a simple program, the AWSFramework invokes an appropriate AP method along with state transition of the harmonized BPM, and behind performs complicated tasks including sending/receiving messages.

```
public class Ap extends AWSFramework {
   public void apOrder(OrderData out) {
      out.item = 'TV-45001'; out.qty = 6; }
   public void apResponse(ResResult in) {
      /* process delivery date (in.date) and price(in.price) */ }
   public void apPay(PaymentData out) {
      out.payDate = payment date; }
   publc Boolean dMatch(String data, Format format) {
      /* check whether data matches with format */ }
}
```

Fig. 6. Example of Application Program

We introduced a XML format "config" file to specify a mapping between operations and AP methods, considering the separation of protocol and programming [3]. Fig.7 is an example of config file corresponding to the program in Fig.6.

```
<operation name="Order"> <method>apOrder</method>
  <parameter>OrderData</parameter> </operation>
<operation name="Response"> <method>apResponse</method>
  <parameter>ResResult</parameter> </operation>
<operation name="Payment"> <method>apPay</method>
  <parameter>PaymentData</parameter> </operation>
```

Fig. 7. Example of Config File

A config file also includes classes to encapsulate details of message data format encoding, called a container class. In Fig.6 for example, AP methods (apOrder, apResponse and apPay) receives container classes (OrderData, ResResult and PaymentData) instead of message texts themselves. Container classes, coded by an application developer, must implement generateMessage() that generates a message text from a container object, and purseMessage() that creates contents of a container object from a message text. AWSFramework invokes them when performs message input/output. Two other methods, initialize() and terminate(), can be included in an application class. They are invoked right after the VL session starts and right before the VL session terminates. In addition, a special method dMatch() must be included which determines whether a message text matches with a given format.

3.2.2 Execution Mechanism in the Framework

The model harmonization layer passes a harmonized BPM objet to the AWSFramework. Successively transiting a status of the BPM object, the AWSFramework selects an appropriate AP method and invokes it with its container object cObj as a parameter. Fig.7 is a pseudo code outlining the process inside the AWSFramework.

```
(vlSession = new VLSession()).start();

bpm.init();
nextOps = bpm.getNextOps().clone();
invoke('initialize');

while(nextOps[0]!='term') {
    if(nextOps.length==1 and getPattern(nextOps[0])=='output')
{
        op=nextOps[0];
        bpm.transit(op);
        nextOps = bpm.getNextOps().clone();
        cObj = genContainerObj(op);
        invoke(getMethod(op),cObj);
        mess = cObj.generateMessage();
        vlSession.send(mess);
    }
    else if(getPattern(op)=='input' for(op:nextOps)) {
        mess = vlSession.receive();
        for(op:nextOps) if(dMatch(getFormat(op),mess)) break;
        bpm.transit(op);
        nextOps = bpm.getNextOps().clone();
        cObj = genContainerObj(op);
        cObj.purseMessage(mess);
        invoke(getMethod(op),cObj);
    }
}
invoke('terminate');
vlSession.terminate();

public getNextOperation() {return nextOps;}
public setNextOperation(ops) {nextOps = ops.clone();}
```

Fig. 8. Processing inside the AWSFramework

After generating and starting a VL session object, setting the status of bpm to the initial status, and invoking initialize(), it enters the main loop transiting the status using bpm.transit(). nextOps in Fig.7 is an array containing next operations. 'term' is set in nextOps if the current status is final. The default value of nextOps is bpm.getNextOps(), a sequence of operations that may occur from the current status. When the length of nextOps is 1 (that is, when next operation is deterministic), or when the length is >1 but all operation patterns are 'input', the next operation(s) are executable. Otherwise, the AP method can restrict possible operations using setNextOperation(). The first "if" clause in the main loop in Fig.7 is the process for 'output' operation and the second "else-if" clause is for 'input'. In the case of 'output', after generating a container object and invoking the AP method, it sends a message text created by generateMessage() by the send() method provided by the messaging layer. In the case of 'input', it first receives a message and determines a corresponding operation op using dMatch(), then injects data into a container object using purseMessage() and invokes the concerning AP method. Note that getMethod(), getContainerObj(), getPattern() and getFormat() are the methods to access the config information, which respectively return the corresponding AP method object, the container class object, the pattern ('input' or 'output') and the format name.

3.3 Messaging Layer

3.3.1 Peer-to Peer Asynchronous Messaging with VL Session

The mechanism of the messaging layer is completely hidden from applications. It provides the peer-to-peer, asynchronous, reliable and stored-forward-type messaging feature between application endpoints to the upper layer. A long term lasting session called a VL session is established between applications from the beginning to the end of a series of transactions (see Fig.3). The VL session is the concept introduced in [3]. The interface from the application framework layer is designed simple - just to use concise methods to a VL session object, e.g., start(), send, receive() and terminate().

3.3.2 Underlying System Configuration and Protocol

The messaging layer supports two types of underlying configuration of systems - a configuration (called a symmetric configuration) where both sides of system have Web servers (Fig. 9), and a configuration (called an asymmetric configuration) where only one side has a Web server (Fig. 10). The former is for usual business transaction exchange between ordinal enterprises, and the latter is for smaller configurations such as for a SME (small and medium enterprise) or a mobile system. In the symmetric configuration, a message data retrieved from the output queue (outQ in the figures) is sent by a HTTP request, and the HTTP response simply acknowledges the results. In the asymmetric configuration, the way of sending a message data from the side without a Web server (system A in Fig.10) to the side with a Web server (system B in Fig.10) is same as the symmetric configuration, but different when sending a message from system B to system A. System A, time to time, sends to system B a HTTP request asking download, and receives message data associated with the HTTP response if outQ in system B has data to be sent.

The messaging protocol was implemented over HTTP and SOAP/Framework, as a simplified form of the ebXML Messaging standard [9]. The reason this standard is not directly applied is that the standard specification is too big and having unnecessary functions for this experimental implementation, and we needed some modification to permit plural number of downloading to improve performance of reliable messaging.

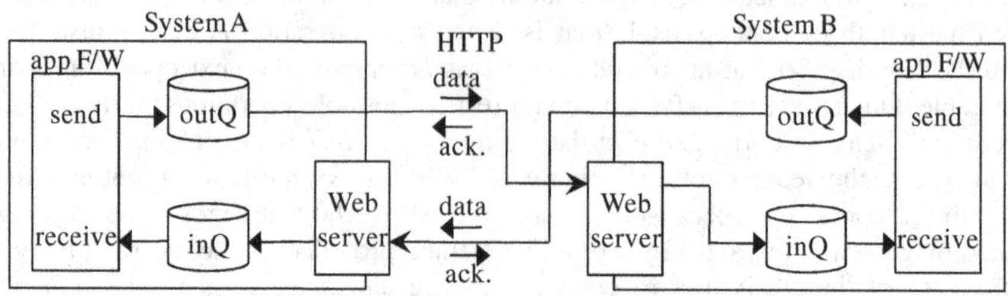

Fig. 9. Symmetric System Configuration

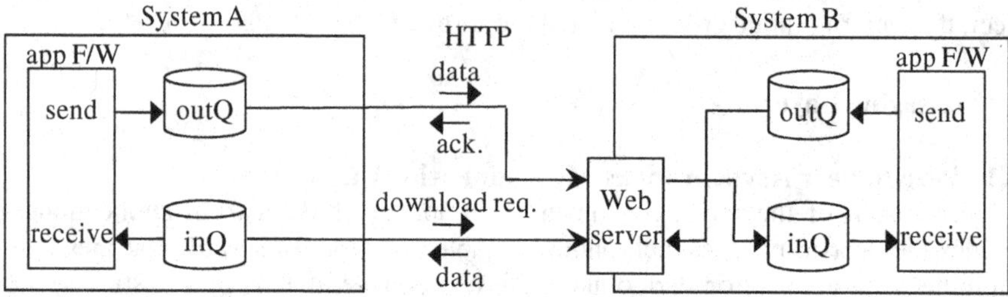

Fig. 10. Asymmetric System Configuration

In addition, the followings were considered at implementing the messaging layer.

- Implementation of queues: Taking account of durability, queues were implemented upon DBMS (PostgreSQL). Eight tables are defined, enabling the retry control and the messaging sequence assurance required in reliable messaging.
- Asynchronization and performance: Multi process/thread structure is applied.
- VL session management: It is a policy of the AWS that no global server manages a session across systems. Therefore, a VL session is managed in individual systems cooperating with each other. A session ID, for example, is generated in conjunction with an opponent system's algorithm.

4 Discussion and Conclusions

4.1 Discussion

The implementation was done using Java. After completing basic software tests, we evaluate the developed AWS middleware from two viewpoints, artificial tests and benchmark tests. In the former viewpoint, theoretically comprehensive BPMs are created and the appropriateness and functionality of the the AWS middleware are verified and evaluated. On the other hand, benchmark tests (Table.1 shows some of them) are created simulating real trading applications and evaluate its availability. A portion of artificial and benchmark tests has been completed by now, and it was confirmed that the implementation of each layer is appropriate and properly works, and the introduced specifications are adequate and enough encapsulate the implementation details.

Table 1. Benchmark Tests (Samples)

Simple01	Basic transaction
Simple02	Multiple step transaction
Fork01	Transaction with a simple branching
Fork02	Multiple branching transaction
Loop01	Simple looping business process
Loop02	Composite looping business process

Let us evaluate the topics of the each layer this paper mentions. We proposed and developed two types of BPM description (see 3.1.1). This provides to application developers free choice of convenient way of description. The proposed specification of the application framework layer (3.2.1) is evaluated through testing as appropriate, and makes an application program codes simpler (such as in Fig.6). AP methods realized as Java methods are automatically invoked by the framework, and input/output data passed to/from applications are encapsulated. The executions mechanism in the framework (mentioned in 3.2.2) was verified through this experimental implementation and testing. At the same time, it was found that more study is necessary in cases an application consists of many processes and/or threads. Several considerations were done at implementing the messaging layer (as mentioned in 3.3), the properness of the solutions was verified through this development.

4.2 Conclusions

Basic ideas and theories of the AWS are the DMH, the application framework based on model driven execution, and the messaging mechanism as their infrastructure. In this study, we implemented the middleware for the AWS. The success of this experimental development proves properness and availability of these ideas, theories and relating technologies. The developed AWS middleware provides the full basic functionality of AWS, and hides the complex implementation details from application programs. The ultimate goal of the AWS is to provide the next generation Web services infrastructure enabling free and flexible business transaction exchanges among independently built autonomously managed systems. Future issues include the dynamic model harmonization among more than three systems, enhancement of capability of a state machine in a behavior, implementation of improved t_match() applying ontology for example, implementation of parallel business processes execution, and security.

Acknowledgement

This implementation was done with cooperation of our students: Hiroteru Otomo, Masamichi Hiramoto, and Kyohei Yoshikawa. This work was supported by the Grant-in-Aid for scientific Research, KAKENHI (21500110).

References

[1] Oya, M., et al.: On Dynamic Generation of Business Protocols in Autonomous Web Services. IEICE Transaction on Information and Systems J87-D-I(8), 824–832 (2004) (in Japanese); Systems and Computers in Japan, vol. 37(2), pp. 37–45. Wiley, Chichester (2006)

[2] Oya, M., Ito, M.: Dynamic Model Harmonization between Unknown eBusiness Systems. In: IFIP I3E, pp. 389–403. Springer, Heidelberg (2005), ISBN:0-387-28753-1

[3] Oya, M.: Autonomous Web Services Based on Dynamic Harmonization. In: IFIP I3E, pp. 139–150. Springer, Heidelberg (September 2008), ISBN:978-0-387-8590-2

[4] Sycara, K., Paolucci, M., Ankolekar, A., Srinivasan, N.: Automatic Discovery, Interaction and Composition of Semantic Web Services. Journal of Web Semantics 1(1), 27–46 (2003)

[5] Martino, B.: An Ontology Matching Approach to Semantic Web Services Discovery. In: Min, G., Di Martino, B., Yang, L.T., Guo, M., Rünger, G. (eds.) ISPA Workshops 2006. LNCS, vol. 4331, pp. 550–558. Springer, Heidelberg (2006)

[6] Chabeb, Y., Tata, S., Belaid, D.: Toward an integrated ontology for web services. In: Proc. of ICIW 2009, Art. no. 5072561, pp. 462–467 (2009)

[7] Oya, M., Ito, M., Tsukamoto, S., Takagi, R., Kimura, T.: AWS, Autonomous Web Services and its Middleware. In: IPSJ 71st Conference Proceedings, pp. 1-503–1-504 (2009) (in Japanese)

[8] Chinnici, R., et al.: Web Services Description Language (WSDL) Version 2.0, W3C Recommendation (2007)

[9] OASIS, ebXML Messaging Services Version 3.0, OASIS Standard (2007)

[10] OASIS, Web Services Business Process Execution Language Version 2.0, OASIS Standard (2007)

[11] Miller, J., et al.: MDA Guide Version 1.0.1, OMG doc. omg/2003-06-01 (2003)

Dynamic Resources Allocation for Delivery of Personalized Services

Adam Grzech, Paweł Świątek, and Piotr Rygielski

Institute of Computer Science
Wroclaw University of Technology
Wybrzeze Wyspianskiego 27
50-370 Wroclaw, Poland
{adam.grzech,pawel.swiatek,piotr.rygielski}@pwr.wroc.pl

Abstract. The aim of this paper is to introduce a problem of e-health services quality management. The process of delivering e-health services to users consists of two major tasks: service personalization and resources allocation. In this paper we introduce a use-cases of e-health system and distinguish services that can be offered. In order to satisfy user requirements one have to manage resources properly especially when communication conditions change (e.g. in an ambulance). An exemplary solution has been presented and conclusions for further work have been formulated.

Keywords: e-Health, Service Oriented Architecture (SOA), service composition, quality of service (QoS), remote monitoring.

1 Introduction

Advances in information and communication technologies allow health service providers to offer e-services in virtually every aspect of health care. The collection of e-health services facilitated by current and future ICT architectures ranges from remote health monitoring, through computer-aided diagnosis, video-consultation, health education, remote surgery and many others [9,11].

Each of possible e-health services is a composition of atomic services provided by either ICT infrastructure or medical personnel. In some scenarios medical personnel can be both service provider and service consumer. Delivery of complex services as a composition of atomic services is the key feature of service oriented architecture (SOA) paradigm [10]. Application of SOA approach in e-health services delivery allows to personalize and flexibly adjust services to individual needs of service consumers.

It also allows to take into account changes in services environment; variable amount of resources implies necessity to reduce amount of services as well as quality of delivered services.

It is assumed that the set of available and required services is known. When the amount of available resources is sufficient all the ranked services may be delivered at assumed quality level. Decreasing amount of resources requires adaptation of

W. Cellary and E. Estevez (Eds.): I3E 2010, IFIP AICT 341, pp. 17–28, 2010.

services delivery scenarios. The gain of such an adaptation is to preserve some services being important form the business process; list of preserved services depends on temporarily available resources. It is assumed that possible lists of services assure continuity of the business process.

According to the SOA paradigm each e-health service is composed of a set of atomic services providing required functionalities, which are delivered in certain predefined order. Each atomic service, which deliver certain functionality may be provided in different versions, which vary in non-functional characteristics such as: response time, security, availability, etc [10,8]. Composition of complex services from different versions of atomic services allows to guarantee required quality of e-health services, which is very often critical in medical applications.

In this paper we present a general framework for QoS-aware SOA-based composition of e-health complex services in varying environment (e.g. varying communication channels capacities). Presented approach is explained with use of an illustrative example – remote monitoring of patients health parameters. The remote monitoring example includes: definition of the remote monitoring problem as a business process, identification of complex services playing major roles in the monitoring process, identification of the set of atomic services necessary to deliver required functionalities and composition of an exemplary complex service.

2 Remote Monitoring of Patients Health

As an example of e-health business process consider the process of remote monitoring of patients health (see Fig. 1).

In this scenario it is assumed, that a patient is equipped with a mobile communication device (e.g. smartphone or PDA), which collects monitored data from sensors placed on patients body. Collected data is preprocessed on patients mobile device and sent for further processing and storage to Digital Health Library.

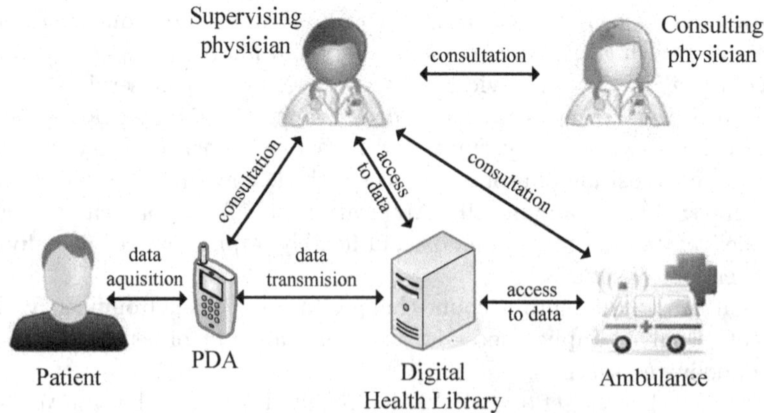

Fig. 1. Remote monitoring of patients health - an overview

Further processing of collected data may involve among others: modelling and identification of physiological processes, updating of medical knowledge base, expansion of medical case study database and decision making for computer-assisted diagnosis. In the last case decision making algorithm may recognize any abnormal situations in patients health and notify medical personnel about such events.

An alarmed physician should have an access to patients health record, their current health state, medical knowledge bases and additional services such as consultation with patient or other physician. After gathering necessary information physician decides whether detected abnormal situation poses a threat to patients health and undertakes appropriate actions, e.g. sends an ambulance to the patient. In the life-threatening situation physician monitors patients status and instructs ambulance crew on how to proceed with a patient.

In the whole process of remote monitoring of patients health three complementary phases may be distinguished as presented on Fig. 2: basic monitoring, supervised monitoring and monitoring in the ambulance.

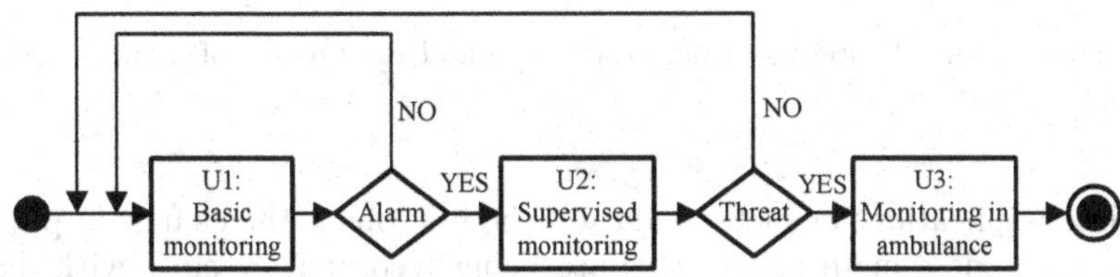

Fig. 2. The process of remote monitoring of patients health

Each of presented monitoring phases is in fact a separate business process composed of one or more complex services. Basic monitoring covers routine day to day monitoring of patients vital parameters (e.g. ECG for post-cardiac patients). Supervised monitoring regards a case when abnormal behaviour of monitored parameters is detected. In this case an alarm is raised and other parameters (e.g.: body temperature, pulse and GPS coordinates) are monitored by physician providing him with information and services necessary to make decisions concerning further actions. Monitoring in ambulance applies to life-threatening situations in which an ambulance was dispatched to collect (possibly unconscious) patient. In this case both ambulance crew and physician should be provided with necessary information and communication services [9].

Processes of supervised monitoring and monitoring in ambulance can be decomposed into separate complex services. Such an exemplary decomposition of considered processes is presented on Fig. 3 a) and b) respectively.

2.1 Supervised Monitoring

The process of supervised monitoring starts at the moment of generation of an alarm concerning misbehaviour of patients health parameters. There are two

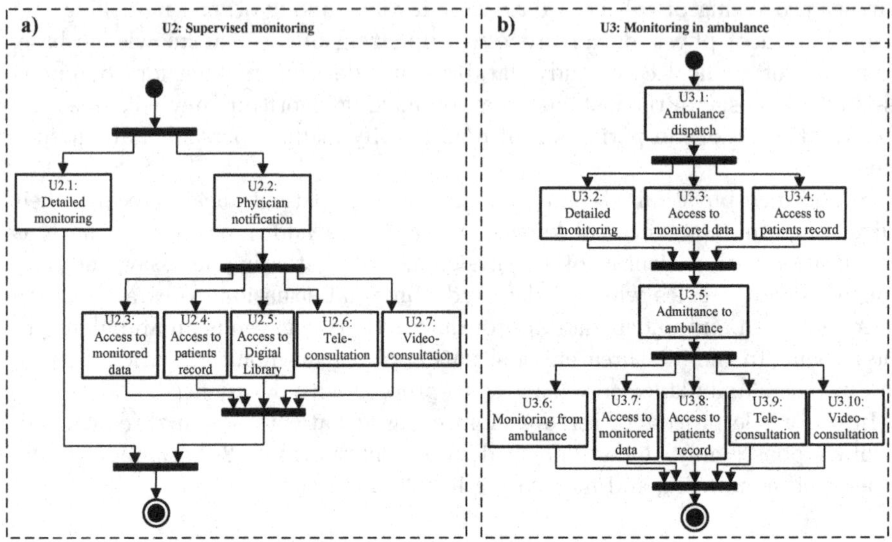

Fig. 3. The process of supervised monitoring (a) and the process of monitoring in an ambulance (b)

immediate implications of such an alarm. The first one is the change in patients monitoring mode - more parameters are being recorded, possibly with denser time resolution. The second consequence is the notification of patients physician about possible health risks. From this moment the physician has access to personalised services allowing him to gather information about current state of the patient and make decision about further actions. These services may include (see Fig. 3 a)): on-line access to monitored health parameters (U2.3), access to patients health record (U2.4), access to Digital Health Library containing knowledge about similar cases (U2.5), and tele- and video-consultation with patient and/or medical experts (U2.6 and U2.7).

2.2 Monitoring in Ambulance

The process of monitoring in an ambulance consists of two stages. The first one starts when supervising physician decides, that patients health is at risk and sends an ambulance to take the patient to the hospital (U3.1). From now on the crew of the ambulance has on-line access to monitored parameters of patients health (U3.3) as well as to the patients health record (U3.4).

After admittance to the ambulance (U3.5) patients monitoring mode changes again. All required patients health parameters are recorded now. Moreover, audio-video monitoring of the patient in the ambulance is performed as well (U3.6). Besides previously accessible services (U3.7 and U3.8) ambulance crew can communicate with supervising physician through tele- and video-consultation services (U3.9 and U3.10).

The process of monitoring in an ambulance may be treated as personalized; it depends both on equipment available in the ambulance as well as on treatment procedures determined by ambulance crew.

3 Remote Monitoring as Business Process

Business process is a series of interrelated activities or tasks that solve a particular problem or lead to achieve specific goal. In the SOA paradigm each of activities constituting in business process is represented as a complex service which delivers certain predefined functionality (see Fig. 4). Complex services, in turn, are composed of atomic services, which provide basic indivisible functionalities. The functionality of a complex service is an aggregation of functionalities of atomic services [5]. Similarly, the goal of a business process (its functionality) is an aggregation of functionalities of performed complex services.

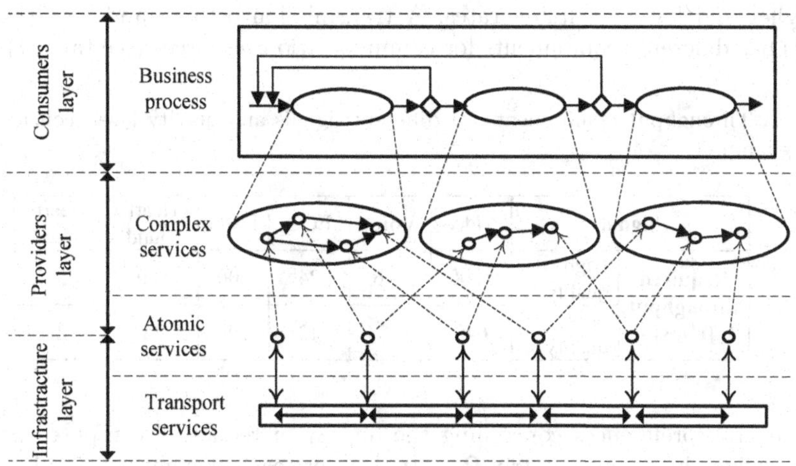

Fig. 4. Composition of business processes

The difference between business process and complex service lies in that the former one is defined and composed by service consumer, while the latter one is delivered by service provider as a whole. Service consumer may influence the choice of particular complex services by specification of Service Level Agreement (SLA) containing functional and non-functional requirements. Service provider, on the other hand, composes complex services from available atomic services basing on requirements stated in the SLA [4].

In special cases the whole business process may be specified by single complex service. Such situations may occur for example when available processes are managed by single entity basing on certain regulations (e.g. medical processes in health care). In general, however, this approach is inefficient and inelastic, since it does not allow consumers to modify their requirements.

4 Services Personalization and Resources Management

Depending on individual needs of service consumers and capabilities of execution environment each of available complex services can be delivered in many versions which differ in non-functional characteristics [2,12]. As an example consider monitoring from ambulance service (U3.6) which allows to transmit monitored signals, voice and video from ambulance to supervising physician. Depending on individual case different health parameters are recorded and transmitted through the network (e.g.: ECG and pulse for cardiac patients or glucose for diabetics). Additionally voice and video transmission may be required by physician. Moreover individual requirements and amount of available system resources may influence the number and the quality of transmitted signals [6,8].

Assume, that there are six signals possible to be measured and transmitted from ambulance to physician: video, voice, ECG, EMG, heart sound (HS) and heart rate (HR). Each signal can be measured and transmitted in two modes - high and low quality. High and low quality of health parameters can be reflected by higher and lower sampling rates. A transmission of high and low quality signals has different requirements for communication resources (see table 1).

Table 1. Throughput requirements for different signals and quality levels considered in the example

Signal		Video	Voice	ECG	EMG	Heart sound	Heart rate
Required throughput [kbps]	High quality	5000	256	24	600	120	5
	Low quality	640	25	12	100	24	2

In general, preferences concerning the quality of requested complex service can be defined by penalty matrix $\mathbf{P}_l = [p_{ij}]$, where each element p_{ij} $(i = 1, ..., I;$ $j = 1, ..., J)$ represents a penalty for not delivering j-th signal in higher than i-th quality levels. The exemplary matrix for six signals considered above and three quality levels is defined by:

$$\mathbf{P}_l = \begin{bmatrix} p_{VID}^{HI} & p_{VOI}^{HI} & p_{ECG}^{HI} & p_{EMG}^{HI} & p_{HS}^{HI} & p_{HR}^{HI} \\ p_{VID}^{LO} & p_{VOI}^{LO} & p_{ECG}^{LO} & p_{EMG}^{LO} & p_{HS}^{LO} & p_{HR}^{LO} \\ p_{VID}^{NO} & p_{VOI}^{NO} & p_{ECG}^{NO} & p_{EMG}^{NO} & p_{HS}^{NO} & p_{HR}^{NO} \end{bmatrix}, \tag{1}$$

where for example $p_{21} = p_{VID}^{LO}$ is the penalty for not delivering high quality video signal and $p_{11} = p_{EMG}^{NO}$ is the penalty for not delivering EMG signal at all. If penalty $p_{ij} = 0$ then i-th quality level of j-th signal is not required.

Denote by $\mathbf{D}_l$ a binary matrix of quality level delivery, where each element d_{ij} $(i = 1, ..., I;$ $j = 1, ..., J)$ is defined as follows:

$$d_{ij} = \begin{cases} 1 & i\text{-th quality level for } j\text{-th signal is delivered} \\ 0 & i\text{-th quality level for } j\text{-th signal is not delivered} \end{cases}. \tag{2}$$

Exemplary matrix $\mathbf{D}_l$ for a complex service in which video and voice signals are delivered at low quality, ECG signal is delivered at high quality, and remaining signals are not transmitted at all is presented below:

$$\mathbf{D}_l = \begin{bmatrix} 0\,0\,1\,0\,0\,0 \\ 1\,1\,0\,0\,0\,0 \\ 0\,0\,0\,1\,1\,1 \end{bmatrix}. \tag{3}$$

Given penalty matrix $\mathbf{P}_l$ and quality delivery matrix $\mathbf{D}_l$ for certain complex service request req_l it is possible to calculate overall penalty p_l for not satisfying consumers preferences as follows:

$$p_l = \sum_{j=1}^{J} \mathbf{p}_{lj} \cdot \mathbf{d}_{lj}^{\mathrm{T}}, \tag{4}$$

where $\mathbf{p}_{lj}$ and $\mathbf{d}_{lj}$ are j-th columns of matrices $\mathbf{P}_l$ and $\mathbf{D}_l$ respectively.

Let $\mathbf{R} = [r_{ij}]$ ($i = 1, ..., I$; $j = 1, ..., J$) denote the matrix of resources consumption, where each element r_{ij} represents the amount of resources required to deliver j-th signal at i-th quality level. In the example considered above resources requirements are stated in terms of required throughput (see table 1). Therefore the exemplary matrix $\mathbf{R}$ is defined as follows:

$$\mathbf{R} = \begin{bmatrix} 5000 & 256 & 24 & 600 & 120 & 5 \\ 640 & 25 & 12 & 100 & 24 & 2 \\ 0 & 0 & 0 & 0 & 0 & 0 \end{bmatrix}. \tag{5}$$

Note, that elements of the last row of exemplary matrix $\mathbf{R}$ are equal to zero since the lowest quality level represents situation in which signals are not delivered at all.

The amount of resources r_l necessary to deliver complex service at quality level represented by certain matrix $\mathbf{D}_l$ can be calculated as follows:

$$r_l = \sum_{j=1}^{J} \mathbf{r}_j \cdot \mathbf{d}_{lj}^{\mathrm{T}}, \tag{6}$$

where $\mathbf{r}_j$ and $\mathbf{d}_{lj}$ are j-th columns of matrices $\mathbf{R}$ and $\mathbf{D}_l$ respectively.

For the model presented above a number of resource management tasks can be formulated. The goal of each task may be different. For example one may want to minimize the average or maximal penalty caused by violation of consumers individual preferences or to maximize consumers satisfaction for each incoming complex service request. Aforementioned tasks can be formulated as follows.

Task 1: Average Penalty Minimization

Given: set $L(t)$ of service requests currently being served, capacity C of the system and matrices of penalties $\mathbf{P}_l$ and resources consumption $\mathbf{R}$.

Find: set of quality delivery matrices $\{\mathbf{D}_l^* : l \in L(t)\}$ such that average penalty caused by violation of consumers individual preferences is minimized:

$$\{\mathbf{D}_l^* : l \in L(t)\} = \arg \min_{\{\mathbf{D}_l : l \in L(t)\}} \sum_{l \in L(t)} \sum_{j=1}^{J} \mathbf{p}_{lj} \cdot \mathbf{d}_{lj}^{\mathrm{T}} \tag{7}$$

with respect to system capacity constraints:

$$\sum_{l \in L(t)} \sum_{j=1}^{J} \mathbf{r}_j \cdot \mathbf{d}_{lj}^{\mathrm{T}} \leq C. \tag{8}$$

Task 2: Maximal Penalty Minimization

This task is similar to Task 1 and can be derived by substitution of objective function in (7) by following formula:

$$\{\mathbf{D}_l^* : l \in L(t)\} = \arg \min_{\{\mathbf{D}_l : l \in L(t)\}} \max_{l \in L(t)} \sum_{j=1}^{J} \mathbf{p}_{lj} \cdot \mathbf{d}_{lj}^{\mathrm{T}} \tag{9}$$

Task 3: Maximization of Service Consumer Satisfaction

Given: the amount of resources $C(t)$ currently available in the system, matrix of preferences $\mathbf{P}_l$ for incoming service request req_l and resources consumption matrix $\mathbf{R}$.

Find: composition of complex service defined by quality delivery matrix $\mathbf{D}_l^*$ such that penalty caused by violation of consumers preferences is minimized:

$$\mathbf{D}_l^* = \arg \min_{\mathbf{D}_l} \sum_{j=1}^{J} \mathbf{p}_{lj} \cdot \mathbf{d}_{lj}^{\mathrm{T}} \tag{10}$$

with respect to system capacity constraints:

$$\sum_{j=1}^{J} \mathbf{r}_j \cdot \mathbf{d}_{lj}^{\mathrm{T}} \leq C(t). \tag{11}$$

The goal of Task 3 is to compose complex services according do consumers preferences. It can be performed each time when new complex service request arrives to the system. It can also be used for request admission control and Service Level Agreement renegotiation. Tasks 1 and 2, on the other hand, are performed in order to optimize utilization of systems resources and to guarantee average or minimal service consumer satisfaction.

4.1 Numerical Example

Consider an example in which two monitoring service requests req_1 and req_2 arrive to the system. Requests req_1 and req_2 are characterized by following preferences matrices:

$$\mathbf{P}_1 = \begin{bmatrix} \times & 0 & \times & 0 & 0 & \times \\ \times & 100 & \times & \infty & 200 & \times \\ \times & \infty & \times & \infty & \infty & \times \end{bmatrix}, \mathbf{P}_2 = \begin{bmatrix} 0 & \times & \times & 0 & 0 & \times \\ 1000 & \times & \times & 100 & 10 & \times \\ \infty & \times & \times & \infty & 200 & \times \end{bmatrix} \quad (12)$$

which mean that request req_1 requires voice and heart sound signal to be delivered at least at low quality and EMG signal to be delivered at high quality. Similarly request req_2 requires video and EMG signal at least at low quality and additional heart sound signal would improve consumers satisfaction.

Assume, that systems capacity is equal to $C = 2510kbps$ and that capacity requirements of available signals are given by matrix $\mathbf{R}$ defined in (5). As a result of minimizing average penalty for not satisfying consumers preferences (Task 1 defined by (7) and (8)) following quality delivery matrices are calculated:

$$\mathbf{D}_1 = \begin{bmatrix} \times & 1 & \times & 1 & 1 & \times \\ \times & 0 & \times & 0 & 0 & \times \\ \times & 0 & \times & 0 & 0 & \times \end{bmatrix}, \mathbf{D}_2 = \begin{bmatrix} 0 & \times & \times & 1 & 1 & \times \\ 1 & \times & \times & 0 & 0 & \times \\ 0 & \times & \times & 0 & 0 & \times \end{bmatrix} \quad (13)$$

resulting in overall penalty $p = 1000$ for not delivering high quality video signal for second service request req_2. Delivery of high quality video signal in this example is impossible because HQ video capacity requirements are higher than overall capacity C of the system. Services composition and resources allocation represented by matrices $\mathbf{D}_1$ and $\mathbf{D}_2$ (13) are illustrated on Fig. 5 (state before moment t_1).

Assume, that at certain moment t_1 a third service request req_3 characterized by matrix $\mathbf{P}_3$ arrives to the system. In order minimize average penalty for not satisfying consumers preferences systems resources have to be reallocated. Final service composition and resources allocation depends on penalty matrices $\mathbf{P}_1$, $\mathbf{P}_2$ and $\mathbf{P}_3$.

In order to show the difference between final resources allocation assume two alternate matrices $\mathbf{P}_3$:

$$\mathbf{P}_3^a = \begin{bmatrix} 0 & 0 & \times & 0 & 0 & \times \\ 1000 & \mathbf{250} & \times & \infty & \infty & \times \\ \infty & \infty & \times & \infty & \infty & \times \end{bmatrix}, \mathbf{P}_3^b = \begin{bmatrix} 0 & 0 & \times & 0 & 0 & \times \\ 1000 & \mathbf{150} & \times & \infty & \infty & \times \\ \infty & \infty & \times & \infty & \infty & \times \end{bmatrix} \quad (14)$$

which differ in the penalty for not delivering high quality voice signal. Two different solutions of resources allocation task are represented by quality level matrices $\mathbf{D}_1^a$, $\mathbf{D}_2^a$, $\mathbf{D}_3^a$ and $\mathbf{D}_1^b$, $\mathbf{D}_2^b$, $\mathbf{D}_3^b$:

$$\mathbf{D}_1^a = \begin{bmatrix} \times & 0 & \times & 1 & 0 & \times \\ \times & 1 & \times & 0 & 1 & \times \\ \times & 0 & \times & 0 & 0 & \times \end{bmatrix}, \mathbf{D}_2^a = \begin{bmatrix} 0 & \times & \times & 0 & 0 & \times \\ 1 & \times & \times & 1 & 1 & \times \\ 0 & \times & \times & 0 & 0 & \times \end{bmatrix} \mathbf{D}_3^a = \begin{bmatrix} 0 & 1 & \times & 1 & 1 & \times \\ 1 & 0 & \times & 0 & 0 & \times \\ 0 & 0 & \times & 0 & 0 & \times \end{bmatrix} \quad (15)$$

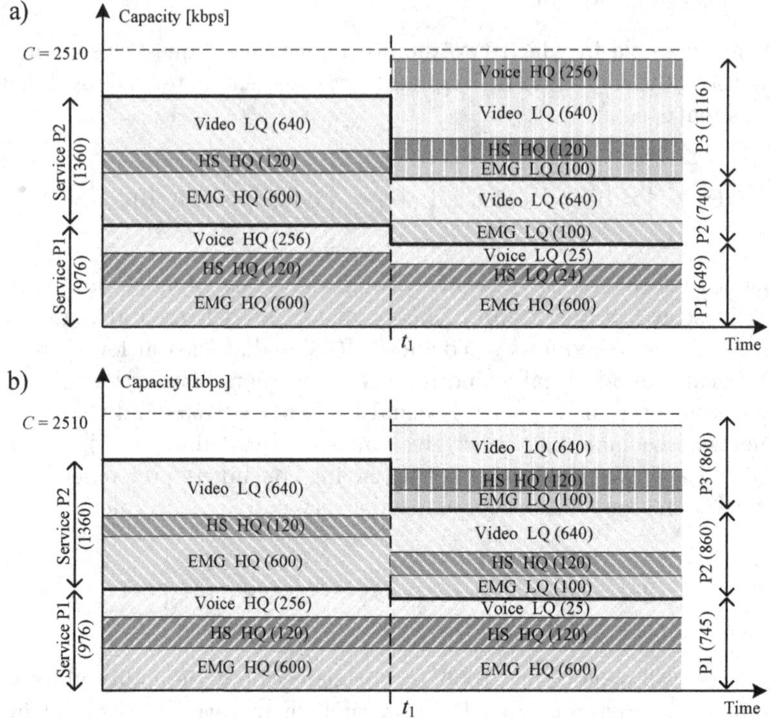

Fig. 5. Services composition and resources reallocation for two versions of third request preferences differing in the value of penalty p_{322} for not delivering HQ voice for request req_3: (a) $p_{322} = 250$, (b) $p_{322} = 150$

and

$$\mathbf{D}_1^b = \begin{bmatrix} \times\ 0 \times 1\ 1 \times \\ \times\ 1 \times 0\ 0 \times \\ \times\ 0 \times 0\ 0 \times \end{bmatrix}, \mathbf{D}_2^b = \begin{bmatrix} 0 \times \times\ 0\ 1 \times \\ 1 \times \times\ 1\ 0 \times \\ 0 \times \times\ 0\ 0 \times \end{bmatrix} \mathbf{D}_3^b = \begin{bmatrix} 0\ 0 \times 1\ 1 \times \\ 1\ 1 \times 0\ 0 \times \\ 0\ 0 \times 0\ 0 \times \end{bmatrix}. \tag{16}$$

Final services composition and resources allocation represented by above matrices are illustrated on figures Fig. 5a) and Fig. 5b) respectively. Note that in the presented example, depending on the penalty for not delivering HQ voice for request req_3, HQ voice in req_3 is traded for HQ heart sound in req_1 and req_2. The threshold value of this penalty is $p_{322} = p_{125} + p_{225} = 210$.

5 Conclusions

In this paper a general problem of e-health services management was introduced. It consists of two major tasks: service personalization and resources allocation. Service personalization allows to flexibly adjust delivered services based on individual needs of service consumers. Resources management allows to reserve and allocate resources necessary to deliver requested services and satisfy consumers preferences. In the presented approach both tasks of personalization and resource allocation are solved simultaneously as single optimization problem in which certain parameters concern the personalization task (penalty matrices), while other parameters regard allocation tasks (resources consumption matrix). Unfortunately formulated tasks are in general NP-hard [3], therefore heuristic algorithms should be applied to effectively control processes of service composition, personalization and resources management [1,7].

Presented approach allows to flexibly compose complex remote monitoring services from a given set of atomic communication services. Service personalization means that complex service components (atomic services) are given certain priorities based on which conflicts are resolved in the case of insufficient resources. Such personalization allows to deliver services with lower quality which still meet consumers requirements.

Reduction of the quality of complex service means deterioration of the quality of atomic service components and/or decrease in the number of utilized service components. Reduction of the quality or the number of service components is performed based on given or acquired knowledge about medical procedures. Acquired knowledge may also address personal experiences, expertise and preferences of systems consumers.

Acknowledgements

The research presented in this paper has been partially supported by the European Union within the European Regional Development Fund program no. POIG.01.03.01-00-008/08.

References

1. Jeannie, A., David, O., Amin, V., Patterson, D.A.: Design and Implementation Trade-offs for Wide-area Resource Discovery. ACM Transactions on Internet Technology, Article 18 8(4) (September 2008)
2. Alrifai, M., Risse, T.: Combining global optimization with local selection for efficient QoS-aware service composition. In: WWW 2009: Proceedings of the 18th International Conference on World Wide Web, pp. 881–890. ACM, New York (2009)
3. Garey, M.R., Johnson, D.S.: Computers and Intractability: A Guide to the Theory of NP-completeness. Publ. W. H. Freeman, New York (1979)
4. Grzech, A., Rygielski, P., Świątek, P.: QoS-aware infrastructure resources allocation in systems based on service-oriented architecture paradigm. In: HET-NETs 2010, Zakopane, Poland, pp. 35–48 (2010)
5. Grzech, A., Świątek, P.: Modeling and optimization of complex services in service-based systems. Cybernetics and Systems 40, 706–723 (2009)
6. Grzech, A., Świątek, P.: Parallel processing of connection streams in nodes of packet-switched computer communication systems. Cybernetics and Systems 39(2), 155–170 (2008)

7. Magnus, K.: Design Rules for Producing Controllable Computer Services. In: Proc. of 10th IEEE/IFIP Network Operations and Management Symposium, pp. 1–14 (2006)
8. Shahadat, K., Li Kin, F., Manning, E.G.: The Utility Model For Adaptive Multimedia Systems. In: International Conference on Multimedia Modeling, pp. 111–126 (1997)
9. Niyato, D., Hossain, E., Diamond, J.: IEEE 802.16/WiMax-based broadband wireless access and its application for telemedicine/e-health services. IEEE Wireless Communications 14(1), 72–83 (2007)
10. Rygielski, P., Świątek, P.: QoS-aware Complex Service Composition in SOA-based Systems. In: SOA Infrastructure Tools: Concepts and Methods. Springer, Berlin (2010)
11. Vergados, D.J., Vergados, D.D., Maglogiannis, I.: NGL03-6: Applying Wireless DiffServ for QoS Provisioning in Mobile Emergency Telemedicine. In: Global Telecommunications Conference, GLOBECOM 2006, November 27-December 1, pp. 1–5. IEEE, Los Alamitos (2006)
12. Tao, Y., Yue, Z., Lin, K.-J.: Efficient algorithms for Web services selection with end-to-end QoS constraints. ACM Trans. Web 1(1) (2007)

Mobile Interfaces for Building Control Surveyors

Jacek Chmielewski, Krzysztof Walczak, and Wojciech Wiza

Poznan University of Economics, Department of Information Technology,
Mansfelda 4, 60-854, Poznan, Poland
{chmielewski,walczak,wiza}@kti.ue.poznan.pl

Abstract. The problem of integrating heterogeneous back-end platforms used in public administration has been widely addressed in a number of research and development projects. In such a complex and heterogeneous environment, application of the SOA paradigm can be particularly beneficial. However, in some application domains – such as the Building Control Administration – there is an additional requirement: integration of heterogeneous front-end platforms – including access through mobile devices. In this paper, a new method of creating adaptable mobile user interfaces for applications based on SOA services is described. In the adaptation process the displayed content is adjusted, the best way of presenting content is selected and interaction methods are adapted to the capabilities of the particular mobile device. Therefore, it is possible to easily make any service accessible on any mobile device – which is of great importance to the Building Control Administration surveyors that operate out of office, directly in the construction field.

Keywords: SOA, adaptation, mobile devices, mobile user interfaces.

1 Introduction

One of the main advantages of using the Service Oriented Architecture (SOA) paradigm [1] to create software is the ability to seamlessly integrate diverse systems running on heterogeneous hardware and software platforms. This feature is of special importance for efficient deployment of systems associated with complex business processes. An application domain which is characterized by intrinsic complexity of the underlying business processes is the public administration. Public administration requires close cooperation of multiple participants representing different domains, playing different roles and having different areas of interest. Moreover, these participants may come from both the private sector and the public sector, therefore, in general, they have different ways of operation and are subject to various regulations and constraints. In such a complex and heterogeneous environment, application of the SOA paradigm can be particularly beneficial. In many cases, this paradigm may enable creation of new types of applications that could not be built based on traditional approaches or, at least, may significantly reduce the software development costs.

The problem of integrating heterogeneous back-end platforms using the SOA paradigm has been widely addressed in a number of research and development projects [2][3][4]. However, in some application domains – such as the Building Control

W. Cellary and E. Estevez (Eds.): I3E 2010, IFIP AICT 341, pp. 29–39, 2010.

Administration for example – there is an additional requirement: integration of heterogeneous front-end platforms. In many cases, work with an application must be performed in several different environments – on a desktop computer in the administration office, on a notebook computer in the construction office, and on a mobile device in the construction field. These devices usually differ significantly in their communication capabilities and processing power, as well as the offered presentation and interaction methods [5]. Access by mobile devices are especially important and – at the same time – the most difficult to integrate.

Apart from addressing different device capabilities, efficiency of work with an application can be significantly improved by allowing users to adjust the application interface and choose the content and the functions, which they need most in given circumstances. In many cases, the method of presentation of the content itself is important as well. Also, users may differ in their privileges to access different types of content and a device may be used in specific context, including geographical position, time of a day, lighting conditions, etc. All these elements should be taken into account in the development of user interfaces for SOA services.

In this paper, we describe a new method of building adaptable user interfaces for SOA services, called *ASIS – Adaptable SOA Interface System*, and provide examples how this method can be used to build SOA based applications for the Building Control Administration. The system is called *BCSS – Building Control Support System* [6].

By the use of the ASIS method it is possible to provide end-users with a convenient and flexible way of accessing available SOA services. The way of accessing the services can be adjusted to the capabilities of the mobile devices used, to users' requirements, and to the current context (place, time, previous interactions). The adjustment is performed automatically, without explicit actions of the user. At the same time, the method is generic and is not bound to any specific set of services or the underlying business logic.

This paper is organized as follows. Section 2 contains an overview of the state of the art in user interface adaptation. In Section 3, an overview of the ASIS system architecture is provided. In Section 4, the ASIS Service Interface Generator is described. Section 5 contains description of the SOIL language used for building adaptable user interfaces. In Section 6, examples of service visualization templates programmed in SOIL are presented. Section 7 concludes the chapter.

2 User Interface Adaptation

The problem of dynamic creation and adaptation of user interfaces has been widely studied. Existing solutions can be broadly divided into four categories. The first category are declarative user interface languages, such as MXML [7], XUL [8] and XAML [9]. Interfaces built with these languages can be highly sophisticated, but at the same time interface descriptions are usually complex and require complicated interpretation engines running on the client side. While this poses no significant difficulties on stationary PC platforms, practical implementations on mobile devices such as PDAs and smartphones are highly problematic due to the diversity of these platforms, low processing power available, and limitations of the communication channel. Therefore, most of the currently built mobile interfaces are based on HTML [10]. The second category of solutions are HTML page generators such as PHP [11], JSP [12] and ColdFusion [13]. These tools can be used efficiently for generation of web pages and in fact are used in many practical applications on the web. However, they are not really well suited for building mobile interfaces for SOA applications as discussed in this paper. Missing features include possibility of automatically integrating fragments of interface description coming from distributed application services, high-level application specific language elements, and XML [14] compliance for easy processing and generation of interface descriptions. Third category of systems simply use different versions of the interfaces for accessing with stationary and mobile devices (e.g. goole.com and google.com/m). This approach is very limited in its applicability, leads to inconsistencies and increases the amount of configuration that needs to be performed by end-users of these systems. Finally, in the fourth category of solutions, HTML interfaces are equipped with dynamic scripting features that enable their adaptation to the device capabilities on the client side. This solution, however, does not take into account full context information during the interface adaptation, significantly decreases bandwidth efficiency, and leads to security problems. Additionally, support for dynamic HTML features on mobile devices varies significantly.

3 ASIS Architecture

The *Adaptable SOA Interface System* (ASIS) is responsible for generating user interfaces for SOA applications adapted to the particular user, the currently used access device and the current context. The ASIS framework creates the interface description content on request received from the end-user device, based on interface templates coded in a specially designed language, called SOIL – *Service-Oriented Interface Language*, parameters of the end-user device – either sent by the device or stored in a local database, and the current context of interface generation. The interface description is then sent to the client device and rendered. At the client device a typical web browser or a specially designed application extending context information can be used. The overall architecture of the ASIS framework is presented in Fig. 1.

The ASIS framework consists of four main elements: SOA Interface Generator Module (SIG), SOIL Interface Templates, Content Access and Adaptation Module (ADAM), and Content Upload and Adaptation Module (UMOD).

The *SOA Interface Generator* (SIG) consists of an interface generation server and a client application. SIG processes interface templates encoded in the SOIL language, generates the interface content and sends the final content to the client devices. The SIG is further described in Section 4.

The *SOIL Interface Templates* enable SOA services to be presented to end-users in a user-friendly way. The templates are encoded in the SOIL language further presented in Section 5. SOIL is based on XML. It provides commands that can control the process of interface generation, communicate between themselves, and execute calls to SOA services. SOIL is independent of the content description language used (e.g. HTML, XML or textual PDF [15]). Examples of SOIL Interface Templates are presented in Section 6.

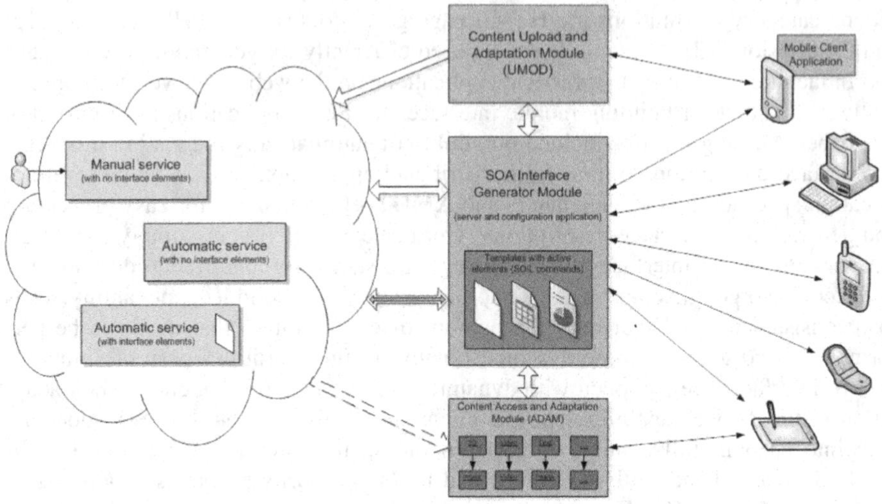

Fig. 1. The overall architecture of the ASIS framework

The *Content Access and Adaptation Module* (ADAM) is responsible for providing access to multimedia objects and adjusting the formats and properties of these objects (type, format, resolution, sampling, precision, compression) to make them suitable for presentation on a particular stationary or mobile device. For example, to display a three-dimensional model of an object on a device, which is not 3D capable, a particular view of the object can be rendered to a 2D raster image. Formatted 2D text can be converted into an image to make the presentation independent of the text presentation capabilities of the particular mobile device.

The *Content Upload and Adaptation Module* (UMOD) is responsible for receiving data from client devices and storing the data in the ASIS Repository or sending it to an application service. In some cases, UMOD can also perform data adaptation operations.

4 The Interface Generator

4.1 Interface Generator Architecture

The overall architecture of the ASIS Service Interface Generator is presented in Fig. 2. The ASIS Service Interface Generator consists of the *SOIL Processor* and a collection of *SOIL command implementations*, and uses a collection of *SOIL interface templates*. The SOIL Processor is the main unit responsible for generation of the user interface. The unit contains the SOIL engine, which can interpret SOIL commands contained in the interface templates (cf. Section 6). In response to a request received from a mobile client, the unit generates the final form of the interface description based on the collection of available interface templates and calls to the available *SOA interface services*, which provide the SOIL processor with all information needed in the process of generating the user interface. It includes information about the templates to be used, their parameters, mobile device capabilities, users and their preferences and privileges, etc.

The interface templates consist of fragments of interface description interwoven with SOIL commands. Implementations of the SOIL commands are provided as a collection of Java [16] classes independent of the main SOIL processor. An XML file provides mapping between the language elements and their implementations in the Java classes.

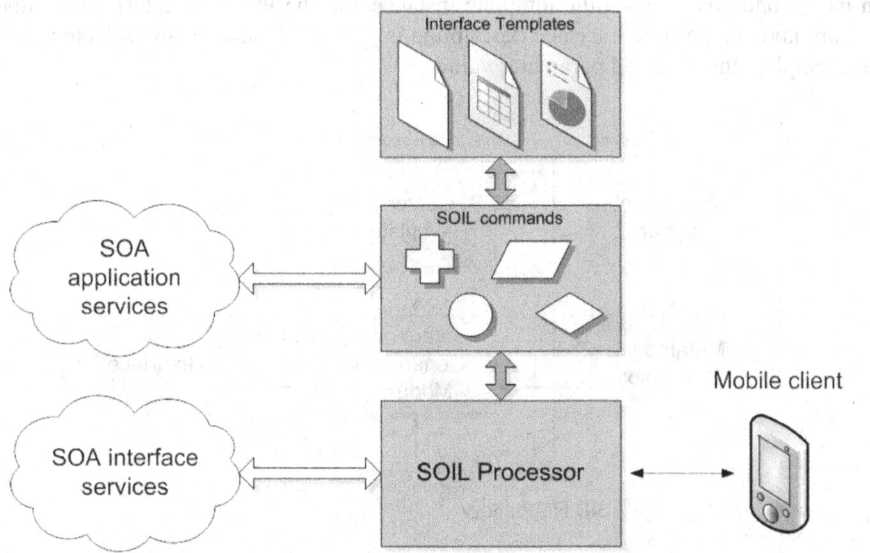

Fig. 2. The overall architecture of the ASIS Service Interface Generator

The SOIL commands can execute *SOA application services*. These are the services, which provide application's business logic. Examples of application services in the BCSS system include retrieval of building information for a given address, retrieval of administrative cases related to the building or storing the list of the selected cases in an electronic 'briefcase' for later access from a mobile device.

4.2 Selection of Templates and Parameters

To enable differentiation of the content presentation method on different target platforms, ASIS employs a notion of *presentation domains*. A presentation domain corresponds to a target environment, a group of users or a usage scenario for a SOA application. In each application context, a number of templates corresponding to different presentation domains can be used. A template assigned to a particular presentation domain along with some of its parameters defined is called a *template instance*. Parameters not defined in the template instance are retrieved from a request sent by the client or the ASIS repository.

To enable automatic selection of template instances based on different and, in general, complex criteria, and to enable automatic setting of template parameter values, a *metamodel processing* phase has been introduced into the interface generation loop (Fig. 3).

With the metamodel approach, the interface content creation process is divided into two phases: *context processing phase* and *interface generation phase*. The context processing phase employs a metamodel, which contains the logic necessary to select appropriate interface template instance and determine values of interface parameters. In the second phase, when the template instance and the values of interface parameters are known, the final interface description is generated based on the selected interface template instance and parameter values.

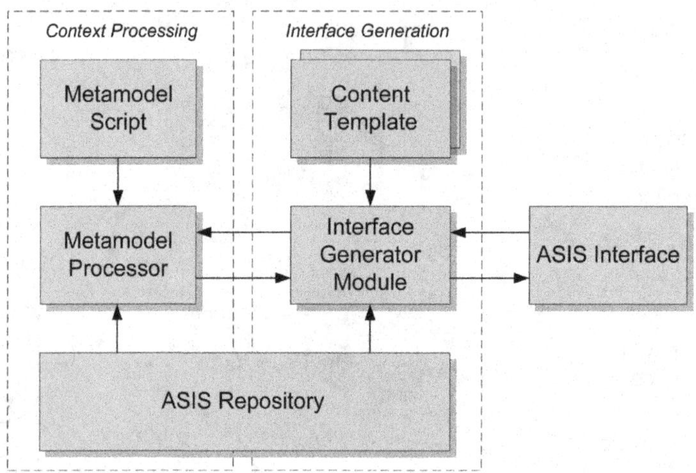

Fig. 3. Metamodel processing in the interface generation loop

5 The SOIL Language

SOIL – *Service-Oriented Interface Language* – is a new interface programming language, which has been designed to enable efficient creation of user interfaces for SOA services and applications. The SOIL language enables creation of interface templates combining static elements and dynamically generated elements including results of calls to SOA services.

The SOIL language is based on XML. A SOIL template is an XML representation of an algorithm that generates the interface description. The template is a program built of SOIL commands. The program can execute calls to SOA services, retrieve or update data from/in a database, use values of template parameters, etc. Examples of SOIL commands are: `set` to assign a value to a variable, `for` implementing a numerical loop, `if/then/else` implementing conditional statements, `db_query` to retrieve data from a database, and `soap_call` to execute external SOA services implemented with SOAP. The SOIL commands are encoded in XML and placed inside the text of the interface description written in HTML, XHTML [17] or any other interface description language.

The target language can be either XML-based or not. All XML elements that are not known to the SOIL processing unit (e.g., use a different namespace) are ignored and included in the outcome as elements of the interface description.

In SOIL, empty XML elements represent single-line commands such as `<set/>` or `<insert/>`. Non-empty elements represent block-statements like loops, conditions, service calls, database queries, iterations, etc. Examples of non-empty elements are `<for>` ... `</for>` and `<soap_call>` ... `</soap_call>`. The non-empty elements can contain fragments of interface description and SOIL code. The code located inside a repeating element may be interpreted multiple times. Parameters for the command execution are provided in the form of values of element attributes. In SOIL, all parameters are expressions and are evaluated prior to command interpretation.

One of the fundamental concepts in the design of SOIL is extensibility. New language elements can be easily added to the language – either implementing some generic operations or operations specific to a particular application domain. The new elements can take the form of new XML SOIL commands or new functions for use in expressions provided as command parameters.

To facilitate management of the SOIL implementation and documentation, the language has been divided into modules. Specialized SOIL modules with functionality specific for particular domain or application can be added to the implementation. In the BCSS system, four SOIL modules are used:

- the Core Module (SOIL CM), which contains basic language elements independent of a particular application,
- the Database Module (SOIL DB), which contains commands that enable retrieving and updating data in databases,
- the Service Module (SOIL SRV), which contains elements enabling executing requests to SOA services implemented for example as SOAP services, and
- the BCSS Module (SOIL BCSS), which contains elements specific to the BCSS application.

6 Service Visualization Templates

Service visualization templates have been designed to enable user-friendly bidirectional communication of users with SOA services. Templates are written in the SOIL language (cf. Section 5). The templates can be either generic or application specific and may provide interfaces for single SOA services or for sets of SOA services. Each template provides interface structure and can influence data adaptation by providing parameters for the data adaptation modules (ADAM and UMOD).

A number of SOIL templates have been implemented for the Building Control Support System (BCSS). Different templates have been designed for different devices supporting adaptation of the application interface. In the BCSS environment sample templates have been prepared for the following end-user devices: desktop PCs, netbooks, Tablet PCs, various types of PDAs and smartphones like Toshiba TG01 [18], Apple iPod Touch [19], HTC Touch Pro2 [20] and others. Templates for desktop PCs were developed with standard web-design guidelines and practices. The real challenge was to design templates for mobile devices, where each device can be radically different than the others.

To generate an optimal mobile user interface for a SOA service, the template has to take into account a number of parameters describing device capabilities. This includes a list of possible interaction channels and values of specific parameters describing these interaction channels. The list of available interaction channels limits the forms of communication that can be used by the final user interface. When the form of communication is selected, values of specific parameters are analyzed to decide about information adaptation procedures.

Information about mobile device capabilities and parameters can be stored in a database or provided directly by the mobile device with each request. In the first case, the device type and model, included in the service request, are decoded by the meta-model into one of predefined device groups. Each device group is linked with a specific set of device capabilities and parameters. Such an approach enables to maintain a complete set of information required by a template regardless of the information provided by a device. In the second approach, a special application running on a mobile device extends standard requests with device capabilities and parameters. In some cases, such information is incomplete and cannot be provided directly to the template, but it is still possible to match a specific device group and thus have access to all information required by the template.

The minimum set of parameters required to start ASIS processing is: identifier of the application interface required by the user and the device type and model. These parameters are included in every incoming service request. The identifier of the application interface maps to a set of template instances implementing this interface in different presentation domains. Information about device capabilities and parameters is used to select one of available presentation domains. Combining information about the required application interface and the presentation domain permits selection of the appropriate template instance.

In the case of the BCSS, it was required to prepare templates that allow the user to interact with the content on both desktop PCs and mobile devices. Templates designed for desktop PCs provide access to building/case search and browse functions. For example, the case browsing interface presented in Fig. 4 contains aggregated information retrieved for a particular case:

- Information about the address (police data);
- Owner data (retrieved from court registers);
- List of associated documents;
- Map retrieved from the geodetic office [21] or Google Maps [22];
- Hierarchy of administrative cases related to the building;
- Staff members involved in the administrative case.

Additionally, each case page contains a briefcase icon. A briefcase is an element permitting a user to select particular case to be included in the mobile interface. By clicking on a briefcase icon the user may select or deselect a given case. By enabling briefcase on selected cases, the user creates a list of cases that will be displayed on his/her mobile device, i.e. that will be accessible outside the office.

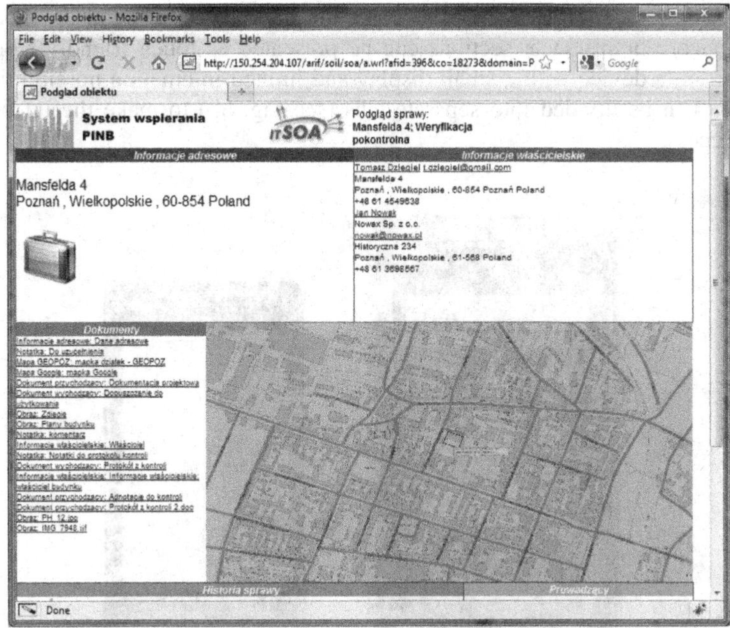

Fig. 4. Case browsing interface for desktop PC

When accessing the BCSS system from a mobile device, the user can see a list of cases that have been previously selected by the use of the briefcase icon. The list is displayed in a form adapted to the current device capabilities and size of the display.

A fragment of a SOIL template responsible for generating such a list is presented below.

```
[...]
<SOIL:FLAG method="GETCO" prop="BRIEFCASE" uid="{#uid}" var="colist"/>
<SOIL:SET name="listsize" value="{sizeOf(@colist)}"/>
<span class="hd1">Cases in the briefcase:</span>
<ul>
  <SOIL:FOR from="0" name="i" to="{$listsize-1}">
    <SOIL:CO_PROPS coId="{@colist[$i]}" prop="CO_NAME" var="objName"/>
    <SOIL:EVALUATE>
      <li>
        <a href="...&domain=BCSS.INFO&co={@colist[$i]}">
        <Insert value="{@objName}"/></a>
      </li>
    </SOIL:EVALUATE >
  </SOIL:FOR>
</ul>
[...]
```

If a user wishes to see a case, he/she can click on a particular link. Then the user is presented with the case browsing interface composed of similar sections as for the desktop PC interface. However in this case, the interface is adapted to the current mobile device. For instance, sections can be presented as touch friendly icons (see Fig. 5a) or, on a device with a small display and limited interaction possibilities, entire content can be divided into separate tabs (see Fig. 5b) to make the information easier to access.

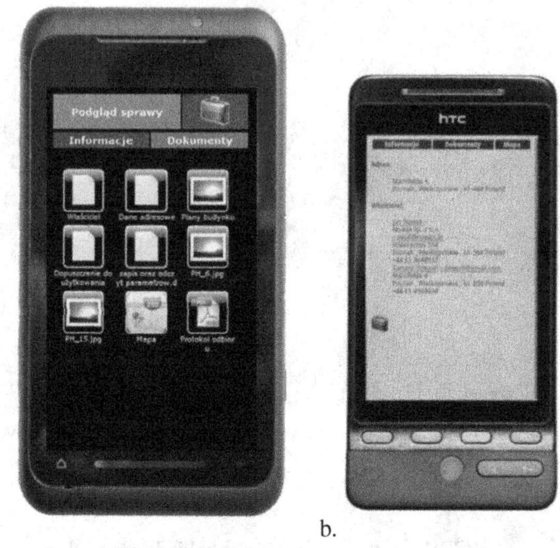

Fig. 5. Case browsing interface on different mobile devices

7 Conclusions

The ASIS solution for building adaptable mobile user interfaces for SOA applications, presented in this paper, is providing a flexible way of accessing SOA services on mobile devices with limited and non-PC like capabilities. Due to the fact that the ASIS Service Interface Generator generates the final user interface on-demand and takes into account capabilities of the particular mobile device, as well as preferences and privileges of the end-user and additional context information like location, it is possible to provide the user with a final interface in the form most appropriate for a given context, without explicit actions of the user. Adjustment of the final user interface is not bound to any specific set of services or underlying business logic, which enables the ASIS system to be used as a front-end interface generation middleware with virtually any system based on the SOA paradigm. Examples provided in this paper are related to the Building Control Administration, however, the method is generic and can be successfully used also in other application domains.

This work has been partially supported by the Polish Ministry of Science and Higher Education within the European Regional Development Fund, Grant No. POIG.01.03.01-00-008/08.

References

1. Bih, J.: Service oriented architecture (SOA) a new paradigm to implement dynamic e-business solutions. In: Ubiquity 2006, p. 1 (August 2006)
2. Martins, A., Carrilho, P., Mira da Silva, M., Alves, C.: Using a SOA Paradigm to Integrate with ERP Systems. In: Advances in Information Systems Development. Springer US, Heidelberg (2007)
3. Barbir, A., Hobbs, C., Bertino, E., Hirsch, F., Martino, L.: Challenges of testing web services and security in SOA implementations. In: Baresi, L., Di Nitto, E. (eds.) Test and Analysis of Web Services, pp. 395–440. Springer, Heidelberg (2007)
4. Karnouskos, S., Baecker, O., de Souza, L.M.S., Spiess, P.: Integration of SOAready Networked Embedded Devices in Enterprise Systems via a Cross-Layered Web Service Infrastructure. In: Proceedings of 12th International Conference on Emerging Technologies and Factory Automation. IEEE Computer Society, Los Alamitos (2007)
5. Cellary, W., Rykowski, J., Chmielewski, J., Walczak, K., Wiza, W., Wójtowicz, A.: Personalised Access to SOA Services. In: ITSOA Project Internal Report (2009)
6. Building Control Administration – Poznań, PINB – Powiatowy Inspektorat Nadzoru Budowlanego dla Miasta Poznania, `http://www.pinb.poznan.pl/`
7. MXML, `http://opensource.adobe.com/wiki/display/flexsdk/MXML+2009`
8. XUL – XML User Interface Language, `https://developer.mozilla.org/en/xul`
9. XAML – Extensible Application Markup Language, `http://msdn.microsoft.com/en-us/library/ms752059.aspx`
10. HTML – HyperText Markup Language, `http://www.w3.org/TR/html4/`
11. PHP: Hypertext Preprocessor, `http://php.net/`
12. JSP – JavaServer Pages, `http://java.sun.com/products/jsp/docs.html`
13. ColdFusion, `http://www.adobe.com/devnet/coldfusion/`
14. XML – Extensible Markup Language, `http://www.w3.org/XML/`
15. Adobe Mars Project, `http://labs.adobe.com/technologies/mars/`
16. Java programming language, `http://java.sun.com/`
17. XHTML – The Extensible HyperText Markup Language, `http://www.w3.org/TR/xhtml1/`
18. Toshiba TG01, `https://www.toshiba-europe.com/mobilerevolution/default.aspx`
19. Apple iPod Touch, `http://www.apple.com/ipodtouch/`
20. HTC Touch Pro2, `http://www.htc.com/www/product/touchpro2/overview.html`
21. Zarząd Geodezji i Katastru Miejskiego GEOPOZ, `http://www.geopoz.pl/`
22. Google Maps, `http://maps.google.com/support/?hl=en`

An Agent-Based B2B Collaboration Platform for Executing Collaborative Business Processes

Edgar Tello-Leal[1,2], Omar Chiotti[2,3], and Pablo D. Villarreal[2]

[1] Universidad Autónoma de Tamaulipas,
Matamoros entre J.B. Tijerina y C. Colón, 87000, Victoria, Tamaulipas, México
etello@uat.edu.mx
[2] CIDISI, Universidad Tecnológica Nacional-FRSF,
Lavaise 610, S3004EWB, Santa Fe, Argentina
pvillarr@frsf.utn.edu.ar
[3] INGAR-CONICET, Avellaneda 3657, S3002GJC, Santa Fe, Argentina
chiotti@santafe-conicet.gov.ar

Abstract. Nowadays, organizations establish Business-to-Business (B2B) collaborations with their business partners. Inter-organizational collaboration is carried out through the execution of collaborative business processes. Organizations are requiring and undergoing the setting up of dynamic B2B collaborations, instead of conducting face-to-face negotiations and agreements for executing collaborative processes. This implies that business partners, maybe without a previous relationship, agree dynamically on the execution of collaborative processes based on predefined models of these processes. In this work, we propose an B2B collaboration platform which provides agent-based systems and interaction mechanisms in order to enable organizations to establish dynamic agreements with their partners and carry out the decentralized execution of collaborative processes. Agents use models of collaborative processes to enact them in a dynamic way. The role an organization performs in a collaborative process is translated into a Petri Net model that a collaboration agent interpret to execute the process.

Keywords: Collaborative Business Process, Business-to-Business, Software Agents, Model-Driven Architecture.

1 Introduction

Nowadays, organizations are focusing on the setting up of Business-to-Business collaborations with their business partners in order to manage inter-organizational collaborations and improve their performance and competitiveness. A B2B collaboration entails a process-oriented integration among heterogeneous and autonomous organizations which must be achieved at a business level and at a technological level [1]. Inter-organizational collaboration is carried out through the execution of collaborative business processes. A collaborative business process defines the global view of the interactions among enterprises to achieve common business goals [1], [2]. The design and implementation of collaborative business processes (CBPs) implies new

W. Cellary and E. Estevez (Eds.): I3E 2010, IFIP AICT 341, pp. 40–50, 2010.

challenges, such as participants autonomy, decentralized management, peer-to-peer interactions, negotiation, and alignment between the business solution and the technological solution [3], [4].

To fulfill the above issues, we proposed a methodology based on a model-driven architecture (MDA) for the design [5], verification, and implementation of CBPs [5], [6]. CBPs are modeled with the UML Profile for Collaborative Business Processes based on Interaction Protocols (UPColBPIP) [5], [6] from which business process specifications can be generated B2B standards such as BPEL or WS-CDL [3]. By using the UPColBPIP language, the behavior of CBPs is modeled through interaction protocols to represent the communicative aspects of B2B interactions.

However, organizations are also requiring and undergoing the setting up of dynamic B2B relationships, instead of conducting face-to-face negotiations and agreements, for executing CBPs. This type of dynamic B2B collaborations implies that business partners find each other and agree on the execution of CBPs based on predefined CBP models. This requires B2B platform and systems that enable organizations to create relationships with their partners and instances of CBPs in a dynamic way, based on predefined CBP models that organizations provide or find either in a partner or public repository. Traditional approaches are only focused on the execution of predefined CBPs based on static agreements among partners [7], [8].

Since the features of software agents such as autonomy, heterogeneity, decentralization, coordination and social interactions are also desirable for organizations involved in B2B collaborations [1], the use of this technology can be considered as appropriate for this domain. The use of software agents to perform CBPs helps to improves process integration, interoperability, reusability and adaptability [9], [8], [10].

Therefore, in this work we propose an agent-based B2B collaboration platform which provides agents and interaction mechanisms in order to enable organizations to establish dynamic B2B collaborations with their partners, and carry out a decentralized execution of CBPs. From a CBP model defined with the UPColBPIP language, a Petri Net model that represents the role a partner performs in the collaborative process is generated for each partner involved in the CBP. Then, collaboration agents representing each partner execute their Petri-Net models to coordinate and manage CBPs in a decentralized way. Thus, all the existing UP-ColBPIP models can be used to enact CBPs in a dynamic way. In addition, our proposal is consistent and integrated with the proposed model-driven development approaches for CBPs and B2B information systems [5], [1].

The remainder of this paper is organized as follows. Section 2 describes an MDA-based methodology for collaborative processes and the modeling approach based on the UP-ColBPIP language. Section 3 describes the architecture and agents that make up the proposed B2B collaboration platform. Section 4 describes the implementation of this platform. Section 5 presents conclusions and future work.

2 MDA-Based Methodology for Collaborative Processes

A methodology, which is based on a model-driven architecture (MDA) [11], was proposed to support the design and implementation of CBPs [6]. This methodology consists of three phases: *analysis and design of collaborative processes*, *verification of collaborative processes* and *generation of B2B specifications*.

The *analysis and design of collaborative processes* consists in the modeling of these processes from a business perspective, i.e. using concepts that are less bound to the implementation technology and are closer to the B2B collaboration domain. The UPColBPIP language [1], [6] is used to model technology-independent CBPs.

The second phase consists in verifying the correctness of CBPs defined in a UPColBPIP model. The purpose is to support the verification of these processes at an early stage of the development, when most of the fundamental decisions of a B2B collaboration are carried out, i.e. previous to the generation of the technological solution. The verification is essential to allow partners to make sure the behavior of collaborative processes is well-defined. To support this, the MDA-based method for generating Petri Net specifications from a UPColBPIP model is applied [12]. Then, interaction protocols are formalized, transformed and mapped into Colored Petri Net (CPN) [13] specifications, which are then verified with CPN Tools.

Finally, the third phase consists in selecting the target implementation technology (i.e. the B2B standards) and generating the B2B specifications (i.e. the business process specifications and interfaces of the partners' systems) that fulfill the CBPs defined in the first phase. The input is a UPColBPIP model that contains CBPs based on interaction protocols and partners' business interfaces. From this model, technology-specific business process models and technology-specific partners' interface models are made. Previous work describes the application of MDA-based methods to generate technological solutions based on the widely used B2B standards: ebXML [1], WS-BPEL [1], and WS-CDL [3].

In this work, we focus on the generation of technological solutions based on software agents in which process models are interpreted by software agents instead of process specifications based on a B2B standard.

2.1 The UPColBPIP Modeling Language

The UPColBPIP language supports the definition of behavior of CBPs through the modeling of interaction protocols. UPColBPIP extends the semantics of UML2 Interactions to model interaction protocols in UML2 Sequence Diagrams. An *interaction protocol* describes a high-level communication pattern through a choreography of business messages between organizations who play different roles. The message choreography describes the global control flow of peer-to-peer interactions between organizations as well as the responsibilities of the roles they fulfill. This also enables the representation of the decentralized management of the interactions between partners.

The conceptual elements used to define interaction protocols are: (a) *Partners* and the *Role* they fulfill, which are represented through lifelines. (b) *Business Messages* that define an interaction between two roles. They contain a *business document* whose semantics is defined by its associated *speech act*, which represents the sender's intention with respect to the exchanged business document. They also indicate that the sender's expectation is that the receptor acts according to the semantics of the speech act. (c) *Control Flow Segments* (CFS), which represent complex message sequences

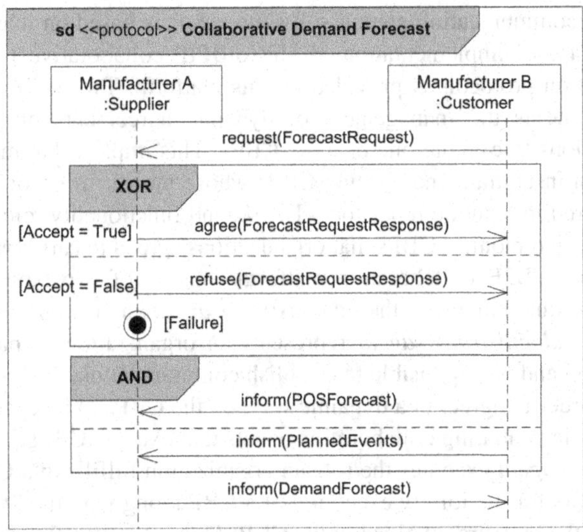

Fig. 1. Collaborative Demand Forecast interaction protocol

They contain a *control flow operator* (such as Xor, And, Or, Loop, etc) and one or more interaction paths. An *interaction path* can contain any protocol elements messages, termination events, protocol references and nested control flow segments. (d) *Protocol Reference*, which represents a sub-protocol or nested protocol. When the sub-protocol is called, the protocol waits until the sub-protocol ends. (e) *Termination event*, which represents an explicit end of a protocol. Termination events are: *success*, which implies the successful termination; and *failure*, which implies that the protocol business logic ends in an unexpected way; and (f) *Time Constraint*, which denotes a duration or deadline that can be associated with: messages, control flow segments or protocols. It represents the available time limit for the execution of such elements.

As an example of an interaction protocol, Figure 1 shows the sequence diagram of the protocol that represents the *Collaborative Demand Forecast* process. This protocol supports a negotiation process between a customer and a supplier to agree on a demand forecast. The process begins with the customer, who requests a demand forecast. The supplier processes the request and may respond by accepting or rejecting it, as it is indicated by the *Xor* control flow segment. If it is accepted, the supplier undertakes to realize the required forecast; otherwise, the process finishes with a business failure. If the supplier accepts the request, the customer informs, in parallel, a sale forecast of its points of sales (POS) and its planned sales, as it is indicated by the *And* control flow segment. Finally, with this information, the supplier generates a demand forecast and sends it to the customer. Then, the process ends.

3 An Agent-Based B2B Collaboration Platform

In this section we propose a B2B collaboration platform based on software agents in order to enable organizations to establish collaborations in a dynamic way and execute

CBPs. Since the communication among software agents is based on interaction protocols, a straightforward implementation of UPColBPIP collaborative process models based on interaction protocols is provided by this platform. Two main functionalities are supported. One is the management of dynamic agreements on collaborations among organizations to execute one or more CBPs. This implies that mechanisms for organizations can instantiate and execute CBPs whose models are provided by an organization or stored in a public repository. The second functionality refers to the capabilities to execute and monitor CBPs that organizations agreed to carry out.

The Agent-based B2B collaboration platform consists of two types of agents to support the above functionalities: the *administrator agent* and the *collaboration agent* (see Fig. 2). An *administrator agent* represents an organization or participant of a B2B collaboration and is responsible to establish communications with other administrator agents in order to agree, in a dynamic way, on the CBPs to be executed. Also, it is responsible for instantiating collaboration agents that execute CBPs.

A *collaborative agent* executes the role an organization fulfills in a CBP, and thus, it is the responsible for the jointly execution of a CBP along with the other collaborative agents from the partners involved in the CBP. Thus, at a specific moment or time, an organization can have many collaborative agents as CBPs being executed on the B2B collaboration (see Fig. 2). The following sections further describe both agents.

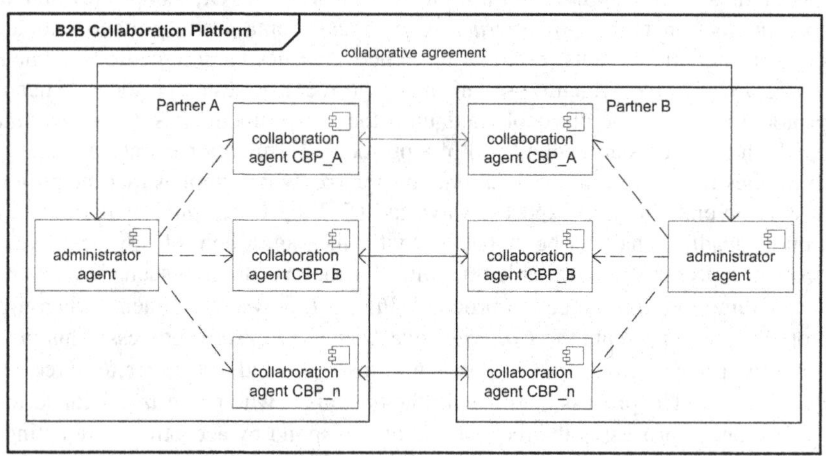

Fig. 2. Agents of the B2B Collaboration platform

3.1 Administrator Agent

Administrator agents are used to create dynamic collaboration agreements and instantiate the collaboration agents that execute CBPs. When an organization wants to establish a dynamic agreement with another organization to collaborate and execute a CBP, its *administrator agent* is used to initiate a conversation with the administrator agent of the another organization. This conversation among agents is carried out by executing a predefined CBP *Request for Collaboration*. Figure 3 shows the UPColBPIP model that represents the interaction protocol of this CBP.

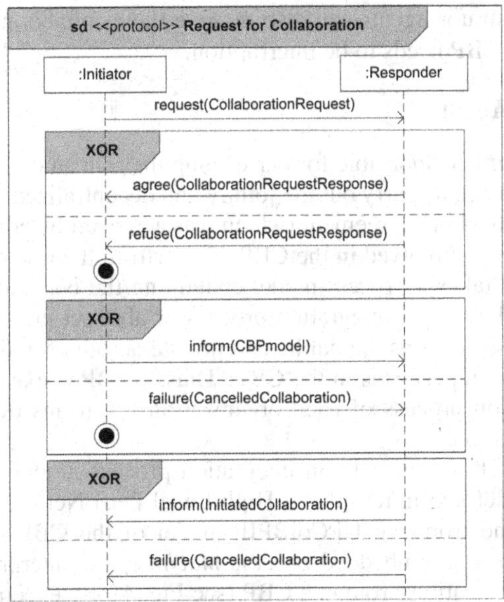

Fig. 3. Request for Collaboration Interaction Protocol

The *initiator* role is performed by the administrator agent of the organization that initiates the conversation. It sends a *request* for collaboration to a *responder* role, which is performed by the administrator agent the other organization which receives the request. This means that an administrator agent can perform the initiator or responder role according to the way that the organization engages in a collaboration agreement.

The request sent by the initiator conveys a *CollaborationRequest* document which contains the UPColBPIP model of the CBP that the *initiator* wants to execute with a responder. The *responder* evaluates the request and responds with a successful *agree* message or a *refuse* message. In the last case, it implies that the responder does not want to establish a dynamic collaboration agreement to execute the CBP, and the protocol finishes. If the responder sends an *agree* message, it waits for the process model that contains the activities that the role is going to execute in the CBP. When the initiator receives the *agree* message, it creates an instance of a collaboration agent, and if it is successful, it sends an *inform* message with the responder's process model. Otherwise, the initiator sends a *failure* message indicating that it could not instantiate its collaboration agent.

Once the responder receives the process model, it immediately instantiates a collaboration agent, and if it is successful, it sends an *inform* message indicating that the collaboration was established, and the protocol finishes. Otherwise, if an error occurs in the instantiation of the collaboration agent, the responder sends a *failure* message indicating that the collaboration was not established, and the protocol finishes. Thus, by executing this protocol administrator agents establish a dynamic agreement to execute a CBP. In case the CBP involves several organizations, the initiator executes the *Request for Collaboration* protocol with each organization that can fulfill the roles of the CBP. Administrator agents can also remove their collaboration agents in case of the execution of a CBP needs to be interruption.

3.2 Collaboration Agent

A *collaboration agent* is responsible for performing the role an organization fulfills in a CBP. Collaboration agents carry out the jointly and decentralized execution of CBPs from an established dynamic agreement (which was achieved by administrator agents) among the organizations involved in the CBP. To perform the role of an organization, a collaboration agent takes a process model containing the behavior of the organization's role, which is known as integration process or abstract process model [5], [1]. An integration process contains the public and private activities and logic that support the role the organization performs in the CBP. Thus, a CBP is executed by the enactment of the integration process of each organization by means of the collaboration agents of the organizations.

In order to interpret and execute an integration process model by a collaboration agent, this model is defined in terms of a High-Level Petri Net (PN) model, which is derived at design-time from the UPColBPIP model of the CBP to be executed. A collaboration agent has an embedded *process machine* that interprets the PN model and executes the organization's role in a CBP (see Fig. 4). By executing this PN model, the behavior of the collaboration agents is generated at run-time. The activities or transitions defined in a PN model represent the actions (i.e. send a message to an other agent, wait for the reception of a message from another agent, execute an internal action) that a collaboration agent has to perform to support the message exchange defined in the interaction protocol of the CBP that is executed, according to the CBP role that the agent performs.

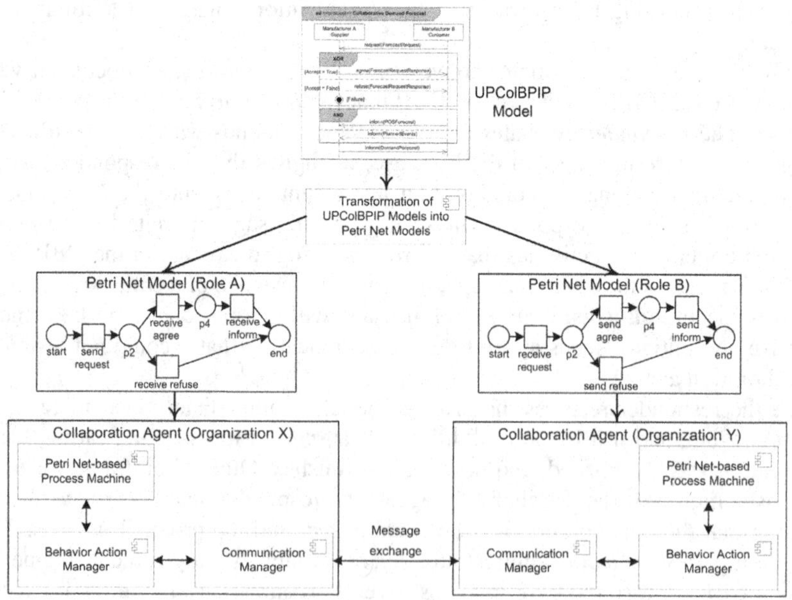

Fig. 4. Collaboration Agents executing a CBP

The behavior of this agent is driven by the *process machine* according to a PN model and it invokes the *behavior action manager* component which is responsible for planning and executing the agent's actions derived from the transitions of the PN model. The sending or receiving of a message from another agent is carried out by the *communication manager* component of the collaboration agent when the *behavior action manager* executes a sending or receiving action message. Tokens in the execution of a PN model contain the *business documents* that are exchanged between the collaboration agents. Thus, *business documents* move through the organizations' collaboration agents when the actions for the sending of messages are executed.

In this way, collaboration agents do not have actions defined at design-time, and they do not require to have the behavior of predefined interaction protocols implemented. The transitions of the PN models execute actions. Such actions are used to activate the behavior of the collaboration agent according to the type of the transition to execute. Different types of transitions (such as send message, receive message, invoke an internal process) were defined to plan and assign the behavior to be executed by the agent. Tokens maintain information about the process in which they were generated (process ID) and business documents which are sent, received, or generated internally. Therefore, the concrete actions (speech acts and business documents) of these agents are obtained at run-time according to the logic defined in PN models. This enables collaboration agents to execute any interaction protocol representing the CBP that organizations want to execute as part of a dynamic collaboration agreement. To generate the PN model that each collaboration agent uses to execute a CBP, a process transformation approach is applied to derive the PN models of the organizations from a UPColBPIP model. This is supported by applying an MDA-based method for generating PN models, as it was proposed in the second phase of the MDA approach for collaborative business processes (see Section 2). However, details of this transformation approach are out of the scope of this work.

4 Implementation of the Agent-Based B2B Collaboration Platform

In this section we describe the implementation of the Agent-based B2B collaboration platform. The software agents were built by using the Java Agent DEvelopment Framework (JADE) [14], which is a physical multi-agent development framework which complies with FIPA specifications and aims at simplifying the development and implementation of multi-agent systems [14]. Therefore, the administrator and collaboration agents are executed on the JADE platform and they use ACL [15] messages to communicate among them.

The *process machine* component of the collaboration agent was implemented by using the Java-based Petri Net framework (JFern). JFern provides an object-oriented Petri Net simulator [16]. It consists of a lightweight Petri Net kernel, providing methods to store and execute Petri Nets in realtime, and for simulation. Further, JFern supports XML based persistent storage of Petri nets and markings. The tokens of PNs contain *business documents*, which are in XML format and they are transported as parts of the content of ACL messages that agents exchange.

The agent-based B2B Collaboration platform includes an administration tool based on Eclipse Rich Client Platform. This tool has to be deployed in each organization and provides the support to: (a) instantiate the JADE platform (b) instantiate the administrator agent of the organization, (c) search, select and retrieve the UPColBPIP and Petri Net models stored in the local repository of the organization; and (d) administrate and monitor the collaboration agents instantiated.

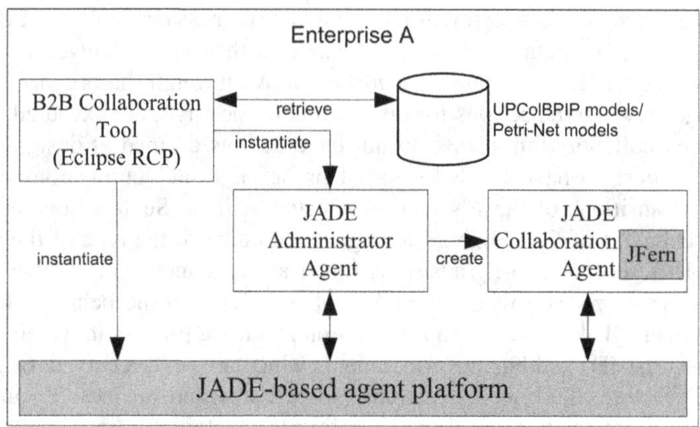

Fig. 5. Agent-based architecture for B2B collaboration

5 Conclusions and Future Work

In this work we have proposed an agent-based B2B collaboration platform which provides agent-based systems and interaction mechanisms in order to enable organizations to establish dynamic B2B collaborations with their partners, and carry out a decentralized execution of collaborative business processes (CBPs). By using this platform, UPColBPIP models can be used directly to enact CBPs in a dynamic way, instead of using process specifications based on a specific technology or B2B standard. Thus, we provide a platform to carry out a model-driven execution of CBPs, which is consistent with model-driven development approaches for CBP and B2B systems proposed in previous works.

The proposed B2B collaboration platform consists of two types of B2B agents: an administrator agent and a collaboration agent. Administrator agents representing the organizations involved in a B2B collaboration establish a collaboration agreement with other organizations by executing the proposed *request for collaboration* interaction protocol. Collaboration agents execute CBPs. We apply High-Level Petri Net models to represent the required behavior of a collaboration agent to perform the role an organization fulfills in a CBP. Petri Net (PN) models are derived from UPColBPIP models of CBPs. Therefore, process models based on Petri Nets, which collaboration agents use, are in compliance with the UPColBPIP models of the CBPs that are executed. Hence, the decentralized execution of a CBP is achieved by the enactment of a PN model carried out by each collaboration agent representing the role of an organization in the CBP. In addition, due to the behavior of collaboration agents is driven by the Petri Net-based process machine, their actions are generated in run-time to support the execution of any interaction protocol representing a CBP. This makes more flexible the architecture of agents for executing CBPs. This is different from the traditional development of agents where actions and interaction protocols that can be executed are beforehand implemented and defined in design-time.

Finally, an implementation of the agent-based B2B platform is based on the JADE agent platform. Also a Petri Net simulator was used to implement the process machine of the collaboration agent. In addition, a distributed B2B collaboration management tool based on the Eclipse platform was developed that enables organizations to manage their agents and their own repository of CBP models.

Future work is about the addition of mechanisms and tools to discover CBP models either in a public or organizations' repositories. In the current implementation of the collaboration agent the private activities or processes of the organizations, which generate or processes the exchanged messages, are simulated. However, a support for a real integration and execution will be developed by integrating Web service technology with agents. Another future work is to establish a mechanism based on CBP *Request for Collaboration*, in which the administrator agent determines if *agree* or *refuse* to establish a dynamic agreement with another organization to collaborate and execute a CBP.

References

1. Villarreal, P.D., Salomone, E., Chiotti, O.: Modeling and Specifications of Collaborative Business Processes using a MDA Approach and a UML Profile. In: Rittgen, P. (ed.) Enterprise Modeling and Computing with UML, pp. 13–45. Idea Group Inc., USA (2007)
2. Roser, S., Bauer, B.: A Categorization of Collaborative Business Process Modeling Techniques. In: 7th IEEE International Conference on E-Commerce Technology Workshops, pp. 43–54 (2005)
3. Villarreal, P.D., Salomone, E., Chiotti, O.: Transforming Collaborative Business Process Models into Web Services Choreography Specifications. In: Lee, J., Shim, J., Lee, S.-g., Bussler, C.J., Shim, S. (eds.) DEECS 2006. LNCS, vol. 4055, pp. 50–65. Springer, Heidelberg (2006)
4. Weske, M.: Business Process Management. Concepts, Languages, Architectures. Springer, Heidelberg (2007)
5. Villarreal, P.D., Salomone, E., Chiotti, O.: A MDA-based Development Process for Collaborative Business Processes. In: European Workshop on Milestone, Models and Mappings for Model-Driven Architecture (3M4MDA) (2006)
6. Villarreal, P.D., Lazarte, I., Roa, J., Chiotti, O.: A Modeling Approach for Collaborative Business Processes based on the UP-ColBPIP Language. In: Rinderle-Ma, S., et al. (eds.) BPM 2009 Workshops. LNBIP, vol. 43, pp. 318–329. Springer, Heidelberg (2010)
7. Liu, C., Li, Q., Zhao, X.: Challenges and opportunities in collaborative business process management: Overview of recent advances and introduction to the special issue. Information Systems Frontiers 11(3), 201–209 (2009)
8. Zinnikus, I., Hahn, C., Fischer, K.: A Model-driven, Agent-based Approach for the Integration of Services into a Collaborative Business Process. In: 7th Int. Conf. on Autonomous Agents and Multiagent Systems (AAMAS 2008), pp. 241–248 (2008)
9. Trappey, C.V., Trappey, A.J.C., Huang, C.-J., Ku, C.C.: The design of a JADE-based autonomous workflow management system for collaborative SoC design. Expert Systems with Applications 36(2), 2659–2669 (2009)

10. Guo, L., Robertson, D., Chen-Burger, Y.H.: A Novel Approach for Enacting the Distributed Business Workflows Using BPEL4WS on the Multi-Agent Platform. In: The 2005 IEEE International Conference on e-Business Engineering (2005)
11. OMG. MDA Guide V1.0.1, http://www.omg.org/cgi-bin/doc?omg/03-06-0103-06-01.pdf
12. Villarreal, P., Roa, J., Salomone, H.E., Chiotti, O.: Verification of Models in a MDA Approach for Collaborative Business Processes. In: 10th Ibero-American Workshop of Requirements Engineering and Software Environments (2007)
13. Girault, C., Valk, R.: Petri Nets for System Engineering: A Guide to Modeling, Verification and Applications. Springer, New York (2001)
14. Bellifemine, F., Caire, G., Greenwood, D.: Developing Multi-Agent Systems with JADE. Wiley, Chichester (2007)
15. FIPA. FIPA Agent Communication specifications deal with Agent Communication Language (ACL), http://www.pa.org/repository/aclspecs.html
16. Nowostawski, M.: JFern - Java-based Petri Net framework (2003)

Compound Web Service for Supply Processes Monitoring to Anticipate Disruptive Event

Erica Fernández[1], Enrique Salomone[1], and Omar Chiotti[1,2]

[1] INGAR – CONICET, Avellaneda 3657, Santa Fe, Argentina, 3000
[2] CIDISI- UTN FRSF, Lavaisse 610, Santa Fe, Argentina, 3000
{ericafernandez,salomone,chiotti}@santafe-conicet.gov.ar

Abstract. The execution of supply process orders in a supply chain is conditioned by different types of disruptive events that must be detected and solved in real time. In this work we present a compound web service that performs the monitoring and notification functions of a supply chain event management system. This web service is designed based on a reference model that we have proposed to improve the event management activity through a deeper analysis of the occurrence and causality of events, leading to anticipate an exception during the execution of a supply process order. The web service composition is defined based on business processes. The ability to proactively detect, analyze and notify disruptive events is given through of a Bayesian network with decision nodes.

Keywords: supply chain, event management, compound web service, Bayesian Networks.

1 Introduction

The execution of supply process orders usually deviates from original plans due to unexpected events. Interdependent processes are affected negatively by these events, and ripple effects in inter-organizational networks are common. These unexpected events (cancellation of an order, failure in a process, change in a process capacity, etc.) must be detected and solved in real time because they can propagate across many levels in the supply chain. Introducing a control mechanism for managing events and responding to them dynamically requires ability to proactively detect, analyze and notify disruptive events. In this scenario, Supply Chain Event Management Systems (SCEM) [1], [2] have been proposed. SCEM is defined as a business process in which significant events are timely recognized, reactive actions are suddenly executed, flows of information and material are adjusted, and the key employees are notified. In other words, SCEM can be seen as a complex control problem. SCEM systems emphasize the need of managing the exceptions by means of short term logistics decisions, avoiding frequent re-planning processes.

Montgomery [3] defines 5 functions that a SCEM system should perform. These are: Monitoring (to provide data in real time about supply chain processes, events and current states of the orders, shipments, production, and supply); Notification (to help

W. Cellary and E. Estevez (Eds.): I3E 2010, IFIP AICT 341, pp. 51–60, 2010.

to support real-time exception management through alert messaging, which proactively warns a decision-maker if an action must be taken); Simulation (to evaluate the effect of actions to be taken); Control (if an exception takes source, to evaluate the changes in the processes proactively); Measurement (to evaluate the supply chain performance).

In this paper, we present a compound web service [4] [5] that performs the monitoring and notification functions of a SCEM system. This web service is designed based on a reference model that we have proposed to improve the event management activity through a deeper analysis of the occurrence and causality of events, leading to anticipate an exception during the execution of a supply process order. The web service composition is defined based on two business processes. The ability to proactively detect, analyze and notify disruptive events is given through of a Bayesian Network with decision nodes.

This paper is organized in the following way. Section 2 discusses related works. Section 3 presents a reference model for monitoring, analysis and notification of events. Section 4 presents the compound web service design. Section 5 presents an example and section 6 presents conclusions.

2 Related Works

In order to provide a SCEM solution, two contributions closely related with this work have been proposed: Speyerer [6] developed a prototype based on web services to detect the root cause of a disruption. After that the disruption has been detected and classified it is compared in the data base to identify the root cause. This prototype also ranks exceptions in order to provide better accessibility and evaluation for operations managers; Maheshwari [7] designed a methodology to analyze business processes with the handling of exceptions suggesting web services to monitor and notify. Other contributions, in the SCEM scenario, have been proposed however, these works have not used web service. Following, some of them are mentioned: In the work of Zimmerman [2] the orders to be monitored are initialized by different triggers: queries from customers, alerts from suppliers and critical profiles. The critical profiles are the orders with high probability of being affected by disruptive events. This SCEM solution is based on a multi-agents architecture to proactively monitoring orders, integrating and interpreting several data gathered from the supply chain members to evaluate and distribute the results. Kurbel [8] proposed a mobile agent-based SCEM system to collect and analyze data provided by a supply chain monitoring system. To detect exceptions, his approach is not only based on target-state comparison, but it includes statistical analysis as well. Tai-Lang [9] proposed a method to analyze and manage the impact of an exception during order execution; Chin-Hung [10] developed a model based on cause-effect relationship to represent the disruptive exception caused by unexpected events in a supply chain. Liu [11] presented a methodology that uses Petri nets to formulate supply chain event rules and analyze the cause-effect relationships among events.

A common feature of these contributions is that the proposed SCEM models do not have the ability to anticipate a disruptive event during the execution of a supply process order. These models detect event in a reactive way and are not predictive.

In the field of event management, Complex Event Processing (CEP) has evolved into the paradigm of choice for the development of monitoring and reactive applications. CEP already plays an important role in many application areas like logistics. CEP addresses two crucial prerequisites to built highly scalable and dynamic systems. CEP-systems support the detection of relationships among events that can be specified by defining models of causal relations [12]. Different types of model can be defined, for instance, they can be defined using statistics and probabilities. Probabilistic models of causality should be supersets of computational causality in the sense that if any two events are causally related by the computation then they must be related by any probabilistic model of cause, but the probabilistic model may also relate other events as well [13]. In the context of this paradigm, this paper presents a reference model for the supply chain domain that contributes to systematizing the generation of models of causal relations among events.

The main difference between Business Activity Monitoring (BAM) and operational intelligence appears to be in the implementation details, real-time situation detection is a feature that only appears in operational intelligence and is often implemented using CEP. Furthermore, BAM focuses on formally modeled processes whereas operational intelligence instead relies on correlation to infer a relationship between different events.

3 Reference Model

We have defined a reference model for monitoring, analysis and notification of events in the supply chain domain. It can be used for monitoring the execution of any supply process order using a monitoring structure based on causal relations, when the total supply process time is of long duration. That is to say, when during the progress of realization of a supply process order is possible to define intermediate check points, so that it can be proactively detected the occurrence of disruptive events.

The reference model is represented as an UML class diagram in Figure 1, it shows that the *Schedule* (provided by the planning system) defines the execution timetable of a set of *Orders* and determines the resources that are linked to a supply process. Each *Resource* has a set of attributes. Associated with each *SupplyProcess*, there are milestones. Each milestone defines a measurement point which is used to assess the progress during its fulfillment. A *Milestone* is a *TimeMilestone* or *StateMilestone* and it has a *PlannedValue* (planned date of achievement of milestone, planned/ordered quantities). The last milestone (in the class diagram is the *Milestone* with *final* role) associated with an order is used by the control structure to anticipate disruptive events. To this purpose, the *ControlStructure* has an assigned *Monitor*. During the plan execution, the *Monitor* determines the *Milestone* to assess where one or more values of the resource *Attributes* or *EnvironmentVariables* can be observed. The *ControlStructureAnalizer* detects the occurrence of an event comparing the *ObservedValue* with the *PlanedValue* of resource *Attributes*. The impact of this event on the following *Milestones* is analyzed by the *ControlStructureAnalizer* using a cause-effect relation network defined by *Nodes* and *CausalRelationArcs*. An *EstimatedValue* of each *Milestone* is obtained. The *Comparator* takes the *EstimatedValue* associated

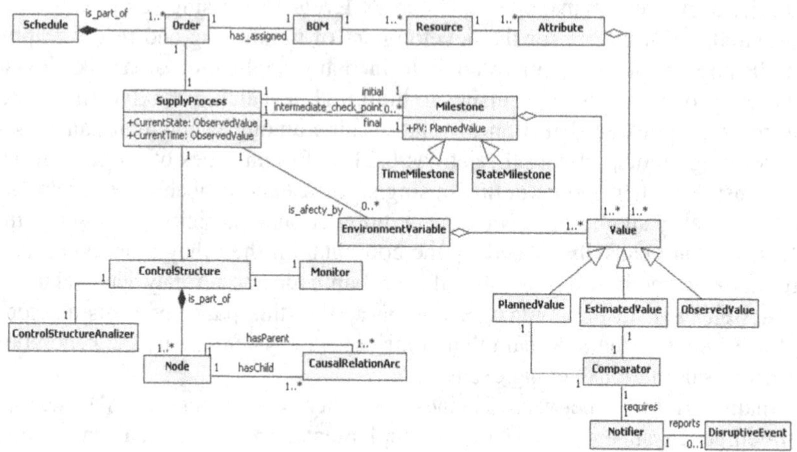

Fig. 1. Reference Model for monitoring, analysis and notification of events

with the last *Milestone* and compares it with its *PlannedValue*. The *Comparator,* based on decision criteria, estimates if a disruption will occur on the last *Milestone*. Upon the occurrence of a *DisruptiveEvent*, the *Notifier* reports it and the monitoring process finishes. Else, the *Monitor* determines the next *Milestone* to assess where one or more values of the resource *Attributes* or *EnvironmentVariables* can be observed. The monitoring process can also finish if the supply process order is completed without problems.

The *DisruptiveEvent* can be: changes in the requirements of an order (quantity of material, deadline), and/or changes in the parameters of a resource (transition time between states, available capacity).

An innovative characteristic of this model is that the network is dynamically constructed in each milestone. That is to say, the monitor, depending on the *EstimatedValues* generated by the *ControlStructureAnalizer*, can extend its monitoring strategy to other milestone including other observed values or eliminating those unnecessary variables.

In this paper, the *ControlStructureAnalizer* has been implemented by means of a Bayesian network with decision nodes. Bayesian networks [14] are a method to represent uncertain knowledge, which allows reasoning based on probability theory.

Mapping the reference model to a Bayesian network requires defining the following nodes in the net: <u>Chance nodes,</u> which describe the set of attributes associated with a resource and a set of environment variables. This type of node can be observed to detect the occurrence of an event. Each node is represented by X: (xi, P(xi)), where xi is a particular value that X (resource attribute or environmental variable) can take, and P(xi) is a conditional probability distribution for each combination of the variables of the parent nodes or a marginal probability distribution. A chance node can be: *Estimated* (its value is calculated from the inference process) or *Observed* (the evidence is captured and propagated through the network, affecting the overall joint distribution). Initially, all chance nodes of a network have likelihoods, which are calculated with a priori information. *Decision nodes* define the chance node that has to be observed to incorporate evidence; *Value nodes* represent utility functions.

The chance nodes and decision nodes are connected in the *ControlStructure* by directed arcs, encoding dependence relations and information precedence.

4 Compound Web Service Design

We have designed a compound web service that has the ability of proactively detect, analyze and notify disruptive events that take source in a supply chain. The composition is defined based on two business processes: Monitoring Service Contract and Order Monitoring Service. A conceptual model of each business process has been developed using the language BPMN (Business Process Modeling Notation) [15]. Theses business processes are described following:

Monitoring Service Contract (Figure 2) defines a contract to use the service. This business process defines the monitoring structure associated to a supply process and the sources from where observed values will be obtained. The process starts with a message reception event where the request service for potential orders monitoring is received. The supply processes are gotten from the model base and are offered in two modes: with standard a prior probability or requestor-defined. The requestor can cancel the request service or can select a supply process. In this case, its monitoring structure is gotten from the model base. Based on the reference model above described, it is determined when and what observed values will be required. The requestor is informed about of these requests and it sends the source from where observed values will can be gotten.

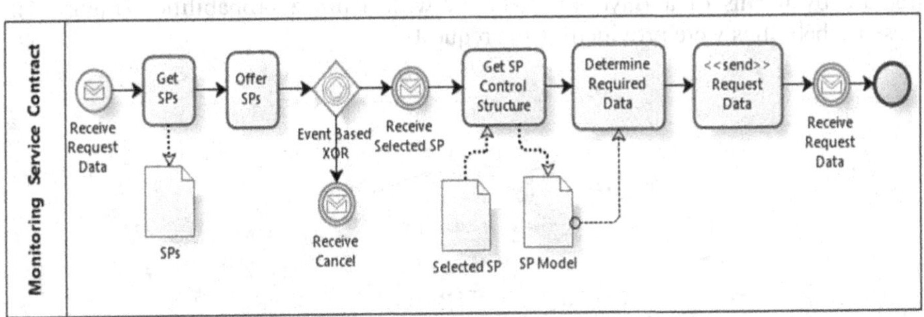

Fig. 2. Business Process Monitoring Service Contract

Order Monitoring Service (Figure 3) monitors orders based on the contract defined. The process starts with a message reception event where the order to be monitored is received. The monitoring structure is instantiated based on the reference model and completed with order parameters (planned values). During the order execution, request of observed values are sent. After receiving the observed values, the inference model is executed. If a disruptive event is detected, the result is notified. Otherwise, the monitoring process continues. Detail about the network dynamics were described in section 2.

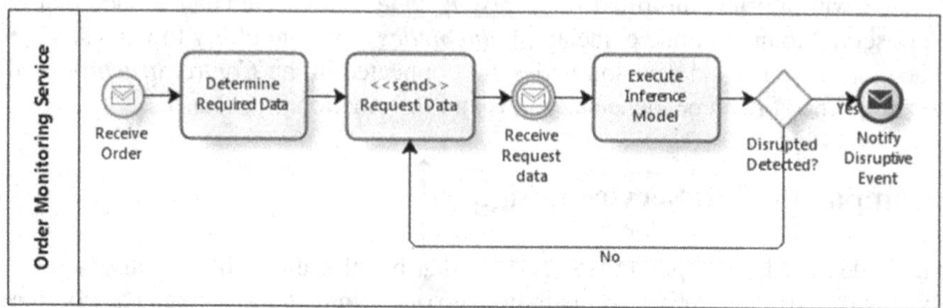

Fig. 3. Business Process Order Monitoring Service

5 An Application Example

As has been said above, the reference model covers monitoring and notification functions. Based on this model, we have designed a compound web service to proactively detect, analyze and notify disruptive events that take source in a supply chain.

An example of a cheese production plant is described to show the behavior of the compound web service and of the reference model. Through the *Monitoring Service Contract* is defined a contract to monitor the cheese production process. In this process, milk acidity is a parameter that can affect the cheese quality. High acidity can produce sandy cheese, bitter cheese or increase the curdling rate causing surface cracks. Low acidity can produce insipid cheese. Normal acidity produces cheese with required quality. Based on the reference model (Figure 1), is defined the monitoring structure by means of a Bayesian Network with a priori probabilities (Figure 4). These probabilities were provided by the requestor.

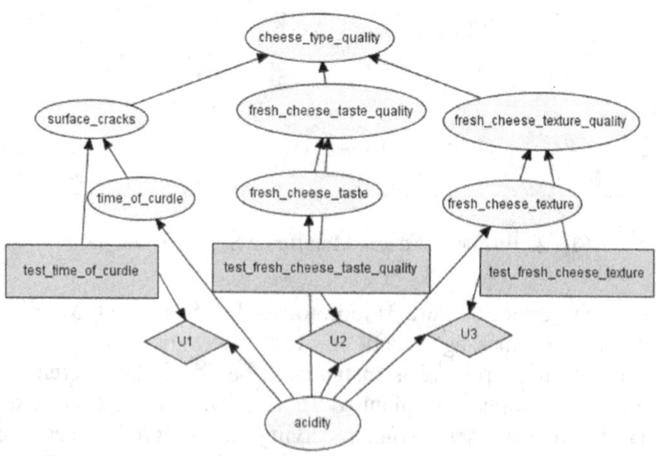

Fig. 4. Monitoring structure based on Bayesian Network

This monitoring structure is composed by the following *nodes*, whose states are represented in braces: *acidity* {normal, low, high}, which is a attribute of resource:*milk; time_of_curdle* {normal, low, high}, *fresh_cheese_texture_quality* {good, bad}, *fresh_cheese _texture* {no_granulated, granulated}, *surface_cracks* {no, yes}, *fresh_cheese_taste* {good, insipid, bitter} and *fresh_cheese_taste_quality* {good, bad}, which are resource attributes of the resource:*cheese_production_plant*; and *cheese_type_quality* {good, bad}, which is a attribute of resource:*cheese_type*. The *decision nodes* are: *test_ time_of_curdle*, *test_ fresh_cheese _texture* and *test_ fresh_cheese _taste*.

The requestor is informed when and what observed values will can be required. In this example the observed values could be the following: *acidity, time_of_curdle, fresh_cheese _texture* and *fresh_cheese _taste*. The requestor sends the source from where observed values will can be gotten.

The Order Monitoring Service starts with a message reception event where an order requires producing a quantity of a cheese type. The monitoring structure is instantiated and adapted to the order parameters (planned values).

The web service notifies changes in the requirement of the order if the probability of the product will be outside the specification is greater than a threshold value (decision criteria). In this example *threshold = 90.0.* The total process time depends on the type of cheese to be produced. In this example *cheese_type* = soft cheese is considered, and the total process time is 240 hours.

Thus, the initial milestone is a *StateMilestone* (start of the supply process) and the monitoring structure (Figure 4) initially includes the node *acidity*. The *acidity* is monitored at the beginning of the process, and for each of its three possible values, different plans of action can be carried out. Following, the action plan when the acidity is high is described.

1. If *acidity == high*, the monitor gets the evidence (from the source specified by requestor), inserts it in the net assigning *acidity:(high, 100)* and executes the inference model. As a result (Fig. 5), the estimated value of the node, *cheese_type_quality:(bad, 85.1)*. Since, *P(bad) = 85.1 < threshold*, the estimated values analyzed are *surface_cracks:(yes,50.75)*, *fresh_cheese_texture_quality:(bad,45)* and *fresh_cheese_ taste_quality:(bad, 45)*. The three values explain the value of the attribute *cheese_type_quality*:

1.1 *surface_cracks:(yes, 50.75)* indicates the probability that the cheese has surface cracks caused by a low time of curdle. Based on this information, the monitor defines the next milestone. *StateMilestone* (finish of the curdle process) and the next process variable to monitor is *surface_cracks*. This is done by assigning to the *decision node test_ time_of_curdle == YES*. This test is made 2 hours after the process has been started. The test has two possible results {*normal, low*}.

1.1.1 If *time_of_curdle == low,* the monitor gets the evidence (from the source specified by requestor) inserts it in the net (Fig. 6) assigning *time_of_curdle:(low, 100)* and executes the inference model. The result is *cheese_type_quality:(bad, 91.68)*. Since *P(bad) = 91.68 > threshold*, which implies high probability that product will be outside the specification, The value of the attribute, *cheese_type_quality*, is notified and the monitoring process finishes. This allows predicting the result 238 hours before the process ends.

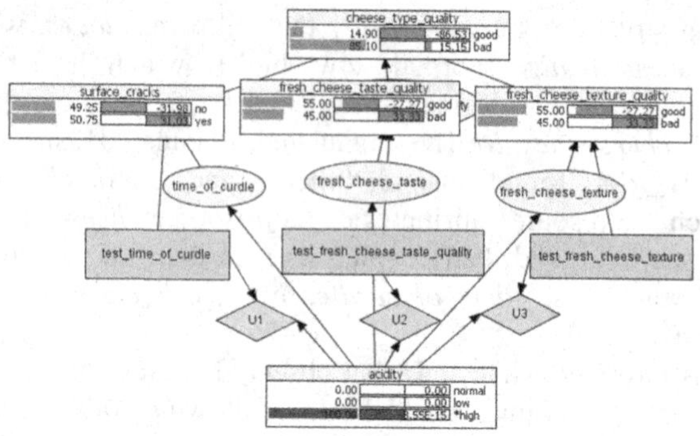

Fig. 5. Monitoring structure based on Bayesian Network with *acidity == high* evidence

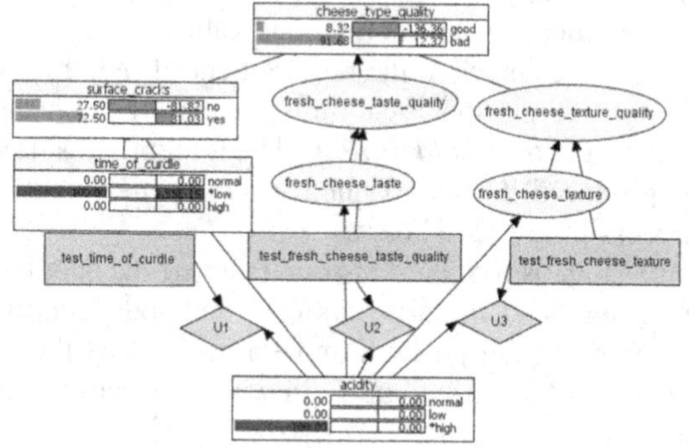

Fig. 6. Monitoring structure based on Bayesian Network with *time_of_curdle==low* evidence

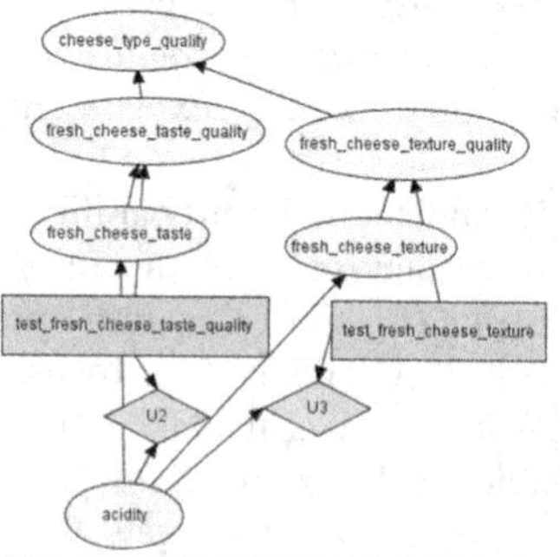

Fig. 7. Monitoring structure based on Bayesian network with the surface cracks branch pruned

1.2 If time*_of_curdle* == *normal,* the monitor gets the evidence (from the source specified by requestor) inserts it in the net assigning *time_of_curdle:(normal, 100)* and executes the inference model. The result is *cheese_type_quality:(bad, 69.7).* Since *P(bad)* = *69.7* < *threshold,* the variables *surface_cracks:(yes,0.0), fresh_cheese_texture_quality: (bad, 45.0)* and *fresh_cheese_taste_quality: (bad, 45.0)* are analyzed. The first variable indicates that there is no risk that the product will have surface cracks and its branch is pruned of the monitoring structure (Figure 7). The two last variables explain the value of the attribute *cheese_type_quality* and these are the next to monitor. The remainder of the monitoring process is similar to explained.

6 Conclusions

In this work we have proposed a compound web service for proactively monitor, analyze and notify disruptive events that take source in a supply chain. Monitoring and notification functions are managed through two business processes. The advantage of using web service technology is that it supports the execution of collaborative and distributed processes in the domain SCEM.

The compound web service is developed based on a reference model for monitoring, analysis and notification of events in a supply chain. Mechanisms based only on ad hoc event management are not acceptable. The generated reference model has two advantages: 1) ability to dynamically change the *network of analysis*. That is to say, after an evidence is obtained, the monitoring strategy can be extended including other parameters and increasing its monitoring frequency; 2) the model can be used to monitor the execution of any supply process order using a monitoring structure based on causal relations, when the total process time is of long duration.

The ability of anticipating disruptive event was implemented defining a Bayesian network with decision nodes representing temporal causality. As has been showed through the example, the model proposed has the ability of anticipating, based on evidences, changes in the values of the attributes of the resource or in the requirements of an order.

Different limitations are mentioned to be taken into account for future work: the approach is limited to a conceptual perspective on SCEM, excluding specific implementation aspects. The application is focused on supply process of long duration (when during the progress of its realization is possible to define intermediate check points) and disruptive events only can be detected during the execution of a supply process order.

References

1. Masing, N.: SC Event Management as Strategic Perspectiva – Market Study: SCEM Software Performance in the European Market. Master Thesis. Universitié du Québec en Outaouasis (2003)
2. Zimmermann, R.: Agent-based Supply Network Event Management. In: Walliser, M., Brantschen, S., Calisti, M., Hempfling, T. (eds.). Whitestein Series in Software Agent Techonologies (2006)
3. Montgomery, N., Waheed, R.: Event Management Enables Companies To Take Control of Extended Supply Chains. AMR Research (2001)

4. Alonso, G., Casati, F., Kuno, H., Machiraju, V.: Web Services - Concepts, Architecture and Applications. Springer, Berlin (2004)
5. Barros, A., Dumas, M., Oaks, P.: A Critical Overview of the Web Service Choreography Description Language (WS-CDL). BPTrends Newsletter 3 (2005)
6. Speyerer, J.K., Zeller, A.J.: Managing Supply Networks: Symptom Recognition and Diagnostic Analysis with Web Services. In: Proceedings of the 37th Hawaii International Conference on System Sciences (2004)
7. Maheshwari, P., Sharon, S.: Events-Based Exception Handling in Supply Chain Management using Web Services. In: Proceedings of the Advanced International Conference on Internet and Web Applications and Services (2006)
8. Kurbel, K., Schreber, D.: Agent-Based Diagnostics in Supply Networks. Issues in Information Systems VIII(2) (2007)
9. Tai-Lang, Y.: An Exception Handling Method of Order Fulfillment Process in the i-Hub Supported Extended Supply Chain. Master's Thesis, National Central University, Institute of Industrial Management, Taiwan (2002)
10. Chin-Hung, C.: Assessing Dependability of Order Fulfillment in the i-Hub Supported Extended Supply Chain. Master's Thesis, National Central University, Institute of Industrial Management, Taiwan (2002)
11. Liu, E., Akhil, K., Van Der Aalst, W.: A formal modeling approach for Supply Chain Event Management. Decision Support Systems 43, 761–778 (2007)
12. Buchmann, A., Darmstadt, T.U., Koldehofe, B.: Complex Event Processing. In: Information Technology (2009)
13. Luckham, D.C., Frasca, B.: Complex Event Processing in Distributed Systems. Stanford University Technical Report CSL-TR-98-754 (1998)
14. Jensen, F.: An Introduction to Bayesian Networks. Springer, New York (1996)
15. OMG/BPMN 1.2: OMG Specification (2009), http://www.omg.org/spec/BPMN/1.2/PDF/

Bridging the Gaps between eTransforming SMEs and SME - ICT Providers

Ana Hol and Athula Ginige

University of Western Sydney, Australia
{a.hol,a.ginige,LNCS}@uws.edu.au

Abstract. Small to Medium Enterprises (SMEs) are struggling to find ICT Providers who could assist them when identifying and implementing adequate Information and Communication Technologies (ICT). Based on this, we conducted a study with 30 SMEs from various industry sectors within Sydney metropolitan region to identify the type of ICT assistance eTransforming SMEs require. Furthermore, to better understand the struggles SMEs go through, we also studied eight ICT Providers. Our findings indicate that in order for the SMEs to successfully eTransform, select and implement appropriate ICT there is need for the ICT Providers to bridge the gaps and understand needs and requirements of the eTransforming companies taking into consideration a holistic view of what eTransforming SMEs need based on their current technology and future business requirements.

Keywords: SMEs, eTransformation, Information and Communication Technology, ICT providers.

1 Introduction

Today, society has changed, and we have become more dependent on technologies that surround us. For the business to be successful they are required to embrace technology. Successful communication with customers and business partners means a successful business. For the customers to be satisfied there is a need for a business to have an online presence. In order to do this, SMEs are required to eTransform, select and implement appropriate ICT.

eTransformation is a process through which companies need to go through so that they can have required skills and technologies to be able to survive in ICT centered world [1]. There are many models that explain oranisational change and ICT implementation [2-11]. One of the models that very comprehensively assess ICT selection and implementation within the organisation is the eTransformation Road Map [1] presented in the table below.

From the table above it can be seen that eTransformation is a staged process and that in order for SMEs to reach a desired level of eTransformation, they need to successfully complete each preceding stage. For example a company's desired stage may

W. Cellary and E. Estevez (Eds.): I3E 2010, IFIP AICT 341, pp. 61–69, 2010.

be Stage 2. To reach Stage 2 they will need to complete all Stage 1 requirements. From this we conclude that in order for the eTransformation process to be successful, ICT Providers would need to take an eTransforming SMEs through each eTransformation stages, step by step. Through this research we explore at what stage current eTransforming SMEs are at and also whether ICT Providers are skilled and able to assist SMEs to eTransform further.

Table 1. eTransformation Stages and Accompanying Technologies - adapted from [1]

Stage		Hardware, Software and Networking infrastructure
Stage 1	Effective Individual	Individuals with stand-alone computers having productivity software such as accounting packages spreadsheets, word processors etc installed. Possibly dial up connection to the Internet for individual email accounts.
	Basic Web Site	Organisation having its own domain name and "Brochure ware" type web site hosted with an ISP.
Stage 2	Effective Team	Computers are networked. People can work in teams using networked applications. Providing email and Intranet capabilities can enhance productivity of a team.
	Interactive Web Site	Organisations having Web sites that provide two-way flow of information. From these Web sites uses should be able to get immediate responses to structured queries such as a quotation for a particular product configuration user has selected. Also another feature would be to provide personalised information to frequent visitors. These types of Web sites though can be hosted with an ISP are better to host on site. This requires a Web server and a high-speed dedicated connection to the Internet.
Stage 3	Effective Organisation	Organisation now uses enterprise wide applications; a single application that supports different sections of the organisation such as purchasing, sales, accounting, manufacturing etc. thus enabling information integration and sharing across enterprise.
	eCommerce Site	At this stage the organisation should have secure Web servers to facilitate financial transactions or a link to a payment get way to get this facility.
Stage 4	Convergence	Organisation has now achieved integration of information that needs to support all its business processes. The flow of information of an organisation that has reached the level of convergence.

2 ICT Requirements as Perceived by eTransforming SMEs

Therefore, to better understand needs and requirements of the eTransforming SMEs, 30 SMEs from Sydney metropolitan region were studied. A list of represented industry sectors is presented in the table below.

Table 2. Industry sectors representing 30 SMEs

Industry Sector	No. of SMEs
Accounting and Consulting	1
Building	2
Community Services and Hospitality	1
Consultancy	4
Construction	1
Education and Training	1
Finance	2
Funeral Services	1
Health and Wellbeing	2
Manufacturing	5
Organic food	1
Photography and Picture Framing	1
Printing	1
Retail, Sales & Speciality	2
Services	1
Tourism Hospitality	3
Training in Sales and Marketing	1
Total	30

Each company that has willingly agreed to participate within the study was interviewed. Interviews lasted about 1h 30min. During the interviews studied SMEs were mapped on the eTransformation Road Map. The results are displayed in Figure 1.

Based on the analysis majority of eTransforming SMEs are currently at level 0 (no website) and 1 (basic website) and a small number on level 2 (interactive site) within the eTransformation Road Map. This means that companies mostly have basic websites, however that there are still those who do not. Furthermore, findings show that studied SMEs use basic productivity tools such as Word, Excel, PDFs. They also use e-mails and file storage media. However, companies are still struggling to integrate their ICT and move towards effective teams.

In addition, studied SMEs were asked to point out the areas of ICT in which they felt that they should improve in. All companies stated that they would need to develop their online identity which would mean design, re-creation and re-shaping of their current websites. Companies also stated that this is extremely hard for them as ICT companies expect them to know exactly what they would like to have on their sites without giving them much opportunity to experiment and identify possibilities.

Furthermore, eTransforming SMEs identified that if they are to move ahead and integrate some of their current systems they are faced with huge challenges. They also report that SME- ICT Providers somehow do not get the full understanding of their requirements. In addition, eTransforming SMEs report that they are struggling to set up networks, share data and establish remote access. They also state that it is extremely hard to identify what type of ICT will be the most beneficial for their own business. Moreover, it is exceptionally hard for the SMEs to keep up with new technology and therefore they need ICT Providers to help them identify what is absolutely crucial for their own business.

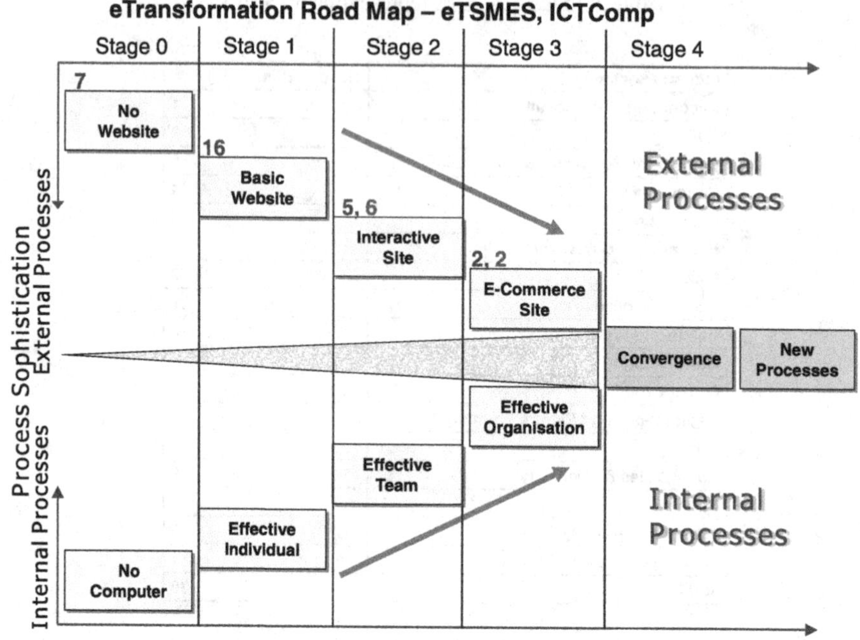

Fig. 1. eTransformation Road Map [1]

ICT Maintenance and Support seem to be a big problem for eTransforming SMEs too. They state that for them it is impossible to find someone who will reliably look into their systems and therefore they are finding that it is the most suitable to rely on help from relatives or friends. They also feel that in order to get some help and advice from the ICT Providers they need to pay for consultations and advice which they are unable to afford and therefore lack holistic support.

In addition, a majority of eTransforming SMEs have identified that in order to survive in the electronic world they will need to undertake training. It appears, based on the data collected via the interviews, that training in handling business online, managing business web pages and communicating via social networking sites with the customers is becoming increasingly important. Moreover, companies feel that they require training in graphical design and document management.

Following the identification that eTransforming SMEs require assistance across both internal and external ICT processes (see Figure 1 for details) and that they are struggling to get it, through this study we aim to identify how best needs and requirements of the eTransforming SMEs can be met by studying a group of SME - ICT Providers.

3 ICT Providers

Following the study with 30 SMEs we have decided to select a group of SME size ICT Providers within a metropolitan Sydney region to identify if these companies are able to meet needs and demands of the eTansforming SMEs.

Eight ICT Provider companies that willingly agreed to participate within the study were interviewed. During the interviews companies were asked about jobs that they performed. Their ability and past experiences were taken into the consideration too. Collated data was used to map ICT Provider companies on the eTransformation Road Map to identify their current ICT development. Results for ICT Providers, shown in red, are depicted in Figure 1. Findings indicate that a majority of ICT Provider companies are in Stage 2 of eTransformation development, that they have interactive websites, are able to manipulate data electronically and are slowly implementing integrated systems.

Based on the data collected and the understanding that ICT Providers have embraced technology more than eTransforming SMEs from other industry sectors we further investigated to what extent ICT companies are able to meet needs and demands of the SMEs requiring technical assistance.

4 ICT Providers: Can They Assist eTransforming SMEs?

Based on the developmental process identified within the eTransformation Road Map each developmental stage (0-4) was converted into a number of questions and based on it given rating. For example, if a studied ICT Provider was able to complete all that was required for the SME to have a website within the Stage 1 the ICT Provider would be given a rating of 1. If the ICT Provider was only partially able to complete the tasks the company would be given a rating of 0.5. This rating would mean that the ICT Provider has answered positively to a minimum of 50% of the questions within this section but less than 100%. If ICT Provider was able to complete activities less than 50% the provider would be given a rating of 0. Table 3 shows the rating for all 8 ICT Providers.

Based on the data within the table it can be seen that none of the 8 providers is able to complete a task across all stages (0-4). Moreover, it can also be seen that even if all resources of the ICT companies are to be combined there would still be areas in which support would be lacking.

From the data depicted in Table 3 it can be seen that only one ICT Provider (company 6) is able to fully complete Stage 1, and that company 8 is missing half a point to be able to do the same. None of the ICT Providers is able to complete Stage 2 in full. The closest one to completing the Stage 2 is company 6 (lacking 1 point). Stage 3 was far from reach for all ICT Providers (company 6 was lacking 3 points). When looking at the collective skills of 8 ICT Provides (Figure 2) it can be seen that Stage 1 and Stage 2 can be completed to almost 70% successfully. Stage 2 however is not well represented and there are many areas that are lacking and do not even reach 50% development, such as infrastructure, application and systems implementation and web set up and support. It can also be seen that Stage 3 can only be completed 30% successfully. Therefore, we conclude that in order for the eTransformation to be successfully carried gaps between eTransformation requirements and ICT Provider skills would need to be bridged.

Table 3. Ratings for ICT Providers

ICT Providers	Comp 1	Comp2	Comp3	Comp4	Comp5	Comp6	Comp7	Comp8	TOTAL	% out of 8
Web design development 1	0.5	1	0	1	1	1	1	1	6.5	81.25
Web set up support 1	0.5	0.5	0	0.5	1	1	1	1	5.5	68.75
Security 1	1	0.5	1	1	1	1	0.5	1	7	87.5
Infrastructure 1	1	0.5	0.5	1	0.5	1	0.5	1	6	75
Training 1	1	1	1	1	1	1	0.5	0.5	7	87.5
Applications systems 1	1	0	1	0.5	0.5	1	0.5	1	5.5	68.75
Web design development 2	0	1	0	1	1	1	1	1	6	75
Web set up support 2	0	0.5	0	0.5	1	0.5	0.5	0.5	3.5	43.75
Security 2	1	0	1	1	0.5	1	0.5	1	6	75
Infrastructure 2	0.5	0	0.5	1	0	1	0	0.5	3.5	43.75
Training 2	0.5	1	1	1	1	1	0	0	5.5	68.75
Applications systems 2	0.5	0	0.5	0	0.5	0.5	0	0.5	2.5	31.25
Web design development 3	0	0.5	0	0.5	1	0.5	1	1	4.5	56.25
Web set up support 3	0	0.5	0	0	0.5	0.5	0.5	0.5	2.5	31.25
Security 3	0	0	0.5	0.5	0	0.5	0	0.5	2	25
Infrastructure 3	0.5	0	0.5	0.5	0	0.5	0	0.5	2.5	31.25
Training 3	0	0.5	0.5	1	0.5	0.5	0	0	3	37.5
Applications systems 3	0.5	0	0.5	0	0.5	0.5	0	0	2	25

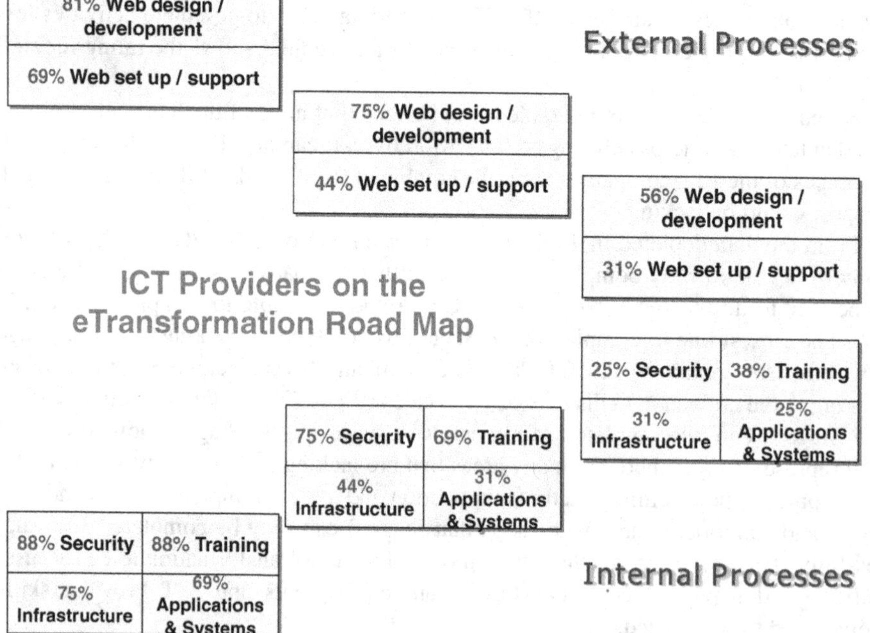

Fig. 2. Grouped Skills of Eight ICT Provides Shown on the eTransformation Road Map

5 Bridging the Gaps between eTransformation Requirements and ICT Providers

Based on the findings it appears that in the form in which ICT Provides are currently operating in, it is virtually impossible for them to fully meet needs and demands of eTransforming SMEs. ICT Providers seem to be specialising in very narrow fields. None of the interviewed providers looks at eTransforming SMEs holistically. They tend to focus only within the area they service. For example, if a company is designing websites they will create the site but will rarely take into the consideration the industry sector the SME needing the website is in, nor other systems the SME has nor the system integration and data and file transfers. Therefore, it becomes very hard for the SMEs to get the appropriate websites and systems. Consequently, to eTransform SMEs are required to see a business analyst, a network specialist, web designer and hardware and software specialists in order to transform. However, even then, it is extremely hard to assure that all components selected will be compatible.

Therefore, we speculate that the way how ICT Providers are assisting SMEs will need to be changed. First of all for the SMEs to get the eTransformation assistance it would be necessary for the businesses to be reviewed holistically. Furthermore, it will be essential for the specialists within the ICT industry to communicate with one another and work with the same understanding of business needs and requirements. They would all need to understand what the SME is intending to achieve by eTransforming. They would also need to know how the SME is planning to work and operate. Are they going to operate online? Will they continue to operate as a brick and mortar company? Furthermore, ICT specialists will need to understand the business operations of the companies they are assisting so that they can guide them in selecting and implementing required ICT. Moreover, it is essential for the ICT Providers to understand systems eTransforming SMEs already have, as well as identify how their existing tools and systems will fit with new system upgrades and applications.

Past research indicates that eTransformation Guide (eT Guide) can be used by SMEs to help them track, guide and measure their eTransformation journey [12]. The eT Guide through a series of questions about *Strategy* – company vision goals and objectives; *Structure* – company departments and divisions followed by *Business Tasks and Processes* – automation, streamlining and integration allows the SME to build a personalised eTransformatgion Report that identifies SMEs current Abilities – what the SME can currently do with the technology they have and the Recommendations – what the SME could do in the future in order to advance and successfully eTransform allows the SMEs to take a charge of their eTransformation journey (Figure 3).

We believe that if eTransforming SMEs are encouraged to take eTransformation initiative and start monitoring their eTransformation journey via the eT Guide they would much easier be able to communicate with ICT Providers. Furthermore, this would also mean that each ICT Provider would be able to understand the company's current eTransformation status and would easier be able to identify tools and systems SMEs would need to successfully eTransform.

We also speculate that for ICT Providers to be able to provide full assistance they could work collaboratively or in clusters. Their operations would be similar to those of toolmaking SMEs example [13] where SMEs would be able to take more complex

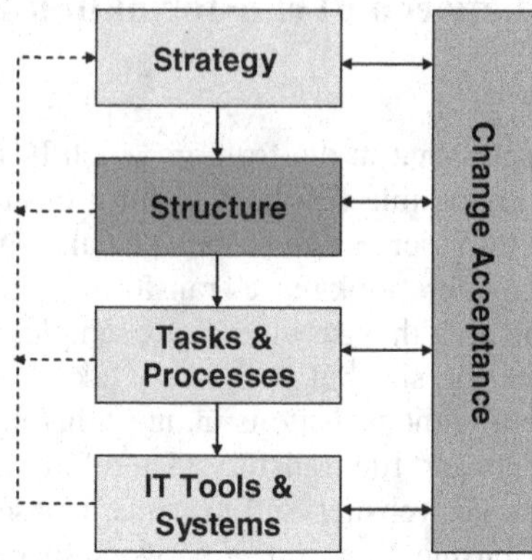

Fig. 3. Iterative Model of eTransformation [12]

and bigger jobs by sharing their equipment and splitting the jobs amongst themselves with the aim of getting bigger projects. Similar could happen with ICT providers were for example analyst, a web developer, a graphic designer, a networking specials and hardware and software specialists search for jobs collectively. Furthermore, they may work collaboratively in a way so that once a business analysis is done for the company depending on their needs and requirements specialists may meet together to discuss the requirements and then split the jobs amongst themselves in accordance to the SME needs.

This further meets with earlier speculations of dynamic enterprise collaborations where companies from same or different industry sectors may meet per project to complete particular tasks or actions. This further indicates that companies within SME sectors will need to create business networks in order to complete tasks and processes and remain competitive within the global markets. However, for the ICT Providers to do so, they will first need to gain an understanding that it is essential to know the business holistically first, before appropriate ICT tools and systems can be selected and implemented. In addition, it can be seen that if the group of eight ICT Providers was to collaborate they would need to be able to identify skills that they as a group have and then identify skills they are missing to be able to assist eTransforming SMEs.

6 Conclusion

It is not surprising to see why eTransforming SMEs are struggling to identify and select required ICT so that they can easily survive in the digital economy. This study identifies that SMEs are experiencing difficulties when required to identify ICT Providers that could help them select and implement ICT tools and systems they need. They are faced with ICT Providers who specialise in specific ICT areas and who are unable to provide holistic guidelines as each ICT Provider is mainly concerned with their own area of expertise and therefore do not take into the consideration eTransforming SME goals and objectives nor their existing tools and systems into considerations while providing support. Furthermore, we also identify that eTransforming SMEs could use the eTransformation Guide to take control of their eTransformation journey and with it also help ICT Providers to understand current state of their eTransformation and so help them identify tools and systems required.

We also identify that in order for the ICT Providers to be able to help eTransforming SMEs holistically they may need to make collaborative arrangements amongst one another as well as with the other related industries to be able to get a more holistic views of the SMEs requirements. The collaborative arrangements could also help ICT Providers meet demands placed by the eTransforming SMEs easier as well as in turn make the SMEs more productive in the electronic environment.

References

1. Ginige, A., Murugesan, S., Kazanis, P.: A Road Map for Successfully Transforming SMEs into eBusiness. Cutter IT Journal 15(5), 13 (2001)
2. Waterman, R.H., Peters, T.J., Phillips, J.R.: Structure is Not Organization. Business Horizons 23(3), 14–26 (1980)
3. Mawson, A.: The Advanced Organisation, New Models for Turbulent Times (2002), `http://www.advanced-workplace.com` (retrieved February 27, 2006)
4. People and Process. Business Crisis Management (2005), `http://www.the-process-improver.com/business-crisis-management.html` (retrieved March 3, 2006)
5. Earl, M.J.: Management Strategies for Information Technology. Burr Ridge, Irwin (1989)
6. Burn, J., Ash, C.: A Dynamic Model of E-business Strategies for ERP Enabled Organisations. Industrial Management & Data Systems 105(8), 1084–1095 (2005)
7. Galliers, R.D., Merali, Y., Spearling, L.: Coping with Information Technology? How British Executives perceive the key information systems management issues in the mid 1990s. Journal of Information Technology 9, 223–238 (1994)
8. McKay, J., Prananto, A., Marshall, P.: E-Business Maturity: The SOG-e Model. In: Proceedings of the ACIS - 11th Australasian Conference on Information Systems, Brisbane, Australia, December 6-8 (2000)
9. Wons, E.: Organisational Change - An Ethical, Means Based, Approach, JPC Training & Consulting LLC, Boston (1999)
10. Nolan, R.L.: Managing the Crises in Data Processing. Harvard Business Review 57(2), 115–116 (1979)
11. Rayport, J.F., Jaworski, B.J.: Introduction to E-Commerce, Boston (2002)
12. Hol, A., Ginige, A.: eTransformation Guide: An Online System for SMEs. In: 3rd IEEE International Conference on Digital Ecosystems and Technologies, Istanbul, Turkey, June 1-3 (2009)
13. Lawson, R., Arunatileka, S., Ginige, A., Hol, A.: A Pilot Project on eCollaboration in the Australian Toolmaking Industry 18th Bled eConference eIntegration in Action, Bled, Slovenia, June 6-8 (2005)

Measuring Accumulated Revelations of Private Information by Multiple Media

Komei Kamiyama[1], Tran Hong Ngoc[2], Isao Echizen[3], and Hiroshi Yoshiura[4]

[1] Department of Human Communication, The University of Electro-Communications, 1-5-1 Chofugaoka Chofu, Tokyo, 182-8585 Japan
[2] Faculty of Information Technology, University of Science, VNU- HCMC227 Nguyen Van Cu, Dist. 5, Ho Chi Minh City, Vietnam
[3] Digital Content and Media Sciences Research Division, National Institute of Informatics 2-1-2 Hitotsubashi, Chiyodaku, Tokyo, 101-8430 Japan
[4] Department of Informatics, The University of Electro-Communications, 1-5-1 Chofugaoka Chofu, Tokyo, 182-8585 Japan
kamiyama@edu.hc.uec.ac.jp, yoshiura@hc.uec.ac.jp

Abstract. A metric has been developed for measuring privacy degradation when various types of media reveal private information about a person. The metric, which is based on joint entropy, quantifies accumulated revelations of information about various personal attributes. Application of this metric to entries posted on a social networking service and to leaks from a company database containing personal information showed that it is effective; that is, it can quantify accumulated revelations of information about multiple attributes and can cope with cases in which the attributes affect each other.

Keywords: Privacy, Privacy metric, Social Networking Service.

1 Introduction

Private information about various attributes of people is acquired, stored, and made available by various types of media in Web2.0 and in ubiquitous networks, and it can be revealed in a number of ways. For instance, friends may disclose private information on social network services (SNSs), third parties may illegally access information residing in databases belonging to public organizations and enterprises, computer viruses may obtain private information residing on PCs and send it over the network, and ubiquitous networks may automatically obtain and reveal personal location information.

Such revelations of private information can lead to serious problems. Leaks of private information may result in a person receiving annoying e-mails, being stalked, or even being fired from their job. Moreover, even if there is no actual damage, people might feel anxious about using network services upon hearing of the danger.

Internet service providers (ISPs) can be the source of revealed private information. The revelations may be unintentional or the result of malicious behaviours by an employees. ISPs must therefore take privacy protection seriously while still ensuring

W. Cellary and E. Estevez (Eds.): I3E 2010, IFIP AICT 341, pp. 70–80, 2010.

system usability. Privacy metrics are therefore important for analysing the trade-off between privacy protection and system usability. Users also reveal their private information carelessly or voluntarily without being able to predict consequence of the disclosure. Thus, privacy metrics are important to detect such revelation by users.

Metrics for quantifying privacy have been proposed for privacy-preserving data mining, location privacy, and e-mail. Most of these metrics are application dependent, but metrics based on k-anonymity and entropy can generally be used. However, such metrics cannot quantify accumulated revelations of information about different attributes. In particular, metrics based on k-anonymity and entropy cannot cope with cases in which multiple attributes are not mutually independent, and, in the real world, such attributes are not usually independent. Assume, for example, that a person posted an entry on his/her SNS page saying "I am struggling everyday to save lives of people" and that he/she is known to graduate from The University of Tokyo from information illegally obtained from a company database. The combination of these two information revelations enables the estimate of his/her occupation (i.e. medical doctor) and his/her educational record (i.e. M.D. conferred by The University of Tokyo). Metrics based on k-anonymity and entropy cannot measure the accumulation of these information revelations.

We have developed a metric for measuring multiple revelations of information by using joint entropy. Section 2 describes the revelation of information about multiple attributes. Section 3 describes related work. Section 4 describes our privacy model. Section 5 describes our metric, and Section 6 describes its application to SNS entries and a company database and evaluates its performance. Section 7 concludes the paper with a brief summary of the key points.

2 Revelations by Various Types of Media

Suppose that a person posts the following entry on an SNS.

Entry 1: I attend a *technical university in Tokyo.*

From this entry, a reader could identify a number of universities that the writer might be attending. The next day, the writer posts another entry.

Entry 2: Next week, I plan to attend the job fair in the West-6 building.

From entry 2, the reader learns that the writer's university has a building named "West-6". If both entries are considered together, the reader can limit the field because only two universities have buildings named "West-6", i.e. UEC (The University of elctro-communication) and Tokyo Tech (Tokyo Institute of Technology). Because the number of students at UEC and Tokyo Tech are 4165 and 4911, the probabilities of the writer attending UEC and Tokyo Tech are 4165/9076 and 4911/9076.

Now, let us suppose that the writer's hometown is in Kyoto and that this information has been leaked from a company database. Moreover, because UEC and Tokyo Tech respectively have 28 and 16 students from Kyoto, the probabilities of the writer attending one of these universities can be calculated more precisely. Numbers of students of UEC and Tokyo Tech as well as those from each prefecture are public data provided by these universities. Therefore any attacker can use these data to estimate the writer's privacy.

Furthermore, we assume that the attacker obtains the record of writer's location at every one hour in daytime of five weekdays, i.e. the attacker has 40 data items of location. If 19 location data items are those of UEC and no data items Tokyo Tech, the confidence that the writer belongs to UEC is increased.

As shown by this example, revelations of private information can have a combinatorial effect. Thus, a privacy metric for the real world should be able to quantify mutually dependent information disclosures.

3 Related Work

Privacy can be quantified as the degree of uncertainty about which private data can be inferred. The metric developed by Agrawal and Srikant et al.[1] for protecting privacy during data mining adds a random perturbation to each attribute of the data including personal information. Privacy is quantified by evaluating how closely the original value of an attribute can be estimated. That is, if the original value can be estimated with c% confidence to lie in interval [a,b], the interval width (b-a) defines the amount of privacy at the c% confidence level. However, they did not consider the distribution of the original data. Therefore Agrawal and Aggarwal et al. improved this metric by using entropy [2].

Sweeney proposed a different approach to privacy protection during data mining: using k-anonymity [3]. If a data table satisfies k-anonymity, every record in that table is indistinguishable from at least k – 1 other records with respect to every set of quasi-identifier attributes. The possible attacks against k-anonymity include homogeneity attacks and background-knowledge attacks focused on the quasi-identifiers. These problems of k-anonymity can be solved by adding l-diversity, which requires that each equivalent class of records in k-anonymity has at least l well-represented values of the sensitive attribute [4]. In t-closeness [5], the distribution of the sensitive attribute values in each equivalent class is close to that in the whole table.

Hoh and Gruteser's [6] location privacy metric uses the expected error in the distance between a person's true location and the attacker's uncertain estimates of that location. Duckham and Kulik [7] defined the "level of privacy" as the number of different location coordinates sent by a user with a single location-based query. Gruteser and Grunwald introduced k-anonymity to location privacy [8] and used k to represent the level of privacy. Hoh et al. [9] quantified location privacy as the duration over which an attacker could track a target person. Some studies on location privacy have taken into account the relationship between location privacy and quality of service[10][11].

Claudia, D. et al.[12] and Andrei, S. et al. [13]proposed metric for E-mail by using entropy. Serjantov et al. also applied their metric to the anonymity of voting system. Ryouke , Y., and Astushi, K., et al proposed probabilistic metric quantifying the degree of personal information disclosure from blog [18].

While most of the above metrics are application dependent, metrics based on k-anonymity and entropy can generally be used to quantify privacy for any kind of media. However, they cannot cope with situations like those described in section 2 because they cannot quantify the accumulated revelations of private information about different attributes and they cannot cope with cases in which the multiple attributes are not independent.

4 Our Model of Privacy

The anonymity metric based on entropy, which was proposed independently by Claudia, D. et al.[12] and Andrei, S. et al. [13], ïfocuses on one particular action. An anonymity set is defined that contains the people who might take the action. For each person, the probability of taking the action is given. The degree of anonymity is defined as the value of the entropy calculated from the anonymity set and the probabilities.

Inspired by this anonymity metric, we propose a privacy metric. We use the symmetry relation between anonymity and privacy [14]. We focus on one particular person, i.e. the subject of our privacy metric. We first consider one attribute of the subject and define a privacy set containing the potential attribute values. The probability that the attribute takes each value is given. The degree of privacy is defined as the value of entropy calculated from the privacy set and the probability (Fig. 1).

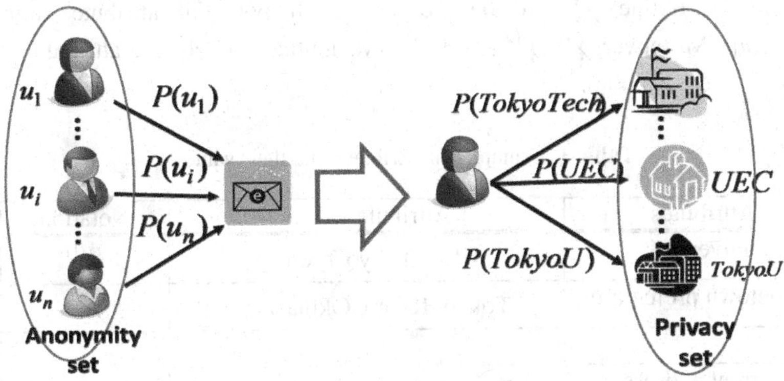

Fig. 1. Anonymity and privacy

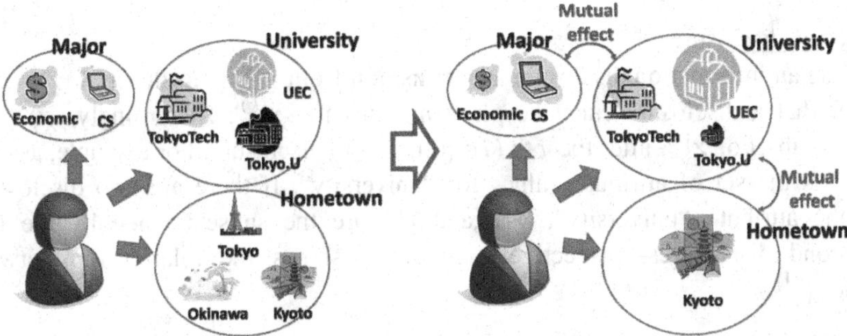

Fig. 2. Privacy of multiple attribute

Next, we consider multiple attributes of the subject and the combination of the privacy sets for the attributes (Fig. 2, left). Finally, we consider the privacy in the case where the attributes affect each other (Fig. 2, right). As described in Section 2, disclosing that the subject's hometown is Kyoto increases the probability that the subject attends UEC. The increase in this probability leads to a decrease in the probability that the subject majors in economics and increases the probability that the subject majors in computer science. We use joint entropy to represent these relations between attributes. Thus, the revelation of private information is quantified in terms of the difference in joint entropy before and after information is disclosed.

5 Metric of Privacy Revelation

5.1 Definition

We first model the problem and define the terms.

Attributes and attribute values

We assume that the person of interest (*the subject of our privacy metric*) has m attributes. We define $\chi^{(k)}$ to be the set of all potential attribute values of $k \in \{1,\ldots,m\}$. Moreover, $\chi^{(1)},\chi^{(2)},\ldots,\chi^{(m)}$ have mutually exclusive attribute values: $\chi^{(1)}\cap\chi^{(2)}\cap\ldots\cap\chi^{(m)}=\varphi$.

Table 1. Examples of attributes and their values

Attributes	Attribute values	Notation
university	UEC, Tokyo Tech,$\cdots$	$\chi^{(1)}$
hometown prefecture	Tokyo, Kyoto, Okinawa,$\cdots$	$\chi^{(2)}$
:	:	:
current address	Tokyo, Kyoto, Okinawa,$\cdots$	$\chi^{(m-1)}$
age	1,2,...,80,$\cdots$	$\chi^{(m)}$

Information disclosure

We define an information disclosure as a transition from $\chi^{(k)}$ to a subset of $\chi^{(k)}$. We consider that a disclosure can take place n times for $\chi^{(k)}$. Accordingly, $\chi_i^{(k)}$ denotes the subset of $\chi^{(k)}$ after the i th ($i\in\{0,1,\ldots,n\}$) disclosure. For example, assume that $\chi^{(1)}$ is the set of attribute values for "university". If there are two disclosures about the attribute "university", $\chi_1^{(1)}$,and $\chi_2^{(1)}$ are the subsets made by the first and second disclosures, respectively. Figure 3 shows the relationship between $\chi_1^{(1)}$ and $\chi_2^{(1)}$.

Joint attribute set

$\tilde{\chi}^{(k)}$ is defined as the intersection of $\chi_1^{(k)},\chi_2^{(k)},\ldots,\chi_n^{(k)}$: $\tilde{\chi}^{(k)}=\bigcap_{i=1}^{n}\chi_i^{(k)}$. In figure 3, $\tilde{\chi}^{(1)}$ is $\tilde{\chi}^{(1)}$ ={UEC, Tokyo Tech}, and $\tilde{\chi}^{(k)}$ is the joint set of n information disclosures.

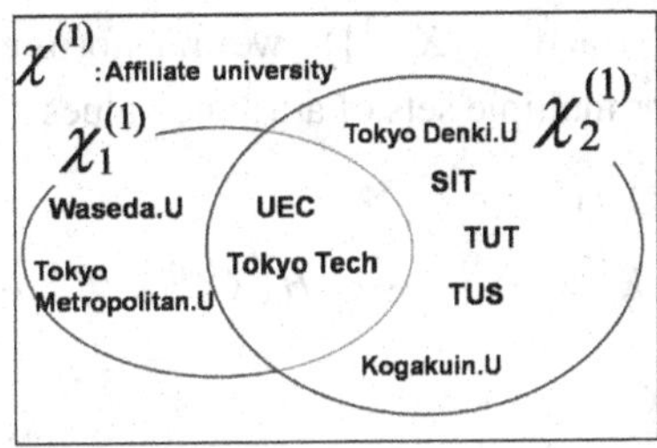

Fig. 3. Sets of attribute values after two disclosures about attribute "university"

5.2 Quantification of Revelations

The revelation of private information is quantified in terms of the difference in entropy before and after information is disclosed. Specifically, joint entropy is used to quantify revelations about a person with multiple attributes.

5.2.1 Privacy Revelations of a Single Attribute

We start by quantifying a revelation of private information about a single attribute. We assume that information about the kth attribute of a person is disclosed.

First, we calculate the entropy before disclosure:

$$H(X^{(k)}) = -\sum_{x} P(X^{(k)} = \mathrm{x}) \log_2 P(X^{(k)} = \mathrm{x}) . \tag{1}$$

Next, we calculate the entropy after disclosure:

$$H(\widetilde{X}^{(k)}) = -\sum_{\mathrm{x} \in \widetilde{X}^{(1)}} P(\widetilde{X}^{(k)} = \mathrm{x}) \log_2 P(\widetilde{X}^{(k)} = \mathrm{x}) . \tag{2}$$

The value of the revelation for the kth attribute is thus

$$\Delta^{(k)} = H(X^{(k)}) - H(\widetilde{X}^{(k)}) \tag{3}$$

5.2.2 Revelations of Multiple Attributes

The total value of all revelations for all attributes is represented by Δ. That is, Δ denotes the difference in the joint entropy of m attributes before and after disclosures.

$$\Delta = H(\{X^{(k)}\}) - H(\{\widetilde{X}^{(k)}\}) \tag{4}$$

The entropy before multiple disclosures is given by

$$H(\{X^{(k)}\}) = H(X^{(1)}, X^{(2)}, \ldots, X^{(k)}) \tag{5}$$

The entropy after multiple disclosures is given by

$$H(\{\widetilde{X}^{(k)}\}) = H(\widetilde{X}^{(1)}, \widetilde{X}^{(2)}, \ldots, \widetilde{X}^{(k)}) \tag{6}$$

To compute $H(\{X^{(k)}\})$ and $H(\{\tilde{X}^{(k)}\})$, we transform equations (7) and (8) into the conditional entropy for multiple sets of attribute values.

$$H(X^{(1)}, X^{(2)}, \ldots, X^{(k)}) = H(X^{(1)}) + H(X^{(2)} \mid X^{(1)}) + \cdots + H(X^{(m)} \mid X^{(m-1)}, \cdots, X^{(2)}, X^{(1)}) \tag{7}$$

$$H(\tilde{X}^{(1)}, \tilde{X}^{(2)}, \ldots, \tilde{X}^{(k)}) = H(\tilde{X}^{(1)}) + H(\tilde{X}^{(2)} \mid \tilde{X}^{(1)}) + \cdots + H(\tilde{X}^{(m)} \mid \tilde{X}^{(m-1)}, \cdots, \tilde{X}^{(2)}, \tilde{X}^{(1)}) \tag{8}$$

$X^{(i)}$ can be exchanged with $X^{(j)}$ for any pair of different i and j ($i, j = 1, \ldots, m$) ($i \neq j$).

6 Application to Privacy Revelation from SNS and Database

Here we consider two attributes for *the subject*: the university he attends and his home prefecture (hometown). In our example, the person is a university student in Tokyo.

We consider three cases:

Case 1: Privacy revealed from SNS (section 6.1).
Case 2: Privacy revealed from company database compromised by third parties (section 6.2).
Case 3: The combination of case1 and case2(section 6.3).

6.1 Privacy Revelation from SNS

6.1.1 One Disclosure of the Affiliated University Attribute

We represent the set of potential universities he is attending as $\chi^{(1)}$. Before disclosure, *the subject* might be attending any university in the set.

The probability that he is attending university x is expressed as follows.

$$P(X^{(1)} = \mathrm{x}) = \frac{(\text{Number of students attending university } x)}{(\text{Number of students attending all universities})}$$

We used university student population data obtained from [15] to calculate $P(X^{(1)} = \mathrm{x})$. The entropy before disclosure was calculated using by using equation (1).

$$H(X^{(1)}) = -\sum_{x} P(X^{(1)} = \mathrm{x}) \log_2 P(X^{(1)} = \mathrm{x}) = 6.0260.$$

There are two entries that disclose information about *the subject*'s university.

Entry 1: Next week, I will attend the job fair in the West-6 building.
Entry 2: I attend a science and technology university in Tokyo.

First, we consider these entries independently.

(I) Entry 1

$\chi_1^{(1)}$ is the subset of $\chi^{(1)}$ after entry 1 is posted. We find that there are four universities that have buildings named "West-6":

$$\chi_1^{(1)} = \{\text{UEC, Tokyo Tech, Waseda Univ., Tokyo Metropolitan Univ.}\}$$

If we consider only this disclosure, $\tilde{\chi}^{(1)} = \chi_1^{(1)}$. $P(\tilde{X}^1 = \mathrm{x})$ is the probability of the subject attending university x.

$$P(\tilde{X}^{(1)} = \mathrm{x}) = \frac{(\text{Number of students attending university } x(\in \tilde{X}^{(1)}))}{(\sum_{x \in \tilde{X}^1} \text{Number of students attending university } x)}$$

$H(\tilde{X}^{(1)})$, which is the entropy after disclosure, is calculated by using equation(2) :

$$H(\tilde{X}^{(1)}) = -\sum_{\mathrm{x} \in \tilde{X}^{(1)}} P(\tilde{X}^{(1)} = \mathrm{x}) \log_2 P(\tilde{X}^{(1)} = \mathrm{x}) = 1.1548 .$$

Thus, once entry 1 is posted, the revelation is quantified as by using equation (3).

$$\Delta^{(1)} = H(X^{(1)}) - H(\tilde{\chi}^{(1)}) = 4.8712$$

(II) Entry 2

$\chi_2^{(1)}$ is the subset of $\chi^{(1)}$ after entry 2 is posted. Since there are seven universities of science and technology in Tokyo,

$$\chi_2^{(1)} = \{\text{UEC, Tokyo Tech, Tokyo Denki Univ., TUT, Kogakuin Univ., TUS, SIT}\}.$$

$H(\tilde{X}^{(1)})$ and $\Delta^{(1)}$ are calculated in a similar fashion by using equation(2) and (3).

$$H(\tilde{X}^{(1)}) = 2.6331,\ \Delta^{(1)} = 3.929$$

6.1.2 Multiple Disclosures about University Attribute

Now consider the case in which entries 1 and 2 are considered in combination. The intersection between $\chi_1^{(1)}$ and $\chi_1^{(2)}$ is

$$\tilde{\chi}^{(1)} = \{\text{UEC, Tokyo Tech}\}.$$

$H(\tilde{X}^{(1)})$ and $\Delta^{(1)}$ are calculated in a similar fashion by using equation(2) and (3).

$$H(\tilde{X}^{(1)}) = = 0.9950 , \Delta^{(1)} = 5.0310$$

6.2 Privacy Revelation from Database

We represent the set of potential values of "hometown" as $\chi^{(2)}$. Before the disclosure, *the subject*'s hometown can be any prefecture in the set. The probability that his hometown is prefecture x is expressed as follows.

$$P(X^{(2)} = \text{x}) = \frac{\text{(Population in prefecture } x)}{\text{(Population in all prefectures)}}.$$

We used data from [16] to calculate $P(X^{(2)} = \text{x})$. The entropy before disclosures is given by using equation (1).

$$H(X^{(2)}) = 5.0842$$

We assume that *the subject*'s hometown is leaked from a company database and that *the subject*'s hometown is in Kyoto. The set obtained from this disclosure is

$$\chi_1^{(2)} = \{\text{Kyoto}\}.$$

We consider only this disclosure; that is, $\tilde{\chi}^{(2)} = \chi_1^{(2)}$ .Because his hometown address is unique now, $H(\tilde{X}^{(2)}) = 0$.
This revelation from a company database is quantified by using equation (3).

$$\Delta^{(2)} = H(X^{(2)}) - H(\tilde{X}^{(2)}) = 5.0842$$

6.3 Multiple Disclosures of Multiple Attributes

The entropy before disclosures about *the subject*'s university and hometown is given by

$$H(\{X^{(2)}\}) = H(X^{(1)}, X^{(2)}) = H(X^{(1)}) + H(X^{(2)} | X^{(1)}) \quad (9)$$

$H(X^{(2)} | X^{(1)})$ is the conditional entropy before disclosure.

$$H(X^{(2)} | X^{(1)}) = -\sum_{\text{x}_q} P(X^{(1)} = \text{x}_q) \bullet \sum_{\text{x}_p} \{P(X^{(2)} = \text{x}_p, X^{(1)} = \text{x}_q) \log P(X^{(2)} = \text{x}_p | X^{(1)} = \text{x}_p)\}$$

$P(X^{(2)} | X^{(1)})$ is the conditional probability of $\chi^{(2)}$ when $\chi^{(1)}$ is known.

$$\text{P}(\text{X}^{(2)} = \text{x}_\text{p} | \text{X}^{(1)} = \text{x}_\text{q}) = \frac{\text{(Number of students attending university } \text{x}_\text{q} \text{ who came from } \text{x}_\text{p})}{\text{(Number of students attending university } \text{x}_\text{q})}$$

For each university, we can determine the number of students who came from each prefecture [17]. Thus, the entropy before disclosure is expressed by using equation (9).

$$H(\{X^{(2)}\}) = 10.1420$$

Now let us consider the case that diary entries 1, 2 are disclosed and revelation from company database.The entropy after the disclosures about the user's university and hometown is expressed by using equation (8)

$$H(\{\tilde{X}^{(2)}\}) = H(\tilde{X}^{(1)}, \tilde{X}^{(2)}) = H(\tilde{X}^{(1)}) + H(\tilde{X}^{(2)} | \tilde{X}^{(1)}) \quad (10)$$

The conditional entropy after these disclosures is calculated as follows

$$H(\tilde{X}^{(2)}|\tilde{X}^{(1)}) = -\sum_{x_q} P(\tilde{X}^{(1)}=x_q) \bullet \sum_{x_p} \{P(\tilde{X}^{(2)}=x_p, \tilde{X}^{(1)}=x_q) \log P(\tilde{X}^{(2)}=x_p \,|\tilde{X}^{(1)}=x_p)\}$$

$$P(\tilde{X}^{(2)} = x_p | \tilde{X}^{(1)} = x_q) = \frac{\text{(Number of students in university } \chi_q \text{ who came from } \chi_p (\in \mathbf{X}^2))}{\sum_{x \in \tilde{X}^2} \text{(Number of students in university } \chi_q \text{ who came from } \chi_p (\in \tilde{\mathbf{X}}^2))}$$

Thus, the entropy after these disclosures is expressed by using equation (10).

$$H(\{\tilde{X}^{(2)}\}) = 0.9950$$

The total value of all the revelations is expressed by using equation (4).

$$\Delta = H(X^{(1)}, X^{(2)}) - H(\{\tilde{X}^{(1)}, \tilde{X}^{(2)}) = 9.1475$$

Table 2 lists the revelation values when disclosures about the university and hometown are independent and dependent.

Table 2. Revelations of information about different attributes

The kind of the attribute and diary entries	Before the disclosure $H\{(X^{(k)})\}$	After the disclosure $H\{(\tilde{X}^{(k)})\}$	Privacy revelation value Δ
Affiliated university (Diary entry 1,2)	6.0260	0.9950	5.310
Hometown address (Revelation from database)	5.0842	0	5.084
Affiliated university and home town address (Diary entry 1,2 and Revelation from database)	10.1420	0.9950	9.147

Thus, our metric quantifies accumulated revelations of information about multiple attributes and can cope with the case in which the attributes affect each other.

7 Conclusion

We have described a framework for quantifying the degree of privacy lost when there are multiple disclosures of information about different attributes of a person. We defined information disclosure as a transition from the possible values of an attribute to a subset of those values. We quantify the privacy revelation in terms of the difference in joint entropy of multiple attribute values before and after disclosures. Our metric can quantify how much private information is revealed as a result of multiple disclosures of information about multiple attributes.

Our metric has two key features: it quantifies accumulated revelations about different attributes and it can handle the case in which the attributes affect each other.

Evaluation using entries posted on a social networking service and leaks from a company database showed that it is effective—it can be used to quantify privacy revelations by various types of media.

References

1. Agrawal, R., Srikant, R.: Privacy preserving data mining. In: Proceedings of the ACM SIGMOD Conference of Management of Data, pp. 439–450. ACM, New York (2000)
2. Agrawal, D., Aggarwal, C.C.: On the design and quantification of privacy preserving data mining algorithms. In: Proceedings of the 20th ACM SIGACT-SIGMOD-SIGART Symposium on Principle of Database System, pp. 247–255. ACM, New York (2001)
3. Sweeney, L.: Achieving k-Anonymity Privacy Protection Using Generalization and Suppression. International Journal on Uncertainty, Fuzziness and Knowledge-based Systems, 571–588 (2002)
4. Ashwin, M., Danier, K., Johannes, G., Muthuramakrishnan, V.: 1-diversity: Privacy beyond k-anonymity. In: Proceedings of the 22nd IEEE International Conference on Date Engineering, Atlanta Georgia (2006)
5. Ninghui, L., Tiancheng, L., Suresh, V.: t-closeness: Privacy beyond k-anonymity and ldiversity. In: Proceedings of the 23nd International Conference on Data Engineering (ICDE 2007), Istanbul, Turkey, April 16-20 (2007)
6. Baki, H., Marco, G.: Protecting location privacy through path confusion. In: Proceedings of the First International Conference on Security and Privacy for Emerging Areas in Communications Networks, Athens, Greece, pp. 194–205 (2005)
7. Duckham, M., Kulik, L.: Simulation of Obfuscation and Negotiation for Location Privacy. In: Cohn, A.G., Mark, D.M. (eds.) COSIT 2005. LNCS, vol. 3693, pp. 31–48. Springer, Heidelberg (2005)
8. Gruteser, M., Grunwald, D.: Anonymous Usage of Location-Based Services Through Spatial and Temporal Cloaking. In: First ACM/USENIX International Conference on Mobile Systems, Applications and Services, pp. 31–42. ACM Press, San Francisco (2003)
9. Hoh, B., et al.: Preserving Privacy in GPS Traces via Uncertainty- Aware Path Cloaking. In: 14th ACM Conference on Computer and Communication Security, Alexandria (2007)
10. Hashem, T., Kulik, L.: Safeguarding Location Privacy in Wireless Ad-Hoc Networks. In: 9th International Conference on Ubiquitous, pp. 372–290 (2007)
11. Krumm, J.: A survey of computational location privacy. Personal and Ubiquitous Computing 13(6) (2008)
12. Claudia, D., Stefaan, S., Joris, C., Bart, P.: Towards measuring anonymity. In: Dingledine, R., Syverson, P.F. (eds.) PET 2002. LNCS, vol. 2482, pp. 54–68. Springer, Heidelberg (2003)
13. Andrei, S., George, D.: Towards an Information Theoretic Metric for Anonymity. Presented at Privacy Enhancing Technologies Workshop, PET (2001)
14. Ken, M., et al.: Role Interchangeability and Verification of Electronic Voting. In: Proc. of SCIS (2006)
15. Nikkei Shingaku Navi, `http://daigaku.shingakunavi.jp/p/`
16. Statistical Database, Statistics Bureau, Director-General for Policy Planning (Statistical Standards) and Statistical Research and Training Institute, `http://www.stat.go.jp/english/data/index.htm`
17. University profile, `http://www3.ibac.co.jp/univ1/mst/info/univinfo_50.jsp`
18. Ryosuke, Y., Astushi, K., Takashi, H., Keiichi, H.: The Metric Model for Personal Information Disclosure. In: Proceedings of Fourth International Conference on Disital Society (ICDS 2010), pp. 112–117 (2010)

A Methodology to Assess the Benefits of Smart Order Routing

Bartholomäus Ende, Peter Gomber, Marco Lutat, and Moritz C. Weber

Goethe-University Frankfurt, E-Finance Lab, Grüneburgplatz 1, 60323 Frankfurt, Germany

Abstract. Smart Order Routing technology promises to improve the efficiency of the securities trading value chain by selecting most favourable execution prices among fragmented markets. To measure the extent of sub-optimal order executions in Europe we develop a simulation framework which includes explicit costs associated with switching to a different market. By analysing historical order book data for EURO STOXX 50 securities across ten European lectronic markets we highlight an economically relevant potential of Smart Order Routing to improve the trading process on a gross basis. After the inclusion of switching costs (net basis), the realisability of this value potential depends on whether the user can directly access post-trading infrastructure of foreign markets or has to make use of intermediaries' services.

Keywords: Electronic Markets, Process Optimisation, Smart Order Router.

1 Introduction

In securities trading, different trading intentions are aggregated at exchanges to discover prices. Until the late 1980s, this process has been conducted by direct human interaction at exchange floors. Then, new trading concepts originated from an IT-driven transformation of trading [1]. Following [2] we measure the potential to generate value of one such IT concept called Smart Order Router (SOR).

The focus of our analysis is the entire *securities trading value chain*: starting from the investment decision it includes all required stages up to the legal transfer of ownership of traded securities (cf. upper horizontal flow path in Figure 1): trading is a traditionally *intermediated* business [3]. Thus, *investors* (step 1) communicate their trade interests to human brokers (step 2) who search for counterparties at exchanges to complete *trades* (step 3). Trade confirmations are communicated to post-trading infrastructure providers: in the *clearing stage* (step 4) settlement obligations are determined for each market participant towards all counterparties. That way clearing provides a risk management function and for efficiency reasons a pooling of multiple trades among counterparties to determine the surplus obligations (netting). *Settlement* (step 5) is "*...the act of crediting and debiting the transferee's and transferor's accounts respectively, with the aim of completing a transaction in securities*" [4, p. 5]. It takes place at a Central Securities Depository (CSD). Custody (step 6) of shares as well as ownership information is provided by a CSD. For domestic settlement each country typically possesses its own CSD whereas International CSDs (ICSDs) enable access to foreign CSDs for international transactions.

W. Cellary and E. Estevez (Eds.): I3E 2010, IFIP AICT 341, pp. 81–92, 2010.

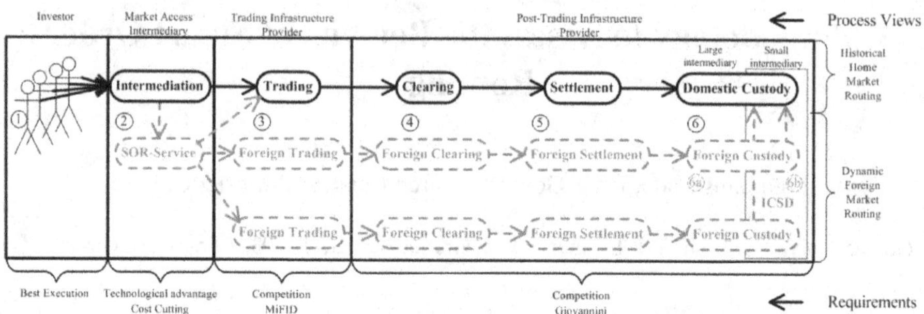

Fig. 1. Traditional securities value chain and changes induced by a SOR

In the US, alternative trading systems have been introduced at the end of the last century, leading to a fragmentation of markets [1]. To enforce best (order) execution, current US regulation (RegNMS) requires mandatory routing of orders from the market initially receiving the order to the one offering the best price. In Europe, no such obligations are in place. Before the Markets in Financial Instruments Directive (MiFID) was introduced in November 2007, stock trading had to take place at national stock exchanges (concentration rule) in various European states. Thus, nearly all trading activity in a security was conducted in its home market [1]. To foster competition and to take advantage of technological developments, MiFID abolished these concentration rules. Besides traditional exchanges, this enables the emerge of so-called multilateral trading facilities (MTFs) like Chi-X, BATS or Turquoise. Relevant market share gains of MTFs [5] in European securities document increasing market fragmentation. To strengthen customer requirements for best execution, MiFID obliges intermediaries to execute customer orders on terms most favourable to the client, i.e. the investor. Within the post-trading stages the European commission aims at fostering competition as it has identified multiple cross-system barriers for cost efficiency [6].

To implement best execution by intermediaries, two alternatives prevail: either to rely on pre-defined static order routing rules, mostly targeting only one market per security (e.g.: the national stock exchange or the respective security's home market) or to employ a dynamic routing by an IT concept called *SOR*. The technological foundation of a SOR is the ability for remote access to multiple markets' electronic order books where available trade intentions are displayed (cf. right hand side of Figure 2). Connectivity is provided by standardised components such as FIX and third party infrastructure like the SWIFT secure IP network. Based on (1) real-time market data, (2) current trading costs information as well as (3) rules representing client preferences, a SOR performs an automated search for trading opportunities across multiple markets. Herein it aims at splitting an order and routing suborders to the most appropriate market combinations: for an incoming parent order (buy 1,000 shares in Figure 2) the SOR determines how it is sliced and how the individual child orders (buy 600 shares at exchange B and 400 at the MTF) are routed to appropriate marketplaces.

[7] reveal best execution implementations to rely mostly on predefined, static routing rules and only a very low usage of real-time SOR solutions up to now. One reason might be the access to post-trading infrastructures: large institutions apply directaccess

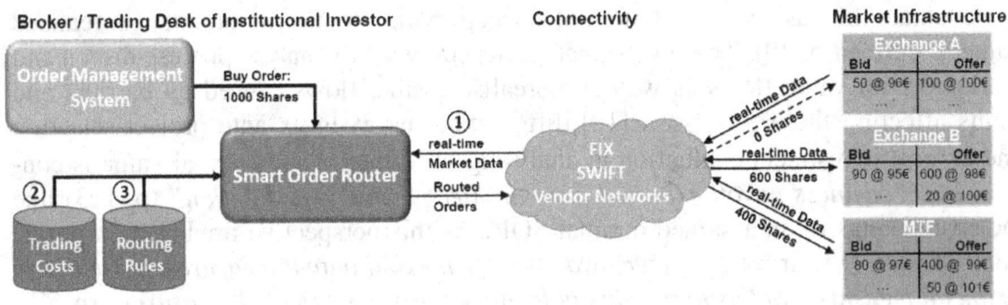

Fig. 2. Operating principle of a SOR Service

(cf. step 6a in Figure 1) whereas smaller ones require intermediaries to the foreign infrastructure by e.g. ICSDs (cf. step 6b in Figure 1) incurring high transfer costs. Therefore, the general question for the business value of SOR arises [8] and the two related research questions for this paper are:

(1) Is a static routing process efficient in fragmented European equity markets?
(2) Does SOR technology enable for relevant efficiency improvements within the trading process?

To answer these questions, we develop a general simulation framework for identifying sub-optimal order executions. It can be applied to public data and accounts for explicit costs associated with switching a trade from the original to a different market in European cross-system trading. To infer cost boundaries, two model users are assumed: one user for an intermediated high-cost scenario and another acting in a low-cost scenario with direct access to the respective post-trade infrastructures. Our framework is then validated on a sample of EURO STOXX 50 constituents.

Applied on a continuous basis our framework provides threefold insights: firstly, intermediaries (brokers and trading desks of institutional investors) can assess the value generation potential of SOR systems on a net basis, i.e. including transaction costs. Secondly, investors can judge the relevance of SOR services for their intermediary choice. Thirdly, regulators can evaluate the effectiveness of the MiFID best execution provisions relative to the RegNMS regime. By comparing the gross (i.e. excluding transaction costs) with the net results the impact of transaction costs, specifically those for clearing and settlement, on the order routing decision is shown.

The remainder of this paper is structured as follows: section 2 reviews related literature, section 3 elaborates on the employed methodology and presents assumptions for the applied transaction cost scenarios. In section 4 the data set is described, followed by our results in section 5. Section 6 concludes.

2 Related Literature

Beside the particular perspective of electronic securities trading, this paper is motivated by multiple cross-domain relations in information systems research:

We evaluate the business value of an IT concept with a focus on potential vs. realised value as defined by [9]. These value categories are used to analyse process-driven and market-driven value flows as well as unrealised value flows caused by barriers and limits affecting these processes. [10] differentiate between ex ante project selection and ex post investment evaluation in analysing IT values. The potential value is construed as *"business payoff expected from an ideal technology solution"* (p. 133) like the cost savings of an assumed optimal SOR. As this perspective implies a corporate point of view [11] argue to *"move away from firm-level output measures, particularly financial measures, of business value in favour of process-oriented measures"* (p. 77). This motivates the process-orientated perspective within our study. Further this choice is substantiated by the limitation incurred by directly measuring at firm-level (but not at process-level) how and where business value is created by IT.

[12] highlight the ability of simulations to serve as a basis for business process optimisation. Their results are backed by [13], who illustrate the impact of integrated process optimisation for multi-criteria stakeholder process views. Both lead to the simulation of business process that is influenced by the criteria of multiple stakeholders (cf. Figure 1). Amongst others, direct measurements and computer simulations are described. Energy cost simulations of globally distributed computer centres by [14] prove possible economic gains of smart routing even outside financial markets. Their results outline potential savings of 40% for data centres which dynamically route their work load to regions with low energy costs. For reliable smart routing simulations, [14]'s analysis shows also the demand for a market scope instead of a firm perspective. At firm-level it is not possible to measure process efficiency for the entire market. On top, firms try to conceal their process strategies to retain their comparative advantages. All three findings strengthen our decision for a market-oriented analysis setup.

Regarding finance literature on SOR technology in particular, [15] argue suboptimal trade executions on security markets to be induced by a lack of automated routing decisions. Empirical studies by [16, 17] investigate the impact of automated order flow on markets. They underline the high percentage of orders originating from Algorithmic Trading. Further, [18] show the business value of algorithms by comparing their overall trading costs with those of human brokers. On top, [19] highlight the importance of overall transaction costs. The latter two investigations' results stress the need to employ an approach including costs.

This paper's contribution to the existing literature is twofold: firstly, it introduces a potential vs. realised value framework for order routing in fragmented markets. Secondly, to the knowledge of the authors it is the first paper which empirically analyses the trading process efficiency after the introduction of MiFID. That way it includes switching costs (i.e. transactions costs) which are relevant for the European case.

3 Methodology and Research Framework

For the empirical analysis of the order execution process, we develop a general simulation framework to calculate the savings per trade (cf. Figure 3). As data including individual market participants' identities and cost structures is only available within

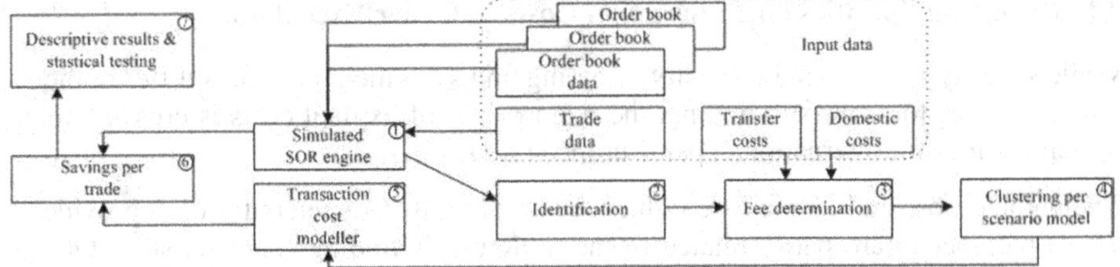

Fig. 3. Research framework simulating SOR and modelling transaction costs

banks, our framework is specifically designed to employ public market data and fees. It is composed of two main artefacts: a *dynamic SOR engine* and a *static transaction cost modeller*. These are described in more detail below:

The SOR engine iterates stepwise through historical trade data, consisting of security names, time stamps, trade price and volume. This data is compared to the historical order book situations of all markets where the trade could have been executed alternatively. According to the information whether a trade could be completed at an alternative market for a better price or not it is classified as executed sub-optimally or optimally respectively (cf. Figure 3, step 1 and Appendix[1] A I for an example).

One might face a situation where some alternative markets offer a better limit price, but with a number of shares insufficient to fully execute the original trade. This kind of sub-optimal execution is sub-classified as *"partial"*. Those sub-optimal executions where the full number of shares might be executed at a better price are labeled as *"full"*. A sub-optimal execution (partial or full) is found if at least one marketplace exists where a strictly positive amount of savings could be realised without considering switching costs. We select the market with the highest potential overall savings for the trade and define the realisable cost difference as *"gross savings"*.

This process improvement information (gross sub-optimal executions) is directed to the transaction cost modeller. This component determines the additional cost to complete the trade at the alternative market. Therefore, cost specific parameters like trade value, security and market characteristics are analysed, as some markets, feature special fees for foreign stocks (cf. Figure 3 step 2). These fees are taken from a database which consists of costs for trading, clearing and settlement in each respective market (domestic costs) and transfer costs among different CSDs (cf. Figure 3 step 3). For reliable results we calculate multiple scenario configurations (cf. Figure 3 step 4). As noticed in [6] it is not trivial to estimate post-trading process costs for European cross-system trades. This is discussed more detailed in the next sub-section which also elaborates on our specific simulation parameters. With the results from clustering by scenarios, specific transaction costs can be determined (cf. Figure 3 step 5). These switching costs are compared to the gross savings generated by using the SOR engine. In the following savings reduced by transaction costs are referred to as "net savings" per trade (cf. Figure 3 step 6) which are aggregated in the last step 7.

[1] The Appendix is available at http://www.efinance.wiwi.uni-frankfurt.de/SOR_Appendix.pdf

3.1 European Specifics on Transaction Costs in Order Execution

While security markets and respective clearing and settlement providers differ in their cost structures for domestic trading, the main driver of explicit costs is cross-system settlement fees for international, pan-European trades:

Trading and post-trading fees are influenced by various parameters for each provider. Those parameters are partly related to the SOR user's trading characteristics. Other parameters concern the characteristics of a specific trade and the market in which it is executed. To reduce complexity we derive the cost contribution of each process activity as depicted in Figure 1. This is consistent with the methodology by [20] who model the variable costs directly related to the execution of trades for the required activity and neglects fix costs. Accordingly, total costs of domestic trading in a specific market for an individual trade are defined as:

$$\text{Costs}_{\text{Total}} = \text{Costs}_{\text{Trading}} + \text{Costs}_{\text{Clearing}} + \text{Costs}_{\text{Settlement}}$$

Detailed cost figures and parameters contributing to the calculation of the domestic transaction costs are presented in the Appendix A II.

Cross-system trading refers to situations where an order is executed in a market/country other than the one where the final settlement takes place (i.e. the domestic CSD of the market where the security is primarily listed). In cross-system trading, clearing and settlement, transaction costs depend on the access setup to the respective CSDs. In order to settle a transaction of a particular security, both counterparties must have access to systems enabling them to deliver and receive the security in question. Thus, the distinctive feature of cross-system settlement is how to gain access to a settlement system in another country and/or the interaction of different settlement systems. [6] lists five different access setups for a SOR user to a foreign CSD. We select those two which can be identified as a lower and an upper boundary for the relevant switching costs and design two scenarios assuming one specific level of costs consistent for all SOR users in that scenario:

1. **Direct access cost scenario:** here the SOR user has direct (non-intermediated) access to foreign CSDs. This means it has direct access to all facilities – trading, clearing and settlement – necessary along the securities trading value chain. Therefore, the direct access cost scenario obviously represents the lower boundary regarding variable switching costs for individual trades.
2. **Intermediated cost scenario:** here the SOR user depends on intermediaries to access the foreign settlement systems. Among the four potential intermediation services reported by [6], our cost analysis identified ICSDs as a realistic upper cost boundary for which price fees are publicly available.

To evaluate whether a sub-optimal execution still holds after the inclusion of switching costs, the fee determination component of our transaction cost modeller artefact delegates the following switching cost information to the scenario clustering component:

For the direct access cost scenario, the switching costs are defined as the difference of the total costs ($\text{Costs}_{\text{Total}}$) for trading, clearing and settlement in the markets, where the trade originally took place to that where it can be executed alternatively. In the intermediated cost scenario this cost difference is extended by additional costs for the transfer of the traded stocks. Thereby it is assumed that the respective securities are kept in the CSD of the alternative market causing costs for a delivery or receive instruction at its CSD and a delivery or receive instruction at the ICSD, i.e. one external instruction to the respective market.

4 Dataset Description and Handling

Our analysis concentrates on actively traded shares on multiple markets in Euro currency. Thus we select the constituents of the Dow Jones EURO STOXX 50 index (as of October 2007). One constituent (ARCELORMITTAL) is not available in the data. Our analysis focuses on simultaneous trading opportunities among multiple markets to be accessible by SORs. This requires markets featuring fully-electronic open central limit order books. In the investigation period, ten European markets are addressed: Bolsa de Madrid, Borsa Italiana Milan, Chi-X, four Euronext (EN) markets (Amsterdam, Brussels, Paris, and Lisbon), NASDAQ OMX Helsinki, SWX Europe and Deutsche Börse Xetra.

For each security/market combination we retrieve trade and order book data from Reuters. Our sample consists of 20 trading days divided into two distinct sample periods with the first from December 10–21, 2007 and the second from January 7–18, 2008, i.e. after the applicability of MiFID. By excluding the last trading days of 2007 and the first trading days of 2008, we avoid potential end-of-year and beginning-of-year trading biases. The collected data contains each best bid/offer limit and trade prices with respective volume and a date as well as time stamps with a granularity of one second. To determine the order book side of the alternative market to be compared with the original trade price, we refer to the following classification: trades executed at the best offer are categorised as buy-initiated and those at the best bid limit are said to be sell-initiated. Trades for which a trade direction cannot be determined unambiguously are removed. Moreover, data lacking essential information (e.g. associated volume) are eliminated. As trading hours among the considered ten electronic markets vary slightly, only the periods of simultaneous trading are analysed. Further, to avoid any bias by strong price movements auctions as well as all trading activity within two minutes around them are removed, such that from a total of 9,163,780 trades, 1,152,875 trades (12.58%) are eliminated.

New limits in a comparison market are considered available when their change arrives within the second of a trade in the original market. Thus they present the most recent order book situation to this trade. With more than one such change within the second of a trade occurrence at one market, the limit resulting in the least savings is taken as a basis for an execution performance comparison in order to retrieve a lower boundary for the improvement potential of the trading process.

Domestic costs for the transaction cost modeller are derived from publicly available data from exchanges, clearing houses and CSDs. Brokerage costs are not included as brokers/trading desks of institutional investors are assumed to constitute the decision point for order routing and consequently their cost structures are taken as the basis of our analysis. The respective transfer costs are derived from the publicly available fee schedules of the two European ICSDs Clearstream Banking Luxembourg and Euroclear Bank (as of late 2007/early 2008).

5 Empirical Results

Our results are based on 8,010,905 trades with a value of 262bn€. They are split into the three cost scenarios: *no cost*, *direct access cost* and *intermediated cost*.

In the no cost scenario, the process optimisation potential allows 6.71% of the orders to be better executed with their full size (6.45% of the orders partially). This enables for total savings of 9.50m€ within our sample period, i.e. 7.54bps relative to total sub-optimal execution value and 0.36bps relative to total traded value. The direct access cost scenario exhibits comparable figures. Even in the intermediated cost scenario, assuming explicit transaction costs like the costs for the transfer of securities, 1.41% of orders can be better executed with their full size (1.34% partially). This enables for total savings of 5.90m€, i.e. 10.17bps relative to the total sub-optimal execution value and 0.23bps relative to the total traded value (cf. Table 1).These potential savings outline inefficiencies within the trading process for all three costs scenarios. To validate these descriptive findings, additional statistical tests have been applied (cf. Appendix A III for details concerning the statistical tests). Table 2 outlines their results in two aggregation perspectives: the *overall perspective* aggregates all sub-optimal executions across all instruments whereas the *security perspective* aggregates individual securities' test results. Checkmarks highlight where savings significantly exceed costs. For the theoretical *no cost scenario* significance can be shown for both perspectives. This is obvious as an idealised SOR is designed to detect saving potentials caused by prevailing market inefficiencies and no switching costs are considered. Thus, when defining best execution as trading at the best available prices our results can be interpreted as significant potential to improve the value chain as far as the trading activity (step 1 – 3 in Figure 1).

Table 1. Descriptive statistics of sub-optimal executions for all instruments

All Instruments	No costs scenario	Direct access cost scenario	Intermediated cost scenario
Number of trades		8,010,905	
Value [m€]		262,313.9	
Value per trade [€]		32,75	
% full sub-optimal execution	6.71	6.60	1.41
% partial sub-optimal execution	6.45	5.30	1.34
Savings [€]	9,502,869	9,709,864	5,908,346
Avg. savings per sub-optimal execution [€]	9.01	10.21	26.83
Savings/sub-optimal execution value [bps]	7.54	7.80	10.17
Savings/trade value[bps]	0.36	0.37	0.23

Table 2. Potential of SOR to improve the efficiency of the securities trading value chain

	No cost scenario	Direct access cost scenario	Intermediated cost scenario
Security perspective	✓	✓	(✓)
Overall perspective	✓	✓	×

To have a more comprehensive perspective we have to extend the focus to the complete value chain, i.e. including all activities (step 4 – 6a / 6b in Figure 1) and considering all applicable costs. Again, for the direct access cost scenario, significant process improvements can be shown for the entire securities trading value chain. This shows that employing SOR leads to an improved process even when considering costs. Unfortunately, the direct access cost scenario is not applicable for all market participants due to their firm size. Small market participants have to employ an additional intermediary (e.g. ICSD) activity (step 6b in Figure 1) providing their access to the alternative markets post-trading infrastructure. Within this intermediated cost scenario results are heterogeneous: whereas on a security perspective for almost one third (16 out of 49) of the considered instruments the potential for process improvement prevails, in the overall perspective no significance can be shown (red X in Table 1). Thus the costs of the additional ICSD activity impede small market participants from taking advantage of the process improvements enabled by SOR.

To highlight an exemplary analysis of this effect for one security, we selected TOTAL as it led the EURO STOXX 50 in terms of market capitalisation (as of December 31st, 2007) and as it exhibits most trades and belongs to the stocks with the highest overall traded value. Detailed statistics are shown in Table 3, where the "Overall" column summarises across all markets. The upper section of Table 3 provides an overview on markets' activity for TOTAL applying characteristic figures which are identical for all cost scenarios.

Trade activity varies heavily for TOTAL among market places. As common for most stocks, the primary market exhibits more than ten times higher trade numbers then the second largest. In the no cost scenario for TOTAL, 14.58% or 42,815 out of 293,729 trades at its home market EN Paris could have been executed in their full size at a better price in (at least) one of the other markets. Again, for the direct access cost scenario the figures are comparable (14.51% or 42,608) whereas in the intermediated cost scenario only 2.98% or 8,752 full sub-optimal executions remain.

For the intermediate scenario (cf. Table 3) we *t*-tested the absolute gross savings (savings of the no cost scenario) against their switching costs. Our findings are heterogeneous among stocks: since this scenario incurs explicit costs for domestic transactions and securities transfer as described in section 3.1, the null hypotheses of no systematic absolute savings cannot be statistically rejected for some stocks like TOTAL. Concerning the significance of our results no systematic pattern can be found (cf. Table 3, intermediated cost scenario, mean costs row). Although EN Bruessel (12.26€) and SWX (165.64€) exhibit the highest gross average savings per sub-optimal execution (Table 3, no costs scenario section), only EN Brussel's savings remain significant after the inclusion of switching costs (intermediated cost scenario section, mean costs). This is due to EN Bruessel's higher observation number and lower mean switching costs in comprision to SWX Europe and Milan. Regarding the additional intermediary activity (e.g. by an ICSD) this supports the thesis that observable gross average savings per sub-optimal execution (overall more than 0.5m€ for TOTAL) are nullified by high ICSD costs. Accordingly, small intermediaries cannot profit from more efficient trading processes enabled by SOR. An overview for all instruments is provided in Appendix A IV.

Table 3. All cost scenarios results for TOTAL

		EN Paris	Chi-X	EN Brussels	Milan	SWX Europe	Overall
Overview	Number of trades	293,729	26,263	465	210	18	320,685
	Volume [million shares]	183.14	8.06	0.09	0.03	0.21	191.53
	Value [m€]	10,299.57	455.75	4.79	1.72	11.86	10,773.68
	Avg. volume / trade [shares]	624	307	183	146	11,725	597.2
	Avg. value / trade [€]	35,065	17,353	10,295	8,167	658,883	33,595.8
No costs scenario	Percentage full sub-optimal execution	14.58	9.52	53.98	53.33	5.56	14.24
	Percentage partial sub-optimal execution	10.88	5.24	4.95	1.90	5.56	10.40
	Number of sub-optimal executions	74,778	3,875	274	116	2	79,045
	Full	42,815	2,499	251	112	1	45,678
	Partial	31,963	1,376	23	4	1	33,367
	Savings [€]	493,219	16,679	3,360	542	331	514,131
	Avg. savings / sub-optimal execution [€]	6.60	4.30	12.26	4.67	165.64	6.50
	Savings / sub-optimal execution value [bps]	4.23	3.33	12.73	8.28	51.19	4.22
	Savings / trade value [bps]	0.48	0.37	7.02	3.16	0.28	0.48
Direct access cost scenario	Percentage full sub-optimal execution	14.51	8.06	53.76	35.24	5.56	14.05
	Percentage partial sub-optimal execution	9.82	3.16	4.52	0.95	5.56	9.26
	Number of sub-optimal executions	71,465	2,946	271	76	2	74,760
	Full	42,608	2,116	250	74	1	45,049
	Partial	28,857	830	21	2	1	29,711
	Savings [€]	516,314	13,114	3,429	464	330	533,651
	Avg. savings / sub-optimal execution [€]	7.22	4.45	12.65	6.10	165.20	7.14
	Savings / sub-optimal execution value [bps]	4.45	2.78	13.05	7.66	51.05	4.41
	Savings / trade value [bps]	0.50	0.29	7.16	2.70	0.28	0.50
Intermediated cost scenario	Percentage full sub-optimal execution	2.98	1.07	20.43	1.90	0.00	2.85
	Percentage partial sub-optimal execution	2.58	0.61	1.94	0.48	5.56	2.41
	Number of sub-optimal executions	16,324	440	104	5	1	16,874
	Full	8,752	280	95	4	0	9,131
	Partial	7,572	160	9	1	1	7,743
	Savings [€]	245,661	4,728	2,243	45	287	252,965
	Avg. savings / sub-optimal execution [€]	15.05	10.75	21.57	8.99	287.34	14.99
	Savings / sub-optimal execution value [bps]	5.01	4.45	12.17	2.67	51.08	5.02
	Savings / trade value [bps]	0.24	0.10	4.69	0.26	0.24	0.23
	H_0: Mean Savings < Mean Costs; H_a: Mean Savings > Mean Costs — observations	74778	3875	274	116	2	79045
	Mean Costs	7.0837	8.4424	7.1177***	25.910	22.3854	7.1783
	t-value	-9.9816	-34.17	2.9928	-28.97	0.9923	-14.005

Null hypothesis is rejected at significance level .10 (*), .05 (**) and .01 (***)

Altogether our results show that investors could have realised significant savings on their trades across all instruments. Those savings result from execution conditions superior to those in the market of the actual trade even when considering different levels of explicit transaction costs. Although those savings obviously shrink under the highest assumed transaction costs (intermediated cost scenario), still one out of a hundred trades could have been executed at better conditions.

6 Conclusion

Concerning the first research question our results imply that the current routing implementations in Europe exhibit potential for improvement. No definitive answer to the second question can be given: although SOR technology enables for relevant improvements, the ability to profit from this potential is limited to large investors, since smaller investors face relevant explicit costs in post-trading.

The implications are threefold: investors should select large market intermediaries enabling them to profit from their potential to provide best execution. Market access intermediaries should use SOR technology to enable cost savings, comparative advantages and best execution for their customers. European regulators shall enforce initiatives to reduce post-trading costs (e.g. the usage of CSD links) to enable even small market access intermediaries to profit from this optimisation potential.

As a future extension of the analysis, inclusion of more detailed data (like order book depth on millisecond basis) will allow to compute the optimisation potential by enhancing the partial sub-optimal execution concept. Concerning the data evaluation period, we are implementing a concept which enables us to compute the sub-optimal execution results on a continuous basis. Beyond the snap shot approach taken in this paper, this will provide insights on how the securities trading value chain evolves and allows to assess how market participants adopt SOR technology and how efforts to reduce post-trading costs help to improve the overall efficiency of the trading process.

Acknowledgment

We thankfully acknowledge the support of the E-Finance Lab, Frankfurt for this work.

References

[1] Schwartz, R.A., Francioni, R.: Equity markets in action: The fundamentals of liquidity, market structure & trading. Wiley, Hoboken (2004)

[2] Hitt, L.M., Brynjolfsson, E.: Productivity, Business Profitability, and Consumer Surplus: Three Different Measures of Information Technology Value. MIS Quarterly, 121–142 (June 1996)

[3] Harris, L.: Trading and Exchanges – Market Microstructure for Practitioners. Oxford University Press, Oxford (2003)

[4] CESAME Sub-Group on definitions, Commission Services Working Document on Definitions of Post-Trading Activities (October 2005)

[5] Fidessa, Fidessa Fragmentation Index (2009), http://fragmentation.fidessa.com/ (last accessed 06/13/2009)

[6] Giovannini Group, Cross-Border Clearing and Settlement Arrangements in the European Union (November 2001), http://ec.europa.eu/internal_market/financial-markets/docs/clearing/first_giovannini_report_en.pdf (last accessed: 08/11/2007)

[7] Gomber, P., Pujol, G., Wranik, A.: The Implementation of European Best Execution Obligations – An Analysis for the German Market, FinanceCom, Paris, France (2008)

[8] Kohli, R., Grover, V.: Business value of IT: An essay on expanding research directions to keep with the times. Journal of the Association for Information Systems 9(1), 23–39 (2008)
[9] Chircu, A.M., Kauffman, R.J.: Limits to Value in Electronic Commerce-Related IT Investments. Journal of Management Information Systems 17(2), 59–80 (2000)
[10] Davern, M.J., Kauffman, R.J.: Discovering potential and realizing value from information technology investments. J. Manage. Inf. Syst. 16(4), 121–143 (2000)
[11] Mooney, J.G., Gurbaxani, V., Kraemer, K.L.: A process oriented framework for assessing the business value of information technology. SIGMIS Database 27(2), 68–81 (1996)
[12] Weyland, J.H., Engiles, M.: Towards simulation-based business process management: towards simulation-based business process management. In: Proc. of the 35th Conf. on Winter Simulation: Driving Innovation, pp. 225–227 (2003)
[13] Yen, V.C.: An Integrated Model for Business Process Measurement. In: CONF-IRM 2008 Proceedings, Paper 9 (2008)
[14] Qureshi, A., Weber, R., Balakrishnan, H., Guttag, J., Maggs, B.: Cutting the electric bill for internet-scale systems. In: Proc. of the ACM SIGCOMM 2009, pp. 123–134 (2009)
[15] Foucault, T., Menkveld, A.J.: Competition for Order Flow and Smart Order Routing Systems. Journal of Finance (63), 119–158 (2008)
[16] Prix, J., Loistl, O., Huetl, M.: Algorithmic Trading Patterns in Xetra Orders. European Journal of Finance 13(8), 717–739 (2007)
[17] Gsell, M., Gomber, P.: Algorithmic trading engines versus human traders – Do they behave different in securities markets? In: Proc. of the 17th European Conference on Information Systems (2009)
[18] Domowitz, I., Yegerman, H.: The Cost of Algorithmic Trading – A First Look at Comparative Performance. In: Bruce, B.R. (ed.) Algorithmic Trading: Precision, Control, Execution, pp. 30–40. Institutional Investor Inc. (2005)
[19] Bakos, Y., Lucas, H.C., Wonseok, O., Viswanathan, S., Simon, G., Weber, B.: Electronic Commerce in the Retail Brokerage Industry: Trading Costs of Internet Versus Full Service Firms, Working Paper Series Stern#1S99-014 (1999)
[20] Oxera. Methodology for monitoring prices, costs and volumes of trading and post-trading activities (July 2007), `http://ec.europa.eu/internal_market/financialmarkets/docs/clearing/oxera_study_en.pdf` (last accessed: 01/15/2008)

Ontology-Based Evaluation of ISO 27001

Danijel Milicevic and Matthias Goeken

Frankfurt School of Finance & Management
IT-Governance-Practice-Network
Sonnemannstrasse 9-11
60314 Frankfurt am Main, Germany
{d.milicevic,m.goeken}@fs.de

Abstract. Information security risks threaten the ability of organizations of reaching their operational and strategic goals. Increasing diversification of the information security landscapes makes addressing all risks a challenging task. Information security standards have positioned themselves as generic solutions to tackle a broad range of risks and try to guide security managers in their endeavors. However, it is not evident if such standards have the required holistic approach to be a solid foundation. In this paper a metamodel of the ISO 27001 security standard explicating its core concepts is presented. We then compare the constructed metamodel with various information security ontologies and analyze for comprehensiveness. We conclude with a discussion of core concepts in the information security domain.

Keywords: Information Security Management, ISO 27001, Metamodeling, Ontologies, Qualitative Data Analysis (QDA), Grounded Theory.

1 Introduction

Regardless if an information system is being planned and used for e-voting, sales via an e-shop or online banking, with all the benefits information systems provide they also come with inherent risks. Information security has gained attention in a number of organizations, be it in the industry or governments. As [2] point out, (exploitable) software vulnerabilities and virus attacks are only two typical threats security managers need to address along with disgruntled employees, social engineering attacks and industrial espionage to name a few. Because security – like a chain – is only as strong as its weakest link, an information security management system requires a holistic approach if one wants to ensure effectiveness [4, 5, 12].

The need for guidance on information security management and common reference points across companies and industries [14] lead to information security standards and best practice frameworks being established. As a collection of best practices on how to deal with most common security risks they provide an overview of the multifaceted information security problem domain [31]. Some researchers have criticized their validity and especially pointed out the lack of depth or content [29]. While depth may be one dimension to scrutinize, we are interested in how comprehensive such information security standards are. To analyze how comprehensive one of the most

W. Cellary and E. Estevez (Eds.): I3E 2010, IFIP AICT 341, pp. 93–102, 2010.

prominent standards – ISO 27001 – is, we derive the information security concepts covered in it and compare them with information security ontologies.

The paper is organized as follows. In the next section we introduce metamodels as one central research artifact [18], discuss their application and present the basic ideas of applying qualitative data analysis (QDA). After a brief overview of related work, we elaborate on our findings from the analyzed source documents (ISO 27001) and present a metamodel. Then we compare the elements of our metamodel with a selection of ontologies before we conclude the paper in the final section with a discussion.

2 Research Methodology

2.1 Metamodels as a Central Artifact of the Research Approach

In IS research we use *models* as design artifacts [18] to abstract from reality and real world objects, the so called universe of discourse (UoD). If the objects of research are models, and not the real world, we create models of models. Usually a "model of a model" is called metamodel. Going from the instance level (real world, UoD), consisting of instances (M0) to the model level (M1) and further to the metamodel level (M2) signifies the application of abstraction mechanisms. The way of abstraction is guided by a metaization principle (see [15] for a broader discussion).

In order to build a metamodel that is on the same semantic level as ontologies we use the ontological metaization. To model some portion of the world (which might be a model), one needs a language as well as a method with procedures, which supports the identification and representation of relevant objects. The language is considered as the "*way of modeling*", the procedures as the "*way of working*" [34]. In IS research, the emphasis is usually on the way of modeling. Here, we use UML class diagrams. Hence, we focus on the static aspects of the framework. In 2.2 we will focus on the *way of working* in order to better support the construction process of metamodels, by making use of ideas from grounded theory and QDA.

In our research program we are using semi-formal models in order to provide the oretical foundation in different domains (for example IT governance in general and IS security in particular). As metamodels represent the underlying, often implicit structure of the models/standards, they can be used in various ways. On the one hand, they are a methodological support for the construction of company specific extensions/adaptations of known standards/models. If extensions are oriented by both, the company specific needs and the metamodel, it will more likely be consistent with the used model/standard. Further aspects, which take into account the use and application of different models and standards in an enterprise, are the relationships between them. A security model of an enterprise should be linked to and integrated into models used for related tasks and initiatives (e.g. IT governance models like COBIT, ITIL ([15])). This linking can be supported by metamodels because they are useful means to integrate different models. On the other hand, the representation of the standards structure on meta-level supports its deeper evaluation, e.g. for comparing it to other models (e.g. a security ontology). In this respect the motivation is analytic in nature.

Of course, a finished metamodel can be used in either way. In the following, we are going to use the metamodel of ISO/IEC 27001 for analytical purpose, e.g. to evaluate for comprehensiveness or completeness.

2.2 Way of Working

In order to support the construction process of metamodels, we refer to ideas and methods used in grounded theory and QDA. Due to page restrictions, we are not able to give a broad introduction (please refer to [7, 8]).

The basic idea in grounded theory (as with most QDA methods) is to work with empirical data like transcripts from interviews, protocols and documents a researcher is confronted with in the field. The focus is on inductively developing a theory, which is 'grounded' in the respective empirical data. One central activity is the "coding", which means conceptualizing qualitative data and assigning categories as well as relations between them. The events and instances a researcher is facing in the data are analyzed as potential "indicators of phenomena … which are thereby given conceptual labels" [8, p. 7]. This conceptualization is very similar to the metaization we referred to above. Our approach is discovering the structure in ISO 27001 by identifying relevant categories/concepts as well as their relations.

Furthermore the abstraction mechanisms used to build concepts and categories are, to the best of our knowledge, not subject of discussions in the relevant methodological literature on QDA and grounded theory. Most approaches only stress its inductive nature. In our metamodelling approach applied in the following section we use inductive categorization in order to derive relevant ontological metamodel components for M2 from the ISO/IEC standard, which is located on model level (M1). We furthermore use QDA software (ATLAS.ti) for coding.

3 Related Work

3.1 Information Security Standards

One of the major challenges in managing information security are incomplete information about the risks the information systems are facing as well as available controls to address them [32]. As such, planning models, checklists and guidelines have been and still are popular. As each organization identifies the threats to their information systems and determines suitable countermeasures, a set of best-practice procedures and techniques emerges. In an attempt to standardize efforts in information security, best-practice frameworks and standards have been developed (e.g. ISO 17799, 2700x, NIST). Due to their origin, these vary in scope and purpose. Furthermore, they vary in depth as well as in the level of detail and granularity. We therefore focus our analysis to the meta level M2.

In our selection of a suitable information security standard we have defined two requirements: 1) the chosen standard must aim to be comprehensive and have a wide scope on information security and 2) the chosen standard should have – even if very limited – a representative character for actual security practice. After considering different standards we chose ISO 27001 [19] for the following reasons: The ISO 27002 standard is the actual guideline on best-practice in information security management. However, as with best practice frameworks in the related field of IT governance, individual controls can be ignored in an attempt to customize the guideline to the actual organizational needs – and in fact this is the common case [24]. By choosing the certification standard ISO 27001 instead, we assume that organizations having completed the certification process accordingly have addressed all concepts incorporated in said standard. Therefore, the chosen standard represents actual security practice in organizations certified based on it. In the next section we will discuss information security ontologies, which will serve as a reference to evaluate our derived metamodel regarding completeness.

3.2 Information Security Ontologies

Ontologies are sets of concepts of a given domain. As explicit specifications of a conceptualization [17] they allow the formalization and transfer of knowledge. This can help to communicate, compare and put in relation to each other the knowledge and findings researchers make. Therefore, defining concepts and the relations between them is one of the primary tasks in any scientific community [5].

Many information security researchers have identified ontologies as a means to structure either the entire information security problem domain or specific subdomains and made contributions (e.g. [1, 10, 23]). In their comparison of thirty security ontologies [6] conclude that the scientific community has not yet reached the goal of establishing a general information security ontology. By building upon an information security standard that is specifically used to certify information security management systems (ISMS) we cannot make the claim to deliver such a contribution either. However, the metamodel of ISO 27001 can serve as a foundation and a starting point to build an information security management ontology which may cover the managerial aspects of information security. After examining several ontologies, we decided to use [12, 21, 23, 25, 27, 33] as reference ontologies based on the shared subject and their broad scope for comparison.

One may ask if ontologies and models can be compared the way we propose. Due to different notions of both, it is impossible to clearly separate 'ontology' and 'model' [3]. E. g. ontologies in literature differ in notation, axiomatic richness and the levels of formality (graphical vs. logic based language; lightweight vs. heavyweight ontologies; machine-readable vs. machine-interpretable); similarly, conceptual modelling languages differ in modelling concepts and their external notation as well as in operators or rules of inference and in their integrity rules. In his ontology spectrum [26] views conceptual models (like the object oriented models of UML) as a kind of ontology, having a medium level of structure and formalization. Partially in contrast, [3] consider every ontology a model. We therefore see our metamodels as comparable to ontologies as long as both are on the same level of abstraction.

4 Metamodeling of the Information Security Standard ISO 27001

Based on our selection of the certification standard ISO 27001 for information security management systems the primary document was defined. We additionally narrowed the QDA approach down to its Annex A, which contains the actual objectives and controls. In order to reduce a potential linguistic bias of the researcher (preferences for certain words), we used in-vivo coding which uses the quoted term itself as code label. By doing this, we have generated 153 codes, which were grounded in 275 quotations. We call this set of codes our base set. Figure 1 shows the steps of our process and the resulting sets of codes.

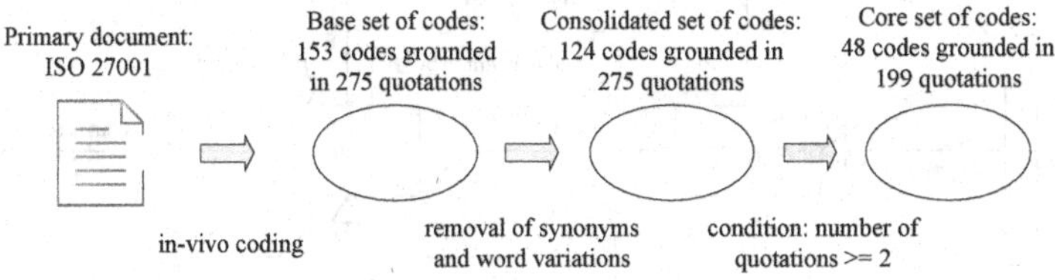

Fig. 1. Inductive Categorization Process

The codes stem from the ISO standard and therefore reside on the M1 level. In a next step we have merged codes based on synonyms and word variations. This way we reduced the number of codes to 124, our so-called consolidated set of codes. During an examination of the remaining codes we noticed that most codes that were grounded only in a single quotation would be considered attributes under a modeling aspect. For example the codes 'information in transit' and 'stored information' embody two states of 'information'. Using the condition of grounding in at least 2 quotations we finalized 48 codes as the foundation for our metaization effort. Once a first version of our metamodel, containing the core set of codes, is established, the excluded 76 codes with singular grounding are re-evaluated and included as either concepts on their own, subconcepts, attributes or ultimately dismissed.

We derive concepts using inductive ontological metaization. These concepts therefore reside on the level M2. We define core concepts as concepts that are not types or subconcepts of other concepts. Amongst the 48 codes we identified the following concepts to be as such: 'asset', 'threat', 'control', 'requirement' and 'role'. The first three concepts did not come as a surprise. Assets represent a value that is deserving of protection for the organization, while threats are the concept that endangers this value and controls (synonymous to countermeasures) are the means to achieve said protection. All three are often cited in security requirements engineering (e.g. [13, 28]).

The concept 'requirements' is represented by three subconcepts we identified in the standard: 1) security requirements, 2) legal requirements and 3) business requirements. These distinctions indicate potential aspects or layers of information security management, as suggested by many information security researchers (see [9]). Figure 2 shows the metamodel of the ISO 27001 standard based on our findings.

In comparison to the other core concepts 'rule' has relatively weak grounding based on the in-vivo coding. However, with 10 quotations the code 'responsibility' is one of the more predominant ones and represents the relation between 'role' and other concepts, mainly 'asset'. To include this emphasis on an ownership-type paradigm we decided to include role as a (supporting) core concept. The relationships among concepts have been derived by analyzing quotations.

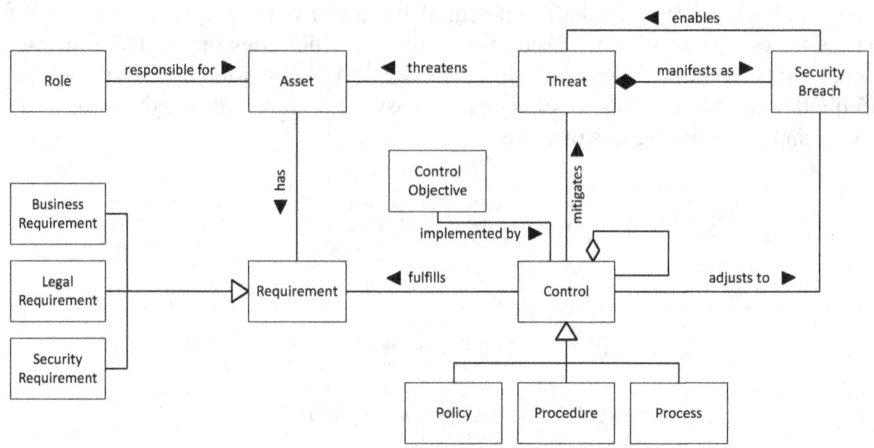

Fig. 2. ISO 27001 Metamodel

After adding the five mentioned core concepts and branching 'requirement' and 'control' into subconcepts, we re-evaluated prior excluded codes with singular occurrences. By doing so we identified three codes that had a semantic similarity: 'security event', 'security incident' and 'security breach'. While interpretation allows to distinct them by varying levels of severity, we decided to merge them together add them as one core concept ('security breach') as an analysis of quotations for the 'control' and 'threat' concept showed that this element played an important part for the control objectives A.8.2, A.10.10 and A.13.2. Additionally we added 'control objective', as it is an important structural element in the standard which groups controls and elaborates on their common purpose.

It is notable, that in the part of the ISO 27001 standard we used for our analysis, measures are not included systematically, even though in the rest of the standard they are mentioned frequently. Furthermore, there is no strong evidence that roles and responsibilities might be assigned to controls or control objectives. From a governance point of view, it would be of central importance to define accountability and decision rights during the implementation of a security standard.

5 Comparison and Findings

To evaluate ISO 27001 using our metamodel we compare it with selected information security ontologies to find out how our identified concepts relate to different sets (e.g. be a super set, subset or an intersection with other sets of concepts). Table 1 shows the security concepts and their correlation to our core concepts of the metamodel. We are aware that it is not possible to evaluate for completeness, but we consider a set of ontologies to be a good proxy evaluating for comprehensiveness.

A review of the selected ontologies shows that the *way of working* differs from our inductive approach, which may be one reason for differences in concepts found. For example [12] identify concepts using a deductive categorization. By surveying existing literature they derive a structure which they fill using multiple source documents such as ontologies of security sub domains (e.g. cryptology) and standards.

Table 1. Comparison of information security concepts

Lee et al. [23]	Karyda et al. [21]	Tsoumas et al. [33]	Fenz et al. [12]	Mouratidis et al. [25]	Raskin et al. [27]	ISO 27001 Metamodel
Asset	Asset	Asset	Asset	Sec. Entities	Object	Asset
Countermeasure	Countermeasure	Countermeasure/Control	Control			Control
Criticality			Rating			
		Impact				
Goal	Objective					Control Objective
			Organization			
		Risk				
Sec. Requirement			Attribute	Security Constraint	Property	Requirement
Source			Location			
Stakeholder	Person	Stakeholder / Threat Agent	Person			Role
Threat	Threat	Threat	Threat			Threat
		Attack/Unwanted Incident			Event	Security Breach
Vulnerability		Vulnerability	Vulnerability			

Comparing these concepts we can find 'asset', 'threat' and 'control' either verbatim in the selected ontologies or in the case of control as a synonym of 'countermeasure'. As we have pointed out before, these concepts are also predominant in security engineering literature and probably can be considered authentic core concepts of the information security discipline. For our 'role' concept we see a semantic equivalent in the two concepts 'organization' and 'person', as well as 'stakeholder' and contextualized in the threat scenario 'threat agent'. Finally, despite its strong grounding in our analysis of the ISO 27001 standard, the 'requirement' concept does not seem to be part of many other ontologies. At best we can find semantic equivalents in the concepts 'security constraints', 'attribute' and 'property'.

One possible reason for this discrepancy might be the difference in the way of working. By building an ontology using a deductive categorization process, the theoretical foundation can pre-determine (bias) elements of the ontology and lead to a different result compared to an inductive process. In their description of the 'attribute' concept [12] describe 'security attributes' as a subconcept, which has e.g. availability or confidentiality as instances – terms that we'd associate with the 'security requirements' subconcept in our metamodel.

Based on the weak grounding of codes like 'internal user' and 'external threat' we did not subsume such codes into a 'source' concept. However, based on its importance in distinguishing threats (by origin) we agree that such an aspect is vital for a comprehensive information security management system. However, it is unclear if 'source' (or 'location') is a concept, a criterion to create subconcepts (e.g. 'internal threat' and 'external threat') or if it is an attribute or property of the 'threat' concept.

For the concepts 'criticality', 'impact', 'organization' and 'risk' we did not find sufficient quotations to derive respective concepts, nor were those concepts found in many of the analyzed ontologies. Contrary the 'vulnerability' concept plays a vital role in the operationalization of ontologies like [12, 33] and should be considered for adoption in a more general metamodel of the information security domain.

6 Conclusion and Future Research

In this paper we attempted to identify relevant concepts in the information security management standard ISO 27001 in order to achieved insight into its structure. As a methodological foundation we applied QDA to enhance transparency and traceability of the metamodeling procedure and, furthermore, showed that metamodels can assist in the analysis and comparison with multiple ontologies.

In their comparison of security ontologies [6] focused on ontological metrics and evaluated essentially the structure of the proposed ontologies, not their content. We contributed by comparing a selection of ontologies and the constructed metamodel based on the concepts therein. Hereby, core concepts in the sense of an intersection of said ontologies could be derived and compared with our findings.

In an extension of the presented research we also see the need to examine the depth (search for instances on meta level M0) and comparison with additional ontologies, which is where e. g. the 'vulnerability' concept may play a crucial role.

We assume that an extended ontology can contribute significantly to the building of a theory core for IS security research. There is a dominance of subjective-argumentative research in information security research, which – according to [30] – indicates that the discipline is still on its way to establish a theory core. We believe that by establishing an ontology not only ambiguity in terminology can be reduced or eliminated, but that ontologies can also serve as a framework for a theory core in the discipline. This consideration is mainly based on the view of theory as "a lens for viewing or explaining the world" [16]. In this respect, the goal of theory is to provide a description of the phenomena of interest, analysis of relationships among concepts, and the definition of constraints. Based on correspondence as well as consensus theory of truth, it could be possible to derive one integrated and reconciled ontology/model which could serve as a theory core for IS security research.

References

1. Amaral, F.d.N., Bazilio, C., Silva, G.M.H.d., Rademaker, A., Haeusler, E.H.: An Ontology-based Approach to the Formalization of Information Security Policies. In: Proc. of the 10th IEEE on International Enterprise Distributed Object Computing Conference Workshops EDOCW 2006. IEEE Computer Society, Los Alamitos (2006)
2. Arief, B., Besnard, D.: Technical and human issues in computer-based systems security. Report No. CS-TR 790, University of Newcastle, UK (2003)
3. Atkinson, C., Gutheil, M., Kiko, K.: On the relationship of Ontologies and Models. In: Second Workshop on Meta-Modelling (WoMM 2006) (October 2006)
4. Baker, W.H., Wallace, L.: Is Information Security Under Control? Investigating Quality in Information Security Management. IEEE Security and Privacy 5(1), 36–44 (2007)
5. Bishop, M.: What Is Computer Security? IEEE Sec. & Privacy 1, 67–69 (2003)
6. Blanco, C., Lasheras, J., Valencia-Garcia, R., Fernandez-Medina, E., Toval, A., Piattini, M.: A Systematic Review and Comparison of Security Ontologies. In: Proc. of the Third International Conference on Availability, Reliability and Security, pp. 813–819 (2008)
7. Bryant, A., Charmaz, K. (eds.): The SAGE Handbook of Grounded Theory. Sage, London (2007)

8. Corbin, J.M., Strauss, A.: Grounded theory research: Procedures, canons and evaluative criteria. Qualitative Sociology 13(1), 3–21 (1990)
9. Dhillon, G., Backhouse, J.: Current directions in IS security research: towards socio-organizational perspectives. In. Systems Journal 11, 127–153 (2001)
10. Donner, M.: Toward a Security Ontology. IEEE Sec. & Privacy 1(3), 6–7 (2003)
11. Eloff, J.H.P., Eloff, M.: Information security management: a new paradigm. In: Proc. of the 2003 Annual Research Conference of the South African Institute of Computer Scientists and Information Technologists on Enablement Through Technology, pp. 130–136 (2003)
12. Fenz, S., Ekelhart, A.: Formalizing information security knowledge. In: Proc. of the 4th International Symposium on Information, Computer and Communications Security, pp. 183–194 (2009)
13. Flechais, I., Mascolo, C., Sasse, M.A.: Integrating security and usability into the requirements and design process. Int. Journal of Electronic Security and Digital Forensics 1(1), 12–16 (2007)
14. Fomin, V., de Vries, H.J., Barlette, Y.: ISO/IEC 27001: Exploring the reasons for low adoption. In: Proc. EUROMOT 2008, Nice/Sophia Antipolis (2008)
15. Goeken, M., Alter, S.: Towards Conceptual Metamodelling of IT Governance Frameworks. Approach - Use – Benefits. In: Proc. of the 42nd Annual Hawaii Int. Conference on System Sciences, Hawaii (2009)
16. Gregor, S.: The nature of theory in information systems. MISQ 3, 491–506 (2006)
17. Grubner, T.R.: Towards principles for the design of ontologies used for knowledge sharing. Int. Journal of Human-Computer Studies 43(5), 907–928 (1995)
18. Hevner, A.R., March, S.T., Park, J., Ram, S.: Design Science in Information Systems Research. MISQ 28(2), 75–105 (2004)
19. International Organization for Standardization and International Electrotechnical Commission, ISO/IEC 27001:2005, information technology - security techniques - information security management systems- requirements (2005)
20. Kankanhalli, A., Teo, H., Tan, B., Wei, K.: An integrative study of information systems security effectiveness. Int. Journal of Information Management 23(2), 139–154 (2003)
21. Karyda, M., Balopoulos, T., Dritsas, S., Gymnopoulos, L., Kokolakis, S., Lambrinoudakis, C., Gritzalis, S.: An ontology for security e-government applications. In: Proc. of the First Int. Conference on Availability, Reliability and Security 2006, pp. 1033–1037 (2006)
22. Kim, A., Luo, J., Kang, M.: Security Ontology for Annotating Resources. In: Proc. of the 4th Int. Conference on Ontologies, Databases and Applications, Agia Napa, Cyprus (2005)
23. Lee, S.-W., Gandhi, R., Muthurajan, D., Yavagal, D., Ahn, G.-J.: Building problem domain ontology from security requirements in regulatory documents. In: Proc. of the 2006 International Workshop on Software Engineering for Secure Systems. ACM, Shanghai (2006)
24. Looso, S., Goeken, M.: Application of Best-Practice Reference Models of IT Governance. In: Proc. of European Conference on Inf. Systems, ECIS (2010)
25. Mouratidis, H., Giorgini, P., Manson, G.: An Ontology for Modelling Security: The Tropos Approach. In: Palade, V., Howlett, R.J., Jain, V. (eds.) Knowledge-Based Intelligent Information and Engineering Systems. LNCS (LNAI), pp. 1387–1394. Springer, Heidelberg (2003)
26. Obrst, L.: Ontologies for Semantically Interoperable Systems. In: Proceedings of the Twelfth International Conference on Information and Knowledge Management, pp. 366–369 (2003)

27. Raskin, V., Hempelmann, C.F., Triezenberg, K.E., Nirenburg, S.: Ontology in information security: a useful theoretical foundation and methodological tool. In: Proc. of the 2001 Workshop on New Security Paradigms (2001)
28. Sindre, G., Opdahl, A.L.: Eliciting security requirements with misuse cases. Requirements Engineering 10(1), 34–44 (2005)
29. Siponen, M., Willison, R.: Information security management standards: Problems and solutions. Information & Management 46, 267–270 (2009)
30. Siponen, M., Willison, R., Baskerville, R.: Power and Practice in Information Systems Security Research. In: Proc. of the Int. Conference on Information Systems, ICIS (2008)
31. Solms, S.H., Solms, R.: Information Security Governance, New York (2009)
32. Straub, D.W., Welke, R.J.: Coping with Systems Risk: Security Planning Models for Management Decision Making. MIS Quarterly 22, 441–469 (1998)
33. Tsoumas, B., Gritzalis, D.: Towards an Ontology-based Security Management. In: Proc. of the 20th Int. Conference on Advanced Information Networking and Applications, vol. 1, pp. 985–992 (2006)
34. Verhoef, T.F., Hofstede, A.H.M.T., Wijers, G.M.: Structuring Modelling Knowledge for CASE Shells. In: Andersen, R., Solvberg, A., Bubenko Jr., J.A. (eds.) CAiSE 1991. LNCS, vol. 498, pp. 502–524. Springer, Heidelberg (1991)

The Importance of Confirming Citizens' Expectations in e-Government

Daniel Belanche[1], Luis V. Casaló[2], and Carlos Flavián[1]

[1] Universidad de Zaragoza, Faculty of Economics, Gran Vía 2, 50.005, Zaragoza, Spain
[2] Universidad de Zaragoza, School of Business Studies, Ronda Misericordia 1, 22.001, Huesca, Spain
{Belan,lcasalo,cflavian}@unizar.es

Abstract. Satisfying consumer needs is a core principle of marketing. However, in the context of e-government, most studies up to now have focused on adoption models such as Technology Acceptance Model or Theory of Planned Behavior, forgetting citizens' needs, demands or expectations. To overcome this, in this work we analyze how confirmation of citizens' expectations may influence citizens' perceptions and behavioral intentions in the e-government context. As well, due to its great influence on consumer behavior, we investigate some factors that may enhance citizens' intention to recommend online public services. Data from 232 citizens reveal that confirmation of expectations and perceived usefulness effectively predicts citizen intention to use online public services. As well, positive word of mouth among citizens is positively affected by confirmation of expectations and intention to use these services. Finally, confirmation of expectations confirms its importance by influencing perceived usefulness too.

Keywords: E-government, intention to use, confirmation of expectations, WOM, perceived usefulness.

1 Introduction

In the last years, governments have increased the offer of public services on the Internet. For example, in Spain the law 11/2007 (Ley 11/2007, de 22 de junio, de acceso electrónico de los ciudadanos a los Servicios Públicos) acknowledges the citizens' right to interact with the Public Administration in an online manner in order to obtain information, make questions or carry out transactions among other tasks in the citizen-government relationship. However, most of these new electronic services offered by governments are still in a starting point and remain unfamiliar for most citizens. The acceptance of these e-services not only by pioneers, but also by follower citizens may allow achieving a critical mass of users that guarantees the success of these e-government initiatives.

Despite widespread acceptance of the importance of e-government initiatives (e.g. Belanche et al. 2009), there is a relative paucity of knowledge about the determinants of citizens' intention to use online public services. Indeed, up to now almost all

W. Cellary and E. Estevez (Eds.): I3E 2010, IFIP AICT 341, pp. 103–111, 2010.

studies in this regard have focused on well-known adoption models such as the Technology Acceptance Model or the Theory of Planned Behavior (e.g. Wu and Chen 2005). Therefore, little consensus exists about what else motivates people to use these online public services. As well, as far as know, there is no empirical assessment of the antecedents of citizens intention to promote these e-government initiatives, which in turn might be one of the most powerful forces in persuading fellow citizens to use these services. Thus, both theoretically and managerially, we require a more in-depth understanding of citizen behavior in the e-government context.

This research contributes to previous literature by addressing two critical issues. First, we examine the role that confirmation of expectations may have on citizens' perceptions and behavioral intentions. It is important to note that citizens have different roles in the complex government-citizen relationship, being one of these the role as a consumer of public services (Steyaert 2000). Sometimes these services are compulsory, but in other cases their use is volitional; so to provide efficient services, citizen needs and requirements should be taken into account. Therefore, the confirmation of citizens' expectations may provide a useful explanation of post-usage behaviors in the e-government context. This variable reflects the degree to which expectations generated on previous occasions have been met, resulting from a person's perception that the benefits received are equal to (or greater than) the expected benefits, increasing the perceived usefulness of using the online public service. As well, met expectations may lead users to feel satisfied and motivated to use repeatedly and promote these online public services. However, to the best of our knowledge, this role of confirmation of expectations has not been analyzed in this context.

Second, due to its great influence on individuals' choices (Chung and Darke 2006), we investigate some factors that may enhance citizens' intention to recommend online public services. In particular, we investigate confirmation of expectations, perceived usefulness, and intention to use the online public service as potential determinants of positive word of mouth [WOM hereafter] among citizens. The reason behind this may be found in the fact that an individual may recommend a product/service if s/he perceives that it is useful or has some kind of affective commitment towards it (these affective ties may be caused by a positive evaluation confirming previous expectations). As well, if citizens have the intention to use online public services, it is likely that they perceive a greater value when using them. In response to that, citizens may also be motivated to promote these services to fellow citizens.

Therefore, this work is structured as follows: First, we formulate the study hypotheses. Second, we describe the data collection process, as well as the methodology we employ. Then, we present the results of the research. Finally, we discuss the main findings, conclusions and managerial implications of the work.

2 Formulation of Hypotheses

First, we expect a positive effect of confirmation of expectations on perceived usefulness. This is explained by the fact that initially, although the lack of experience involves uncertainty, citizens have some perceptions about the level of usefulness of the service. If they finally use it and general expectations about service's performance are confirmed, citizens will perceive higher levels of positive website attributes (such us usefulness) than previously thought. Then, citizens may use their experience as a basis to form more precise perceptions and adjust their expectations. This reasoning is supported by the Cognitive Dissonance Theory (Festinger 1957), which suggests that rational individuals try to eliminate the dissonance between pre-acceptance thoughts and actual performance evidences by modifying previous expectations in order to be more consistent with reality. Broadly speaking, in our case, confirmation of expectations should serve to increase perceived usefulness of using an online public service, while negative disconfirmation should reduce perceived usefulness. Indeed, this link has been proved in the Information System Continuance Model developed by Bhattacherjee (2001). Therefore, we propose our first hypothesis:

H1: Confirmation of expectations has a positive effect on the perceived usefulness of using an online public service.

In addition, the intention to use an information system is primarily determined by consumer satisfaction with prior usage experience (Bhattacherjee 2001). More specifically, satisfaction reflects that benefits derived from using a system are, at least, equal to the expected ones. Thus, if these expectations are met, the individual will be motivated to continue using the system. To be precise, expectations provide the baseline level against which perceived performance is compared in order to determine the consumer evaluative response. In this sense, confirmation of expectations implies the realization of the expected benefits, while disconfirmation leads to dissatisfaction since it denotes failure to achieve expectation (Bhattacherjee 2001). Therefore, in our context of analysis, we may expect that confirmation of expectations motivates citizens to continue using an online public service. Bearing in mind these considerations, we propose the second hypothesis:

H2: Confirmation of expectations has a positive effect on the intention to use an online public service.

Traditionally, several authors have stated that satisfaction leads to an increased probability that consumers will talk in a favorable manner about an organization and recommend the firm to other customers (e.g. Dolen et al. 2007). Broadly speaking, due to the fact that satisfied consumers confirm their expectations and demands when using an organization's products/services, these customers may be effective promoters of the organization (Dolen et al. 2007). Therefore, it seems reasonable to think that citizens that confirm their expectations when using an online public service will be more likely to promote the service, thanks to positive comments about it made to fellow citizens, rather than those that experience a negative disconfirmation. Bearing these considerations in mind, we propose the following hypothesis:

H3: Confirmation of expectations has a positive effect on citizens' positive WOM.

In turn, the Technology Acceptance Model (e.g. Davis et al. 1989) proposes that perceived usefulness not only influences the acceptance intention indirectly (through attitude), but it also has a direct effect on intention to use. Indeed, individuals also form their behavioral intentions according to the expected productivity associated to that behavior (Davis 1989). For instance, Vroom (1964) noted that good performance within an organizational context is usually rewarded by monetary gains or promotions. Therefore, in this context, information systems may be seen as means to reach that end, so that the adoption of information systems among workers may be enhanced. Analogously, focusing on our context of analysis, online public services may be seen as a worthwhile mean in order to carry out regular citizen's task by saving time and costs. Thus, the intention to participate in this kind of citizen-government relation may be enhanced due to its usefulness. Consequently, we propose the following hypothesis:

H4: Perceived usefulness of using an online public service has a positive effect on the intention to use that service.

Following East et al. (2007), positive WOM is not only caused by consumer satisfaction, but many other stimuli may motivate WOM communications. Among these, WOM most usually appears when the receiver of the communication has a special need and asks for specific information (Mangold et al. 1999). In this situation, the communicator will likely recommend the most useful option according to the receivers' needs. Thus, it is reasonable to think that, in the context of e-government, citizens will more likely recommend the use of online public services if these services are perceived as useful and valuable. Indeed, Mangold et al. (1999) found that value and quality –two concepts very close to usefulness– are the product/service attributes that stimulate most WOM communication. Therefore, we propose the following hypothesis:

H5: Perceived usefulness of using an online public service has a positive effect on citizens' positive WOM.

Finally, the intention to use a product/service reflects favorable consumer attitudes towards it and the organization that provides it (e.g. Evanschitzky et al. 2006). In this respect, one of the consumer behaviors that might benefit the organization derived from this favorable disposition is the development of positive WOM and recommendation (Hallowell 1996) by emphasizing the main attributes of the organization products and services. This is motivated by the fact that the intention to use the service is the result of the individual's beliefs that the quantity of value received from consuming a product or service is greater than the value of non-consuming (Hallowell 1996). Thus, in response to this greater value obtained, the individual is motivated to use the service again and to promote it by, for instance, positive WOM behaviors. Indeed, this fact will reinforce the suitability of the decision to use that service and enhance the idea of being a good citizen that try to spread the benefits of a public resource among fellow citizens in his/her community. Therefore, taking these considerations into account, we propose in our last hypothesis that intention to use an online public service may favor the development of positive WOM among citizens:

H6: The intention to use an online public service has a positive effect on citizens' positive WOM.

3 Data Collection

We collected the data for this study from a Web survey of Spanish-speaking citizens. This method is consistent with common research practices online (e.g., Steenkamp and Geyskens 2006). To obtain responses, we included a link on a Spanish Governmental Agency which collaborated in the research promotion. When potential interviewees entered the study Web site, they found the research questionnaire and additional information about the research project. We finally collected 232 valid questionnaires (after eliminating atypical cases, repeated responses, and incomplete questionnaires).

The study subjects chose the online public service they analyzed (among those offered in the collaborating agency), because we work to assess citizens' behaviors regardless of the specific characteristics of the public service. We simply required the respondents to have used the online public service selected at least once in the last year. Respondents then answered several questions about their levels of confirmation of expectations, and perceived usefulness of the online public service, as well as their intentions to use the system again and recommend it to fellow citizens. These measures use a seven-point Likert type response format, and respondents rated them from 1 ("completely disagree") to 7 ("completely agree").

4 Measures Validation

An in-depth review of the relevant literature concerning relationship marketing and e-marketing was developed to propose an initial set of items to measure the latent constructs. This review helped guarantee the content validity of the scales. We also tested face validity –the degree that respondents judge that the items are appropriate to the targeted construct– through a variation of the Zaichkowsky method (1985). Following this method, each item was qualified by a panel of experts as "clearly representative", "somewhat representative" or "not representative of the construct of interest". Finally, items were retained if a high level of consensus was observed among the experts (Lichtenstein et al. 1990).

The first step in the process of measures validation was an exploratory analysis of reliability and dimensionality. In this sense, the Cronbach's alpha indicator –considering a minimum value of .7 (Nunnally 1978)–, the item-total correlation –considering a minimum value of .3 (Nurosis 1993)–, and principal components analysis were used to assess the initial reliability and dimensionality of the scales. All items were adjusted to the required levels and only one factor was extracted from each scale: confirmation of expectations, perceived usefulness, intention to use and positive WOM.

In order to confirm the dimensional structure of the scales, we used the Confirmatory Factor Analysis. For these tasks, the statistical software EQS v.6.1 was employed and we used Robust Maximum Likelihood as an estimation method. The criteria proposed by Jöreskog and Sörbom (1993) were followed in order to depurate the scales. Following these recommendations, we obtained acceptable levels of convergence, R^2 and model fit (Chi-square = 46.861, 29 d.f., p = .01923; Satorra-Bentler Scaled Chi-square = 30.1946, 29 d.f., p = .40434; Bentler-Bonett Normed Fit Index =.98; Bentler-Bonett Nonnormed Fit Index =.99; Comparative Fit Index (CFI) =.99; Bollen (IFI) Fit Index =.99; Root Mean Sq. Error of App. (RMESA) =.013; 90% Confidence Interval of RMESA (.000, .052)).

Additionally, we used the composite reliability indicator to asses construct reliability (Jöreskog 1971). We obtained values above .65 (see table 1), exceeding the benchmarks that are suggested as acceptable (Steenkamp and Geyskens 2006). Finally, convergent validity, which indicates whether the items that compose a scale converge on one construct, was tested by checking that the factor loadings of the confirmatory model were statistically significant (level of .01) and higher than .5

points (Steenkamp and Geyskens 2006). As well, we used the Average Variance Extracted (AVE) to contrast the convergent validity and obtained acceptable values greater than .5, which implies that items that compose a determined scale contain less than 50% error variance and converge on only one construct (Fornell and Larcker 1981). On the other hand, discriminant validity, which reveals whether a determined construct is significantly distinct from other constructs that are not theoretically related to it, was tested by comparing the square root of the AVE with the correlations among constructs. That is, we checked that the construct shares more variance with its own measures than the variance it shares with the other constructs in the model (Wiertz and De Ruyter 2007). The results show acceptable levels of discriminant validity since all diagonal values exceed the inter-construct correlations.

5 Results

To test the hypotheses, we developed a structural equation model, which offers the results in Figure 1. All hypotheses are supported at the .01 level, unless hypothesis 5 which is not confirmed. As well, model fit achieves acceptable values (Chi-square = 46.861, 29 d.f., p = .01923; Satorra-Bentler Scaled Chi-square = 30.1872, 29 d.f., p = .40470; Bentler-Bonett Normed Fit Index =.98; Bentler-Bonett Nonnormed Fit Index =.99; Comparative Fit Index (CFI) =.99; Bollen (IFI) Fit Index =.99; Root Mean Sq. Error of App. (RMESA) =.013; 90% Confidence Interval of RMESA (.000, .052); normed Chi-square = 1.6159).

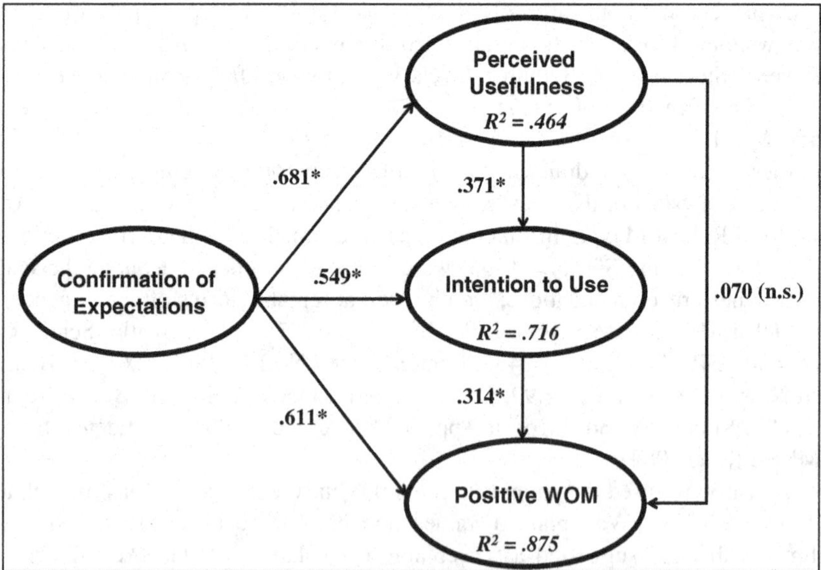

Fig. 1. Structural equation model: Standardized solution. Note: "*"Coefficients are significant at .01 level; (n.s.) coefficients are non-significant.

Firstly, in accordance with standardized coefficients, it has been proved that confirmation of expectations positively affects perceived usefulness of an online public service ($\lambda = .681$, $p < .01$), intention to use that service ($\lambda = .549$, $p < .01$), and intention to recommend it –positive WOM– ($\lambda = .611$, $p < .01$), in support of hypotheses 1, 2 and 3, respectively. Secondly, perceived usefulness also shows a positive effect on the intention to use an online public service ($\beta = .371$, $p < .01$), confirming hypotheses 4. Finally, positive WOM among citizens is positively affected by intention to use an online public service ($\beta = .314$, $p < .01$), but contrary to expected it is not significantly influenced by perceived usefulness of the service ($\beta = .070$, $p > .1$). As a result, we accept hypothesis 6, but hypothesis 5 could not be confirmed.

We further remark that this simple model can partially explain the endogenous variables of the study: perceived usefulness of using an online public service ($R^2 = .464$), citizen intention to use that service ($R^2 = .716$) and, especially, citizen intention to recommend the use of the system –positive WOM– ($R^2 = .875$).

6 Discussion

The results of this research have helped to remedy, to a certain extent, the lack of empirical studies that analyze: (1) citizens' motivations to use online public services (apart from the adoption models used up to now), and (2) the positive WOM development in the e-government context. Indeed, the analysis of WOM in this context is especially relevant since WOM is more important and influential in the services context because of their intangibility (Murray and Schlacter 1990). Thus, citizens may appreciate WOM because in this situation fellow citizens are seen as more objective and reliable than other information sources.

Specifically, in this study, we first have seen that intention to use online public services is determined by both confirmation of expectations and perceived usefulness. The effect of perceived usefulness on intention to use is coherent with previous applications of Technology Acceptance Model to the e-government context (e.g. Wu and Chen 2005). As well, the positive influence of confirmation of expectations is also in line with previous research in other contexts, since it has been widely used to explain post-usage behaviors such as intention to use again a product/service (e.g. Oliver 1980). In addition, in line with the Information System Continuance Model (Bhattacherjee 2001), perceived usefulness is influenced by confirmation of expectations, which in turn may also have an indirect effect on intention to use through perceived usefulness. As a result, the citizen's affective state derived from the confirmation of his/her expectations seems to have a deeper impact in developing citizen behavioral intentions, which might be considered as a first contribution of this study.

Secondly, positive WOM is mainly influenced by confirmation of expectations and, in a lesser extent, by the intention to use online public services. On the other hand, the direct effect of perceived usefulness seems to be non-significant. Although these results are quite surprising, we consider they are in line with previous findings in the e-commerce context. Indeed, Casaló et al. (2008) already found that, rather than individual beliefs about a service, affective feelings are the strongest precursor of positive WOM in the e-banking business. In our case, this affective state arises from the confirmation of citizens' expectations; that is, from satisfying citizens' demands.

To sum up, we may conclude that, in the context of e-government, the confirmation of expectations directly affects citizens' behavioral intentions, in terms of preference for future use of online public services and recommendation to fellow citizens, which may therefore affect the probability of e-government success in a positive way. Therefore, this research offers several alternatives to increase the citizens' intentions to both use and recommend online public services, so that governments can develop and implement e-government initiatives more easily.

1. Firstly, governments should try to maximize the satisfaction of their citizens by confirming their expectations when using online public services. Customer satisfaction will be generated if the customer's expectations about the relationship are met. Therefore, governments should try to identify the needs of their citizens (e.g. in terms of services offered, design of the website, etc.) in order to offer them what they want in an efficient way. Thus, confirming citizens' expectations will lead to satisfied citizens that will be motivated to continue using these online services. In addition, satisfying customers may serve to avoid the negative WOM generated by dissatisfied customers. This fact is especially relevant since negative actions have a more intense impact on the individual than positive ones. However, it is important to note that the process of satisfying citizens is not an easy task; there is a wide spectrum of citizens with different abilities and needs, so that satisfying all of them may be a difficult issue. In this way, we recommend to prioritize ease-of-use in website design, promoting access to these services (e.g. by offering free wifi zones in public buildings and spaces, etc.) in order to overcome the access barriers that exist in some groups of the population, and constantly analyze the evolution of citizens' needs and demands.
2. Secondly, perceived usefulness has revealed as a crucial aspect in forming citizens' intention to use online public services. The degree of perceived usefulness can also be improved through some strategies. However, online public services may be considered as experience goods so their usefulness is difficult to perceive until they have been used. To overcome this obstacle, it is necessary to promote the test and the benefits that citizens can obtain by using them (e.g. saving time and cost, less paper waste –ecological concern–, etc.). To do that, the Public Administration can contact citizens directly (e.g. by post mail, e-mail, etc.) or conduct promotional campaigns in mass media in order to explain these benefits in more detail. In this way, it will be possible to create an external influence that increases citizen's perceptions that it is useful and trendy to use online public services.

Thus, improving the confirmation of citizens' expectations and the perceived usefulness of online public services will promote citizens' intentions to use and recommend online public services. As a consequence, the success of e-government initiatives will be more likely.

References

1. Belanche, D., Casaló, L.V., Flavián, C.: Citizen adoption of e-government based on TAM and TPB models. In: VIII International Congress on Public and Non Profit Marketing, Valencia (2009)

2. Wu, I.L., Chen, J.L.: An extension of Trust and TAM model with TPB in the initial adoption of on-line tax: An empirical study. Int. J. Hum.-Comput. Stud. 62, 784–808 (2005)
3. Steyaert, J.: Local governments online and the role of the residents. Government shop versus electronic Community. Soc. Sci. Comput. Rev. 18(1), 3–18 (2000)
4. Chung, C.M.Y., Darke, P.R.: The consumer as advocate: Self-relevance, culture and word-of-mouth. Mark. Lett. 17, 269–279 (2006)
5. Festinger, L.A.: A Theory of Cognitive Dissonance. Stanford University Press, Stanford (1957)
6. Bhattacherjee, A.: Understanding Information Systems Continuance: An Expectation/Confirmation Model. MIS. Q. 25(3), 351–370 (2001)
7. Dolen, W.M., van Dhabolkar, P.A., De Ruyter, K.: Satisfaction with Online Commercial Group Chat: The Influence of Perceived Technology Attributes, Chat Group Characteristics, and Advisor Communication Style. J. Retail. 83(3), 339–358 (2007)
8. Davis, F.D., Bagozzi, R.P., Warshaw, P.R.: User Acceptance of Computer Technology: A Comparison of Two Theoretical Models. Manag. Sci. 35(8), 982–1003 (1989)
9. Davis, F.: Perceived Usefulness, Perceived Ease of Use and User Acceptance of Information Technology. MIS. Q. 13(3), 319–340 (1989)
10. Vroom, V.H.: Work and Motivation. Wiley, New York (1964)
11. East, R., Hammond, K., Wright, M.: The relative incidence of positive and negative word of mouth: A multi-category study. Int. J. Res. Mark. 24(2), 175–184 (2007)
12. Mangold, G.W., Miller, F., Brockway, G.R.: Word-of-mouth communication in the service marketplace. J. Serv. Mark. 13(1), 73–89 (1999)
13. Evanschitzky, H., Gopalkrishnan, R.I., Plassmann, H., Niessing, J., Meffert, H.: The relative strength of affective commitment in securing loyalty in service relationships. J. Bus. Res. 59, 1207–1213 (2006)
14. Hallowell, R.: The relationships of customer satisfaction, customer loyalty and profitability: an empirical study. Int. J. Serv. Ind. Manag. 7(4), 27–42 (2006)
15. Steenkamp, J.B.E.M., Geyskens, I.: How Country Characteristics affect the perceived value of a website. J. Mark. 70(3), 136–150 (2006)
16. Zaichkowsky, J.L.: Measuring the Involvement Construct. J. Consum. Res. 12(4), 341–352 (1985)
17. Lichtenstein, D.R., Netemeyer, R.G., Burton, S.: Distinguishing coupon proneness from value consciousness: an acquisition—transaction utility theory perspective. J. Mark. 54, 54–67 (1990)
18. Nunnally, J.C.: Psychometric Theory, 2nd edn. McGraw-Hill, New York (1978)
19. Nurosis, M.J.: SPSS: Statistical Data Analysis. Spss Inc. (1993)
20. Jöreskog, K., Sörbom, D.: LISREL 8 Structural Equation Modeling with the SIMPLIS Command Language. In: Scientific Software International, Chicago-Illinois (1993)
21. Jöreskog, K.: Statistical analysis of sets of congeneric tests. Psychom. 36(2), 109–133 (1971)
22. Fornell, C., Larcker, D.: Structural Equation Models With Unobserved Variables and Measurement Error. J. Mark. Res. 18, 39–50 (1981)
23. Wiertz, C., De Ruyter, K.: Beyond the Call of Duty: Why Consumers Contribute to Firm-hosted Commercial Online Communities. Organ. Stud. 28(3), 347–376 (2007)
24. Murray, K.B., Schlacter, J.L.: The Impact of Services versus Goods on Consumers's Assesment of Perceived Risk and Variability. J. Acad. Mark. Sci. 18(1), 51–65 (1990)
25. Oliver, R.: A Cognitive Model of the Antecedents and Consequences of Satisfaction Decisions. J. Mark. Res. 14, 495–507 (1980)
26. Casalό, L.V., Flavián, C., Guinalíu, M.: The role of satisfaction and website usability in developing customer loyalty and positive word-of-mouth in the e-banking business. Int. J. Bank. Mark. 26(6), 399–417 (2008)

E-Democracy and Network Externalities – The Case of Websites of Finnish Members of Parliament

Reima Suomi

University of Turku, Finland

Abstract. Effective communication between voters and members of parliament is a key success factor democracy. Fortunately, modern information technology is giving a lot of new channels to take care of this communication. Traditionally, Members of Parliament have maintained static www-sites, but nowadays more dynamic and interactive forms of communication, such as blogs, Facebook and Twitter are almost a must for the Members of Parliament, especially in the case of less popular politicians. As in any technology application, even in www-presence of Members of Parliament network externalities occur: unexpected consequences of web-presence. This article sets out some preliminary concepts and ideas on what these network externalities might be.

Keywords: e-democracy, Member of Parliament, web-sites, network externalities.

1 Introduction

Not even political life can escape the power of the Internet. Indeed, web presence has become a critical key to success in the playfields of Internet, as the election of Barrack Obama shows. [1-2] [3] puts it very clearly: "*An exciting new technology like the World-Wide-Web is simply too much for a politician to overlook*" Internet with its various communication platforms becoming strong channels for providing political information and for conducting political activities and decision-making.

The applications of www-technology in politics are many. Different tools are being developed through which electors can compare and weigh up the manifestos and opinions of political decision-makers. [4] Internet is a mainstream platform for political journalism. [5] In many countries, Internet is an important channel for political fund-raising. [6] Politicians beyond their active phase can use websites to maintain their political life. [7] Websites are a major channel for political activism. [8].

As in any technology application and adoption environment, learning happens [9-10] and during the technology adoption process, unexpected results occur. These unexpected results can also be called network externalities.

Our article unfolds as follows. In section 2, we perform a conceptual analysis of eDemocracy. In the section 3 we discuss network externalities. In the section 4, we hypothesise what network externalities could be in the case of Internet-presence of Members of Parliament. In section 5, the state of the art of the websites of Finnish Members of Parliament in 2006 and 2008 is analysed based on some collected data. Finally, in section 6 conclusions are drawn.

W. Cellary and E. Estevez (Eds.): I3E 2010, IFIP AICT 341, pp. 112–117, 2010.

2 e-Democracy

eDemocracy refers to support of democratic practice and processes through the potential of cyberspace. Päivärinta and Sæbø [11] note that eDemocracy can be harnessed to support many different models of democractic processes. They introduce the models of Liberal, the Deliberative, the Partisan, and the Direct Democracy. eDemocracy is an integral part of eGovernment [12].

The Internet is without doubt the most important public political sphere available today, and the only really international one [13]. Online public spaces can provide flexible and interactive outlets for dialogue, and document the dynamic, as values shift and demands for transparency increase [14]. Schuler [15] also emphasises the effect of modern ICT on democratic processes: *"ICT provides tools for strong democracy, such as email, forums and online access to documents."* Rheingold [16] also states that new media can help *"to gather critical information, organize political action, sway public opinion and guide policy making"*.

Williamson [17] defines a five-level maturity model of eDemocracy:

1	access	getting access to discussion and material
2	literacy	understanding the material and the media restrictions
3	content	having meaningful and relevant content
4	creation	taking part in content creation oneself
5	dissemination	publishing new material beyond individual community boundaries.

Welch [18] defines two goals for eGovernment applications to support eDemocracy: transparency and interactivity. The more transparent and interactive an institution's web-pages are, the more they encourage trust in citizens. Mahrer and Krimmer [19] refer to the fact that Internet-presence of politicians supports multiple and complicated democracy goals.

On the worst case, Internet can also turn out to be a buffer between citizen and Members of Parliament [20]. One big challenge for Members of Parliament as well as for other politicians is to be able to maintain deep and credible enough presence in the Internet. Old and outdated material on the Internet is no receipt for success for a politician.

Members of Parliament are very central actors in the eDemocracy field. So their application the Internet is an important topic. We found widely-published empirical academic research on the topic in just one article. Jackson and Lilleker [21] report, among other things, on the websites of British Members of Parliament. They conclude that websites and e-mail still remain under-utilised communication tools for Members of Parliament.

3 Network Externalities

Network externality has been defined as a change in the benefit, or surplus, that an agent derives from a good when the number of other agents consuming the same kind of good changes. [22]. The roots of the network effect research are in the marketing discipline, where it was understood that the success of a product or service is a phenomenon strengthening itself. The phenomenon was called the bandwagon effect by which was meant *"the extent to which the demand for a commodity is increased due to the fact that others are also consuming the same commodity. It represents the desire of people to purchase a commodity in order to get into 'the swim of things'; in order to conform with the people they wish to be associated with; in order to be fashionable or stylish; or, in order to appear to be 'one of the boys."*[23] Still today, the network effect is often connected the act of buying and selling, and not the act of consuming, as above: *"A positive consumption externality (or network externality) signifies the fact that the value of a unit of the good increases with the number of units sold"* [24]. Another definition stressing buying is that of: *"Network externalities arise when a consumer values compatibility–often stemming from ability to take advantage of the same complements–with other consumers, creating economies of scope between different consumers' purchases"* [25].

One should make a difference between network effect and network externality. Network externalities should not properly be called network externalities unless the participants in the market fail to internalize these externalities [22]. An **externality** is the effect of a transaction between two parties on a third party who is not involved in the carrying out of that transaction. Internalizing an effect means that it is no more directed towards a third party.Network externalities can be direct or indirect, and positive or negative.

Direct network externalities exist when an increase in the size of a network increases the number of others with whom one can "communicate" directly. Indirect network externalities exist when an increase in the size of a network expands the range of complementary products available to the members of the network [26].

Network externalities can be positive or negative. A typical negative network effect is a traffic jam. All too often network externalities are understood just as positive. The same phenomenon can be both positive and negative, depending on the role of the observer. To take an example, to a railway operator having a lot of customers is a good thing (more revenue), but for the customer the same situation can mean congestion, also a negative effect.

The enchantment of network externalities is that they often come out as surprise and as a byproduct that was not calculated or foreseen in any way.

4 Network Externalities and Member of Parliaments' Web-Presence

In Figure 1, we illustrate some network externalities that come out from the use of electronic media in political communication. Please note that this is not analyzing the very basic goal and purpose of political communication: better democratic processes. This is the expected and natural outcome of web-presence of politicians, not something unexpected, not also externalities. Figure 1 concentrates on unexpected outcomes of using web-based technologies for democratic processes.

Please note that the classification is tentative and very rudimentary. In general, classification of network externalities is difficult: Externalities for one party or

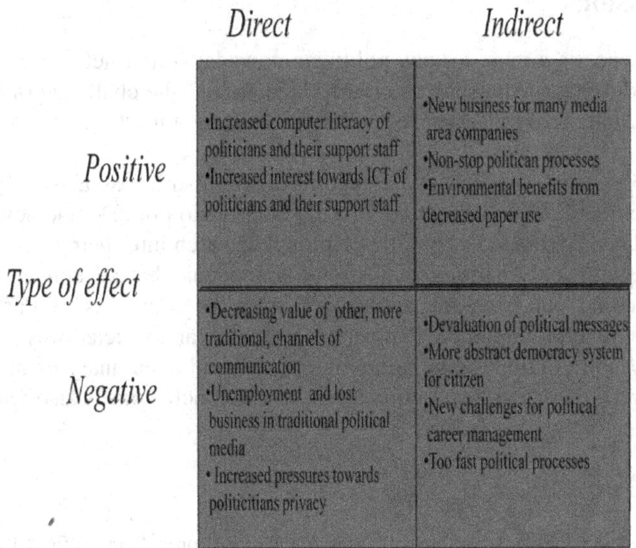

Direct
Indirect
Positive
Type of effect
Negative
•Increased computer literacy of politicians and their support staff
•Increased interest towards ICT of politicians and their support staff
•New business for many media area companies
•Non-stop politican processes
•Environmental benefits from decreased paper use
•Decreasing value of other, more traditional, channels of communication
•Unemployment and lost business in traditional political media
• Increased pressures towards politicitians privacy
•Devaluation of political messages
•More abstract democracy system for citizen
•New challenges for political career management
•Too fast political processes

Fig. 1. Network externalities in the case of www-presence of politicians

stakeholder might be negative, and the very same externalities can be positive for some other party or stakeholder. In the same way, differentiation between what is direct and what is indirect is very vague.

Positive effects are foremost the increased interest and skills of members of parliament and their staff in ICT-issues. This is very positive for the whole ICT-industry and cluster. When realizing their web-presence, Members of Parliament need a lot of support, which fact gives new business opportunities for many experts and companies with media skills. As in any e-activity, even in eDemocracy the goal is to substitute paper communication with electronic communication, which is good from the environmental point of view.

The Internet never sleeps. Activity takes place on a 24/7 hour basis. This will have an unexpected effect on the political processes as well. Might be that in some cases the speed of activities becomes too fast, which could potentially decrease the quality of political processes. Indeed, this is a real externality, which consequences are yet hard to predict.

Negative externalities can most likely be seen in the valuation of other channels of communication, especially if we think that the amount of real and affordable communication has some maximum amount that is already achieved. Might of course be that political issues cannot gain any more human attention in our society, where attention is a scarce resource [27]. We already now see signs that the traditional political media is worried about its status in the political sphere. Again, is this good or bad is surely not a straightforward issue.

Internet activity is always a threat for privacy [28]. Politicians are by definition in the focus of public interest, and their lives are followed up in great detail. Heavy Internet presence will surely cause a further privacy threat for them.

5 Conclusions

Internet presence is a must for any politician nowadays. Internet is even more important than traditional media such as press, TV or radio. The challenge of Internet is its global reach, interactivity and speed. Politicians have a hard time answering to these challenges.

In our conceptual analysis, we categorised eDemocracy as a sub-topic of eGovernment. Members of Parliament are in a central position in eDemocracy, but the academic world has conducted very little empirical research into their websites.

In our network externalities analysis we found out, that several unexpected outcomes can come out from the active web-usage of Members of Parliament, also outcomes not touching upon the democratic system in an expected way.

Our study will continue with more complicated and deep analyses of the collected data. Additional theory to give ramifications to the conclusions is also required.

References

1. Stirland, S.: Propelled by internet, barack obama wins presidency. Wired Blog Network 4 (2008)
2. Talbot, D.: How obama really did it. TCR 111(5), 78–83 (2008)
3. Berghel, H.: Digital politics. Communications of the ACM 39(10), 19–25 (1996)
4. O'Leary, M.: Project vote smart helps confused voters. IFT 17(2), 14–15 (2000)
5. Reilly, A.: The allure of the web. Nieman Reports 58(1), 27–28 (2004)
6. Wilner, E.: Network web sites influence political reporting. Nieman Reports 58(1), 28 (2004)
7. Jarvis, M.: Spinning history. Foreign Policy (134), 102 (2003)
8. Brown, D.: Screen-to-screen activists. Inter@ctive Week 7(4), 80 (2000)
9. Sun, H.-C.: Conceptual clarifications for 'organizational learning', 'learning organization' and 'a learning organization'. Human Resource Development International 6(2), 153–166 (2003)
10. Hibbert, P., Huxham, C.: A little about the mystery: Process learning as collaboration evolves. European Management Review 2(1), 59 (2005)
11. Päivärinta, T., Sæbø, Ø.: Models of e-democracy. Communications of the Association for Information Systems 17(1), 37 (2006)
12. Borins, S.: A holistic view of public sector information technology. Journal of E-government 1(2), 3–29 (2005)
13. Coleman, S., Norris, D.: A new agenda for e-democracy. International Journal of Electronic Government Research 1(3), 69 (2005)
14. Geiselhart, K.: Digital government and citizen participation in international context. In: Pavlichev, A., Garson, G.D. (eds.) Digital Government: Principles and Best Practices, pp. 320–343. IDEA Group Publishing, Hershey (2004)
15. Schuler, D.: New communities and new community networks. In: Gurstein, M. (ed.) Community Informatics: Enabling Communities with Information Communication Technologies. IDEA Group Publishing, Hershey (2000)
16. Rheingold, H.: Electronic democracy. Whole Earth Review, 4–13 (Summer 1991)
17. Williamson, A.: Getting ready for edemocracy: A five-stage maturity model for community ict. In: The Australian Electronic Governance Conference, Melbourne, Victoria. Centre for Public Policy, Victoria (2004)

18. Welch, E.W.: Internet use, transparency and interactivity effects on trust in government. In: Hawaii International Conference on System Sciences, HICSS 2003. IEEE, Los Alamitos (2003)
19. Moreno-Jiménez, J., Polasek, W.: E-democracy and knowledge. A multicriteria framework for the new democratic era. Journal of Multi-Criteria Decision Analysis 12(2-3), 163–176 (2004)
20. Mahrer, H., Krimmer, R.: Towards the enhancement of e-democracy: Identifying the notion of the 'middleman paradox'. Information Systems Journal 15(1), 27–42 (2005)
21. Jackson, N.A., Lilleker, D.G.: Just public relations or an attempt at interaction. European Journal of Communication 19(4), 507–533 (2004)
22. Liebowitz, J., Margolis, S.E.: Network externalities (effects). In: The New Palgrave's Dictionary of Economics and the Law (1998)
23. Leibenstein, H.: Bandwagon, snob, and veblen effects in the theory of consumers' demand. The Quarterly Journal of Economics (May 1950)
24. Economides, N.: The economics of networks. International Journal of Industrial Organization 14(2) (1996)
25. Farrell, J., Klemperer, P.: Network effects and switching costs. In: Durlauf, S.N., Blume, L.E. (eds.) The New New Palgrave Dictionary of Economics. Palgrave Macmillan, Basingstoke (2006) (forthcoming)
26. Besen, S.M.: Innovation, competition and the theory of network externalities. Charles River Associates, Hingham (2006)
27. Davenport, T., Beck, J.C.: Getting the attention you need. Harvard Business Review, 119–126 (September-October 2000)
28. Cranor, L.: Internet privacy. Communications of the ACM 42(2), 28–38 (1999)

Educateca: A Web 2.0 Approach to e-Learning with SCORM

Rebeca P. Díaz Redondo, Ana Fernández Vilas, and Jose J. Pazos Arias

Department of Telematics Engineering. University of Vigo. 36310 Vigo, Spain
{rebeca,avilas,jose}@det.uvigo.es

Abstract. This paper introduces the *Educateca* project, a Web 2.0 approach to e-learning. The project refactors SCORM, the *de facto* e-learning standard, to embrace the two main shifts in Web 2.0: the WOA (Web Oriented Architecture) and the social trends in user involvement. In this new context of the Internet, flexibility is a must and so big and static e-learning content are no longer effective enough. Thus, we propose a more dynamic approach where small pedagogical units are offered as services to be combine on-the-fly, whenever needed. Social aspects are currently another key and so we propose to adapt the e-learning ecosystem to allow students to innovate and create new content and/or assess the existent one. Clearly, in this new philosophy, recommendation is essential to avoid overwhelming users with too much educative content that are not able to filter, asses and/or consume.

Keywords: e-learning 2.0, SCORM, SaaS, Web Service.

1 Introduction

E-learning and its related technologies and standards are destined to accept the two main paradigm shifts in the Web 2.0 era [1,2]: the programmable Web and the social Web. In the programmable Web vision, the topology behind WOA (*Web oriented Architecture*) makes invalid the typical scenario where an organization stores learning materials locally in an LCMS (*Learning Content Management System*) and deliver them through an LMS (*Learning Management System*) to the learner's device. Instead, learning organizations should publish and even share their material in the cloud so that learners can access them directly. In the same way, the LMS is becoming another SaaS (*Software as a Service*) in the cloud so that the student can select a LMS according to the LMS's features and his/her preferences. To sum up, learner, content and LMS are not necessarily in the same domains or from the same providers in a WOA. As the different elements move toward service based approaches, consumers (learners in our case) may opt to mix and match a variety of tools from multiple providers to build an environment that will work best for them.

Apart from these architectonic changes, the Web 2.0 era is characterized by a strong social component. The cloud has to be a place where the learning content is easily generated and published by both teachers and learners so that the collective intelligence of users encourages a more democratic use.

W. Cellary and E. Estevez (Eds.): I3E 2010, IFIP AICT 341, pp. 118–126, 2010.

With the above motivation, this paper introduces the *Educateca* project, a Web 2.0 approach to e-learning. As it is mandatory in an interoperable environment, standards (Web standards, e-learning standards and mobile standards) are the essential ingredient. Especially in the enhanced learning field, the recognition of needs for standards in e-learning can be tracked back to its origins. Today, ADL SCORM [3] (*Shareable Content Object Reference Model*) has become the *de facto* standard to allow content developed within one learning system to be exported and used in all other systems. Despite the fact that SCORM encourages the reusability and remixability in Web 2.0 vision, some aspects of SCORM are not ready to Web 2.0 immersion [4]. With the aim of tackling these shortcomings, *Educateca* project refactors SCORM infrastructure to provide e-learning in the Web 2.0 arena.

The paper is organized as follows. In the next section we briefly introduce the changes we propose in the SCORM to properly accomplish both social and WOA aspects of the Web 2.0. Section 3 overviews the *Educateca* vision in the new context of the cloud and in Section 4 we detail the proposed architecture. Finally, conclusions and future work is exposed in Section 5, as well as a comparison between our approach and other works about bringing Web 2.0 to e-learning.

2 SCORM Shifts to Web 2.0

In this section we introduce the changes we propose to SCORM content and SCORM LMSs to accomplish the architectonic and social shifts in Web 2.0. First, we include a brief overview about SCORM standard. After having established the SCORM jargon and its essential components, we explain our approach to bringing SCORM closer to both architectonic and social characteristics in Web 2.0.

2.1 Brief SCORM Overview

Although SCORM is a vast standard that deals with any aspect related to any *e-learning* aspect, we only focus on SCORM CAM (*Content Aggregation Model*) and SCORM RTE (*Run-Time Environment*), the two most relevant components for our approach.

On the one hand, the SCORM CAM defines three main elements used to build a learning experience from learning resources: (1) SCO (*Shareable Content Object*), a single launchable learning object that utilizes SCORM RTE to communicate with a LMS; (2) Content **Organization**, a map that represents the intended use of the content through structured units of instruction; and (3) Metadata that should be used to describe these elements in a consistent manner; SCORM strongly recommends the use of the IEEE LOM (see Figure 1). Besides, Content Aggregation is an entity used to deliver both the structure and the resources that belong to a course in a Content Package, which consists of a compressed file with the physical resources of educational content and at least one XML file — called manifest — that embodies a structured inventory of the content of the package: its organization *(<organizations>)* and metadata *(<metadata>).*

On the other hand, SCORM RTE defines: (1) the launch process as a common way for LMSs to start SCOs; (2) the API as the mechanism for exchanging data between

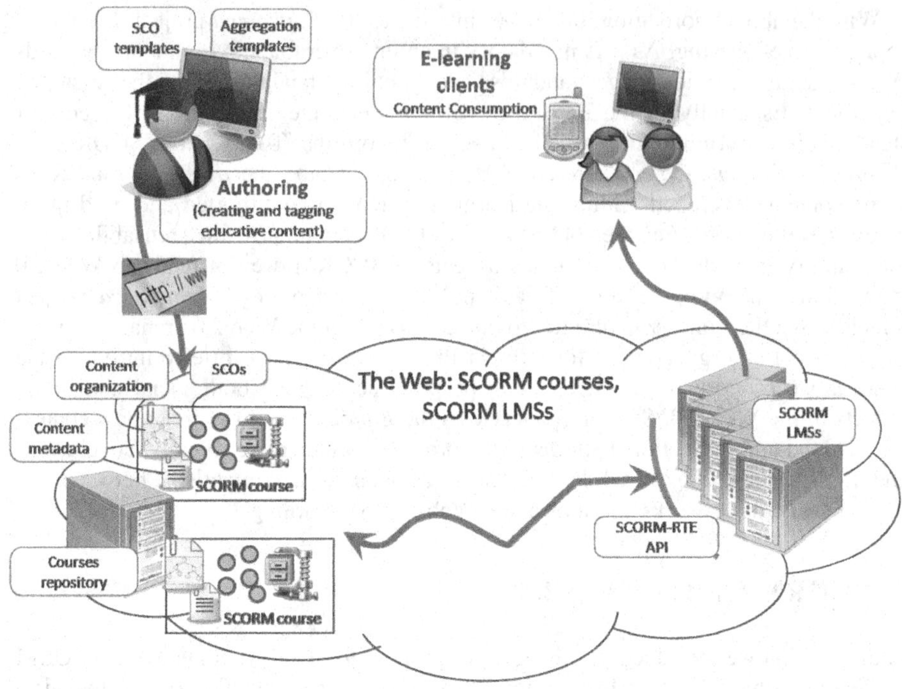

Fig. 1. Typical architecture for any SCORM-compliant e-learning platform

the LMS and the SCO; and (3) a data model as a standard set of elements to define the information tracked for a SCO

2.2 Architectonic Shift: Driving SCORM to the WOA

The concept of cloud computing arose as consequence of both the progressive price reduction of consumer electronic devices with computing capabilities and the growing availability of broadband connectivity. Although in origin the cloud was conceived as a way to allow users to access their documents and applications from anywhere and using any device as a lightweight client, this vision has expanded to embrace the so-called *Everything as a Service* (EaaS or XaaS) trend. Thus, in addition to applications for on-demand use (*Software as a Service*), the offer encompasses computation, storage, development and communication resources (*Platform as a Service, Communication as a Service*) and, at the same time, it integrates whichever services may be provisioned through the e-commerce technologies, including human resources in any areas of activity (what we may term *User as a Service*). Therefore, the cloud lodges arbitrary resources that appear as high-granularity services that may be composed in a flexible manner in response to complex necessities. In this new context, both learning software and content should not be delivered in a packetized way anymore. Instead, we propose to offer these elements as autonomous ones with the aim of being available to be used separately according to the users' needs.

Therefore, to integrate SCORM content and processes in the WOA cloud we propose the following modifications. First, the compressed file structure of a SCORM course (learning content) would be replaced by set of independent pedagogical units able to communicate to the SCORM RTE to be run (independently or cooperatively) whenever needed. Thus, each SCO becomes an SCS (*Sharable Content Service*) according to the SaaS conception. Besides, the organization of a SCORM course remains, but it is separated from the learning objects itself. This provides more flexibility to users which finally decide if they prefer a pre-established course definition or an *ad-hoc* composition of pedagogical units according their interests.

Secondly, the SCORM RTE itself (learning software) is deployed as a set of Web Services offering the SCORM API. Finally, the SCORM CAM (*Content Aggregation Model*) is replaced by a SAM (*Service Aggregation Model*), a service (learning software) in the cloud that provides access to a set of SCSs according to a specific organization.

2.3 Social Shift: Collaborative SCORM

Social networks appear as a true social and cultural phenomenon on the Internet, whose impact is evident in any social sector. In fact, there are millions of users who already engage in online social interactions as part of their daily lives: sharing information, exchanging experiences and opinions, tagging elements, ratting content and services, even creating or uploading their own content to be shared to other users. Thus, social networks have facilitated a notable change of attitude in users: from a more passive to a really active on. This change is not only restricted to the social networks context, it has spread out to any aspect in the Internet, and e-learning cannot stand aside.

Consequently, we propose an environment where learners have a more leading role in a context where they are no longer passive receivers of information given by a teacher, but active participants whose opinions are took into account. Thus, we revise two main aspects in m-learning. Firstly, describing and cataloguing learning objects is no more responsible for the teaching committee. On the contrary, learners tag and rate learning objects as they use the platform. Secondly, not only tagging but authoring also moves from teachers to learners so that these can create or modify content to contribute to the learning distributed repository. Besides, users can create and share course organizations combining pedagogical units created by them or by any other user.

This vision of providing a suitable space for active learners comes up against the SCORM conception. SCORM was created assuming a single authority (usually a teacher) that creates and assigns metadata for a collective of students. This metadata theoretically allows searching and combining learning objects to make them accessible for other purposes, but, in practice, SCORM content hardly include metadata. Consequently, it is difficult for a community to alter or add metadata tags within SCORM infrastructure, and it is currently impossible for a learner to contribute to a course by adding or altering its content.

Therefore, we propose to change the processes which affect metadata and organization specification to support this environment of participation with SCORM-compatible infrastructures. Apart from distributing authoring (both of learning objects and organizations), a Web 2.0 approach requires an open access from students to metadata so that both learning objects and organizations are collaboratively tagged.

3 *Educateca* Vision

Figure 2 depicts the *Educateca* interpretation of Web 2.0 principles in the e-learning field. One of the aspects that must be highlighted is how the teacher and student roles change in this new model. Whereas in the traditional model (Figure 1) both roles are totally separated, in this new approach students are expected to adopt a *prosumer* attitude. Thus, students are not more those who receive courses and pedagogical units and whose only obligation is learning the provided content and demonstrate their new knowledge resolving an exam; instead they have now the opportunity of providing new educative content.

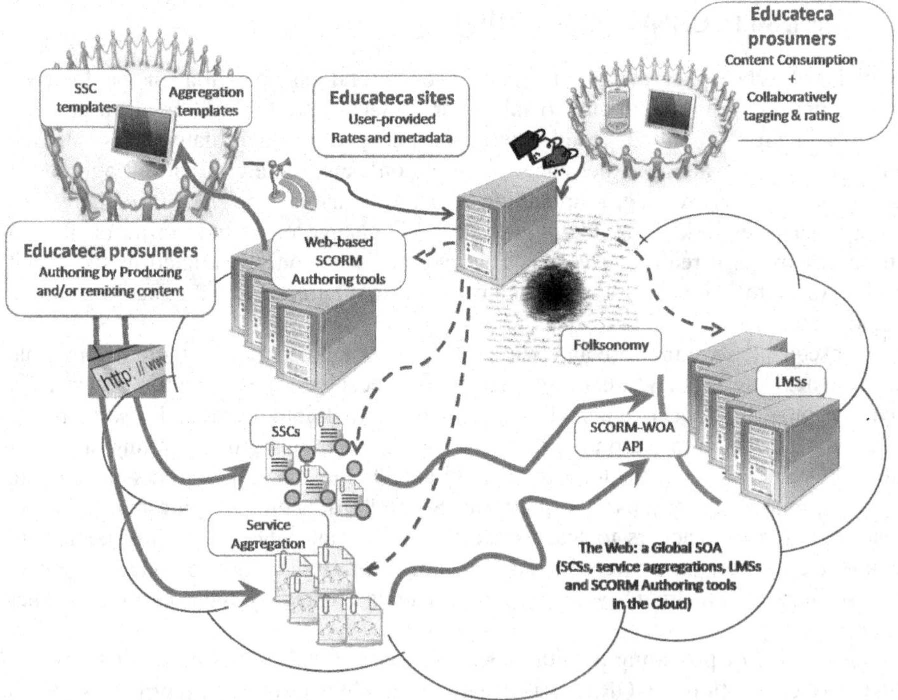

Fig. 2. Proposed architecture for SCORM-compliant e-learning 2.0

According to the WOA interpretation of a SCORM course, their two main components are the SAM (*Service Aggregation Model)* and SCS (*Sharable Content Service*), respectively mirrors of CAM and SCO. The CAM service maintains the structure and location of the SCSs in a course but not the SCSs themselves; whereas a SCS consists mainly of an XML template of the learning content, the metadata describing that content and the location of the resources (assets) in the template.

Consequently, the creation of new educative contents can be done by prosumers in two ways: (i) creating their own pedagogical units (SSCs) and (ii) defining new service aggregations that combine already developed SSCs. With this aim, and according the WOA in the Web 2.0, they may use any SCORM-complaint authoring tool that is offered as a service in the cloud. Teachers, on another hand, continue taking their typical role and, as experts in the field, they create, tag (using metadata) and upload both new pedagogical units as self-content educative services (SSCs) and service aggregations.

The active role of students goes further than creating new elements: *prosumers* have also the possibility of given their opinion about other SSCs and service aggregations as well as labeling them. Tags given by *prosumers* allow creating and dynamic updating a folksonomy which support a mechanism to classify and search educative units whenever needed. In fact, users look for pedagogical content according to key-words and their decision of choosing one or another will be likely based on the rates each unit has received. So, instead of having an environment where the quality of content is assumed (like in classical models), this new model entails a certain degree of competition where the opinion of consumers gives a measurement of the quality. Finally, and for courses consumption, users may use any SCORM-complaint LMS having a Web-based interface, just according to the main SCORM principles that claims for open e-learning environments.

To conclude, *Educateca* sites maintain information about all the previously mentioned elements: the folksonomy, references to locate SCSs and service aggregations, and references to locate LMSs and authoring tools. Therefore, any prosumer, after login the *Educateca* system using a Web navigator (in any suitable device: a computer, a mobile phone, etc.), may use the educative environment to create, tag, rate and/or consume pedagogical units in a totally transparent way. Simply the *Educateca* site recommends the most suitable LMSs to represent properly the educative content according to the user's device.

4 Details of the Proposed Architecture

The work introduced in this paper involves the transfer of previous approaches of our research group to the new paradigms in the Web. Being inspired by the personalized e-learning platform T-MAESTRO [5], we have added social and WOA conceptions, central milestones of the Web 2.0. Especially, it is remarkable the following technical aspects in this work. Firstly, users have the possibility of choosing the characteristics they ask to a LMS to operate with or delegate this election to a LMS raking, consequence of third parties' rates. Secondly, it is possible to obtain personalized recommendations of the available content. Given the social nature of our proposal, *Educateca* joins together formal SCORM metadata (usually provided by expert users, teachers mainly) and informal free-tags (usually given by less expert users, students mainly). Integrating both kind of data entails having a plain structure (folksonomy) which will be the base to establish user's profiles and to run the recommendation algorithm. Thirdly, discovering any element in the proposed architecture over a service philosophy entails redefining SCORM aggregations as BPEL specifications that orchestrate content coming from different SCORM organizations.

4.1 Exporting LMs as a Virtual Web Service

E-learning in the cloud should give the illusion of infinite resources available on demand, eliminating the students need to plan far ahead for e-learning provisioning and following a pay-as-you-go model. With this illusion, infinite LMS would be available in the cloud with different features: cost, efficiency, level of personalization, etc. In the proposed architecture, student delegates the process of discovering and selecting an appropriate LMS to *Educateca* sites so that some form of SLA (*Service Level Agreement*) between the student and the *Educateca* provider has to be defined. Concretely, *Educateca* sites virtualize LMS by offering a Virtual Web Service, in the sense defined in our previous work in [6, 7], which we call VLMS (Virtual-LMS). Client Device uses the V-LMS as any other service in the cloud and only *Educateca* sites are aware of the virtual nature of the service and materialize the service in a real LMS by incorporating user-defined preferences, load-balancing, availability, caching, etc.

4.2 Social Content Discovery and Recommendation

In order to support e-learning community, *Educateca* sites incorporate mechanisms to assist the users in a personalized access to e-learning material (discovering and recommendation). To be precise, *Educateca* strategy is based on collaborative tagging. Folksonomy-like structures are maintained for users and e-learning material in the cloud which support social collaborative filtering for the discovery and recommendation of e-learning material.

The *Educateca* community collaborate in creating, sharing and describing contents so that students and teachers tag their own contents but also the ones incorporated by others. Each SCS, SAM or even LMS is associated with a set of weighted tags (tagcloud). Similarly, the users in *Educateca* community have their own tagcloud, representing his/her profile. The user's tagcloud-profile registers the tags of e-learning material he/she has rated and the weights which resume these ratings and so the user's interest. The social collaborative filtering strategy implements an algorithm of tag cloud comparison which is mathematically described in [8].

4.3 Introducing BPEL in SAMs

As we have mentioned before, using BPEL4WS in the definition of the SAM components of our model is the natural way of turning an aggregation of SCORM contents (SCOs) into an aggregation of SCORM service (SCSs). As service composition becomes the main concern of the application development process in XaaS paradigm, it is also the case in "e-learning as a service". At this respect, BPEL4WS and its related specifications [9] provide the standard mechanism for defining service compositions in the form of choreographies of Web services, that is, in the form of aggregation of services according to certain rules, e-learning rules in our case. These e-learning rules are the ones defined in *SCORM 2004 Sequencing and Navigation* specification, derived from *IMS Simple Sequencing* (IMS SS) specification. Sequencing is what happens when learner exits a SCO, that is, sequencing is responsible for determining what happens next. Further, it orchestrates the flow and status of the course as a whole. This orchestration consists of the *sequence definition* itself, a set of rules, and the *tracking data* which records the current state of the e-learner activity.

In brief, our BPEL-style solution to SCORM WOA is as follows. Firstly, the SCORM aggregation is translated into a set of <partnerlink> and <invoke> definitions in BPEL. Secondly, sequencing rules (if-then conditions), limit conditions, constraint choice controls, etc. in a typical SCORM manifest, are translated into BPEL structure activities <sequence>, <flow>, <switch>, <while> and <pick>. Finally, tracking data is registered as a set of <variable> elements which are used in the BPEL specification of the course to restrict the BPEL process which implements the course.

Architectonically speaking, the actual process of sequencing SCORM occurs whenever a course is launched, whenever a SCO exits or whenever the learner makes a navigation request through the LMS. For that, a typical SCORM- compatible LMS implements a set of defined algorithms that apply the sequencing rules to the current set of tracking data to determine which activity should be delivered next. *Educateca* incorporates these algorithms in the LMSs by integrating *ActiveBPEL Engine*[1]. However, we cannot obviate that content authoring turns into social so that every user in the community should be able to publish a new course organization or a modified version of an existing one. To facilitate this scenario, we provide SAM templates in *Educateca* sites.

5 Conclusions

There are some other approaches in the literature which transfers e-learning platforms to a service-oriented approach and even to cloud e-learning. In [10], Vossen & Westerkamp discuss typical problems of SCORM-related standards and propose a service-oriented approach as a solution, but any specific architecture or implementation is introduced. In [11,12] *Dong* proposes the use of cloud computing as a base for modern e-learning by introducing the *BlueSky* cloud framework which virtualizes physical machines for e-learning systems. Similarly, *CoudIA* (Cloud Infrastructure and Application) project [13] runs private cloud infrastructure for e-learning and collaboration in the university environment of HFU (*Hochschule Furtwangen University*). With a lab-oriented application, *Virtual Computing Laboratory* (VCL) [14] (by North Carolina State University) enables students to reserve and access virtual machines (VMs) with a basic image or specific applications environments, such as *Matlab* and *Autodesk*. Meanwhile the above works focus on the infrastructure dimension of cloud-based e-learning, our proposal gives a more ambitious conception for e-learning in the cloud. Not only the infrastructure but the content and the metadata are freely in the cloud and then reassembled on demand by *Educateca* sites. Apart from that, the social dimension of e-learning in the cloud is considered by turning students and teachers into a peer-to-peer community.

The *Educateca* project is one more step towards new perspectives for enhanced learning with SCORM. The *Educateca* site and the online authoring tool are based on our previous work in t-MAESTRO [5], a SCORM-compatible infrastructure for personalized t-learning experiences combining TV programs and learning contents in a personalized way, with the aim of using the playful nature of TV to make learning more attractive and to engage TV viewers in learning. To be precise, we have adapted the functionality and architecture of the t-MAESTRO ITS (Intelligent Tutoring

[1] http://www.activevos.com

System) which constructs the t-learning experiences by applying semantic knowledge about the t-learners; and the A-SCORM Creator Tool, the authoring tool which allow teachers to create adaptive courses with a minimal technical background. The processes in the back office of Educateca site are also based in our work in [8, 15] where we introduce a folksonomy based approach to e-learning 2.0.

References

1. Chatti, M.A., Jarke, M., Frosch-Wilke, D.: The future of e-learning: a shift to knowledge networking and social software. International Journal of Knowledge and Learning 3(4/5), 404–420 (2007)
2. Downes, S.: e-learning 2.0. eLearn. 10 (October 2005)
3. Advanced Distributed Learning (ADL): Sharable Content Object Reference Model, SCORM 2004, 3rd edn. (2004), `http://www.adlnet.org`
4. Rogers, C.P., Liddle, S.W., Chan, P., Doxey, A., Isom, B.: Web 2.0 learning platform: Harnessing collective intelligence. Online Submission 8, 16–33 (2007), `http://www.eric.ed.gov/ERICWebPortal/detail?accno=ED498811`
5. Rey López, M., Díaz Redondo, R., Fernández Vilas, A., Pazos Arias, J., López Nores, M., García Duque, J., Gil Solla, A., Ramos Cabrer, M.: T-MAESTRO and its Authoring Tool: Using Adaptation to Integrate Entertainment into Personalized T-learning. Multimedia Tools and Applications 40(3), 409–451 (2008)
6. Fernández Vilas, J.A., Pazos Arias, J.J., Fernández Vilas, A.: Virtual Web Services: An Extension Architecture to Alleviate Open Problems in Web Services Technology, pp. 74–94. IGI Global (October 2008)
7. Fernández Vilas, J.A., Pazos Arias, J.J., Fernández Vilas, A.: VWS: Applying Virtualization Techniques to Web Services. International Journal of Computer Science and Network Security 6(5B), 120–128 (2006)
8. Rey López, M., Díaz Redondo, R., Fernández Vilas, A., Pazos Arias, J.J.: T-learning 2.0: a personalized hybrid approach based on ontologies and folksonomies. In: Computational Intelligence for Technology Enhanced Learning. Springer, Heidelberg (2010)
9. Curbera, F., Khalaf, R., Mukhi, N., Tai, S., Weerawarana, S.: The next step in Web services. Communications of the ACM 46 (October 2003)
10. Vossen, G., Westerkamp, P.: Why service-orientation could make e-learning standards obsolete. International Journal of Technology Enhanced Learning 1(1/2), 85–97 (2008)
11. Dong, B., Zheng, Q., Yang, J., Li, H., Qiao, M.: An E-learning Ecosystem Based on Cloud Computing Infrastructure. In: 9th IEEE International Conference on Advanced Learning Technologies, ICALT 2009, pp. 125–127 (July 2009)
12. Dong, B., Zheng, Q., Qiao, M., Shu, J., Yang, J.: BlueSky Cloud Framework: An E-Learning Framework Embracing Cloud Computing. In: 1st International Conference on Cloud Computing (CloudCom 2009), Beijing, China (December 2009)
13. Sulistio, A., Reich, C., Dölitzscher, F.: Cloud Infrastructure & Applications – CloudIA. In: Proceedings of the 1st International Conference on Cloud Computing (CloudCom 2009), Beijing, China, December 1-4 (2009)
14. Vouk, M., Averitt, S., Bugaev, M., Kurth, A., Peeler, A., Shaffer, H., Sills, E., Stein, S., Thompson, J.: Powered by VCL - Using Virtual Computing Laboratory (VCL). In: Proc. 2nd International Conference on Virtual Computing (ICVCI), pp. 1–10 (May 2008)
15. Rey López, M., Díaz Redondo, R., Fernández Vilas, A., Pazos Arias, J.: Use of Folksonomies in the Creation of Learning Experiences for Television. In: Upgrade. Monograph: Technology-Enhanced Learning, vol. IX(3), pp. 21–26 (June 2008)

Achieving Meaning Understanding in E-Marketplace through Document Sense Disambiguation

Jingzhi Guo and Guangyi Xiao

Department of Computer and Information Science, University of Macau,
Av. Padre Tomás, Pereira, S.J., Taipa, Macau
{jzguo,ya97409}@umac.mo

Abstract. E-marketplace has a very important requirement of achieving mutual meaning understanding between sellers and buyers. To meet this requirement, this paper has proposed a novel SD-DSD approach, which enables to disambiguate senses between a sender and a receiver for their sent and received documents. This approach has developed five novel strategies for sense disambiguation. Based on them, new document representation models for message exchange are devised, together with their sense consistency control procedures and sense interpretation evaluation method.

Keywords: Meaning understanding, sense disambiguation, business document, e-marketplace, XML Product Map (XPM).

1 Introduction

E-marketplace is a rapidly evolving research area and has been received significant attentions from academia and industry (e.g., [3, 10, 16, 13], emarketservices.com). It is a common business information space (CBIS) and is an infrastructure of e-market where buyers and sellers at various enterprise information systems conduct business online [4]. It has a very important requirement of achieving mutual meaning understanding between sellers and buyers. *Meaning understanding* refers to reaching a certain level of semantic agreement between the communicating parties of human through underlying disparate messaging systems over various networks or Internet. This requirement for meaning understanding has to be implemented in e-marketplace. This is because sellers and buyers can conduct business if and only if they well understand what they are talking about and have no misunderstanding on their exchanged messages with each other.

Consider a case as follows: Seller S sends a valid offer of fridge to Buyer B and Buyer B confirms the offer by sending back an offer acceptance. In this legally valid offer-acceptance business cycle, the Seller's offer is made in Table 1 and the Buyer's offer acceptance is made in Table 2. Both tables are generated based on their local databases and the messages in exchange. Now, the problem happens such that Seller S deems that it sells a mini household refrigerator in US$250, but Buyer B believes it confirms an offer of camping fridge only worth of HK$250. Definitely, this is a legally-flawed offer-acceptance cycle and will cause legal consequences.

W. Cellary and E. Estevez (Eds.): I3E 2010, IFIP AICT 341, pp. 127–138, 2010.

Table 1. A valid offer of Seller S

Offer No.	Commodity	description	Quantity	Price	Total
S111	Fridge	orange, low temperature	100 pieces	$250	$25,000
This offer is valid before 2009/12/15.					

Table 2. A valid offer acceptance from Buyer B

Acceptance No.	Commodity	description	Quantity	Price	Total
B222	Fridge	orange, low temperature	100 pieces	$250	$25,000
This acceptance confirms the offer no. S111 on 2009/12/10.					

Technically speaking, the above case can be easily avoided if the offer-acceptance cycle is processed by human. Nevertheless, when a trading process is automatically handled by autonomously developed software systems, the business document sense disambiguation becomes a tough research problem and must be resolved.

Trading process automation is a very important topic and long been recognized in e-commerce research area [8, 12, 14, 15]. It is the design foundation of modern e-marketplace that saves business costs and increases efficiency of sellers and buyers. At the core of trading process automation is the document sense disambiguation that helps reach mutual meaning understanding between buyers and sellers for their smooth conducting electronic business. *Document sense disambiguation* (DSD) is a specialized research of word sense disambiguation (WSD) [11], focusing on identifying the meaning of a document to generate a correctly interpreted document. For example, in the above case, in order to avoid a legally-flawed offer-acceptance cycle, Buyer B must equip with a DSD tool to test whether its interpretation on the document of Seller S is accurate, following the original meaning of Seller S. Document sense ambiguities during interpretation are often caused by document systems autonomy, which can happen in the levels of document design, document communication and document execution [5:15-18]. Thus, the sense disambiguation methods can also be classified in these three levels. In addition, the target document for sense disambiguation can be an unstructured document (UD) (e.g. an article in plain text) or a structured document (SD) (e.g. an invoice or an offer sheet in tabular form). Traditionally in natural language processing, a most important task is to enable machines to process unstructured textual information and transforms them into data structure that can be analyzed to determine the underlying meaning. Such computational identification of meaning for words in context is called *word sense disambiguation* (WSD), which is an AI-complete problem [11] when a text is an unstructured document (UD).

This paper aims to propose a novel SD-based document sense disambiguation (SD-DSD) approach to resolve the ambiguous interpretation problem that causes the gap of meaning understanding between sellers and buyers. It resolves the problem in design phase and attempts to turn an AI-complete problem of WSD [11] into a relatively easy problem through constructing business documents in a uniquely identified concept hierarchy. It assumes that both sellers and buyers in e-marketplace are sufficient to utilize a certain structured document (SD) for achieving mutual meaning understanding during trading communication. It is, thus, contented that a solution to SD-based document sense disambiguation suffices to achieve the goal of this paper if and only if an SD-based document can be transformed into a uniquely identified concept hierarchy, initially described in [5, 6] for constructing interoperable electronic product catalogues.

The rest of the paper is arranged as follows. Section 2 proposes a novel approach of SD-based document sense disambiguation to achieve mutual meaning understanding between sellers and buyers in e-marketplace. Section 3 implements the proposed MD document data model in XPM format. In Section 4, an evaluation method is suggested to evaluate the interpretation accuracy for any incoming MD document. Section 5 briefly describes the related work of the proposed approach. Finally, a conclusion is made together with contributions and future work.

2 Structured Document Based Sense Disambiguation

The traditional sense disambiguation often targets at unstructured free text. It takes a whole piece of free text as the input and then tries to make sense on what the input text means. The hardness of the problem is AI-complete [11]. However, under the circumstances of e-marketplace trading activities, a free text is not necessary for conveying the business meaning between sellers and buyers. A structured tabular document suffices for meaning understanding in most trading cases. For example, an inquiry can be designed as a structured tabular inquiry sheet, constituting a set of concept pairs of an abstract concept and its reified concept such as (color, red) or (price, 100). This provides an opportunity to turn an AI-complete problem of WSD into an easier problem that is suitable to be solved to identify explicit and consistent meanings of a structured document. We shall call such an easier problem as a *one-to-one match problem*, which means that as long as any concept of a text matches a one-to-one correspondence in an interpreted text, the text is capable of sense disambiguation. Thus, the problem of WSD is transformed into a problem of SD-based document sense disambiguation (DSD) with the task of finding a one-to-one match-able document, in which each concept is explicit and consistent.

2.1 Problem Description

By observation, most e-marketplace documents are in tabular form that is structured. A one-to-one concept match problem, which could describe the senses ambiguity of a *structured tabular document* (SD), can be described as follows:

Structured tabular document (SD) $\Rightarrow$ One-to-one match document (MD) (1.1)

This problem states that, if a concept match document MD could be found to have a one-to-one correspondence with SD document in concept match, then the one-to-one concept match problem could be solved as (1.1). Given the problem (1.1), our research task is to find a one-to-one match document MD from an existing structured tabular document SD. For example, given a table SD1 as shown in Table 1, we need to find a one-to-one match document MD1 as shown in Table 3, where each concept of MD1 can exactly match with each concept of SD1.

Table 3. An ideal MD1 file for SD1 as shown in Table 1

Concept	Word	Definition
1	offer	A scheme of payment for providing products
2	No.	A series of numerals or symbols used for reference or identification
3	S111	A particular series of numerals or symbols used for reference or identification
4	commodity	Something useful that can be turned to commercial or other advantage
5	fridge	An appliance for storing food or other substances at a low temperature.
6	description	The act, process, or technique of describing
7	orange	A kind of color
8	low	Below average in degree, intensity, or amount
9	temperature	A specific degree of hotness or coldness to a standard scale
10	quantity	A specified number
11	1000	A numerical value
12	pieces	A unit of quantity
13	price	The amount as of money, asked for or given in exchange for something else
14	$	United States dollar
11	250	A numerical value
16	total	A sum of all parts
14	$	United States dollar
11	25,000	A numerical value

The MD1 of Table 3 suggests a mapping A that in document SD1 only one sense S can be assigned to each word $w_i \in$ SD1 such that:

$$|\,A(i)_S\,| = 1 \ (i \in 1\ldots n). \quad (2.1)$$

where i refers to a word w_i and s refers to the corresponding senses of i. The $A(i)_S$ means that every w_i in an SD1 corresponds to its senses to derive a map A. □

If this $|\,A(i)_S\,|= 1$ holds, we say that the sense of SD1 is fully disambiguated or the interpretation of SD1 could be 100% accurate. Generically, achieving $|\,A(i)_S\,|= 1$ for SD will, thus, solve the problem of SD-based document sense disambiguation.

2.2 Strategies of Achieving | A(i)S | = 1

To achieve (2.1) of $|\,A(i)_S\,| = 1$, this paper proposes five strategies, which are concept identification, concept hierarchy, concept atomization, concept pairing, and concept matching. In the following, we discuss these strategies one by one to show how we disambiguate the sense of a tabular SD document to 100% accuracy.

Strategy 1. (*Achieving sense uniqueness by concept identification*): Given any word $w \in$ SD and any concept $c \in$ MD, w is uniquely sensed if and only if $w \Leftarrow c$ and $c \Leftarrow rt$, where rt is a unique identifier. □

By this strategy, the sense of each word has been assigned a corresponding uniquely identified concept. This makes it possible to construct a one-to-one match document, where word sense can be disambiguated. For example, the concept like "orange" in MD1 is uniquely identified by "7" and it will not be interpreted as fruit.

Nevertheless, unique concept identification is not enough. In real practice, many concepts are group concepts such as "price", which means "price(currency, amount, unit)". In fact, the flawed offer-acceptance cycle of the introduction case, shown in Table 1 and Table 2, happens due to the fact that "price" concept has not been well defined by missing the clear definition of "$". In many existing databases, the use of "$" or omission of "$" is popular since the database designers assume a local context in data design. Such implicit concepts have to be explicitized when accurate sense of word is required. Strategy 2 is a method of resolving this problem.

Strategy 2. (*Achieving sense explicitization by concept hierarchy*): Given any word $w \in$ SD and a set of concepts $c, c_1^{\,1}, c_i^{\,2}, \ldots, c_i^{\,k}, \ldots, c_i^{\,n} \in$ MD, w is explicitly sensed if and only if $w \Leftarrow c$ and $c = (c_1^{\,1}, c_i^{\,2}, \ldots, c_i^{\,k}, \ldots, c_i^{\,n})$, where c is a hierarchy with $c_1^{\,1}$ as the root node and $c_i^{\,k}$ as a descendant node (i, k refer to a sibling and a level of hierarchy, respectively). □

Strategy 2 assumes that every concept is a group concept by default, though most concepts only contain only a root node concept such that $c = c_1^{\,1}$. With this assumption, it requires every concept to be explicitized by decomposing itself into member concepts until any member concept contains only a root concept. This strategy can effectively eliminate implicit concepts that cause interpretation ambiguity, for example, "price = price(currency, amount, unit)".

Strategy 3. (*Achieving sense independence by concept atomization*): Given any two words $w, w' \in$ SD and any two concepts $c, c' \in$ MD, w is independently sensed if and only if $w \Leftarrow c \parallel w' \Leftarrow c'$, where "||" is an independence relationship. □

This strategy is to ease the execution complexity of any concept. A uniquely, explicitly and independently sensed word remains the same sense in whatever place even outside of the document. The principle of concept atomization states "What you are saying is what you have said". For example, an independently sensed "orange" in MD1 can be permanently recognized as "fc: orange, cid: boo.com::docDB#S11.7, rt:voc.com::vocDB#2222". The sense of the word can always be disambiguated against the reference vocabulary in voc.com and found in boo.com as historical archive unless they have been deleted. By this strategy, everything becomes a history. Apparently, it well fits for business needs of tracking and verification from the perspective of legality.

Strategy 4. (*Achieving sense reification by concept pairing*): Given any two words $w_1, w_2 \in$ SD and any two concepts $c_1, c_2 \in$ MD, w_2 is a reified sense of w_1 if and only if $\exists 1\ Pair(w_1 \Leftarrow c_1, w_2 \Leftarrow c_2)$ and $c_1 \rightarrow c_2$, where c_1 and c_2 are called abstract concept and reified concept, respectively, and "→" is reification relationship. □

This strategy helps build a correct context for a reified concept. While a context of an abstract concept in MD is explicit and can be described by its parent concept, the context of a reified concept is, sometimes, implicit. For example, a concept such as "$25000" in Table 1 is difficult to be associated any concept if no mechanism disambiguates it. A pair-wise mechanism, described in Strategy 4, is a means of achieving it. For instance, if we have a paired concept (total, value((currency, USD), (amount, 25000)), we can easily derive the correct association of (total, USD25000), where USD25000 if a reification of "total" concept.

Strategy 5. (*Achieving sense making by concept matching*): Given $w_i \in$ SD and $c_j \in$ MD ($i, j \in 1\ldots n$), MD makes sense against SD if and only if $\forall w_i, c_i, c_i \Rightarrow w_i$. □

This strategy ensures that all words in a structured tabular document can be transformed into the unique, explicit and independent concepts in a one-to-one match document. For example, the document of Table 1 can be transformed into another document shown in Table 3 (note: the definition can be replaced by a reference to a commonly shared vocabulary).

2.3 Document Representation Models

Employing the above strategies of SD-based document sense disambiguation, we can create two document representation models for representing both SD document and MD document. The former must satisfy the business user requirement for a tabular document presentation, while the latter opts for adapting to solve one-to-one match problem. With these in mind, our document representation models are designed as follows:

Definition 1. (*Document presentation model*): A document presentation model SD for business users is a tabular document model, defined as follows:

$$\mathrm{SD} = (\mathrm{w}_{11}, \mathrm{w}_{12}, \ldots, \mathrm{w}_{ij}, \ldots, \mathrm{w}_{mn}), i, j \in 1\ldots\mathrm{N} \quad (3.1)$$

$$\mathrm{w}_{ij} = (\mathrm{WID}, \{\mathrm{FC}\}, [\mathrm{GF}]) \quad (3.2)$$

where SD is a tabular model, in which w_{ij} is a cell, i is a row number and j is a column number. Each cell is a tuple, in which WID is cell ID, {FC} is a set of words expressing w_{ij}, and [GF] is local graphic features. When a word $w_{ij} \neq$ NULL, the cell(w_{ij}) is active and implies a valid word, otherwise the null cell is considered as inactive and neglected. □

This tabular model well fits for the existing business practices for document template design and reification.

Definition 2. (*Document data model*): A document data model MD for storing one-to-one matching concepts of SD is a hierarchically structured document model, defined as follows:

$$\mathrm{MD} = (c_1{}^1, (c_a, c_r[k])_{\mathrm{i}}{}^2, \ldots, (c_a, c_r[k])_{\mathrm{i}}{}^{\mathrm{j}}, \ldots, (c_a, c_r[k])_{\mathrm{i}}{}^n \quad (4.1)$$

$$c_a = (\mathrm{WID}, \{\mathrm{FC}\}, \{\mathrm{RT}\}, \mathrm{PC}, \mathrm{DP}) \quad (4.2)$$

$$c_r = (\mathrm{RID}, \{\mathrm{FC}\}, \{\mathrm{RT}\}, \mathrm{OP}) \quad (4.3)$$

where MD is a hierarchical form, in which $c_1{}^1$ is document root, (c_a, $c_r[k]$) is a pair of an abstract concept and a set of reified concepts in k number, and i and j refer to any sibling concept and any MD level.

In each concept pair following Strategy 4, the abstract concept c_a is a tuple where WID is a unique document concept classifier extracted from SD, {FC} is a set of words of a WID-ed cell, {RT} is a set of unique concept identifiers one-to-one corresponding to {FC} and referenced in common vocabularies (VOC). DP = “yes/no” such that if yes {FC} is displayed else hide. PC points to the parent WID.

The reified concept c_r is also a tuple, in which RID, notated as WID-i pointing to WID. OP defines how {FC} and {RT} are related and presented in SD.

Document data model MD enable all data of SD document to be accurately and hierarchically represented, in which sense ambiguities are disambiguated by RT.

2.4 Transformation between SD and MD Documents

SD and MD are two different models. The SD model is to provide a model that is similar to existing tabular document model while MD model is to provide a storage model. it is necessary to provide a tool to enable mutual transformation such that:

$$SD \Leftrightarrow MD \qquad (5.1)$$

In this paper, a set of rules are designed to enable the transformation between SD and MD. These rules are provided as follows to govern the design of both SD and MD when models of Definition 1 and Definition 2 are followed:

Definition 3. (*Common concept reference rule*): While adopting *Strategy 1*, for any concept $c \in$ MD and any cell $w \in$ SD, there exist a set of unique concept definitions $an_i \Rightarrow rt_i \in$ VOC such that:

$$rt_i \Rightarrow fc_i \qquad (6.1)$$

The (6.1) guarantees that for $\{rt_i\} \Rightarrow \{fc_i\} \Rightarrow c_j$ and $\{rt_i\} \Rightarrow \{fc_i\} \Rightarrow w_j$ hence $c_j = w_j$ of Strategy 1, a group c and a cell w share a set of unique and consistent word senses by *rt*.

Definition 4. (*Common group concept classifier rule*): while adopting *Strategy 2*, for any concept $c \in$ MD and cell $w \in$ SD, there exists a common group concept classifier *wid*, such that:

$$(wid \in c) = (wid \in w) \qquad (7.1)$$

The (7.1) guarantees that the sense of w and c are equivalent by *wid* and thus transformable. In addition, it also solves one presentation problem of SD, that is, how to properly present w in tabular form. The solution is to utilize wid as hierarchical classifier such that wid = wid(wid). For example, if there are cells with classifiers 1.5.8.1, 1.5.9.2, 1.5.9.2-3, 1.5.8.1-2 and 1.6.8, then words of 1.5.8.1, 1.5.9.2, 1.5.9.2-3 and 1.5.8.1-2 is a group having a common root concept 1.5. Within this 1.5 group concept, 1.5.8.1-2 is the second value (reified concept) of 1.5.8.1, and 1.5.9.2-3 is the third value (reified concept) of 1.5.9.2. By this concept grouping rule, all words can be properly aligned in a tabular form such that a group of siblings can be placed in the same row or column and their value can be placed just under or right of column cells or row cells. The detailed presentation approach for SD is beyond the discussion of this paper will be elaborated elsewhere.

2.5 Procedures of Achieving $| A(i)_S | = 1$

Procedurally, the semantic consistency of the transformation from SD to MD can be validated through a semantic consistency check procedure as follows.

Procedure 1. (*Sense Consistency Check*): For any $id_i = (wid_i \mid rid_j) \in$ SD $(i \in 0 \ldots m)$ and $id_j = (wid_j \mid rid_j) \in$ MD $(j \in 0 \ldots n)$, a sense consistency check can be made to semantically validate both SD and MD, as defined in the following:

```
count = 0;
for(i=0, i<m, i++)
{
        if (id_i = Search(id_j, MD))
```

```
            MD = MD – id_j
            else
            {
                        InconsistentSD = count + 1;
                        LogSD[InconsistentSD -1] = id_i;
            }
    }
    InconsistentMD = Count(MD);
    LogMD[InconsistentMD -1] = Enumerate(MD);
    Inconsistent = InconsistentSD + InconsistentMD;
```

This procedure validates the sense consistency between cell semantics of SD and group concepts of MD. It provides the information about the sense inconsistent status. The InconsistentSD means that the sense inconsistency is caused by SD document while the InconsistentMD means that the sense inconsistency comes from MD document. Besides the above procedure, for each cell of SD, its corresponding group concept must also be checked whether $rt_i \Rightarrow fc_i$ exists. This is the task of Procedure 2.

Given the sense consistent SD and MD, when a recipient receives an MD document from the sender, this MD document must be semantically validated again to disambiguate document senses. We provide a sense existence match procedure to semantically validate an incoming document.

Procedure 2. (*Sense Existence Match*): For any incoming document MD such that $rt_i \in$ MD, $iid \in$ dbVOC, $i \in (1 \ldots m)$, a semantic validation is defined as follows:

```
count = 0;
for(i = 0, i < m, i++)
{
    Search(iid, dbVOC);
    {
            if rt_i = iid
                        Continue()
            else
    {
                        NonExistent = count + 1;
                        log[NonExistent -1] = rt_i;  } } }
```

The above defined procedure semantically validates the incoming MD document from a trading partner. If NonExistent = 0, the MD document is 100% consistent for interpretation as the sender's meaning understanding. In this case, $| A(i)_S | = 1$ has been achieved. The interpretation accuracy is reduced or interpretation ambiguity is increased as number of NonExistent increases.

3 XPM Implementation of Document Data Model

The key to achieving $| A(i)_S | = 1$ is to derive a semantic consistent MD from SD. In this paper, the MD document designed in Section 2 is implemented in an XPM document model, which is initiated in the research of [5, 17]. The original XPM model describes a document as a set of hierarchical concepts, in which each concept is denoted as a denotation by a set of elementary structures. Every denotation is an independent concept. Several concepts are grouped by connotation such that a sequence of sibling denotations is connotations of their parent concept's denotation. Simply, XPM document model can be defined as follows:

```
<!ELEMENT concept (#PCDATA | concept)*>
<!ATTLIST concept
        iid ID #REQUIRED
        an CDATA #REQUIRED
>
```

In this document model, a concept is denoted by *iid* and *an*, and is connoted by (#PCDATA | concept)* in which each concept is recursive for deriving a hierarchy.

The simple structure of XPM is its advantage to combat complexity of the existing business world. Its denotation and connotation relationship enables this specification to separate all description of a concept (i.e. denotation) into an <ATTLIST> without the need of associating with other concept as described by an <ELEMENT>. Concept grouping (i.e. connotation) as a composite concept is achieved by the sub-hierarchy of any <ELEMENT>.

MD document model designed in this paper maintains these good features, which can be described as follows:

```
<!ELEMENT doc (concept*)>
<!ELEMENT concept (concept | values)*>
<!ELEMENT values (value*)>
<!ELEMENT value (#PCDATA)>
<!ATTLIST doc       cid CDATA #FIXED "d" rt CDATA #REQUIRED fc CDATA #REQUIRED
            comment CDATA #IMPLIED>
<!ATTLIST concept  cid ID #REQUIRED  rt CDATA #REQUIRED fc CDATA #REQUIRED
        pc CDATA #REQUIRED dp (yes | no) "yes" oc CDATA #IMPLIED>
<!ATTLIST values    rid ID #REQUIRED  oc CDATA #IMPLIED ch CDATA #REQUIRED>
<!ATTLIST value     rid ID #REQUIRED  rt CDATA #IMPLIED op (EQ | LessThan | LargerThan |
LessEq | LargerEq | PlusMinus | IS | NOT | MF | FN) "IS"
        dt (string | number | decimal | scientific | const | serial | symbol) "string">
```

Fig. 1. XPM MD Document Data Model (mddoc.dtd)

Applying the model of Figure 1, the MD1 document of Table 3 following SD1 of Table 1 can be instantiated as a reified XPM MD document, as shown in Figure 2.

```
<!DOCTYPE doc SYSTEM "mddoc.dtd">
<doc cid="d" rt="100" fc="Offer Sheet" comment="An offer sheet answering an inquiry sheet.">
  <concept cid="d.1" rt="100;;200" pc="d" fc="Offer No." dp="yes">
   <values rid="d.1-v"><value rid="d1.1-v1" dt="serial" op="IS">S111</value></values>
  </concept>
  <concept cid="d.2" rt="400" pc="d" fc="Commodity" dp="yes">
   <values rid="d.2-v"><value rid="d.2-v1" rt="500" dt="string" op="IS">Fridge</value></values>
  </concept>
  <concept  cid="d.3" rt="600" pc="d" fc="Description" dp="yes">
    <values rid="d.3-v" oc="3">
         <value rid="d.3.-v1" rt="700" dt="string" op="IS">orange</value>
         <value rid="d.3.-v2" dt="symbol" op="IS">,</value>
         <value rid="d.3-v3" rt="800;;900" dt="string" op="IS">low temperature</value>
    </values></concept>
  <concept cid="d.4" rt="1000"  pc="d"  fc="Quantity" dp="yes">
   <values rid="d.4-v" oc="2" ch="all">
         <value rid="d.4-v1" dt="number" op="EQ">100</value>
         <value rid="d.4-v2" rt="1200"  dt="string" op="IS">pieces</value>
```

Fig. 2. XPM MD1 Reified Document (md1.xml)

```
  </values></concept>
 <concept cid="d.5" rt="1300" fc="price" pc="d" dp="yes">
  <values rid="d.5-v" oc="4" ch="all">
        <value rid="d.5-v1" rt="1400" dt="const" op="IS">$</value>
        <value rid="d.5-v2" dt="decimal" op="EQ">250.00</value>
        <value rid="d.5-v3" dt="symbol" op="IS">/</value>
        <value rid="d.5-v4" rt="1200" dt="string" op="IS">piece</value>
  </values></concept>
 <concept cid="d.6" rt="1600" fc="total" pc="d" dp="yes">
  <values rid="d.6-v" oc="2" ch="all">
        <value rid="d.6-v1" rt="1400" dt="const" op="IS">$</value>
        <value rid="d.6-v2" dt="decimal" op="EQ">25,000.00</value>
  </values></concept>
</doc>
```

Fig. 2. (*continued*)

4 Evaluation Method of Sense Interpretation Accuracy

The accuracy of SD document interpretation can be evaluated using a newly devised evaluation method, which takes consideration of interpretation inaccuracy from both the transformation of SD⇒MD and the sense match between MD and dbVOC.

Definition 5. (*Transformation Inaccuracy TI between SD and MD*): When an SD document is transformed to an MD document, the transformation inaccuracy TI happens such that for $wid_i \in$ SD and $wid_j \in$ MD, $wid_i \neq wid_j$, $i \in 0\ldots m$, $j \in 0\ldots n$. The number of TI can be calculated from N_{TI} = Inconsistent of Procedure 1.

Definition 6. (*Match Inaccuracy MI between MD and Vocabulary dbVOC*): When all the concepts of an MD document are compared with the concepts of a vocabulary dbVOV, the sense match inaccuracy MI happens such that $rt_i \in$ MD and $iid_j \in$ dbVOC, $rt_i \neq iid_j$, $i \in 0\ldots m$, $j \in 0\ldots n$. The number of MI can be calculated from N_{MI} = NonExistent of Procedure 2.

Definition 7. (*Sense Interpretation Accuracy SIA*): The total sense interpretation accuracy of an MD, where $rt_i \in$ MD ($i \in 1\ldots n$), during achieving $|\ A(i)_S\ | = 1$, can be measured as follows:

$$SLA = \frac{T - N_{TI} - N_{MI}}{T} \tag{8.1}$$

where $T = Count(\sum_{i=1}^{n} rt_i)$, and N_{TI} and N_{MI} are defined in Definition 5 and 6, respectively.

The evaluation form SIA is useful to evaluate the sense making of any incoming MD document. Against SIA formula, the evaluation result of the above incoming offer sheet (md1.xml) is the 100% sense interpretation accuracy since both N_{TI} and N_{MI} are zero such that SIA = 1 = 100%. It must be noted that a comparative evaluation against existing other approaches such as ontology will not be discussed here. The reason is that ontology and the vocabulary used within this paper has substantial difference. The vocabulary used in this paper is collaboratively created and is cross-domain [5, 6] while Ontology is domain-wide. This is also why SIA can equal 1.

5 Related Work

The SD-DSD approach in general, relates to the sense disambiguation technology [7, 11], which is often applied in the area of machine translation, information retrieval, hypertext navigation, content and thematic analysis, grammatical analysis, speech processing, and text processing. The general steps of achieving sense disambiguation are: (1) determining all the different senses for every relevant word in a text, and (2) assigning an appropriate sense to each occurrence of the word in a text.

The methods of taking the first step often require a list of predefined senses in sorts of vocabularies such as taxonomy (e.g., taxonomystrategies.com), thesaurus [1] (e.g., visualthesaurus.com), glossary (e.g., [9] and glossary.com), machine-readable dictionary (e.g. WordNet at wordnet.princeton.edu), ontology (e.g., [2] and geneontology.org), and collaborative concepts [6]. These vocabularies define different senses of each word that possibly occurs in a document needing disambiguation. The methods for Step (2) can be classified as context-based and knowledge-based [7] or unsupervised and supervised [11]. In practice, context and knowledge are both utilized in assigning the sense to words.

Particularly, SD-DSD approach is context- and knowledge-based [7]. In designing SD-DSD approach, different contexts of creating SD and MD documents are aligned and mediated through a collaborative editing system that links to an external common vocabulary exactly known by SD creator and MD interpreter. Through this editing system, a unique sense of any word is assigned to both SD and MD documents without sense ambiguity. It is achieved by applying a set of collaborative concepts [5, 6], i.e. CONEX concepts, which are mutually agreed in meaning by document senders and receivers, assuming both of them are in a same e-marketplace.

6 Conclusion

This paper achieves the meaning understanding of exchanged business documents between unknown sellers and buyers in e-marketplace by proposing a novel structured tabular document sense disambiguation approach (SD-DSD). In this approach, it has developed five sense disambiguation strategies, which guide designing two document representation models: structured tabular document (SD) presentation model, and one-to-one match document (MD) data model. Two procedures of sense consistency check procedure and sense existence match are developed to control the sense disambiguation. The MD document data model is implemented in a newly devised XPM scheme, where example of its reification is described. The interpretation accuracy between SD creator and MD user is validated, considering both factors in SD-MD transformation and MD interpretation.

This paper has contributed a novel approach to tabular document sense disambiguation, achieving a unique sense of $| A(i)_S | = 1$. It has eased the difficult problem in word sense disambiguation (WSD) area by strategies of sense uniqueness, sense explicitization, sense independence, sense reification and sense making, and made the problem-solving possible.

SD-DSD approach is fundamental and important to e-marketplace semantic information exchange. Future work will use this research result for designing tools and applications of business document interchange.

References

1. Aitchison, J., Clarke, S.D.: The Thesaurus: A Historical Viewpoint, with a Look to the Future. Cataloging & Classification Quarterly 37(3/4), 5–21 (2004)
2. Gruber, T.R.: A translation approach to portable ontologies. Knowledge Acquisition 5(2), 199–220 (1993)
3. Guo, J.: Business-to-Business Electronic Marketplace Selection. Enterprise Information Systems 1(4), 383–419 (2007)
4. Guo, J.: A Term in Search of the Infrastructure of Electronic Markets. In: Research and Practical Issues of Enterprise Information Systems II, vol. 2. IFIP, vol. 255, pp. 831–840 (2007)
5. Guo, J.: Collaborative Concept Exchange. VDM Publishing, Germany (2008)
6. Guo, J.: Collaborative Conceptualization: Towards a Conceptual Foundation of Interoperable Electronic Product Catalogue System Design. Enterprise Information Systems 3(1), 59–94 (2009)
7. Ide, N., Véronis, J.: Introduction to the special issue on word sense disambiguation: the state of the art. Computational Linguistics 24(1), 2–40 (1998)
8. Kaleta, M., Pałka, P., Toczyłowski, E., Traczyk, T.: Electronic Trading on Electricity Markets within a Multi-agent Framework. In: Nguyen, N.T., Kowalczyk, R., Chen, S.-M. (eds.) ICCCI 2009. LNCS (LNAI), vol. 5796, pp. 788–799. Springer, Heidelberg (2009)
9. Malkin, G.: RFC1983: Internet Users' Glossary, RFC Editor, USA (1986)
10. Michalak, T., Tyrowicz, J., McBurney, P., Wooldridge, M.: Exogenous coalition formation in the e-marketplace based on geographical proximity. Electronic Commerce Research and Applications 8(4), 203–223 (2009)
11. NavigliI, R.: Word Sense Disambiguation: A Survey. ACM Computing Surveys 41(2), Article 10 (2009)
12. Ncho, A., Aimeur, E.: Building a Multi-Agent System for Automatic Negotiation in Web Service Applications. In: ACM Proc. of AAMAS 2004, pp. 1464–1465 (2004)
13. Serban, C., Chen, Y., Zhang, W., Minsky, N.: The concept of decentralized and secure electronic marketplace. Electronic Commerce Research 8(1-2), 79–101 (2008)
14. Stohr, E.A., Zhao, J.L.: Workflow Automation: Overview and Research Issues. Information Systems Frontiers 3(3), 281–296 (2005)
15. Unitt, M., Jones, I.C.: EDI - The Grand Daddy of Electronic Commerce. BT Technology Journal 17(3), 17–23 (1999)
16. Wang, S., Zheng, S., Xu, L., Li, D., Meng, H.: A literature review of electronic marketplace research: Themes, theories and an integrative framework. Information Systems Frontiers 10(5), 555–571 (2008)
17. XPM, http://www.sftw.umac.mo/~jzguo/pages/resource.html

Automatically Detecting Opportunities for Web Service Descriptions Improvement

Juan Manuel Rodriguez[1,2], Marco Crasso[1,2], Alejandro Zunino[1,2], and Marcelo Campo[1,2]

[1] ISISTAN Research Institute, Universidad Nacional del Centro de la Provincia de Buenos Aires (UNICEN), Campus Universitario, Tandil (B7001BBO), Buenos Aires, Argentina
[2] Consejo Nacional de Investigaciones Científicas y Técnicas (CONICET), Argentina
rodriguez.juanmanuel@gmail.com

Abstract. Mostly *e*-business and *e*-applications rely on the Service Oriented Computing paradigm and its most popular implementation, namely Web Services. When properly implemented and described, Web Services can be dynamically discovered and reused using Internet technologies, pushing interoperability to unprecedented levels. However, poorly described Web Services are rather difficult to be discovered, understood, and reused. This paper presents heuristics for automatically detecting common pitfalls that should be avoided when creating Web Service descriptions. Experimental results with ca. 400 real-world Web Services, empirically show the feasibility of the proposed heuristics.

Keywords: Web Service modeling, Web Service discoverability anti-patterns.

1 Introduction

The success encountered by the Internet encourages practitioners, companies and governments to create software that utilizes information and services that third-parties have made public in the Web. This, besides encouraging the aforementioned actors to offer their information and services in the same way, spreads into a new kind of software, namely *e*-applications, *e*-business, and *e*-government [1]. Nowadays, the *Service Oriented Computing* (SOC) paradigm [2] is used for developing this kind of software.

With SOC, software development involves a service provider, who offers services and advertises them in a public registry, and service consumers, who use such a registry to find the services that they need [3]. Using open standards, such as SOAP, HTTP, and XML, to implement the SOC paradigm is by now commonplace in the software industry because these standards allow the integration of different pieces of software independently of their platform and location. Basically, providers describe their services using Web Service Description Language (WSDL), which is an XML-based language, and advertise them using Universal Description, Discovery and Integration (UDDI), which uses XML for representing services meta-data and SOAP for querying it. The term Web Services refers to these standards that support SOC across the Web [4].

W. Cellary and E. Estevez (Eds.): I3E 2010, IFIP AICT 341, pp. 139–150, 2010

SOC and Web Services have been broadly embraced by the software industry. The ever-growing number of publicly available services represents "either more freedom or more chaos for service consumers" [5], mainly because of the limited search capabilities of UDDI, the incorrect usage of standards to describe Web Services, and that they do not consider the semantics of services in an explicit and non-ambiguous way [6]. Several registry enhancements have been proposed to improve the experience of service consumers. The approach to service discovery that bases on exploiting every possible piece of information conveyed in standard service descriptions, has shown favorable outcomes [7]. This approach bases on the fact that when WSDL documents are well-written the signatures and associated comments of their offered operations, convey keywords relevant to index the services [7]. Well-written WSDL documents are essential for not only such approach, but also service consumers because if they do not understand what a service does, they would not select the service. Unfortunately, despite such importance and Foster's words "Web Services have little value if other cannot discover, access, and make sense of them" [8], it seems that providers tend not to care about Web Services discoverability and understandability, as pointed by [9, 10, 11].

In our previous work [10], we introduced a catalog of WSDL-based Web Services discoverability anti-patterns. Besides measuring the impact of each anti-pattern on discovery, the study assesses the implications of anti-patterns on users' ability to make sense of WSDL documents. The catalog consists of eight anti-patterns having a name, a problem description, and a soundly refactor procedure. However the results of the study motivate anti-patterns refactoring, manually looking for an anti-pattern in WSDL documents might be a time consuming and complex task. Thus, this paper presents heuristics to automatically detect the anti-patterns of the catalog. These heuristics have been experimentally validated with a real-world data-set, showing an averaged accuracy of 98.5%. Therefore, the main contribution of this paper is:

- The definition and validation of novel heuristics for automatically detecting anti-patterns that already have been proven to be opportunities for improving the discoverability and understandability of Web Services in [10].

The rest of the paper is organized as follows: Sect. 2 explains the essential characteristics of the WSDL, the service discovery process, and the Web Services discoverability anti-patterns, Sect. 3 explains the proposed heuristics, while Sect. 4 reports conducted experiments, finally Sect. 5 presents conclusions and opportunities of future research.

2 Background

WSDL is an XML-based language that allows providers to describe the service functionality as a set of *port-types*. A port-type arranges different *operations* whose invocation is based on exchanging *messages*: one message with input data, other with the result, and another with error information, optionally. Port-types, operations and messages, must be named with unique names. Messages consist of *parts* that are arranged according to specific data-types defined using the XML Schema Definition (XSD) language. XSD offers constructors for defining simple types (e.g., integer and string), and more elaborate mechanisms for defining complex elements. Data-type definitions can be put into a WSDL document or into a separate file and imported from any WSDL document afterward. The grammar of the WSDL[1] can be summarized as follows:

```
<documentation .... />?
<types>?
    <documentation .... />?
    <schema .... />*
</types>
<message name="nmtoken">*
    <documentation .... />?
    <part name="nmtoken" element="qname"? type="qname"?/>*
</message>
<portType name="nmtoken">*
    <documentation .... />?
    <operation name="nmtoken">*
        <documentation .... />?
        <input name="nmtoken"? message="qname">?
            <documentation .... />?
        </input>
        <output name="nmtoken"? message="qname">?
            <documentation .... />?
        </output>
        <fault name="nmtoken" message="qname">*
            <documentation .... />?
        </fault>
    </operation>
</portType>
```

UDDI[2] was originally defined as the discovery protocol of Web Services. However, UDDI has been proven to be an ineffective discovery method for large registries because it is a keyword based discovery method [12]. As a result two approaches to discovery have been taken, the first one relies on an extended WSDL to include ontology based descriptions of the service. Although this approach allows automatic service discovery, the industry has not adopted because the high effort required for implementing it [13]. The second direction is applying informationretrieval (IR) techniques to WSDL documents for allowing search Web Service [7]. The main strength of using IR is that there is no need of modifying existent WSDL documents. However, this is also a drawback because many of those documents are not well-written.
Although the importance of well-designed WSDL document has been identified as a central concern in Web Service reuse [14, 15], different studies have pointed out the existence of widespread problems in documentation [16], naming [11] and interface design [9, 17] in real-life WSDL documents.

---

[1] Note that "?" means optional and "*" means none or many.
[2] UDDI http://uddi.xml.org/

Table 1. Catalog of Web Service discoverability anti-patterns

Anti-pattern	Symptoms	Manifest
Enclosed data model	Occurs when the data-type definitions are placed in WSDL documents rather than in separate XSD ones.	Evident
Redundant port-types	Occurs when port-types offer the same set of operations.	Evident
Redundant data models	Occurs when many data-types for representing the same objects of the problem domain coexist in a WSDL document.	Evident
Whatever types	Occurs when a data-type represents any object of the domain.	Evident
Inappropriate or lacking comments	Occurs when (1) a WSDL document has no comments, or (2) comments are inappropriate and not explanatory.	(1) Evident, or (2) Not immediately apparent
Low cohesive operations in the same port-type	Occurs when port-types have weak semantic cohesion.	Not immediately apparent
Ambiguous names	Occurs when ambiguous or meaningless names are used for denoting the main elements of a WSDL document.	Not immediately apparent
Undercover fault information within standard messages	Occurs when output messages are used to notify service errors. Sometimes (1) whatever types are returned and operation comments suggest anti-pattern occurrence. Otherwise (2) it is necessary to analyze service implementation.	(1) Not immediately apparent, or (2) Present in service implementation

In [10], we have explicitly addressed the quality of WSDL documents from the perspective of a discoverer, pursuing recurrent problems that attempt against the understandability and discoverability of services. To do this, we have studied publicly available WSDL documents looking for common problems. As a result, the study presents a catalog of bad practices that frequently occur in the analyzed corpus, along with hints about how to detect problem symptoms, and refactoring guidelines to solve them. Specifically, each observed bad practice has been described in a general way that includes a description of: the problem, its solution, and an illustrative example, thus we refer to the catalog as a catalog of Web Services discoverability *anti-patterns* [18].

Table 1 summarizes the identified anti-patterns. The "Symptoms" column describes the bad practice associated with an anti-pattern. The column named "Manifests" presents a classification based on how an anti-pattern can be detected. Anti-pattern manifestation can take three values: *Evident*, *Not immediately apparent*, and *Present in service implementation*. An anti-pattern is *Evident* if it can be detected by analyzing only the structure, or syntax of the WSDL document. *Not immediately apparent* means that detecting the anti-pattern requires a semantic analysis as well. Finally, *Present in service implementation* anti-patterns may not show themselves in the WSDL document, thus requiring the execution of the associated service to be detected. This classification drives the approach to detect an anti-pattern, as will be explained in next section. It is worth noting that two anti-patterns are classified in many categories, and that the proposed heuristics detect them when they manifest according to their 1st classification.

3 Automatic Discoverability Anti-pattern Detection

Our anti-pattern detection approach bases on an incremental process, in which a WSDL document is passed through eight different heuristics. Each heuristic deals with the detection of a particular anti-pattern. The idea of having individual detection heuristics stems from the fact that anti-pattern occurrences are mutually independent [10]. In other words, the occurrence of one anti-pattern does not imply the occurrence of another one. Below, the heuristics are discussed regarding the way each anti-pattern manifests.

3.1 Evident Anti-patterns

The detection of Evident anti-patterns is based on rules, which are applied to the WSDL document grammar, because the manifestation of these anti-patterns is syntactical.

To detect Enclosed data model anti-pattern, it is necessary to know if the data-types exchanged by service operations are defined in the WSDL document or imported from some where else. To do this, our heuristic checks if the <types> tag is present in a WSDL document. If it is not present, the data model is not defined in the WSDL document; therefore, the anti-pattern is not present. Instead, when the WSDL document contains the <types> tag, the heuristic analyzes whether the tag is empty or it contains one or more <schema> tags. If the <types> tag is empty, it again means that no type is defined, which suggests that the anti-pattern is not present. On the other hand, if the <types> tag has <schema> tags defined, it is necessary to check each <schema> tag. If all <schema> tags are empty, the anti-pattern is not present, otherwise it is present.

```
Function Redundant (element1, element2)  //The first time
//receives two data definitions
          if(!HaveSameAttributes(element1, element2))
            return false
          end if
          children1←GetChildren(element1)
          children2←GetChildren(element2)
          if(Size(children1)!=Size(children2))
            return false
          for i=0;i<Size(children1);i++ do
            child1←children1[i]
            child2←children2[i]
            if(!Redundant(child1,child2))
              return false
            end if
          end for
          return true
end function
```

Algorithm 1. Heuristic for detecting *repeated data model anti-pattern*

The detection of *Redundant port-types* anti-pattern requires to revise if a port-type is defined several times in the same WSDL document. Usually, to support another invocation method for a service, providers tend to repeat a port-type, but using data-types specially designed for the new invocation method [10]. Consequently, it is not possible to detect anti-pattern occurrences by looking for exact matching between two port-types. Therefore, the heuristic analyzes if two port-types have the same number of operations and if they have the same names, skipping any message similarity checks.

Redundant data model anti-pattern manifestation is different from *Redundant port-type* anti-pattern manifestation. With *Redundant data model* anti-pattern, the names of the elements that describe the data-type are likely to change, but not the structure of the data-type. Thus, the detection of this anti-pattern involves comparing the structure of each defined data-type. Algorithm 1 shows how two data-type definitions are compared.

The two commonest forms in which the *Whatever type* anti-pattern manifests itself are: (1) when a data-type is defined using the XSD primitive type "anyType", (2) when a data-type definition includes the <any> tag. Both cases allow developers to leave a data-type part undefined because any valid XML content can be inserted afterward in such an undefined part. Therefore, the corresponding heuristic analyzes if <any> tag is present, or some tag have "anyType" as a value of its "type" property.

Finally, another heuristic checks that that all operations within a WSDL document have associated the <documentation> tag and its content is not empty, otherwise an evident occurrence of *Inappropriate or lacking comments* anti-pattern is present.

3.2 Not Immediately Apparent Anti-patterns

Not immediately apparent anti-patterns cannot be detected by syntactically analyzing the WSDL grammar. Instead, their detection requires analyzing the semantics of comments and names present in WSDL documents [10]. Therefore, the rules for detecting anti-patterns of this group are more complex than those of the previous section.

In order to detect if the *Low cohesive operations in the same port-type* anti-pattern occurs in a service description, it is necessary to verify that port-type operations belong to the same domain. Broadly, the heuristic aims to deduce the domain of each individual operation, and then compares deduced domains looking for mismatches. Since the information available of the operations are their names, comments, messages and data-types, which are textual information, our heuristic reduces the problem of classifying operations according to their domain to the well-known problem of classifying text.

Current implementation of the heuristic employs a variation of Rocchio classifier, called Rocchio TF-IDF, because a previous work [19] has empirically shown that Rocchio TF-IDF outperformed other classifiers for the Web Services context. Rocchio TF-IDF represents textual information as vectors, in which each dimension stands for a term and its magnitude is the weight of the term related with the text. Having represented all the textual information of a domain as vectors, the average vector, called centroid, is built for representing the domain. Then, the domain of an operation is deduced by representing it as a vector and comparing it to each domain centroid. Finally, the domain of the most similar average vector is returned as being the domain of that operation. For the sake of conciseness, the reader asking for deep explanations and details about gathering textual information from WSDL documents, representing it as vectors, centroid construction and similarity calculations should refer to [19].

Using Rocchio TF-IDF, operations can be easily classified and if a port-type contains operations that belong to different domains the anti-pattern is considered to be present. The main disadvantages of using Rocchio TF-IDF are that the classifier is only able to classify operations in known domains, and requires an expert to classify a training-set of operations according with their domain. Thus, for the experiments we employed a corpus of WSDL documents that have been previously classified.

The *Ambiguous names* anti-pattern is another Not immediately apparent anti-pattern, which deals with non-explanatory WSDL element names. The first step to detect naming problems in a WSDL document is to check whether the length of any name is neither too short nor too long. Thus, the associated heuristic checks if the length of any name is between a fixed range of characters, otherwise the name is considered as an occurrence of the anti-pattern. For the experiments, we set the range in [3:30] characters.

Second, several words have been identified to be related with non-explanatory or too general names [11]. The unrecommended words are: *thing, class, param, arg, obj, some, execute, return, body, foo, http, soap, result, input, output, in, out*. A name that has any of these words probably is too general; therefore if a name contains one of these words, the corresponding heuristic detects it as an ambiguous name.

Third, each name should have an adequate grammatical structure. The name of an operation should be in the form: <verb> "+" {<noun>|<noun phrase>} because an operation is an action, but in the case of exchanged data (e.g. a message part), its name should be a {<noun>|<noun phrase>} because it represents a concept [10].

To grammatically analyze the structure of a name, our heuristic applies a probabilistic context free grammar parser [20] to operation and part names. With this kind of parsers, a sentence is analyzed and associated with rules that form one or more parsing trees as in traditional context free grammar, but each rule has an independent probability. Therefore, it is possible to calculate the most probably parsing tree for a given sentence by multiplying the probability of all the rules of each derived parsing tree.

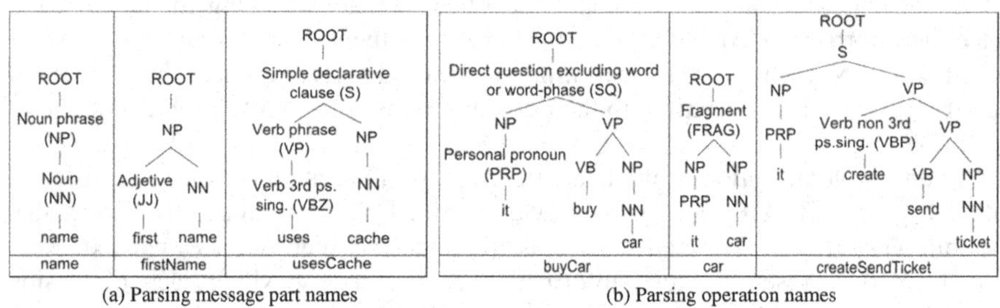

(a) Parsing message part names (b) Parsing operation names

Fig. 1. Parsing tree examples

The heuristic to analyze a message name is to check if the parsing tree derived by the parser has no verb tags. For example, Fig. 1.a depicts the parsing tree of three message names: "name", "firstName", and "usesCache". The first and second names are correct, because their parsing trees do not contain verbs. However, the name "usesCache", starts with a verb so it represents an action and thus it is not correct.

When analyzing an operation name, the heuristic adds to the operation name the word "it" at the beginning of the name to indicate the noun that it should be missing in the name of an operation. For instance, if the operation is named "buyCar", the sentence analyzed by the parser is "it buy car". Although the sentence is not grammatically correct, it is closed enough to the correct sentence because having probabilistic rules makes the parser able to handle malformed sentences [20]. Then, our heuristic counts the number of verbs in the parsing tree. If the number of verbs is different from one, the *Ambiguous name* anti-pattern is detected. Figure 1.b represents parsing trees for three different operation names with the "it" pronoun added as explained above. The first name, which is "buyCar", is correct because it gives the idea that the operation performs one and only one action. In contrast, the second name, which is "car", is a noun then is incorrect because the name has not semantics of what the operation does. Finally, the third operation name, which is "createSendTicket", is also incorrect because it has two verbs meaning that the operation actually performs two actions.

Finally, the last heuristic aims at detecting Not immediately apparent occurrences of *Undercover fault information within standard messages* anti-pattern. Commonly, this anti-pattern has footprints in WSDL documents, but sometimes it requires to analyze service implementation. Our heuristic only detects this anti-pattern when is the first case. To do this, the heuristic verifies whether an operation has a <fault> message defined that means that the errors are handled in the correct manner [10]. Consequently, the presence of a <fault> message is considered enough evidence that the operation presents no symptom of the anti-pattern. If this not the case, the heuristic looks for an occurrence of the Whatever type anti-pattern in the output, and keywords in the operation comments that indicate the presence of the anti-pattern. The set of keywords is: *fault, error, fail, overflow, exception, stackTrace*.

4 Experimental Evaluation

Previous section describes the proposed heuristics for automatically detecting the discoverability anti-patterns introduced by [10]. This section describes the experiments that have been conducted to evaluate the detection effectiveness of these heuristics.

Table 2. Confusion matrixes for the detection of anti-patterns

Automatic detection results per anti-pattern		**Manual detection results**	
		Negative	Positive
Enclosed data model	Negative	116	6
	Positive	0	270
Redundant port-types	Negative	161	4
	Positive	0	227
Redundant data models	Negative	221	2
	Positive	3	166
Whatever types	Negative	339	0
	Positive	3	50
Lacking comments	Negative	135	0
	Positive	0	257
Low cohesive operations in the same port-type	Negative	272	10
	Positive	78	32
Ambiguous names	Negative	67	0
	Positive	9	316
Undercover fault information within standard messages	Negative	351	3
	Positive	4	34

The followed evaluation methodology involves manually analyzing each WSDL document to identify the anti-patterns it has, peer-reviewing manual results (at least three different people reviewed each WSDL document), automatically analyzing the WSDL document using the proposed heuristics, and finally comparing both manual and automatic results. These results are organized per anti-pattern, in which if a WSDL document has the anti-pattern it is classified as "Positive", otherwise it is classified as "Negative". When the manual classification for a WSDL document is equal to the automatic one, it means that the heuristic accurately operates for that document. Achieved results are shown using a confusion matrix. Each row of the matrix represents the number of WSDL documents that were automatically classified using the heuristic associated with a particular anti-pattern. The columns of the matrix show manual classifications, i.e. the number of WSDL documents that has the anti-pattern actually.

The described methodology was followed using the data-set of 392 WSDL documents that it is described in [10]. This data-set[3], which was gathered by Hess et al. [21], has been selected because it is an snapshot of publicly available Web Service on Internet. Once each heuristic was fed with the data-set and its results computed, we built the confusion matrixes. Then, we assessed the accuracy, and false positive/negative rates for each matrix. Table 2 shows the confusion matrixes.

The accuracy of each heuristic was calculated as the number of classification matching over the total of analyzed WSDL documents. For instance, the accuracy of the Redundant data model heuristic was $\frac{221+166}{221+3+166} = 0.987$. The heuristic for detecting Low cohesive operations within the same port-type anti-pattern achieved the lowest accuracy: 0.755. This could be caused by errors that the classifier introduced. Nevertheless, the averaged accuracy for all heuristics was 0.958.

The false positive rate is the proportion of WSDL documents that a heuristic wrongly labels them as having the corresponding anti-pattern. At the same time, the false negative rate is the proportion of WSDL documents that a heuristic wrongly labels as not having the corresponding anti-pattern. A false negative rate equals to 1 would mean that a detection heuristic missed all anti-pattern occurrences. For these rates, the lower the achieved values the better the detection effectiveness. The averaged false positive rate was 0.036, and the averaged false negative rate was 0.052.

We individually analyzed each WSDL document that was wrongly classified by the heuristics. Afterward, we detected that the reason behind 16 incorrect classifications was that those WSDL documents adhere to the 2001 WSDL standard, whereas the implementation of the heuristics depends on the 1999 standard. Therefore, 16 mismatches were caused by current implementation of the heuristics and not by a heuristic itself.

5 Conclusions and Future Work

Many Web Service problems for being discovered and re-used, have been recognized as having their roots in WSDL discoverability anti-patterns [10]. This paper presents novel heuristics for detecting these anti-patterns. Proposed heuristics have been

[3] Data-set: http://www.andreas-hess.info/projects/annotator/index.html

employed for analyzing a corpus of real-world Web Services, which had been manually analyzed. Reported experiments show that the averaged accuracy of the heuristics was 0.958, and the false positive and false negative averaged rates of 0.036 and 0.052, respectively. All in all, the proposed heuristics represent an advance in the creation of Web Services that are easier to be understood and discovered, which by themselves symbolize the basic blocks for *e*-applications relying on the SOC paradigm or the new wave of service-oriented software systems, such as Cloud Computing [22], SaaS or PaaS [23].

The anti-pattern detector can minimized the impact of the commonest bad practice by helping developers to detect potential problems in their services before they are made available. In addition, Web Service registries may use the anti-pattern detector for informing service developers about possible problems in their services, so developers can be aware of those problems for avoiding them in future versions of the services.

More experiments should be done in the future, since the reported results cannot be generalized, in particular those related to Not immediately apparentanti-patterns. In this sense, we are planning to employ the heuristics with a recently published repository of real Web Services [24]. Besides, this work will be extended to incorporate a heuristic for analyzing the descriptiveness of comments present in WSDL documents. Currently, we are evaluating a heuristic that combines WordNet, an electronic lexical database, and a natural language parser. Preliminary results are encouraging.

Another line of future research involves the synchronization between changes in WSDL documents and service implementations, because removing the identified anti-patterns from a service description may imply changes in the underlying software. Furthermore, some version support technique is necessary to allow consumers that use the old WSDL document version to continue using the service until they migrate to the improved WSDL document [25].

Acknowledgments

We thank Pablo Inchausti and Daniel Molero for helping us to implement the heuristics. Also, thanks to ANPCyT for supporting this research through grants PAE-PICT 2007-02311 and PAE-PICT 2007-02312.

References

1. Janowski, A.O.T., Estevez, E.: Rapid development of electronic public services: a case study in electronic licensing service. In: Proceedings of the 8th Annual International Conference on Digital Government Research (DG.O 2007), pp. 292–293 (2007)
2. Bichler, M., Lin, K.-J.: Service-Oriented Computing. Computer 39(3), 99–101 (2006)
3. Papazoglou, M.P., Van Den Heuvel, W.-J.: Service-oriented design and development methodology. International Journal of Web Engineering and Technology 2(4), 412–442 (2006)
4. Grefen, P.W.P.J., Ludwig, H., Dan, A., Angelov, S.: An analysis of Web Services support for dynamic business process outsourcing. Information & Software Technology 48(11), 1115–1134 (2006)
5. Chung, J.-Y., Lin, K.-J., Mathieu, R.G.: Guest editors' introduction: Web Services computing–advancing software interoperability. Computer 36(10), 35–37 (2003)

6. Mateos, C., Crasso, M., Zunino, A., Campo, M.: Adding semantic Web Services matching and discovery support to the Movilog platform. In: Proceedings of the IFIP 19th World Computer Congress (IFIP 2006). IFIP, vol. 217, pp. 51–60 (2006)
7. Crasso, M., Zunino, A., Campo, M.: Combining query-by-example and query expansion for simplifying Web Service discovery. Information Systems Frontiers (2009) (in Press)
8. Foster, I.: Service-oriented science. Science 308(5723), 814–817 (2005)
9. Fan, J., Kambhampati, S.: A snapshot of public Web Services. SIGMOD Rec. 34(1), 24–32 (2005)
10. Rodriguez, J.M., Crasso, M., Zunino, A., Campo, M.: Improving Web Service descriptions for effective service discovery. Science of Computer Programming 75(11), 1001–1021 (2010)
11. Brian Blake, M., Nowlan, M.F.: Taming Web Services from the wild. IEEE Internet Computing 12(5), 62–69 (2008)
12. Garofalakis, J., Panagis, Y., Sakkopoulos, E., Tsakalidis, A.: Contemporary Web Service Discovery Mechanisms. Journal of Web Engineering 5(3), 265–290 (2006)
13. McCool, R.: Rethinking the Semantic Web, part II. IEEE Internet Computing 10(1), 96, 93–95 (2006)
14. Dong, B., Qi, G., Gu, X., Wei, X.: Web service-oriented manufacturing resource applications for networked product development. Advanced Engineering Informatics 22(3), 282–295 (2008); Collaborative Design and Manufacturing
15. Beaton, J., Myers, B.A., Stylos, J., Ehret, R., Karstens, J., Efeoglu, A., Jeong, S.Y., Xie, Y., Busse, D.K.: Improving Documentation for eSOA APIs through User Studies. In: Pipek, V., Rosson, M.B., de Ruyter, B., Wulf, V. (eds.) IS-EUD 2009. LNCS, vol. 5435, pp. 86–105. Springer, Heidelberg (2009)
16. Pasley, J.: Avoid XML schema wildcards for Web Service interfaces. IEEE Internet Computing 10(3), 72–79 (2006)
17. Beaton, J., Jeong, S.Y., Xie, Y., Jack, J., Myers, B.A.: Usability challenges for enterprise service-oriented architecture APIs. In: IEEE Symposium on Visual Languages and Human-Centric Computing (VL/HCC), pp. 193–196 (September 2008)
18. Brown, W.J., Malveau, R.C., McCormick, H.W., Mowbray, T.J.: AntiPatterns: Refactoring Software, Architectures and Projects in Crisis. John Wiley, Chichester (1998)
19. Crasso, M., Zunino, A., Campo, M.: AWSC: An approach to Web Service classification based on machine learning techniques. Revista Iberoamericana de Inteligencia Artificial 37(12), 25–36 (2008)
20. Klein, D., Manning, C.D.: Accurate unlexicalized parsing. In: Proceedings of the 41st Annual Meeting on Association for Computational Linguistics (ACL 2003), pp. 423–430 (2003)
21. Heß, A., Johnston, E., Kushmerick, N.: ASSAM: A tool for semi-automatically annotating semantic Web Services. In: McIlraith, S.A., Plexousakis, D., van Harmelen, F. (eds.) ISWC 2004. LNCS, vol. 3298, pp. 320–334. Springer, Heidelberg (2004)
22. Buyya, R., Yeo, C.S., Venugopal, S., Broberg, J., Brandic, I.: Cloud computing and emerging it platforms: Vision, hype and reality for delivering computing as the 5th utility. Future Generation Computer Systems 25(6), 599–616 (2009)
23. Zaplata, S., Lamersdorf, W.: Towards mobile process as a service. In: Proceedings of 25th ACM Symposium on Applied Computing (SAC 2010), pp. 372–379 (March 2010)
24. Al-Masri, E., Mahmoud, Q.H.: Qos-based discovery and ranking of Web Services. In: Proceedings of the 16th International Conference on Computer Communications and Networks (ICCCN 2007), pp. 529–534 (2007)
25. Juric, M.B., Sasa, A., Brumen, B., Rozman, I.: WSDL and UDDI extensions for version support in Web Services. Journal of Systems and Software SI: Architectural Decisions and Rationale 82(8), 1326–1343 (2009)

Exploiting the Social Capital of Folksonomies for Web Page Classification

Daniela Godoy[1,2] and Analía Amandi[1,2]

[1] ISISTAN Research Institute, UNICEN University
Campus Universitario, Paraje Arroyo Seco, CP 7000,
Tandil, Buenos Aires, Argentina
[2] CONICET, Buenos Aires, Argentina
{dgodoy,amandi}@exa.unicen.edu.ar

Abstract. Collaborative tagging systems (CTSs), also known as folksonomies, have grown in popularity on the Web and social tagging has become an important feature of many Web 2.0 services. It has been argued that the power of tagging lies in the ability for people to freely determine the appropriate tags for resources without having to rely on a predefined lexicon or hierarchy. The free-form nature of tagging causes a number of problems in this social classification scheme, such as synonymy and morphological variety. However, social tagging can be a valuable source of information to help in the organization of Web resources. In this paper we present an empirical analysis carried out to determine the importance of social tagging in Web page classification. Experimental results showed that tag-based classification outperformed classifiers based on full-text of documents.

Keywords: Social Tagging Systems, Web Page Classification, Folksonomies.

1 Introduction

Collaborative tagging systems (CTSs) are one of the most popularized content sharing applications associated with Web 2.0 and an important feature of many Web 2.0 services. The practice of collectively creating and managing tags to annotate and categorize content, has achieved widespread success on the Web as it allows to easily browse and search huge volume of shared resources. In sites such as *Del.icio.us*[1], *Technorati*[2] or *Flickr*[3] users annotate a variety of resources (Web pages, blog posts or pictures) using a freely chosen set of keywords in order to improve search and retrieval of such information.

Folksonomies [7] are the primary structure of the novel social classification scheme introduced by tagging systems and are usually contrasted with traditional predefined taxonomies used on the Web. This scheme relies on the convergence of

[1] http://del.icio.us/
[2] http://technorati.com/
[3] http://www.flickr.com/

W. Cellary and E. Estevez (Eds.): I3E 2010, IFIP AICT 341, pp. 151–160, 2010.

tagging efforts of a large community of users to a common categorization system that can be effectively used to organize and navigate large information spaces. In fact, the term folksonomy is a blend of the words taxonomy and folk, and stands for conceptual structures created by the people [6].

In spite of the novel mechanisms for finding interesting resources in vast information spaces provided by collaborative tagging systems, problems associated with the completely unsupervised nature of social tagging (ambiguity, synonymy, noise, etc.) may reduce its efficiency in content indexing and searching, thereby hindering the task of users.

In order to effectively organize on-line information, however, distributed classification provided by folksonomies might become an essential and value resource. In this sense, social tagging can help to automatize or assist the time consuming and laborious task of manually classifying documents into a set of pre-defined categories. Hammond et al. [5] and Guy and Tonkin [12] agree that tagging can play a complimentary role alongside more formal types of organization.

In this paper we empirically evaluate social tagging information, consisting of collaboratively generated, open-ended tags, to categorize content such as Web pages. For this purpose, we carried out a number of experiments using a collection of pages categorized by experts in a Web directory and the tag assignments given by non-expert users in a folksonomy. Several representations of tag vectors as well as pre-processing operations over tags were also evaluated.

The rest of the paper is organized as follows. Section 2 presents the empirical analysis carried out to compare content-based with tag-based classification of Web pages. Section 3 briefly reviews related research. Finally, our findings are summarized in Section 4.

2 Empirical Evaluation

To investigate the role social tagging can play in Web page categorization we performed an empirical analysis using *Social-ODP-2k9* [13] dataset, which basically links Web pages with their corresponding categories in a Web directory such as the Open Directory Project (ODP)[4] and tags assigned to these pages by users in a popular social bookmarking site such as *Del.icio.us*.

The Open Directory is one of the largest, most comprehensive human-edited directory of the Web. It is maintained by an international community of volunteer editors who evaluate sites for inclusion in the directory and categorize each Web document into one or more predefined and hierarchically organized categories. In *Del.icio.us*, in contrast, users store, share, and discover bookmarks using a non-hierarchical classification system in which they tag their bookmarks with freely chosen index terms.

Social-ODP-2k9 [13] is a dataset created during December 2008 and January 2009 with data retrieved from *Del.icio.us*, *StumbleUpon*[5], the ODP and the Web. This dataset contains 12.616 unique URLs, all of them annotated by at least 100 users to ensure Web

[4] http://www.dmoz.org/

[5] http://www.stumbleupon.com/

page popularity. For each of these Web pages the dataset has the corresponding category from the ODP as well as the number of users that annotate them, the top 10 list of assigned tags, the full tag activity (FTA) and also notes and reviews about the page.

In this paper we used the category assigned for ODP to Web documents as ground-truth or expert categorization, to compare with tagging of non-expert users provided by *Del.icio.us* folksonomy. For classification we used the 17 categories in the first level of the ODP taxonomy. In regards to social tagging information we used from the dataset both the list of the 10 most popular tags, including their number of occurrence, and the full tag activity (FTA) listing all tags assigned to a resource, which is limited to the latest 2000 users.

2.1 Content-Based Classification

In order to establish the relative importance of content and tags in Web page classification, we first evaluated the performance of text classifiers over the full text of documents as well as their titles.

From the total 12.616 Web pages in the *Social-ODP-2k9* dataset, experiments reported in this paper were performed over the 9.611 English-written pages identified using the classification approach presented in [3]. The content of these Web pages was filtered using a standard stop-word list and the Porter stemming algorithm [11] was applied to the remaining words.

Table 1 summarizes the resulting Web pages collection and its main statistics. The notation used for reporting these statistics is based on the formal definition of folksonomies. These social structures can be defined as a tuple $\mathbb{F}:=(U,T,R,Y,\prec)$ which describes the users *U*, resources *R*, and tags *T*, and the user-based assignment of tags to resources by a ternary relation between them, i.e. $Y \subseteq U \times T \times R$ [6]. In this folksonomy, $\prec$ is a user-specific sub-tag/super-tag-relation possible existing between tags, i.e. $\prec \subseteq U \times T \times T$.

Web pages were randomly partitioned into a training set of approximately 70% of the collection, 6.727 pages, and the remaining 30% for testing, 2.884 pages. In the experiments we compared the performance of three classifiers *k*NN (considering *k*=100), Naïve Bayes and SMO, a sequential minimal optimization algorithm for training a Support Vector Machines (SVM) classifier using a polynomial kernel [10]. For evaluating the classifiers we used the standard precision and recall summarized by F-measure as well as accuracy [2].

Figure 1 depicts the scores of F-measure achieved by the three classifiers per class and in average. SMO outperforms Naïve Bayes in all cases and *k*NN showed a very poor performance. As a result of the highly unbalanced distributions of examples in the 17 classes some categories obtained high scores, such as *Computers*, whereas classifiers failed to recognize examples in other categories, like *Adult*. Figure 2 shows the results when the classifiers were trained using the title of documents only. In this case, the results observed the same trends, although with inferior performance than full-text classification.

Table 1. Summary of statistics for Web pages in the dataset used for experimentation

Category	|R|	# unique words in text content	# unique words in title	|T| in the top 10 lists	|T| in the FTA
Adult	25	2.841	94	25	2.920
Arts	920	46.006	1.657	1.524	62.081
Business	427	18.313	1.096	1.125	37.127
Computers	2.922	80.117	3.908	3.051	165.485
Games	232	18.953	544	566	15.571
Health	95	7.760	298	351	9.815
Home	216	15.750	536	529	19.773
Kids and Teens	311	13.383	651	778	30.839
News	115	11.812	265	305	16.857
Recreation	249	16.215	662	728	21.211
Reference	521	22.625	914	1.064	55.266
Regional	1.158	38.208	2.225	2.371	78.707
Science	662	31.248	1.214	1.333	58.376
Shopping	412	19.953	1.269	945	27.037
Society	842	37.335	1.572	1.654	65.275
Sports	84	12.039	271	269	4.901
World	420	27.616	1.248	1.271	45.160
All categories	9.611	199.968	10.865	8.932	426.086

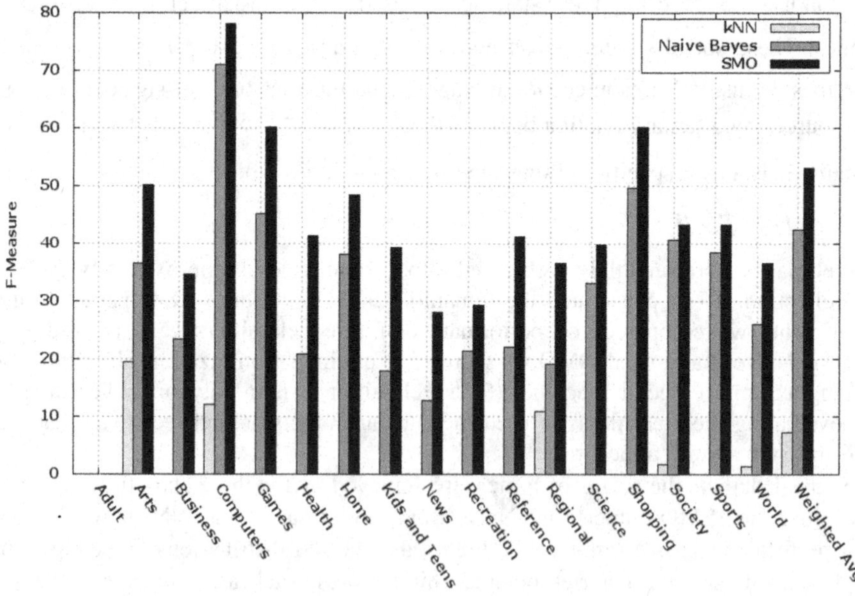

Fig. 1. F-measure scores per class for several text classifiers applied to Web page contents

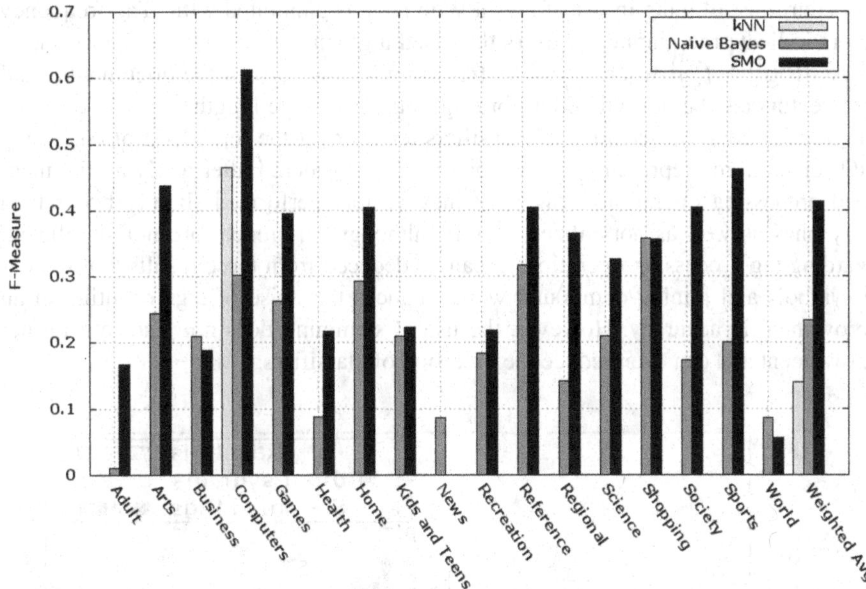

Fig. 2. F-measure scores per class for several text classifiers applied to the titles of Web pages

2.2 Tag-Based Classification

In social classification schemes, raw tags are noisy and inconsistent as they are not introduced according to a controlled vocabulary. In consequence, to determine whether tags are a valuable source of information for classification of Web page some filtering techniques were considered and compared.

Tags variations can be attributed to several factors [12,4]:

- compound words consisting of more than two words that are not grouped consistently. Often users insert punctuation to separate the words, for example *ancient-egypt*, *ancient_egypt* and *ancientgypt*.
- use of symbols in tags, symbols such as # , - , + , /, : _, &,! are frequently used at the beginning of tags to cause some incidental effect such as forcing the interface to list some tag at the top of an alphabetical listing
- morphological problems given by the use of singular, plural or other derived forms of words. For example, blog, blogs and blogging.

Other factors that might account for tag variations include misspelling and incorrect encodings.

Experimental evaluation was performed to determine the effect of two processing operations over tags tending to normalize them. The original raw tags were filtered to remove the symbols mentioned before as well as join compound words in a first processing considered. Then, tags were stemmed to their morphological roots using Porter stemmer algorithm.

In these experiments we also compared different weighting schemes for the resulting tags. Binary vectors were constructed to indicate the occurrence or non-occurrence of a tag in list of tags a Web page is annotated with. Tag frequency vectors indicate the number of users that used a given tag to annotate the resource, this is $(\log(1+f_{ij}))$ where f_{ij} is the frequency of the tag i in the document j, and these vectors can be normalized according to their average length.

Figure 3 shows the accuracy of classifiers leaned over the top 10 list of tags using SMO for the three representations of tag vectors considered after applying the mentioned processing operations. Tag frequency vectors performed slightly better than binary ones as well as normalized vectors, although differences are not significant. Regarding tag processing operations it can be deduced from these results that removing symbols and joining compound words reduces the noise of tags resulting in an improvement in accuracy. However, the use of stemming does not lead to a further improvement and can even reduce the precision of classifiers.

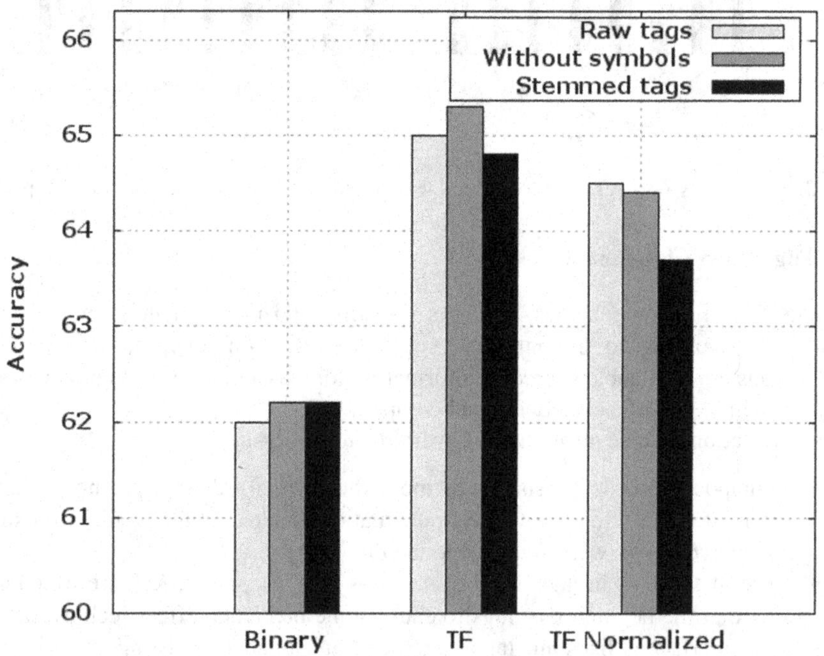

Fig. 3. Classification accuracy using tags in the top 10 list

Figure 4 depicts the results using the same configuration of experiments but applied to tags in the full tag activity (FTA). FTA leads to a larger list of tags in spite of being limited to the 2000 last users. In consequence, normalization of TF vectors improves the performance of classifiers. In contrast to the previous experiments with the top 10 list of tags, raw tags in these experiments reach better accuracy levels than other representations, although differences are not significant. Stemming of tags in this situation seems to improve the accuracy of classification.

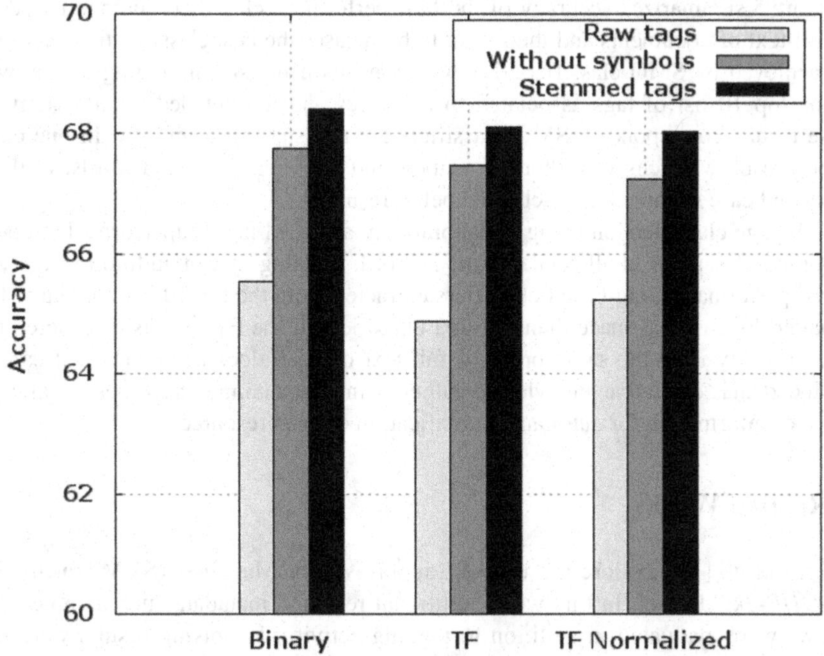

Fig. 4. Classification accuracy using tags in the FTA

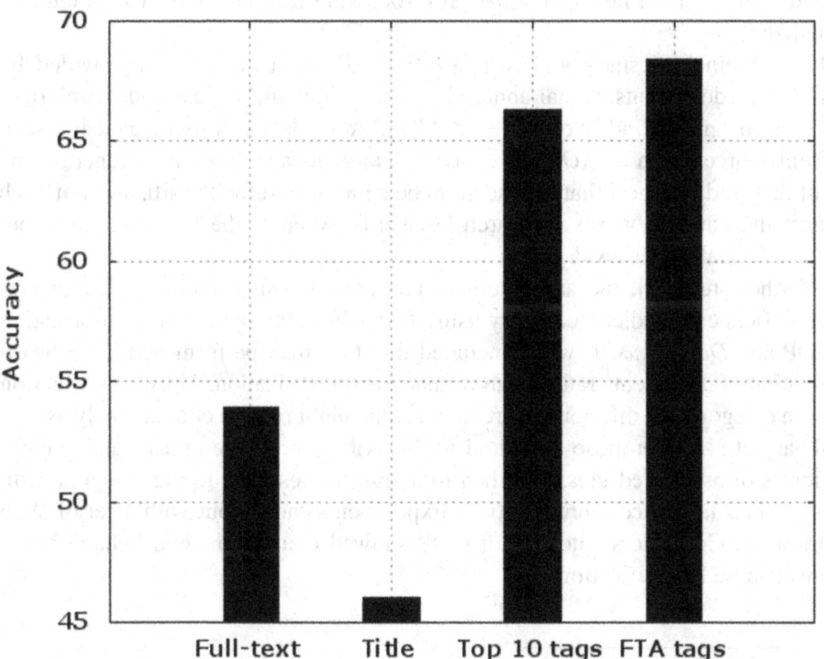

Fig. 5. Comparison of classification accuracy of content-based and tag-based classifiers

Figure 5 summarizes accuracy of the best performing classifiers learned based on the full-text of documents and their title. In both cases the best classification accuracy was achieved by SMO classifiers. Likewise, results using social tagging are showed for the top 10 list of tags associated to resources and the detailed tagging activity. These results correspond to SMO classifiers learned starting from tags. In one case, the best result was achieved filtering symbols and unifying compound words, while in the second case stemmed tags achieved better results.

Web page classification using collaboratively assigned tags outperforms both content-based classifiers in all scenarios. It is worth noticing that in addition to the improved performance, tag-based classifiers extracted from the top 10 list are learned in a smaller dimensional space than full-text classifiers. If the FTA tag is considered the dimensionality is in the same order of full-text of Web documents. Thus, it can be concluded that collective knowledge gathered in folksonomies becomes a valuable source of information for automatic classification of Web resources.

3 Related Works

Zubiaga et al. [13] explore the use of Support Vector Machines (SVM) in the *Social-ODP-2k9* dataset. In this work additional resource metadata such as notes and reviews were evaluated in addition to tagging activity. Promising results were obtained using tags and comments for Web page classification. In contrast to this work, we concentrate the evaluation in the tagging activity of users within a folksonomy and evaluate the impact of some pre-processing techniques over tags tending to normalize them.

Noll and Meinel [9] study and compare three different annotations provided by readers of Web documents, social annotations, hyperlink anchor text and search queries of users trying to find Web pages. *CABS120k08*[6] dataset was created for such study from sources such as *AOL500k*, ODP, *Del.icio.us* and *Google* in general. The results of this study suggest that tags seem to be better suited for classification of Web documents than anchor words or search keywords, whereas the last ones are more useful for information retrieval.

In a further study [8], the same authors analyzed at which hierarchy depth tag-based classifiers can predict a category using *DMOZ100k06*[7] dataset with information from ODP and *Del.icio.us*. It was concluded that tags may perform better for broad categorization of documents rather than for narrow categorization. Thus, classification of pages in categories at inferior hierarchical levels might require content analysis.

Aliakbary et al. [1] propose a method for describing both Web pages and categories in terms of associated tags, and then to assign the resource to the category with the most similar tag-space representation. Experiments carried out with a set of Web pages from the Computers category of ODP showed that the method behave better than content-based classification.

[6] http://www.michael-noll.com/wiki/CABS120k08/

[7] http://www.michael-noll.com/wiki/DMOZ100k06

4 Conclusions

In this paper we presented an empirical analysis to establish the ways in which social tagging can contribute to automatic Web document classification, then, helping to bridge the gap between the strict structure of taxonomies and the completely open nature of folksonomies. Experimental results obtained with a collection of Web pages categorized by experts in a Web directory not only showed that tag-based classifiers outperformed content-based ones in broad level categories, but also that pre-processing tags operations such as removal of symbols, compound words and reduction of morphological variants have a discrete impact on classification performance. The first operations improve classification accuracy in most experiments. However, stemming demonstrate to reduce accuracy when fewer tags were used (the top 10 tags assigned to resources), whereas it showed to be useful when more tags were involved in classification. Other operations over tags that we will investigate in future works are the correction of misspelled words and enconding variations. Even tough Web page organization in directories is an interesting application for tag-based classification, other prominent application in which social tagging can be exploiting is personalized Web classification (for example, interesting/uninteresting Web pages).

Acknowledgements

This research was supported by The National Council of Scientific and Technological Research (CONICET) under grant PIP Nº 114-200901-00381.

References

1. Aliakbary, S., Abolhassani, H., Rahmani, H., Nobakht, B.: Web page classification using social tags. In: Proceedings of the 2009 International Conference on Computational Science and Engineering (CSE 2009), pp. 588–593 (2009)
2. Baeza-Yates, R., Ribeiro-Neto, B.: Modern Information Retrieval. Addison-Wesley Longman Publishing, Amsterdam (1999)
3. Cavnar, W., Trenkle, J.: N-gram-based text categorization. In: Proceedings of 3rd Annual Symposium on Document Analysis and Information Retrieval, Las Vegas, USA, pp. 161–175 (1994)
4. Echarte, F., Astrain, J., Córdoba, A., Villadangos, J.: Pattern matching techniques to identify syntactic variations of tags in folksonomies. In: Lytras, M.D., Carroll, J.M., Damiani, E., Tennyson, R.D. (eds.) WSKS 2008. LNCS (LNAI), vol. 5288, pp. 557–564. Springer, Heidelberg (2008)
5. Hammond, T., Hannay, T., Lund, B., Scott, J.: Social bookmarking tools (i): A general review. D-Lib Magazine 11 (2005)
6. Hotho, A., Jáschke, R., Schmitz, C., Stumme, G.: Information retrieval in folksonomies: Search and ranking. In: Sure, Y., Domingue, J. (eds.) ESWC 2006. LNCS, vol. 4011, pp. 411–426. Springer, Heidelberg (2006)
7. Mathes, A.: Folksonomies - cooperative classification and communication through shared metadata. Computer Mediated Communication (2004)

8. Noll, M.G., Meinel, C.: Exploring social annotations for Web document classification. In: Proceedings of the 2008 ACM Symposium on Applied Computing (SAC 2008), pp. 2315–2320 (2008)
9. Noll, M.G., Meinel, C.: The metadata triumvirate: Social annotations, anchor texts and search queries. In: IEEE/WIC/ACM International Conference on Web Intelligence and Intelligent Agent Technology, vol. 1, pp. 640–647 (2008)
10. Platt, J.: Fast training of support vector machines using sequential minimal optimization. In: Burges, C., Schoelkopf, B., Smola, A. (eds.) Advances in Kernel Methods - Support Vector Learning. MIT Press, Cambridge (1998)
11. Porter, M.: An algorithm for suffix stripping program. Program 14(3), 130–137 (1980)
12. Tonkin, E., Guy, M.: Folksonomies: Tidying up tags? D-Lib 12(1) (2006)
13. Zubiaga, A., Martínez, R., Fresn, V.: Getting the most out of social annotations for Web page classification. In: Proceedings of the 9th ACM Symposium on Document Engineering (DocEng 2009), Munich, Germany, pp. 74–83 (2009)

Guidelines to Transform Industry Clusters in Virtual Organization Breeding Environments – A Case Study

Fabiano Baldo[1] and Ricardo J. Rabelo[2]

[1] Department of Computer Science, Santa Catarina State University, Zip Code 89223-100, Joinville, Brazil
[2] Department of Automation and Systems, Federal University of Santa Catarina, PO Box 476, Zip Code 88040-970, Florianópolis, Brazil
baldo@joinville.udesc.br, rabelo@das.ufsc.br

Abstract. This paper encompasses the specific problem of how transforming industry clusters in environments prepared to create Virtual Organizations. This kind of coalitions is known as Virtual Organization Breeding Environments (VBEs). In order to reach the envisaged objective a set of guidelines for implementing VBEs has been proposed and its current results have been presented here. These guidelines are strongly based on modeling frameworks. This approach is being tested in a cluster of moulds and dies producers from Brazil. In the future, it is intended to use these guidelines as a structured approach to systematize the implementation of any type of VBE.

Keywords: Virtual Organization, Virtual Organization Breeding Environment, Members Preparedness, VBE Implementation Methodology.

1 Introduction

Recently, Brazilian Small and Medium size Enterprises (SME) are increasingly establishing alliances with local competitor in order to increase their national and international competitiveness. The importance of strategic alliances has been pointed out by many authors as a way to augment industries' competitiveness [1]. Pursuing the advantages brought by strategic alliances, in 1990's Brazilian industry clusters started to create strategic alliances over the country based on a so-called local productive arrangement concept. Despite of the benefits of this initiative, it has been realized that this form of alliance is limited to face some new business requirements, as volatility of economics, commercial barriers, global competition and innovation needs. [2]. New forms of alliances have been recently arisen to cope with these requirements under the scope of the conceptualization called Collaborative Networked Organizations (CNO).

Considering the original goals of local productive arrangements, among the new collaboration forms identified by Camarinha-Matos et al. [3], VBE has been seen as its natural evolution. Virtual Organization Breeding Environments (VBEs) can be defined as a long-term alliance of organizations aimed at offering conditions to

W. Cellary and E. Estevez (Eds.): I3E 2010, IFIP AICT 341, pp. 161–172, 2010.

support the rapid configuration of virtual organizations (VO) to attend given business opportunities [4]. Among many competitive advantages, VBEs have the potential to enhance collaboration and knowledge sharing among members, to decrease costs and risks, to leave them more competitive acting jointly and to reach new markets.

The establishment of a VBE is a very complex task regarding the number of technical and non-technical aspects to embrace. Existing VBEs have fundamentally been created by *ad-hoc* approaches, which have created some obstacles for their proper scalability and configurability during their typical evolution [5] [6]. In the last years, a relevant number of works have presented more solid theoretical models for CNO formation, including VBE creation. An important contribution to answer this question has been proposed by Romero et al. [7]. In this work it has been devised a methodology to create VBEs based on a reference framework for modeling CNOs. Although presenting more concrete sequence of actions to create VBEs, it is too generic yet to be applied indeed. Therefore, it requires an additional effort when trying to build VBEs using it. This additional effort is mainly required to harmonize the considerable discrepancy of preparedness among VBE members candidate. Afsarmanesh et al. [4] state that candidate members' preparedness is a crucial element for the successful creation of VBEs. As can be seen, it is not sufficient to have methodologies to implement VBE if these methodologies do not take into consideration the VBE candidates' preparedness. So, the problem is how to take into account candidate's preparedness when specifying the VBE implementation methodology?

In order to contribute to answer this question, it is assumed as hypothesis that a more correct identification of candidates' preparedness would speed-up the VBE creation process and decrease launching costs, as well as increase members' confidence and their overall preparation. In this sense, this paper presents a set of guidelines to transform industry clusters in VBEs where the candidates' preparedness has the central hole in the specification of the VBE implementation methodology. The contributions of this work are been tested in a case study performed in a cluster of moulds and dies producers from Brazil.

In this paper, section 2 presents the guidelines proposed to implement VBEs. Section 3 describes the VBE model specified for the case study. Section 4 depicts the characteristics to assess VBE member candidates. Section 5 shows the evaluation of the VBE member candidates. Section 6 specifies the VBE implementation methodology. Finally, section 7 presents some conclusions and future work.

2 Guidelines for VBE Implementation

This section presents the set of guidelines for implementing VBEs. This approach has been developed based on previous modeling frameworks and implementation methodologies that will be presented in section 3. The structure approach is composed of the following steps presented in Figure 1:

1. VBE Model Specification. This step aim at specifying a model to represent every key-element to be considered for implementing a VBE for a particular cluster. This specification should be based on reference frameworks, so that, a complete reviewing of the state-of-the-art is needed. This representation provides a better understanding of all elements involved in the VBE implementation.

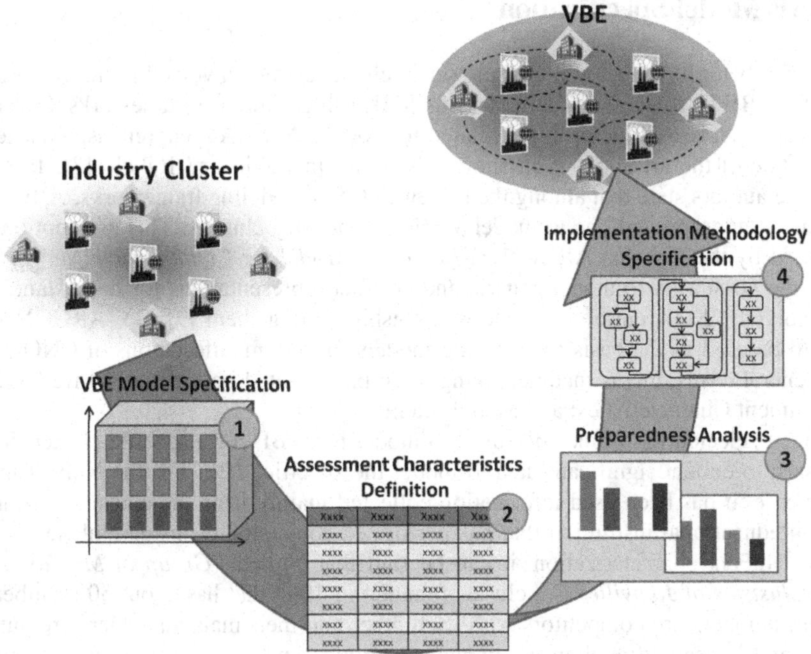

Fig. 1. Steps for VBE Implementation

2. Assessment Characteristics Definition. This step defines the assessment characteristics that are going to be used to check cluster members' preparedness. Based on the model previously specified, this step intends to describe the relevant characteristics that should be considered when assessing actual organizations' preparedness to be part of a VBE. These characteristics should be classified according to some predefined perspectives.
3. Preparedness analysis. This step aims at applying individual assessment in order to map the main weakness and strengths of each organization and thus to have a more comprehensive and precise overview about the global organizations' needs. This assessment can be performed using questionnaires specified based on assessment characteristics defined in step2 and its main propose is to provide a more tuned plan to implement the methodology for the VBE implementation.
4. Implementation Methodology Specification. This step specifies the methodology for implementing the VBE for the specific group of organizations. This methodology identifies the activities, their relationships and the involved actors involved in the VBE implementation. This methodology is specified based on the organizations' preparedness analysis done in step 3.

Next sections detail these steps applied in a case study performed in a cluster of moulds and dies producers called NuFerJ that is located in Joinville – Brazil.

3 VBE Model Specification

In order to better understand the whole set of characteristics involved in the construction of a VBE it is necessary to model this VBE using reference frameworks. Several works have addressed the problem related to model CNOs. A comprehensive review of the state-of-the-art about such subject is found in Baldo and Rabelo [8]. In this work, the authors state that among the reviewed CNO modeling frameworks, ARCON is the most appropriated one to model VBEs for industry clusters. This assumption is supported by the fact that ARCON (*A Reference Model for Collaborative Networks*) brings the possibility to model generic and abstract representations for understanding the involved CNO's entities and the relationship among them [9]. So, ARCON intends to be used as the basis for deriving models for any manifestations of CNOs. In very general terms, this is made applying three inter-related perspectives: Life Cycle; Environment Characteristics; and Model Intents.

Having selected the framework used to model the VBE for a specific cluster, it is necessary to collect significant data to model the specific VBE. For the NuFerJ particular case, it has been used information collected mainly from the cluster itself and from an educational institution that has performed some studies inside NuFerJ. Concerning NuFerJ characterization, it can be said that NuFerJ (*Group of Moulds and Dies Industries of Joinville*) is a cluster founded in 1993 that has about 50 members. Several members are competitors with each other and their main customers are automobile and household appliance companies. Moulds and dies are very unique parts that are produced only once and each one of them uses to be very complex to manufacture. This kind of industry uses high-speed CNC machines to transform large blocks of steel in complex moulds [10]. Considering the increasing and extreme hard world-wide competition, NuFerJ is looking for an alternative model which allows its members to better and more effectively prepare themselves for this new reality.

Taking into account ARCON modeling framework, a NuFerJ VBE Model has been created. This model classifies every element necessary to design the NuFerJ VBE, which in turn will guide the work towards its implementation. Baldo and Rabelo [8] presents the VBE model created for NuFerJ, considering all the characteristics and elements involved in the Endogenous and Exogenous ARCON's subspaces [11].

4 Assessment Characteristics Definition

As mention before, to implement a VBE it is necessary first to know quite well the cluster and its members in order to specify the implementation methodology. A way to perform such recognition is doing an assessment of the cluster members. This assessment evaluates the cluster members' preparedness to be part of a VBE. Conceive assessment strategies, e.g. questionnaires, base of the information available at the VBE model is to complex due to its broad coverage. So, to overcome this obstacle it is proposed to extract from the model the relevant characteristics and to organize them into perspectives of assessment. Table 1 shows the assessment characteristics extracted from the NuFerJ VBE model and used to assess NuFerJ members' preparedness.

Table 1. Perspectives and Characteristics for NuFerJ Members' Assessment

Business Process	Organizational Structure	Resources (human and ICT)	Organizational Culture	Market
- Production planning process - Production control process and data collection (for performance assessment) - Purchase process - Supplier selection process (enterprises and logistics operator) - Budget specification process - Raw material quotation process - Service providers search process - Financial management process - Work power hire process - Third-part hire process and production control - Software acquisition, deployment and maintenance process	- Departments well-defined and structured - Functions and responsibilities defined - Low accumulation of functions per employee - Flexible structure and with few levels - Methodology for performance measurement and assessment well-defined and deployed	**ICT** - High utilization of ICT - Enterprise resource planning system - Internet resources - Internet utilization, systems via Web - Collaborative systems utilization (e-mail, chat, skype, wflow, forum, etc.) - Enterprise website (used as an Intranet service) - Customer relationship management system - CAE/CAD/CAPP/CAM systems - Budget specification system - History record system - Systems for production control and data collection - Logistics system - Stock and resource management systems Humans - Qualified Employees - Employees with good education (including other languages) - Employees adapted to work with technology - Employees with flexibility for chancing Equipments - CNC machines - Industrial networks - Data collectors	- Resource utilization optimization - Quality prioritization - Pro-activity - Standards and norms utilization (including technology and process models) - Partnership stimulation (interns and externs) - Processes and conducts documentation - Group working - Creativity motivation - Employee satisfaction fostering - Participation in events with other enterprises - Exchange experiences with other enterprises - Sharing of information with service providers - Record of past experiences - Past knowledge utilization - Work with enterprises or customers of other countries - Participation in any type of strategic alliance	- Target market well-defined - Market strategy well-defined - Customer interaction (post-sales) - Product advertisement (Marketing) - Brand enrichment - Long-term planning - Co-creation of products (i.e. with customers)

5 Preparedness Analysis

The characteristics contained in the perspectives presented in section 4 can be used to specify questions for evaluating how prepared an industry is to be part of a VBE. Roughly, it can be said that each question is based on a characteristic presented in Table 1. It means, each characteristic in Table 1 has been written as a question in order to ask for each candidate if it presents such VBE requirement. However, when appropriated, some characteristics have been combined into a single question due to their intrinsic correlation. Figure 2 presents an example of question.

1. Does the organization have a defined production planning process?
☐ **Yes** ☐ Excellent ☐ Good ☐ Not good ☐ Bad ☐ **No**
Comments: ______________________________

Fig. 2. Example of question presented in the questionnaire

The questionnaire conceived contains 45 questions divided into five perspectives as follows:

- **Business Process**: 9 questions;
- **Organizational Structure**: 4 questions;
- **Resources (human and ICT)**: 14 questions;
- **Organizational Culture**: 13 questions;
- **Market**: 5 questions.

Each question has been conceived in a way to estimate the level of preparation of an industry. This level is estimated through a scale of values on which the industries should fit in one of them. This scale is composed of the following values: excellent, good, not good and bad. Besides that, each question has two check boxes containing yes and no values, respectively. These options are necessaries in situations where a question is not applied for a specific industry or the industry does not have any manifestation of such characteristic stated in the question.

Having the questionnaire prepared it is time to start the interviews. The questionnaire has been applied to six industries that participating in the NuFerJ cluster. The choice of those six has been aided by a manager that knows pretty well most of the industries and it has been chosen medium size industries with high organizational degree and small size industries with low organizational degree.

The results obtained through the interviews have been first charted and afterwards analyzed and finally graphically plotted. In order to chart the obtained data the scale presented in the questionnaire has been converted as follows: "excellent" → 4; "good" → 3; "not good" → 2; "bad" → 1; "no" → 0.

Figure 3 shows an overview about the industries' preparedness. Considering the business process perspective, in general terms the industries are not much prepared, as it can be seen in Figure 3 where the average has reached 2.28. It means that they do not have a good systematization of daily performed business processes. This interferes negatively to reach industries' common business processes definition. Concerning the organizational structure the industries have reached a better level of

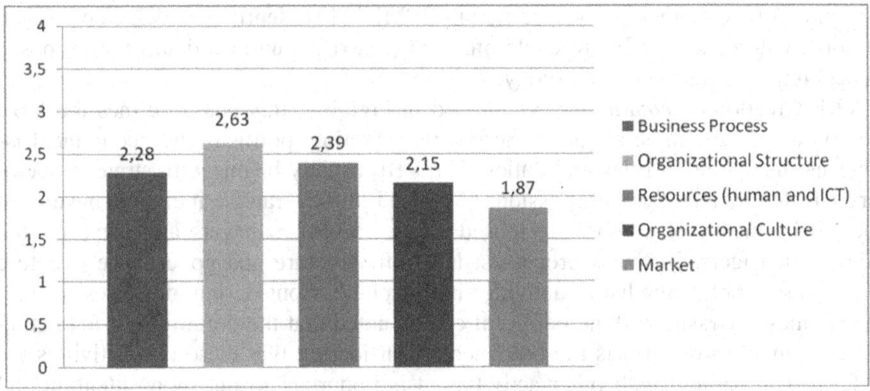

Fig. 3. Industries' Preparedness for each Analyzed Perspective

preparation, getting an average of 2.63. This result has been obtained because most of the industries are well-structured in departments physically separated, and their employees have well-defined functions. This characteristic is essential for industries that want to be part of a VBE because it supports their inter-organizational communication. Regarding the human and ICT resources it can be verified that the industries utilize them in a moderated way, reaching 2.39 as average. However, assessing each industry separately it could be verified that there is a considerable difference among them, where some of them are highly automated while others are poorly automated. This discrepancy impacts negatively in the VBE implementation process because everyone needs to have a minimal ICT bases to collaborate.

Considering the organizational culture, it could be observed in Figure 3 that most of the industries do not stimulate neither internal nor external collaboration. This low preparedness, with 2.15 of average, represents the biggest problem to implement the VBE for NuFerJ because to slight improve this perspective it is necessary a deep change in institutional and organizational principles, and this takes a long time to present results. About the market, this perspective has reached the lowest average among all the perspectives evaluated, which is 1.87. This has been cased mainly because the industries are not habituated to make strategic planning. For instance, several industries do not have budget planning longer that one year. The industries should improve this aspect before applying to take of a VBE.

6 Implementation Methodology Specification

The last step of cluster mapping is to design the VBE implementation methodology. This methodology aims at identifying all the activities, and their sequence of execution, necessary to cope with the main aspects modeled in the VBE model. The activities presented in the methodology are specified based on the main issues stated in the NuFerJ VBE model [8] (see section 3). However, the activities positioning inside the methodology is guided by the preparedness assessment done previously and presented in section 5. The methodology specified in BPMN[1] [12] identifies which steps should be done within each VBE life cycle phase [4]. Next paragraphs detail the proposed NuFerJ implementation methodology.

VBE Creation (*Foundation*): As showed in Figure 4, this phase defines the VBE mission and goals, its strategies in terms of marketing, political and economical issues, and its operating rules and duties. The VBE usually begins with strategic members selected by a sort of commission. In NuFerJ, these strategic members have been selected by means of a board composed of the NuFerJ managers and some invited industry managers. Business processes, ICT infrastructure and governance structure definitions complete the list of activities in this phase. Considering industries' market preparedness assessment done before, it can be noted that the definition of marketing and economical strategies is the bottleneck. Considering that these two activities are performed in parallel with other activities, it is important to put more attention and workforce in such activities in order to do not delay the whole methodology deployment. So, it would be suitable contract external marketing and financial consulting considering that the cluster does not present expertise about such subjects inside it.

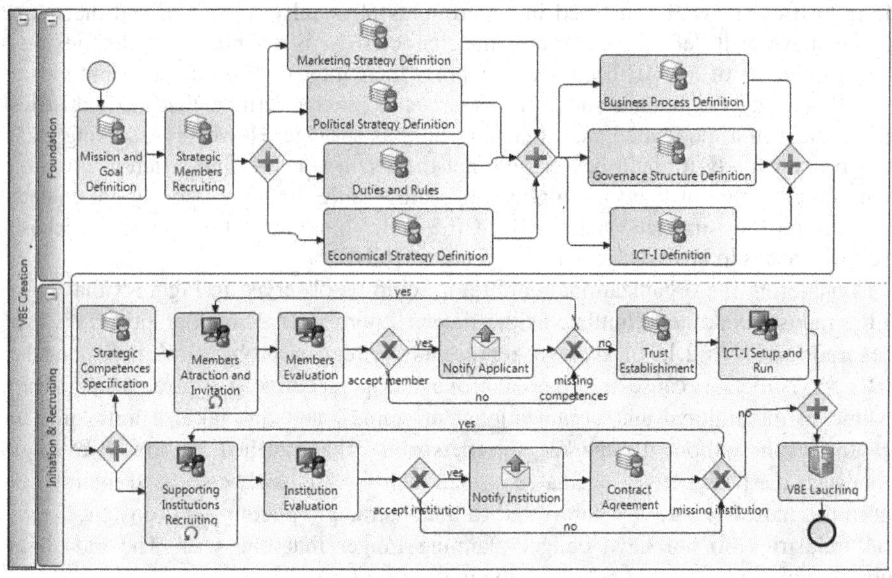

Fig. 4. NuFerJ Implementation Methodology – Creation phase

VBE Creation (*Initiation & Recruiting*): As can be seen in Figure 4, this phase is concerned to recruiting the VBE members and the VBE supporting institutions (e.g. educational and financial institutions). Considering the VBE members, the envisaged competences should be firstly specified in order to invite the right members. Every candidate should be empowered with basis knowledge on how to work in a VBE, which includes the aspect of trust, governance, etc. Once a given industry is

[1] BPMN – Business Process Modeling Notation (www.bpmn.org).

considered prepared to become a member, its ICT infrastructure is prepared. Having all this prepared, the VBE can be launched. Based on the organization culture preparedness it can be identified that the establishment of trust will take time. In fact, this is one of the main barriers when people or entities are collaborating. There are no standard strategies to establish trust. Therefore, in NuFerJ the strategy is to stimulate the good relationship among the preselected strategic members, and through punctual initiatives tries to aggregate more members in this reliable and trustworthy group.

VBE Operation (VBE management): Figure 5 shows that VBE management comprises the activities related to deploy VBE business processes and systems. In NuFerJ the processes (and further systems) of Membership and ICT infrastructure management should be introduced first. Profile and Competence Management comes after and includes the deployment of a system to register and maintain VBE members' information. After that, a number of activities can start in parallel: Financial, Marketing, Performance, Acquisition, Trust, VO inheritance and Customer Relationship management. Considering the resource assessment done previously, it could be observed that NuFerJ members have a high difference of ICT resource utilization. It implies that some of the involved industries need to allocate more efforts to reach the same level of preparedness presented by the other members (such preparedness is mandatory to deploy the aforementioned systems). This preparation can imply to spend money to buy new technologies. That is a critical issue when talking about SME and it can make some of the participants to give up the process. Besides that, acquisition management is critical for NuFerJ because it has a tremendous impact on the mould final cost, so it can represent to win or lose the business. Therefore, this is a concrete aspect where working collaboratively (i.e. buying together) can bring advantages.

VBE Operation (VO creation): Figure 5 shows that VO creation encompasses activities devoted to initiate new VEs once new collaboration opportunities are identified. Typically, Opportunity Identification management is deployed first. This seems natural as it is responsible for brokering business opportunities. Opportunity Quotation management is the next one. Based in the business process assessment, this is another critical task that must be paid attention because most of the quotation employees do not know how to exactly quote a mould. They used to do this either by feeling or based on quotations done by other industries in a round of quotation. Following the methodology, the next step is to deploy the partners selection management. For that, it is necessary first the deployment of performance and trust management. As already mentioned, trust is specially complicated when talking about collaboration. So, the deployment of trust management process and system will take time mainly due to the fact that it will be hard to reach a common agreement among the involved industries about how this process should be constituted and handled. The remaining activities are performed in sequence: Contract Negotiation management (among VO members, and between the VBE and the customer), VO Planning management (to specify which partners will do what and when), VO Registration (to prepare the VBE's repositories to store VO's information for further inheritance), and Launching management (to coordinate the VO starting). Considering this last set of activities, contract negotiation management has to be carefully performed because it includes not only technical, but also legal issues. So, as legislations and bylaws can change rapidly, this process and system should be flexible to quickly attend and assimilate such changes.

As can be seen in Figure 4 and Figure 5 the methodology has a suitable number of activities what implies that it would take long to be entirely deployed. However, meanwhile, some economical, legal or financial facts can change in the country, or even in the world, and these things could affect the normal VBE deployment. So, these changes should be rapidly assimilated by the methodology during its deployment process. Although not explicitly represented in the methodology, any activity can be replaned or changed, even if this implies replanning the remaining activities. Moreover, if an activity impacts backward in the execution flow, this feedback should be passed to the previous executed activities and, if necessary, these affected activities should be replanned and executed again.

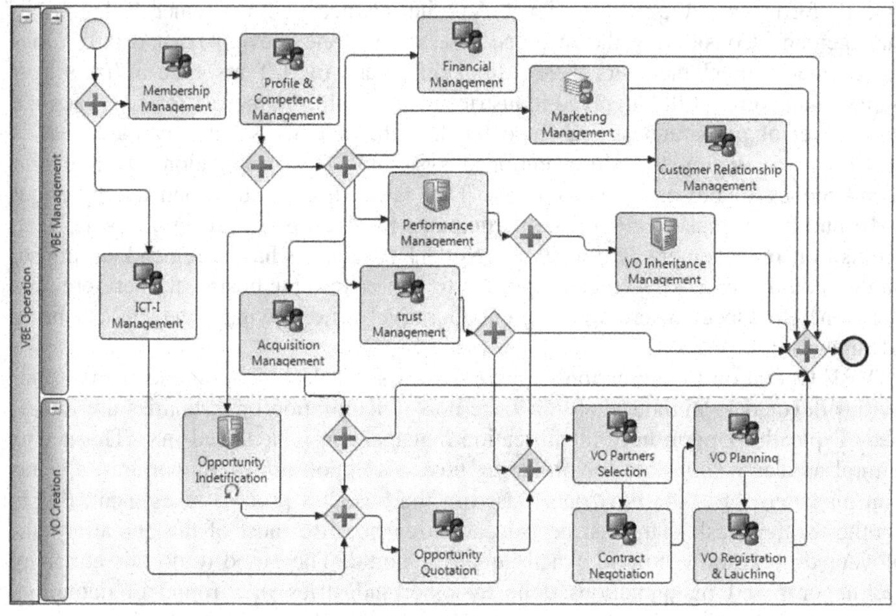

Fig. 5. NuFerJ Implementation Methodology – Operation phase

7 Conclusions

This paper presents a set of guidelines conceived to transform industry clusters in VBEs. Its main contribution is to systematize the whole process that concerns the implementation of a VBE when the organizations are previously arranged as a cluster. It also presents the first results of this ongoing research that is being applied in a case study for more than one year.

In this work it has been applied a top-down approach to derive comprehensive instances of VBEs based on CNOs reference models. This standardized support facilitates further VBE scalability and configurability because the VBE model is conceptually created considering most of the aspects related to a VBE, even if some of these aspects are not been considered in a first stage. The proposed set of guidelines have been devised mainly to supporting the implementation of VBEs from the mould and die sector. But, its natural evolution is to be extended and adapted to be used as guideline to transform in VBE any kind of cluster.

In fact, the aim of this set of guidelines is to support a better specification of the VBE implementation methodology. However, the deployment of this methodology depends on the particularities and preparedness level of the candidates to became VBE members. This means that the methodology's steps can present different levels of complexity and take different times to be implemented. In a first estimation, it is planned that the entire execution of the methodology with the creation of the first VO would take almost three years to be concluded.

Due to its practical conceptualization, even based on reference frameworks, there are no formal methods to evaluate the set of guidelines, especially the methodology, in order to assess its correctness and effectiveness. This assessment will be gradually done during its execution, not only in NuFerJ cluster, but also in many other study cases. So, only this real assessment can provide suitable feedback to ensure the guidelines correctness, or provide valuable information to fix and / or improve them.

Next steps of this work are mainly concerned to a deeper evaluation of the methodology considering a larger number of NuFerJ's members as well as applying this set of guidelines in other clusters that want to become a VBE or even creating a VBE from scratch (where its members do not belong to a previous established cluster). This last initiative should be carefully evaluated, because the set of guidelines have not been structured to create VBE from scratch, and thus it could not be prepared to perform such thing. However, its utilization can be tested and some adaptations may be proposed.

Acknowledgements. This work has been partially supported by Brazilian Council for Scientific and Technological Development – CNPq. The authors thank NuFerJ's managers, in particular Mr. Alexandre Wanzuita and Mr. Christian Dihlmann, as well as the industry managers that are participating and providing contribution for this work.

References

1. Porter, M.E., Fuller, M.B.: Coalitions and global strategy. Competition in Global Industries 1(10), 315–343 (1986)
2. Vallejos, R.V., Lima, C.P., Varvakis, G.: Towards the development of a framework to create a virtual organisation breeding environment in the mould and die sector. Journal of Intelligent Manufacturing 18(5), 587–597 (2007)
3. Camarinha-Matos, L.M.: Emerging Collaboration Forms And Further Research Needs. In: Methods and Tools for Collaborative Networked Organizations, pp. 513–528. Springer, New York (2008)
4. Afsarmanesh, H., Camarinha-Matos, L.M.: A Framework for Management of Virtual Organization Breeding Environments. In: Sixth IFIP Working Conference on Virtual Enterprises. Springer, Valencia (2005)

5. Galeano, N., et al.: VBE Pilot Demonstrators. In: Camarinha-Matos, L.M., Afsarmanesh, H., Ollus, M. (eds.) Methods and Tools for Collaborative Networked Organizations, pp. 405–430. Springer, New York (2008)
6. Romero, D., et al.: Towards the Next Generation Collaborative Networked Organizations: International Challenges, Trends and Research Opportunities (2009), http://www.uninova.pt/~prove09/2009/presentations/PRO-VE09_Special_Panel_Session_ebook.pdf (cited 2010 03/10/2010)
7. Romero, D., Galeano, N., Molina, A.: A Virtual Breeding Environment Reference Model and its Instantiation Methodology. In: Ninth IFIP Working Conference on Virtual Enterprises. Springer, Poznan (2008)
8. Baldo, F., Rabelo, R.J.: For a Methodology to Implement Virtual Breeding Environments – A Case Study in the Mold and Die Sector in Brazil. In: Tenth IFIP Working Conference on Virtual Enterprises. Springer, Thessaloniki (2009)
9. Camarinha-Matos, L.M., Afsarmanesh, H.: The ARCON Modeling Framework. In: Camarinha-Matos, L.M., Afsarmanesh, H. (eds.) Collaborative Networks: Reference Modeling, pp. 67–82. Springer, New York (2008)
10. SOCIESC, Projeto Pesquisa de Mercado Interno para o APL Metalmecânico de Joinville. SOCIESC - Educational Society of Santa Catarina, Joinville, p. 57 (2007)
11. Camarinha-Matos, L.M., et al.: ARCON Reference Models for Collaborative Networks. In: Camarinha-Matos, L.M., Afsarmanesh, H. (eds.) Collaborative Networks: Reference Modeling, pp. 83–112. Springer, New York (2008)
12. White, S.: Introduction to BPMN. IBM Cooperation, p. 2008–029 (2004), http://www.bptrends.com/publicationfiles/07-04%20WP%20Intro%20to%20BPMN%20-%20White.pdf (accessed in 02/03/2010)

A Research Framework on Social Networking Sites Usage: Critical Review and Theoretical Extension

Kathy Ning Shen and Mohamed Khalifa

University of Wollongong in Dubai, PO Box 20183, Dubai, United Arab Emirates
{kathyshen,mohamedkhalifa}@uowdubai.ac.ae

Abstract. Despite the worldwide popularity and rapid proliferation of social networking sites (SNS), e.g., Facebook, our understanding about what drive people to SNS and how they use them remains limited. This study aims at establishing a theoretical framework guiding the research on SNS usage. Built upon the Theory of Acceptance and Use of Technology (UTAUT), the framework makes following major extensions: 1) taking a feature-centric perspective in conceptualizing SNS usage; 2) adopting uses and gratifications paradigm to specify the performance expectancies; 3) accounting for the other important social influences (identification and group norms); 4) accounting for the role of anticipated emotions; and 5) accounting for habituation by including prior usage.

Keywords: Social networking sites; post-adoptive behavior; use and gratification theory; social influences; goal-oriented behavior.

1 Introduction

According to Boyd and Ellison [1], social networking sites (SNS) are "web-based services that allow individuals to 1) construct a public or semi-public profile within a bounded system, 2) articulate a list of other users with whom they share a connection, and 3) view and traverse their list of connections and those made by others within the system." Since their introduction, SNS, e.g., Facebook, MySpace, and Hi5, have been rapidly expanding and profoundly affecting our society. They have become an inescapable part of our lives, which is more evident among young people. In the past couple of years alone, SNS such as Frienderster, MySpace, and Facebook have become immensely popular among adolescents and emerging adults, and play an important role in shaping their identities, affecting psychological well-being, and changing their social networks [2-4].

While most people take such technologies for granted, our understanding about SNS is very limited [2]. First, most existing studies on SNS remain descriptive, focusing on what people do with SNS and user-reported reasons for using those sites, e.g., [2, 3]. Little research has strived for establishing causal claims, which prevents designing effective interventions for SNS. Secondly, despite the abundant research on IT adoption in general, our understanding about the post-adoptive behavior is still at the early stage [5]. Moreover, the uniqueness of SNS from the other IT applications may requires and also gives rise to further theoretical extension.

W. Cellary and E. Estevez (Eds.): I3E 2010, IFIP AICT 341, pp. 173–181, 2010.

In this study, we try to address these issues related to SNS usage by developing a theoretical framework that extends the existing IT adoption theories, e.g., the Theory of Acceptance and Use of Technology (UTAUT) [6], to accounts for the uniqueness of SNS usage. Particularly, the proposed framework advances research on SNS in several ways. First, by taking a feature-centric perspective rather than considering IT as a black-box, we focus on the pattern of SNS usage, i.e., diversified interaction between users and features in SNS. Secondly, the resulting framework extends the existing theories to capture the specificity in social computing contexts of SNS by developing a more comprehensive conceptualization of social influences. Thirdly, different from the most prior studies on SNS that are descriptive and exploratory, this study attempts to establish a base theory to explain the antecedents of SNS usage, which can readily guide future empirical research to uncover the causality in SNS usage in particularly and the other similar Internet applications in general.

The article is organized as follows. The second session will offer a critical review on IT adoption/usage and identify the theoretical gaps. Then the theoretical framework is proposed and discussed. Finally, we conclude the article by discussing the implications and possible future research opportunities.

2 A Critical Review: Research on IT Adoption/Usage

Since SNS are a kind of IT applications, of particularly relevant to the research on this phenomenon might be existing studies examining the adoption and use of new IT applications [6], which has evolved into one of the richest and most mature research streams in Information Systems (IS) field. There are five competing perspectives, which share much in common. The first one originates from the theory of reasoned action (TRA) [7], which predicts behavior as a function of behavioral intention depending upon attitude toward behavior and subjective norm. David [8] applied this theory to explain individual acceptance of technology and developed the Technology Acceptance Model (TAM) and TAM2 [9], which predicts information technology acceptance and usage on the job with perceived usefulness, perceived ease of use, and subjective norm. Ajzen [10] extended TRA by adding the construct of perceived behavioral control and the resulting theory, the Theory of Planned Behavior (TPB), has also been widely used to explain usage of various technologies. The second perspective in IT acceptance and usage research is from motivational theories. Davis et al. [11] explained new technology adoption and use with extrinsic and intrinsic motivation (see also [12]). The third perspective relies on Rogers' [13] Innovation Diffusion theory (IDT), which has been used to explain different innovations. In the context of IT adoption and usage, the predictive validity of innovative characteristics, e.g., relative advantage, visibility, compatibility, results demonstrability and ease of use, were supported [14]. The forth competing perspective is largely derived from Triandis' theory of interpersonal behavior [15]. According to this theory, behavior in any situation is a function of the intention, the habitual responses, and the situational constraints and conditions. Since this theory is developed to explain the choice behavior, in the context of IT adoption and usage, its direct application is limited. Most frequently, only selected constructs, e.g., perceived consequences [16], are adopted and integrated with TPB and/or TRA to explain IT adoption and usage. The fifth perspective takes roots in social cognitive theory [17]. Compeau and Higgins [18] applied this theory to the context t of computer utilization. In this theory, expectations, self-efficacy, affect and anxiety are proposed to influence the computer usage. Realizing the overlaps among the above fifth perspectives, Venkatesh et al. [6] synthesize these prominent theories into the Unified Theory of Acceptance and Use of Technology (UTAUT) that capture the essential elements of established models into four core predictors, i.e., performance expectancy, social influences, effort expectancy, and facilitating conditions.

Although insightful, certain theoretical gaps remain in applying existing theories directly to SNS. First, much of this research has been focusing on the initial adoption of IT and the reflective cognitive processing (e.g., a technology's usefulness and ease of use) associated with individuals' pre-adoption activities, the adoption decision, and initial use behavior. However, the usage of SNS goes beyond the initial adoption stage and should be considered as post-adoptive behavior which may not be fully explained by existing theories [5]. Particularly, the Information Systems literature has argued that rational task-technology fit models might better explain pre-adoption and adoption behaviors while political and learning models might better explain post-adoptive behaviors [19]. Secondly, IT applications in such studies are more considered as a black box rather than as a collection of specific features sets; while SNS integrate various features, which in the social construction of technology [20-22] are interpreted differently by individual users. Since it is specific features that influence and determine the outcomes [21], it is necessary to take a feature-centric view of technology [5] in examining SNS. Thirdly, emphasizing on the reflective cognitive processing, most prior research on IT usage has overlooked the role of emotions in affecting user behavior [23]. Recent research shows that negative anticipated emotions influence the individual's intentions over and above the cognitive variables [24]. According to the model of goal-oriented behavior [23], individual users tend to take into account the emotional consequences, termed as anticipated emotions. Finally, developed in the context of organizational IS, most existing theories, e.g., the Unified Theory of Acceptance and Use of Technology (UTAUT) [6], may not be able to capture the specificity of social computing applications such as SNS. For instance, while the equivocal results have been reported regarding the effect of social influences on IT usage in organizational contexts [6], social influences are frequently cited as an influential factor in social computing contexts [25].

Recently, some theoretical advancement has been made to address the above gaps. Taking a feature-centric view, Jasperson et al. [5] proposed the construct of post-adoptive behavior in the context of IT-enabled work systems, defined as the "myriad feature adoption decisions, feature use behaviors, and feature extension behaviors made by an individual user after an IT application has been installed, made accessible to the user, and applied by the user in accomplishing his/her work activities" (pp. 531). It is a function of prior usage and individual cognitions, contingent upon individual differences. Prior usage accounts for the impact of habituation, which also echoes the argument made by Triandis [15] that behavior in any situation is a function partly of the habitual responses. Individual cognitions involve both processes and content. According to Jasperson et al., the four predictors in UTAUT capture the cognitive content and are more likely to influence post-adoptive intentions. However, Jasperson, et al's model remains a conceptual work, lack of empirical support.

Moreover, their theory is developed for working systems which are significantly different from SNS. For instance, while the contextual influences in [5] are mainly from organizations; in SNS, from various social sources. While the expectations in the context of work systems are mainly related to work performance; those in SNS are far more diversified. While the post-adoptive behavior in the context of work systems might be mandatory; that in SNS is completely voluntary. Finally, incorporating UTAUT predictors fails to account for the role of emotions in affecting user behavior, as discussed above.

Based the critical literature review, we anchor our research framework with UTAUT and Jasperson et al.'s work [5] because these two theories represent the up-to-date and comprehensive understanding of IT acceptance and usage, covering from acceptance, initial usage to post-adoption stages. However the limitations in these theories suggest further theoretical development remain relevant and necessary to account for the specificity of SNS.

3 Theoretical Framework on SNS Usage

In this section, we will discuss the conceptual framework (See Figure 1) explaining antecedents of SNS usage. The overarching theory explaining the antecedents is the UTAUT [6]. The main extensions of the UTAUT are: 1) taking a feature-centric perspective [5] in conceptualizing SNS usage; 2) specifying the performance expectancies by adopting uses and gratifications paradigm which has been widely used in explaining media usage [26]; 3) accounting for the other important social influences (identification and group norms) [27]; 4) accounting for the role of anticipated emotions [23]; and 5) accounting for habituation by including prior usage [5, 15].

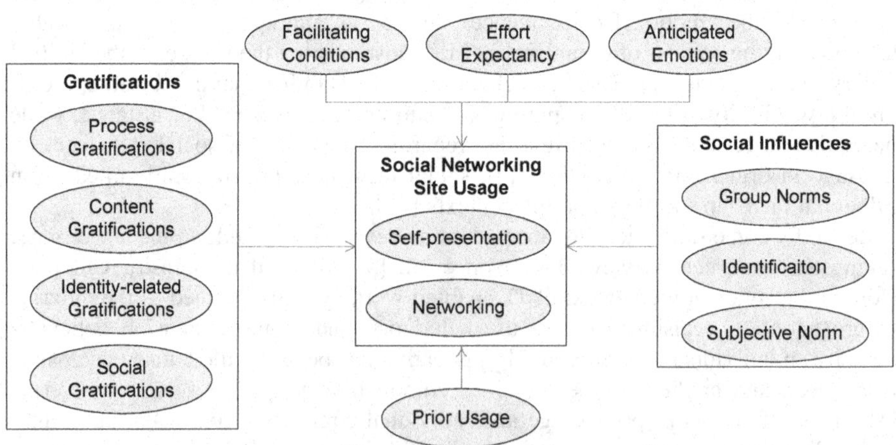

Fig. 1. Theoretical Framework

Due to its integrated technical context, it is not appropriate to assume usage of SNS as uni-dimensional. According to the definition by Boyd and Ellison [1], SNS usually provide three functions, i.e., self-presentation, social networking, and information sharing, from which we derive the usage behaviors that are relevant for SNS. First, self-presentation refers to a person's effort to express a specific image and identity to others [28]. Users may follow different strategies in presenting themselves, e.g., Authentic, Authentic Ironic and Fakesters [29]. By using different features, users may determine the level of identity information discloser (ranging from screen names only to full-fledged profiles) as well as enforce access control (from open to public to completely private). As for networking, it refers to a person's effort to develop and maintain his/her social networks, as indicated through the quantitative characteristics (the amount of connections), the nature of networks (who are connected), networking activities (e.g., cross-posting and sending/receiving invitations).

Synthesizing eight prominent models, the UTAUT [6] articulates four strong predictors for use behavior, i.e., performance expectancy, social influences, effort expectancy, and facilitating conditions.

Performance expectancy is defined as the degree to which an individual believes that using the system will help him or her to attain gains in job performance. Although SNS may not be related to job performance, applicable is the same logic that positive utilitarian expectancies lead to more usage [30]. To account for the specificity of SNS, we rely on the uses and gratifications paradigm (U&G) to identify a set of relevant expectancies. According to the U&G [26], individuals interact with media in a goal-oriented fashion to fulfill a core set of motives or gratifications, which are similar to performance expectancies. This theory has been applied to study Internet usage because of the Internet and its applications' media-like characteristics [26, 31]. Since SNS are a typical Internet application, we also adopt the similar approach. In [26], three categories of gratifications were identified and empirically validated, i.e., process, content and social, covering both website interaction and social interaction. Although more comprehensive than the other typologies, these gratifications fail to capture the ones related to identity-related motives. SNS have been portrayed to be a great venue for people to look for self [32-34]. Existing research on motivation has suggested some identity-related motives, such as feared and/or desired selves [35], self-verification [36], self-enhancement [25, 37], and self-exploration [33]. Thus, we incorporate identity-related gratifications into the original set of gratifications proposed by [26] and, together, they specify the performance expectancies in SNS.

Another major extension of the UTAUT is to account for multiple routes for social influences [27]. While UTAUT only focuses on subjective norm which is a normative influence of others' expectations, individual behavior is also subject to the other two group-level influences, i.e., internalization (i.e., congruence of one's goals with those of group members), and identification (i.e., conception of one's self in terms of the group's defining features). The effects of these three social influences have been examined in the context of virtual communities [38]. Although virtual communities examined in [38] are built around content while SNS, around users, social influences remain relevant.

The third extension of the UTAUT is to account for the role of emotions in affecting use behavior. Anticipated emotions are derived from the model of goal-oriented behavior [23] and defined as prefactual appraisals in which the individual imagines the emotional consequences of achieving and not achieving a goal. The forward-looking positive emotions when the users imagine the pleasant aspects of the upcoming experience from using SNS will significantly predict the actual usage.

The forth extension of the UTAUT is to account for habituation by including prior usage, defined as existing experiences with certain SNS features. It is suggested that as individuals gain experience with what was initially a novel behavior (e.g., first usage of a SNS), they tend to engage less frequently in reflective processes and simply reply on previous patterns of behavior to direct future behavior [39, 40]. Accordingly, for most regular users of SNS, their interaction is likely to reflect a habitualization of action that occurs more or less automatically [5, 41].

The last two predictors according to UTAUT are effort expectancy and facilitating conditions. Effort expectancy refers to the degree of ease associated with the use of the system (in this case, a SNS). Facilitating conditions are defined as the degree to which an individual believes that an organizational and technical infrastructure exists to support use of the system. In SNS, facilitation may come from online help offered by the site itself, or the other users of the same site, which removes barriers to use. We adapt the same conceptualizations in SNS not at the system level, but at the feature level to be consistent with the feature-centric perspective. Some features are easier to use than the others. The more facilitating conditions perceived by the users regarding specific features, the more likely they extend the usage of those features.

4 Implications and Future Research

In this study, we attempted to extend the existing theories to explain SNS usage by: 1) taking a feature-centric perspective in conceptualizing SNS usage; 2) adopting uses and gratifications paradigm to specify the performance expectancies; 3) accounting for the other important social influences (identification and group norms); 4) accounting for the role of anticipated emotions; and 5) accounting for habituation by including prior usage. The proposed framework entails significant theoretical and practical implications.

First, by conceptualizing SNS usage as post-adoptive behavior at the feature level, our framework will better uncover the complexity in SNS usage. While most information systems have integrated various features along with different users' appropriation, same information system may generate distinct usage patterns and interpretations. Although the framework focuses on SNS usage, the same approach should be applied in investigating information systems in general. Second, built upon the UTAUT [6] and Jasperson et al.'s work [5], the proposed framework provides a more integrated understanding about the antecedents of SNS usage by accounting for both cognitive and affective factors, both rational and habitual reasons, and both personal and social influences. Again, we believe that this integrated approach will be useful in investigating the other social computing systems. Finally, the proposed framework is ready to guide further hypothesis development and empirical validation, which will well complement the void of research on causality in SNS research. Particularly, while the majority studies were conducted with US/European samples, limited understanding has been achieved outside the developed countries. Given the rapid increase in SNS usage in regions such as Asia and Middle East where people may use SNS for different purposes, and the SNS usage may incur different implications. Therefore, we encourage researchers to examine the samples in various cultural/national contexts and to bring the local specificities into the SNS research.

In terms of future extension, we would suggest considering important moderators, such as gender and culture. For instance, prior research has realized the gender differences in affecting users' interaction with IT (e.g., [42-45]. In the context of SNS gender differences may be present in following ways. First, although the existing evidence has not uncovered significant gender differences in the amount of usage of SNS; but gender differences were reported in the pattern of usage. For instance, Manago et al. [46] reported that male–female differences in self-presentation parallel, and possibly intensify, gender norms offline. Similarly, Magnuson and Dundes [47] reported that some traditional gender roles also exhibit online in SNS, as indicated by different patterns in their user profiles. Fogel and Nehmad [48] reported general privacy concerns and identity information disclosure concerns are of greater concern to women than men. Greater percentages of men than women display their phone numbers and home addresses on SNS; and greater risk taking attitudes exist among men than women. Second, gender has been identified as one of major moderators in UTAUT [6]. Significant gender differences were reported for the effects of performance expectancy, effort expectancy, and social influences. The effect of performance expectancy is stronger for men than women; while that of effort expectancy and social influences is stronger for women than men. Particularly, Thelwall [49] reported in MySpace, females are more interesting in friendship, males are more interested in dating. Given strong cultural notions of gender, there is no reason to assume equal adoption and pursuit of SNS between the male and female users. Moreover, investigating gender differences in SNS usage will be a gateway to explicate more complicated cultural differences.

References

1. Boyd, D., Ellison, N.B.: Social network sites: Definition, history, and scholarship. Journal of Computer-Mediated Communication 13, 210–230 (2008)
2. Pempek, T.A., Yermolayeva, Y.A., Calvert, S.L.: College students' social networking experiences on Facebook. Journal of Applied Developmental Psychology (2009)
3. Subrahmanyam, K., Reich, S.M., Waechter, N., Espinoza, G.: Online and offline social networks: Use of social networking sites by emerging adults. Journal of Applied Developmental Psychology 29, 420–433 (2008)
4. Steinfield, C., Ellison, N.B., Lampe, C.: Social capital, self-esteem, and use of online social network sites: A longitudinal analysis. Journal of Applied Developmental Psychology 29, 434–445 (2008)
5. Jasperson, J., Carter, P.E., Zmud, R.W.: A comprehensive conceptualization of post-adoption behaviors associated with information technology enabled work systems. MIS Quarterly 29, 525–557 (2005)
6. Venkatesh, V., Morris, M.G., Davis, G.B., Davis, F.D.: User Acceptance of Information Technology: Toward a Unified View. MIS Quarterly 27 (2003)
7. Fishbein, M., Ajzen, I.: Belief, Attitude, Intention and Behavior: An Introduction to Theory and Research. Addison-Wesley Publishing Company, Reading (1975)
8. Davis, F.D.: Perceived Usefulness, Perceived Ease of Use and User Acceptance of Information Technology. MIS Quarterly 13, 319–340 (1989)
9. Venkatesh, V., Davis, F.D.: A Theoretical Extension of the Technology Acceptance Model: Four Longitudinal Field Studies. Management Science 46, 186–204 (2000)
10. Ajzen, I.: The Theory of Planned Behavior. Organizational Behavior and Human Decision Processes 50, 179–211 (1991)

11. Davis, F.D., Bagozzi, R.P., Warshaw, P.R.: Extrinsic and Intrinsic Motivation to Use Computers in the Workplace. Journal of Applied Social Psychology 22, 1111–1132 (1992)
12. Venkatesh, V., Johnson, P.: Telecommuting Technology Implementations: A Within- and Between- Subjects Longitudinal Field Study. Personnel Psychology 55, 661–687 (2002)
13. Rogers, T.B.: The Psychological Testing Enterprise. Brooks/Cole Publishing Company, Pacific Grove (1995)
14. Moore, G.C., Benbasat, I.: Integrating Diffusion of Innovations and Theory of Reasoned Action Models to Predict Utilization of Information Technology by End-Users. In: Kautz, K., Pries-Hege, J. (eds.) Diffusion and Adoption of Information Technology, pp. 132–146. Chapman and Hall, London (1996)
15. Triandis, C.H.: Values, Attitudes and Interpersonal Behavior. In: Howe, H.E. (ed.) Nebraska Symposium on Motivation, 1979: Beliefs, Attitudes and Values, pp. 159–295. University of Nebraska Press, Lincoln (1980)
16. Limayem, M., Khalifa, M., Frini, A.: What Makes Consumers Buy from Internet? A Longitudinal Study of Online Shopping. IEEE Transactions on Systems, Man and Cybernetics—Part A: Systems and Humans 30, 421–432 (2000)
17. Bandura, A.: Social Foundations of Thought and Action: A Social Cognitive Theory. Prentice Hall, Englewood Cliffs (1986)
18. Compeau, D.R., Higgins, C.A.: Application of Social Cognitive Theory to Training for Computer Skills. Information Systems Research 6, 118–143 (1995)
19. Robey, D., Ross, J.W., Boudreau, M.: Learning to Implement Enterprise Systems: An Exploratory Study of the Dialectics of Change. Journal of Management Information Systems 19, 17–46 (2002)
20. Orlikowski, W.J.: The Duality of Technology: Rethinking the Concept of Technology in Organizations. Organization Science 3, 398–427 (1992)
21. Griffith, T.L.: Technology Features as Triggers for Sensemaking. Academy of Management Review 24, 472–488 (1999)
22. DeSanctis, G., Poole, M.S.: Capturing the Complexity in Advanced Technology Use: Adaptive Structuration Theory. Organization Science 5, 121–147 (1994)
23. Perugini, M., Bagozzi, R.: The role of desires and anticipated emotions in goal-directed behaviours: Broadening and deepening the theory of planned behaviour. British Journal of Social Psychology 40, 79–98 (2001)
24. Bagozzi, R.P., Dholakia, U.M., Basuroy, S.: How Effortful Decisions Get Enacted: The Motivating Role of Decision Processes, Desires, and anticipated Emotions. Journal of Behavioral Decision Making 16, 273–295 (2003)
25. Dholakia, U.M., Bagozzi, R.P., Pearo, L.K.: A Social Influence Model of Consumer Participation in Network- and Small-Group-Based Virtual Communities. International Journal of Research in Marketing 21, 241–263 (2004)
26. Stafford, T.E., Stafford, M.R., Schkade, L.L.: Determining uses and gratifications for the Internet. Decision Sciences 35, 259–288 (2004)
27. Bagozzi, R.P., Lee, K.H.: Multiple Routes for Social Influence: The Role of Compliance, Internalization, and Social Identity. Social Psychology Quarterly 65, 226–247 (2002)
28. Joinson, A.N.: Understanding the Psychology of Internet Behaviour: Virtual Worlds. Real Lives Palgrave Macmillan, New York (2003)
29. Marwick, A.: I'm a lot more interesting than a Friendster profile: Identity presentation, authenticity, and power in social networking services. In: Internet Research 6.0, Chicago, USA (2005)
30. Raacke, J., Bonds-Raacke, J.: MySpace and Facebook: Applying the Uses and Gratifications Theory to Exploring Friend-Networking Sites. CyberPsychology & Behavior 11, 169–174 (2008)

31. Diddi, A., LaRose, R.: Getting hooked on news: Uses and gratifications and the formation of news habits among college students in an Internet environment. Journal of Broadcasting & Electronic Media 50, 193–210 (2006)
32. Tong, S.T., Van der Heide, B., Langwell, L., Walther, J.B.: Too much of a good thing? The relationship between number of friends and interpersonal impressions on Facebook. Journal of Computer-Mediated Communication 13, 531–549 (2008)
33. Valkenburg, P.M., Schouten, A.P., Peter, J.: Adolescents' identity experiments on the internet. New Media & Society 7, 383–402 (2005)
34. Zhao, S., Grasmuck, S., Martin, J.: Identity construction on Facebook: Digital empowerment in anchored relationships. Computers in Human Behavior 24, 1816–1836 (2008)
35. Cesario, J., Grant, H., Higgins, E.T.: Regulatory fit and persuasion: Transfer from "feeling right". Journal of Personality and Social Psychology 86, 388–404 (2004)
36. Swann Jr., W.B., Polzer, J.T., Style, D.C., Ko, S.J.: Finding Value in Diversity: Verification of Personal and Social Self-Views in Diverse Groups. Academy of Management Review 29, 9–27 (2004)
37. Pfeffer, J., Fong, C.T.: Building Organization Theory from First Principles: The Self-Enhancement Motive and Understanding Power and Influence. Organization Science 16, 372–388 (2005)
38. Bagozzi, R.B., Dholakia, U.M.: Intentional Social Action in Virtual Communities. Journal of Interactive Marketing 16, 2–79 (2002)
39. Bargh, J.A., Peitromonaco, P.: Automatic Information Processing and Social Perception: The Influence of Trait Information Presented Outside of Conscious Awareness on Impression Formation. Journal of Personality and Social Psychology 43, 437–449 (1982)
40. Verplanken, B., Aarts, H., van Knippenberg, A., Moonen, A.: Attitude versus General Habit: Antecedents of Travel Mode Choice. Journal of Applied Social Psychology 24, 285–300 (1994)
41. Khalifa, M., Limayem, M., Liu, V.: A Contingency Theory for Online Consumer Retention: the Role of Online Shopping Habit. In: Hunter, G., Tan, F. (eds.) Advanced Topics in Global Information Management, vol. 3, pp. 39–55. Idea Group Publishing, Hersey (2004)
42. Venkatesh, V., Morris, M.G.: Why Don't Men Ever Stop to Ask for Directions? Gender, Social Influence, and Their Role in Technology Acceptance and Usage Behavior. MIS Quarterly 24, 115–139 (2000)
43. Munro, M.C., Huff, S.L., Marcolin, B.L., Compeau, D.R.: Understanding and Measuring User Competence. Information & Management 33, 46–57 (1997)
44. Gefen, D., Straub, D.W.: Gender Differences in Perception and Adoption of E-Mail: An Extension to the Technology Acceptance Model. MIS Quarterly 21, 389–400 (1997)
45. Gefen, D., Ridings, C.M.: If you spoke as she does, Sir, Instead of the Way you do: A sociolinguistics perspective of gender differences in virtual communities. The DATA BASE for Advances in Information Systems 36, 78–92 (2005)
46. Manago, A.M., Graham, M.B., Greenfield, P.M., Salimkhan, G.: Self-presentation and gender on MySpace. Journal of Applied Developmental Psychology 29, 446–458 (2008)
47. Magnuson, M.J., Dundes, L.: Gender differences in "social portraits" reflected in MySpace profiles. Cyber Psychology & Behavior 11, 239–241 (2008)
48. Fogel, J., Nehmad, E.: Internet social network communities: Risk taking, trust, and privacy concerns. Computers in Human Behavior 25, 153–160 (2009)
49. Thelwall, M.: Social networks, gender, and friending: An analysis of MySpace member profiles. Journal of American Society for Information Science and Technology 59, 1321–1330 (2008)

A Digital Platform for Marketing Communications in the Mobile and Social Media Space

Otto Petrovic

Karl Franzens University, Institute for Information Science and Information Systems, Universitätsstraße 15/G3, 8010 Graz, Austria
otto.petrovic@uni-graz.at

Abstract. This paper presents a digital platform for marketing communications developed during the last years. Functionalities of the platform are described according to different categories and by means of case studies together with related results. Also further development strategies are discussed, e.g. the planned enlargement of the platform in the field of social media will include three new modules. A browsing module will enable multidimensional browsing in selected social media. The measurement module will facilitate creation of individual social media portfolios. Finally, the engagement module realizes a uniform user interface between the platform and social media.

Keywords: digital marketing platform, mobile advertising, social media marketing, mobile communications.

1 Introduction

The digital platform for marketing communications presented in this paper was designed and developed under the guidance of the author in the last four years as well as the strategy for the future development. Compared with other solutions the original contribution of that platform is mainly based on innovations in three areas. Firstly, the presented platform enables an integration of communications via mobile messaging with numerous other digital media, e.g. mobile websites, mobile clients for iPhone and Android, iPad apps, e-mail, RSS feeds and social media. All that channels are used and controlled from the backend functionality described below. Secondly, due to the strong tendency to integrate digital communications with classical media like print, TV, and outdoor advertising, the presented platform supports the linkage between those classical media and new digital media. Thirdly, the platform has an elaborated range of backend functionalities. Those deliver CRM functions for selecting target group together with a wide range of rule based handling of customer interaction.

An important aim of the paper is to present the current development status of the platform by describing the wide range of functionalities in different areas. For each group of functionalities a real life case accomplished by the author is presented together with obtained results. The third aim is to discuss future challenges for

W. Cellary and E. Estevez (Eds.): I3E 2010, IFIP AICT 341, pp. 182–192, 2010.

marketing communications in the digital space and, as a consequence, further development directions of the platform.

2 Changes in Marketing Communications

The amount of time that people spend with media has almost tripled within the past four decades and averages ten hours by now [11]. A variety of new media types has evolved simultaneously and communication behavior is becoming more and more inhomogeneous and multifaceted. Two trends are observable in this context. Former key media – TV and radio – are predominately used by older target groups whereas young people turn towards interactive media. Additionally user generated content that is distributed in networks gains significance compared to editorial content that is distributed via broadcasting.

Especially two media gained importance. No communication media was distributed as fast during the past decades and changed communication realities that strong as the mobile phone. Absolute user numbers as well as rate of growth are significantly higher than those of internet. The 4 billion mark of users was passed by the end of 2008 which accounts for about 60 percent of world population [5]. Next to that social media like Facebook, Twitter and Youtube gained importance. Two thirds of all internet users already use social media regularly and time that is spent increases three times as fast as for other internet activities. 93 percent of internet users expect companies to be represented in social media. The analysis of age structure shows that social media is also comprehensively used by senior target groups older than 49 years [10]. Spending for marketing communications align to these new communication realities only step-by-step. United Kingdom was the first big country where internet marketing communications spending for internet with 23,5 % surpassed those for TV accounting for 21,9 % of all spending in the first half of 2009 [13].

In order enable marketing communications to measure up to this changed framework there is need for a digital platform that facilitates management of this constantly increasing complexity. Important tasks in this context are central control of different media, cross-media communication, collecting and using of customer data as well as integration of existing systems such as CRM and ERP. Whereas there already exist commercial systems in the area of classical media and traditional Internet usage, first systems for usage of mobile communication [12] and social media [6, 9] are developed in research. Those include hardly any cross-media functionalities and are not evaluated in real usage yet. The purpose of this paper is a contribution to close this gap.

3 Functionalities of the Platform

3.1 Messaging

The basic form of marketing communications via mobile phone is *information broadcast*. SMS is qualified to reach almost all users of mobile phones independent from device type.

Functionalities. In addition to SMS, the platform facilitates further message types: MMS enables transfer of multimedia content and WAP Push is a link that leads to a website which was optimized for display on mobile phones. Another possibility is transmission of emails, which are mobile communication for those recipients who receive emails on their mobile phones. Free choice of message type concerning the single recipient ensures optimum choice of communication form depending on objectives, target groups, and budget.

In order to avoid unwanted messages for the recipient the backend that is explained later offers comprehensive query mechanisms. It is possible to decide who receives certain messages and when. The central messaging administration is also used for quality assurance of messages that are to send.

An additional functionality of the platform is the response option for recipients of the message. It allows the recipient to reply to SMS, MMS and email immediately from the mobile phone. Implementation of mechanisms that allow the sender of the message further processing of responses is especially challenging. Very often only one or two employees are engaged with message transmission and processing of thousands of responses is therefore quite demanding. The platform facilitates automatic conversion of responses into emails and their forwarding according to definable processes.

Even more complex mechanisms of interaction in the area of message transmission are enabled using the mechanism of information and content request by the customer. The customer requests information or other content using a pull mechanism. Certain information or other content is then transmitted using the message types SMS, MMS, email or social media to this customer or to a third party according to the customer data that is stored in the backend and to rules for the processing the dialogue.

Case: Customer Relationship Management of a Retail Bank. The business aims for this retail bank are: low-cost increase of customer contact rate, dedicated services for young target groups and brand image improvement regarding innovation leadership. They decided to use the mobile channel as a fourth channel of communication towards the customer besides over-the-counter business, self service area and telebanking. Requirements were that existing customer data from the CRM system is comprehensively used and that an interface with the core banking system (transaction system) is implemented. This ensures the entire integration of marketing communications via the mobile channel into the bank's other activities. The emphasis was placed on avoidance of spam-messages that could seriously damage the bank's image as a trustworthy partner via the especially sensitive mobile communication channel. Therefore opt-in mechanisms and processes for highly personalized interaction were developed and implemented very carefully. The control cockpit in the backend which is described later takes up a leading role in this context. Essential forms of system usage are: invitations to events, transmission of coupons with the possibility to forward them to friends, personalized information, context-oriented market research, personalized congratulations on birthday, appointment reminder, and incentives for inviting further participants.

A pilot test was conducted in several branch banks in September 2006. The area-wide rollout in 380 branches followed in 2009. 150.000 customers were acquired for system usage within twelve months showing an upward trend. This value represents a share of 12,5 % of the total population of the target area. One million additional customer contacts could be generated at the same time because of carefully planned communication and interaction activities. The opt-out ration is below three percent. Accompanying market research (n=759) indicates positive values of system acceptance. 71 % think that the system is either very good or good, 60 % recommended it to someone but only 2 % rated it as bad. Concerning effects on brand image there is a significant improvement in the areas of innovation and customer satisfaction observable. At the same time there was no decrease in trustworthiness which indicates that the especially sensitive mobile channel has been used advisedly.

3.2 Mobile Market Research

Market research on the mobile phone offers the essential advantage that a survey can be initiated in a certain context unlike other methods. Examples are surveys concerning customer satisfaction with the check-in service at the airport immediately after checking in or a certain mobile service immediately after using it.

Functionalities. An activity of the participant at the point of sale or usage of a mobile service triggers the transmission of a WAP Push link that is leading to a mobile website. Alternatively an SMS dialogue can be initiated. Then the participant will be able to answer several sets of questions via mobile phone. Different types of questions are available including Likert scale, multiple choice, multiple answer options, numeric questions and yes/no questions. The questions are arranged in blocks that allow adaptive handling depending on answer behavior, using jump orders and filter channels. Direct integration into the backend of the platform enables simplified composition of questionnaires as well as rule-based arrangement and deliver of questions, transmission of immediate feedback, resumption of answering after break-off as well as generating different reports.

Case: Measurement of Perceived Service Quality for a Mobile Network Operator. Main goal of the study [14] was the measurement of customer satisfaction concerning the content download service provided by a mobile network operator immediately after usage. Design of the questionnaire and definition of messaging type for the WAP Push link were processed in the backend. Immediately after the customer's usage of the service the questionnaire is configured according to rules that were defined in the backend of the platform then personalized and transmitted adapted to mobile phone type using the rendering engine in an optimized way. The response rate of this mobile survey was 6,4 % which is four times higher than the response rate of the online survey (1,7 %) that was conducted for reasons of comparison. 53 % of the participants who finished the WAP survey within seven days actually completed it within one hour after start in contract to the online survey where only 27 % of the participants finished the survey within the first day. These facts indicate that an addressee of a mobile survey decides to take part either immediately after receiving the invitation link or not at all.

3.3 Interactivation of Traditional Media

Traditional media of marketing communications such as newspaper, advertisement, TV spots, or billboards basically follow a broadcast approach. A message is distributed to as many members of the target group as possible. Interaction is not intended or only indirectly possible like in form of letters to the editor or calls by viewers or listeners. Interactivation of traditional media enables utilization of the mobile phone as an immediate feedback channel for marketing communications in traditional media and hence turns them into interactive media.

Functionalities. In a first step the company creates a physical medium for their advertising message. This could be a newspaper advertisement, billboards, a TV spot or an object like a t-shirt or the wall of a building. After that, an interface with the mobile phone is implemented on this medium. The platform supports SMS numbers, 2D-codes [7], Bluetooth [8], and Near Field Communication (NFC) [4]. Depending on type and configuration of the implemented interface the customer receives a call for interaction when coming closer to the vehicle of the advertising message (Push-technology) or can initiate interaction himself (Pull-technology). Access of a mobile website, content download and SMS dialogue are supported forms of interaction. The profound integration into the backend of the platform allows definition of detailed rules for starting and processing the interaction as well as generation of comprehensive reports concerning customer behavior.

Case: Interactivation of Billboards using 2D Codes and Bluetooth. A billboard campaign was interactivated for the exhibition of a 25.000 year-old statue in a museum of historical art using this module of the platform. Main purposes were increasing attention to the billboard, invite for interaction and stimulating viral effects. The billboards were therefore equipped with 2D codes. Activation of an applicable reader on the mobile phone enabled passers-by to download a game that was especially created for mobile phones including information concerning the statue. They could also forward the game to friends and acquaintances immediately from their mobile devices. Additionally a Bluetooth interface was implemented in order to call attention of passers-by with enabled Bluetooth recognition to the possibility to get further information concerning the statue on their mobile phones. Within three weeks 3.200 mobile phones with enabled Bluetooth recognition were detected. Invitation for download was accepted 630 times which represents a response ratio of 20 %.

3.4 Mobile Websites and Mobile Apps

The increasing penetration with smart phones and their ability to display mobile websites and execute special application on the device fosters demand for mobile websites and mobile apps [3]. This effect is enforced by low-cost data tariffs provided by mobile network operators often in form of flat fees. This is why mobile websites and mobile apps increasingly replace SMS-based forms of marketing communications [2].

Functionalities. In contrary to usage of websites via PC there is no uniform standard for their usage on mobile phones. Devices differ a lot concerning data formats for pictures and videos that are supported, display size, screen resolution and browser functionalities. For this concern a Rendering Engine was implemented into the platform which recognizes the type of mobile device and enables optimized delivery of the website. At the moment the Rendering Engine includes 5.000 different types of mobile devices while this base is continuously updated and enlarged. It enables output of the website at the best concerning markup language, resolution, display size and data format. Data from websites gets into the Rendering Engine either via a dedicated mobile website, via integration of existing data using an RSS feed or via direct integration of the Rendering Engine into the particular Content Management System (CMS).

Because of increasing processing power of smart phones the number of mobile apps that are developed and used also increases. These apps enable usage of a particular mobile device's functionalities as well as offline usage of applications and data. Moreover the user perceives an emotional quality of actually "possessing" something which positively affects willingness to pay for it. This assumption is supported by enormous sales volumes e.g. for Apple AppStore where more than one billion apps were downloaded within nine month after opening [1]. The plattform is able to deliver messages, information and coupons into a mobile application based on rules for every single user of a certain application. Further functionalities of the platform are access to customer data, triggering of interaction via other channels, direction of interaction and content of the app as well as a comprehensive reporting.

Case: Launch of a New Car Model and Development of a Mobile Loyalty Card. The launch of a new car model was supported by a mobile website. This website could be accessed either via directly inserting the URL or via 2D codes in newspaper advertisings. Next to current news concerning the model this website included a comprehensive description of the new model as well as of alternative models, the range of products and the possibility to contact a nearby merchant in order to make an appointment for a test drive. In the case of GPS enabled devices the nearby merchant was immediately suggested. A comprehensive reporting system between merchants and automotive manufacturer was implemented in order to centrally collect and analyze the customer data generated subsequent to test drives. The mobile website had 2.500 visits within 30 days and 8.000 page views. 90 % of the visitors accessed the mobile website using the 2D codes integrated in newspaper advertising. The most visited areas were those concerning the newly launched car model.

Additionally a mobile app in form of a mobile loyalty card was developed integrated in the platform. Depending on the stored interaction mechanics the backend enables transmission of personalized content to each single customer according to deposit on the loyalty card. It is also possible to transfer personalized coupons to the app. Clicking a certain coupon initiates display of a customary EAN code that can be read by standard scanners on the point-of-sale.

4 The Backend

4.1 Functionalities of the Backend

An essential functionality of the backend is the control cockpit. *Communication Planning* enables selection of customers with whom a certain form of communication is to be initiated. Next to demographic criteria drawn from customer master data also behavior-oriented data and transaction data is used. For instance certain messages are only sent to those customers that are younger than 20 years and who did not buy a product within the past two months. The functionalities concerning content selection support personalization of content like personalized address on the one hand and on the other hand quality assurance of sent content in decentralized organizations. For example it is possible that the communication department defines various standard contents like birthday messages, messages in case of expiration of a contract or a message addressing negative news coverage concerning the company. The particular departments or branches can then use these drafts for sending messages to their customers. At the same time the module for communication planning displays costs related to the particular selection of target groups and content like for outgoing SMS.

The *Reporting Module* conduces to analysis of customer behavior. Examples are response ratios for certain transmitted messages or surveys, redemption rates of coupons, access numbers of mobile websites or forwarding rate of viral content. All reports can be displayed either on mobile devices or in the web. The reports are supplemented by a thorough monitoring of system performance. A further module is dedicated to *User Administration*. It includes definition of groups, roles and authorization in order to define who is allowed to administer which system transactions. *Campaign and Program Control* is used for grouping if single activities that are topically related. It is possible to define rules for editing customer feedback concerning sent messages and also to decide on certain types of content according to customer behavior. All these functionalities are at the disposal of all communication channels illustrated above. Integration possibility of the backend into existing IT-systems is of paramount importance in order to avoid isolated solutions. Fig. 1 shows the integration of the platform into existing ERP- and CRM-systems, transaction systems at the point-of-sale, call center activities and campaign management software.

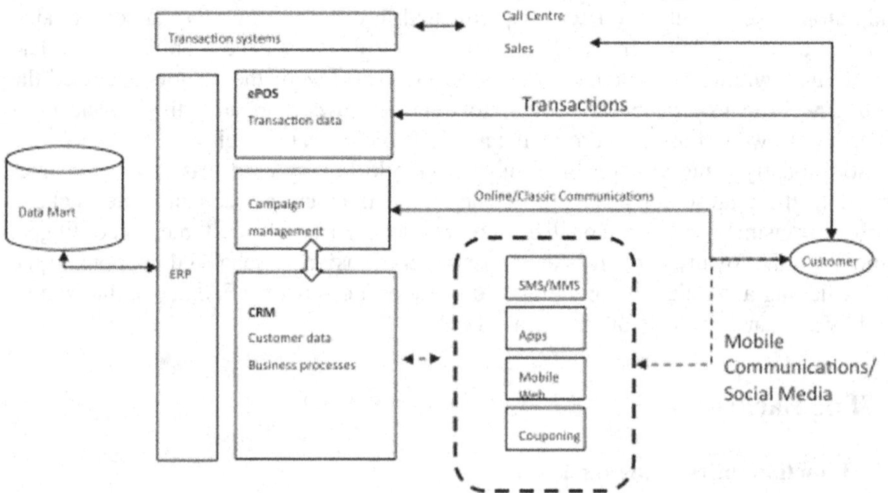

Fig. 1. Integration of the platform in other IT-Systems

4.2 Technical Implementation of the Backend

The technical implementation is done in Java as far as possible and reasonable. For interactions that are adaptable during runtime Groovy, which is based on JDK (Java Development Kit) and therefore enables integration into the platform, is used as script language. The server system is based on the specifications of the Java platform Enterprise Edition. This covers following aspects of platform software: web-container-infrastructure, administration of transactions and relational data base access. Integrating platform (middleware): Apache Tomcat. Data base: In order to allow secure and scalable administration of a huge amount of users MySQL (data base engine: InnoDB) is used. Web-applications-framework: Struts-framework to ensure a uniform user interface with a MVC-structure (model-view-controller). Object-relational mapping: Data base tables are configured by means of Hibernate-library and implemented in Java-object structure. Therefore business logics and actual data storage are uncoupled in the coded areas of the platform. Reporting-tool: Reports are generated using the reporting tool BIRT. Views are defined that allow uncoupling of report queries and actual table structure.

5 Future Development

5.1 From Messaging to Cross-Media Communications and Dedicated Adservices

One important factor for further development of the platform is the advent of smart phones together with mobile broadband connectivity and flat fees for using the internet. That bundle of innovation leads to a relative gain of mobile internet-based communications in form of mobile websites, mobile clients and social media via traditional short message services. The main challenge is to enable consistent brand strategies and consumer interaction mechanisms independent from differing digital media used by the target group. The most important challenge is not only to support the communication of a company with its clients but also to handle all the responses as well as to influence the communication among brand relevant peer groups in social media. Additionally upcoming dedicated ad-services like Google's AdMobs or Apple's iAd will challenge the interface of the current platform. Monitoring Systems like flurry.com deliver completely new consumer insights in the field of application usage and thus new communication opportunities. But the most important challenge will come from social media.

5.2 Future Deployment of Social Media

Marketing communications gained a totally new dimension caused by social media (e.g. Facebook, Twitter, Blogs, Wikis, and further more). It is not about developing messages and then penetrating the market any more but about engaging in existing, hard to control communication processes of (potential) customers and stakeholders that are relevant to the brand. In order to use these new possibilities the platform is currently enlarged by three additional modules.

Browsing Module: This module includes a freely configurable dashboard that enables multidimensional browsing in social media of one's own choice. Dimensions can be for instance brand values. The Browsing Module displays relevant activities in social media (postings, uploaded videos and photos) multidimensional on the screen in real-time. The creative department can now browse through this space and get an emotionally loaded picture of the activities that are of high relevance to his own or his client's brand values.

Measurement Module: This module facilitates creation of own portfolios of relevant social media. The Social Media Marketing Engine will then automatically access transaction data from the chosen websites which replaces manual research. Certain key data are listed for each social medium (e.g. number of followers, tweets, friends, watchers, stickiness, time on site). This functionality causes identification of those social media that are of high importance to the enterprise as well as of opinion leading users and content that is especially influential and often virally passed on.

Engagement Module: By means of a uniform user interface it is possible to communicate within the sites that are listed in the Social Media Portfolio. Various activities in social media (search, upload, matching of posts and profiles, tagging, voting, categorization, administration of authorization) can be administered by using APIs that are provided by the particular operator. The module particularly supports the following forms of communication design in social media: direct dialogue with customers, distribution of viral content via seeding (spreading of media content targeted especially at opinion leaders), creation of a mass appeal by brand owners, complaint management.

5.3 Technological Implementation of the Integration of Social Media

The interfaces between the platform and external systems will be adapted to and enlarged according to APIs that are used in leading social networks. Main purpose is to create a central interface between the platform and the networks and then use it for all functionalities described above. Following APIs will be implemented: *Twitter*: usage of simple http accesses via GET/POST. It is necessary to implement REST API to enable access to core data as well as access via Streaming API. Processing of the responses is conducted in XML/JSON respectively via http status codes for malfunction reports. Usage of existing Open Source Java Libraries (Twitter4J, Java-twitter, jwitter) is planned. *Facebook*: Facebook Connect is used as the central API in order to access all functionalities. Existing JavaScript SDK is used for the development of the frontend. Usage of existing Open Source Java Libraries (Facebook-Java-API) is planned. *Youtube*: Different APIs are available enabling data access and integration of players. The focus is on Data API that offers access to manifold functionalities. Data API uses http accesses as well as XML and additionally Java Client Libraries can be used. Fig. 2 shows the technical implementation of the platform enlarged by integration of social media.

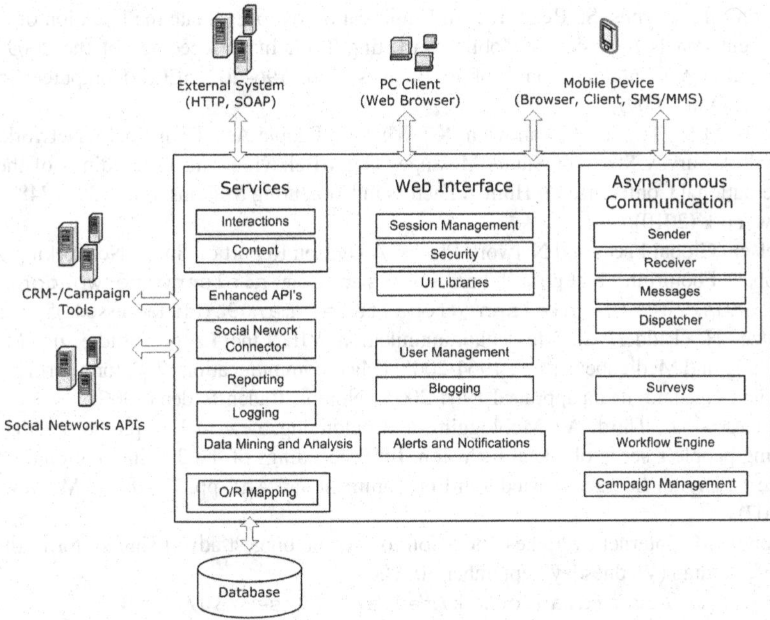

Fig. 2. Technical implementation of the platform enlarged by integration of social media

Acknowledgments. The developer teams of the evolaris foundation and of scoop and spoon did the programming of the platform. The team of scoop and spoon will code the future development. All that work is strongly appreciated.

References

1. Apple, `http://www.apple.com/at/itunes/billion-app-countdown/` (accessed 05.05.2010)
2. Little, A.D.: Exane BNP Paribas: Mobile Internet: blessing or curse? 9th edn. (2010)
3. Businesswire: GetJar Reveals That Mobile Apps Will Outsell CDs (2012), `http://www.businesswire.com/portal/site/home/permalink/?ndmViewId=news_view&newsId=20100316007140&newsLang=en` (accessed 05.05.2010)
4. Finkenzeller, K., Kenneth, C.: RFID Handbook: Fundamentals and Applications in Contactless Smart Cards. In: Identification and NFC. Wiley, UK (2010)
5. International Telecommunication Union: Mobile Phone Subscribers Pass 4 Billion Mark, `http://www.itu.int/ITU-D/ict/newslog/Mobile+Phone+Subscribers+Pass+4+Billion+Mark.aspx` (accessed 18.05.2009)
6. Jansen, B.J., Sobel, K., Cook, G.: Gen X and Ys attitudes on using social media platforms for opinion sharing. In: Proceedings of the 28th International Conference on Human Factors in Computing Systems, pp. 3853–3858. ACM, New York (2010)
7. Kato, H., Tan, K.T., Chai, D.: Barcodes for Mobile devices. Cambridge University Press, Cambridge (2010)

8. Maron, M., Magnus, S., Read, K.: An Empirical Study to Evaluate the Location of Advertisement Panels by Using a Mobile Marketing Tool. In: Proceedings of the 2009 Eigth International Conference on Mobile Business, pp. 196–202. IEEE Computer Society, Washington (2009)
9. Morris, M.R., Teevan, J., Panovich, K.: What Do People Ask Their Social Networks, and Why? A Survey Study of Status Messages Q&A Behaviour. In: Proceedings of the 28th International Conference on Human Factors in Computing Systems, pp. 1739–1748. ACM, New York (2010)
10. Nielsen: Global Faces and Network Places: A Nielsen Report on Social Networking's New Global Footprint, http://blog.nielsen.com/nielsenwire/wp-content/uploads/2009/03/nielsen_globalfaces_mar09.pdf (accessed 05.05.2010)
11. Reitze, H., Ridder, C.: Massenkommunikation VII. Eine Langzeitstudie zur Mediennutzung und Medienbewertung 1964-2005. (Mass communications 7. A long-term study of media usage and media appraisal 1964-2005.) Nomos, Baden-Baden (2006)
12. Richardson, I., Third, A.: Moblogging and belonging: new mobile phone practices and young people's sense of social inclusion. In: Proceedings of the 2nd International Conference on Digital Interactive Media in Entertainment and Arts, pp. 73–78. ACM, New York (2007)
13. Sweney, M.: Internet overtakes television to become biggest advertising sector in the UK, The Guardian (Wednesday September 30, 2009), http://www.guardian.co.uk/media/2009/sep/30/internet-biggest-uk-advertising-sector (accessed 05.05.2010)
14. Wallisch, A., Maxl, E.: A customer satisfaction study for Vodafone live. In: Maxl, E., Döring, N., Wallisch, A. (eds.) Mobile Market Research. Neue Schriften zur Online-Forschung 7 (New papers concerning online research 7), pp. 276–283. Herbert von Halem Verlag, Cologne (2009)

Reusing Geographic E-Services: A Case Study in the Marine Ecological Domain

Patricia Pernich[1,*], Agustina Buccella[1], Alejandra Cechich[1], Maria del Socorro Doldan[2], and Enrique Morsan[2]

[1] GIISCO Research Group
Departamento de Ciencias de la Computación
Universidad Nacional del Comahue
Neuquen, Argentina
patricia.pernich@gmail.com,
{abuccel,acechich}@uncoma.edu.ar
[2] Instituto de Biología Marina y Pesquera "Almirante Storni"
Universidad Nacional del Comahue - Ministerio de Producción de Rio Negro
San Antonio Oeste, Argentina
{msdoldan,qmorsan}@gmail.com

Abstract. Software product line engineering aims to reduce development time, effort, cost, and complexity by taking advantage of the commonality within a portfolio of similar products. This may benefit the development of applications in several domains, and particularly in geographic information systems (GIS). Reusing services for GIS challenges developers to produce assets highly adaptable to various service clients and contexts. For that, service variability must carefully be modeled by considering different recommendations such as well-established standards. This paper presents an approach that facilitates variability implementation, management and tracing by integrating product-line and GIS development. Features are separated following standard recommendations and composed on a platform-oriented framework. The presented concepts are illustrated with a case study of a marine ecological system.

Keywords: Geographic Information Systems, Software Product Lines, Services, Marine Ecology.

1 Introduction

During last years, information about geographic aspects has been widely regarded as crucial part of every information system. With the new emerging technologies, such as GPS devices or remote sensing techniques, the work of capturing geographic information is becoming easier. In addition, there exists hundred of proprietary and open source software to store this type of information in an efficient way.

* This work is partially supported by the UNComa project 04/E072 (Identificación, Evaluación y Uso de Composiciones Software).

W. Cellary and E. Estevez (Eds.): I3E 2010, IFIP AICT 341, pp. 193–204, 2010.

Thus, several organizations are interested in implementing interactive web portals or stand-alone systems that allow users to query and manage this type of information. In Geographic Information Systems (GIS) applications, there exists a set of geographic e-services that several organizations need. Identifying this common set of services and making them flexible to be implemented by the organizations might help reduce costs in development, staffing, maintenance, etc. With this goal in mind, we looked at two main areas of different research lines: software product line engineering and geographic information systems (GIS).

Within the first area, a system decomposition into high-level components is defined by considering the concepts of reuse and of family of products [1] (introduced firstly by Parnas [2] in 1976). In the literature there are several definitions of software product line engineering. One of them, defined in [3], introduces the concept of product lines as *a set of systems sharing common features and satisfying specific needs of a segment of a market.* The main characteristics involved in this new discipline are [4]: *variability*, in which individual systems are considered as variations of a common part; *architecture-based*, in which the software must be developed by considering the similarities among individual systems; and *two-life cycles approach*, in which two engineerings in every software product line process must be considered: *domain engineering and application engineering* [4,5].

In the second area to be analyzed, GIS have emerged to allow the storage and manipulation of geographic information in spatial domains or with geographic characteristics. The special nature of geographic information results in a set of characteristics that must be taken into account in the development of a GIS application. In addition, there have been many research and industrial efforts to standardize many aspects of GIS technology, particularly by the Open Geospatial Consortium[1] (OGC) and the ISO Technical Committee 211[2] (ISO/TC 211, Geographic Information/Geomatics). For instance, the Service Architecture standard (defined in OpenGIS Service Architecture)[3]and the ISO/DIS 19119[4] std. define a taxonomy of geographic services in which each service of a particular system should be classified into one or more categories (depending on whether it is a simple or aggregate service).

In this work, we introduce a methodology for creating software product lines for GIS applications by combining the advantages of two widely referenced methodologies in the literature [1, 5]. The main goal is to create a software product line taking into account the set of common e-services of GIS software within a specific domain (in this case, the marine ecological domain). These common e-services are firstly defined by using the standard information provided in the ISO 19119. We also propose the creation of a framework to support the generation of new products within the line. The framework acts as a platform allowing developers to reuse implementation of common e-services, instantiate variable e-services, and implement product-specific e-services.

This paper is organized as follows: Section 2 describes our methodology to create the product-line for GIS applications and briefly describes related works in

[1] `http://www.opengeospatial.org`

[2] `http://www.isotc211.org/`

[3] The OpenGIS Abstract Specification: Service Architecture, 2002.

[4] Geographic information. Services. International Standard 19119, ISO/IEC, 2005.

this area. Then, we describe the instantiation of the product line applied to an real project. Future work and conclusions are discussed afterwards.

2 A Software Product Line Specification for GIS

For many years, the Open Geospatial Consortium (OGC) and the International Organization for Standardization (ISO) had worked independently to reach overlapping goals, but nowadays both converge towards a common solution. The ISO/TC 211 deals with long-term, abstract, static standards, meanwhile the OGC works on industry-oriented, technology-dependent, evolving standards. Thus, the development of GIS applications can be done by following these standards in order to improve interoperability among systems. However, although software reuse among different systems could be improved when these standards are applied, they are not created for this purpose. Special efforts must be done to reach effective reuse.

Secondly, in the literature there exists several techniques proposing methodologies to develop a software product-line. Some of the most referenced proposals are [1, 3–5]. All of them propose a division into common and variable aspects of the product line, and a set of tasks or activities that must be done to specify and implement these aspects. For example, in [3] and in [4, 5] authors propose the same type of phases but with different names and activities. In [4, 5] the phases, named as *domain engineering and application engineering*, define common and variable aspects, and derive the product line from the platform defined in the first phase. Other recent proposals are analyzed in [6]. Here, authors compare four methodologies that involve specific goals to improve different aspects of a software product line development. For example, FAST (Family-Oriented Abstraction, Specification, and Translation) [7] defines a methodology based on a software engineering process trying to improve some aspects such as production costs, time-to-market, etc.

To the best of our knowledge, the two sets of work, GIS standards and software product lines, are not related in the literature. The creation of software product lines for GIS products is only seen as another application of a product line development. In addition, there are few references applying these concepts together. However, geographic software shares a set of common services that are essential for every application; therefore these common services might be identified and modeled as part of the product line together with different variations.

Our work is based on the creation of a software product line to be used by organizations working within the marine ecological domain that are interested in implementing geographic e-services. In order to build the software product line we combined characteristics of two methodologies defined in [1, 5]. Each methodology presents a set of processes to perfom this task. We have combined both proposals in order to take advantage of their best-defined processes. In particular, we modified the main process, named domain engineering, from the software product line engineering framework defined in [5]. We have defined a different set of six subprocesses by applying activities defined in both methodologies. Figure1 shows these subprocesses together with their main tasks.

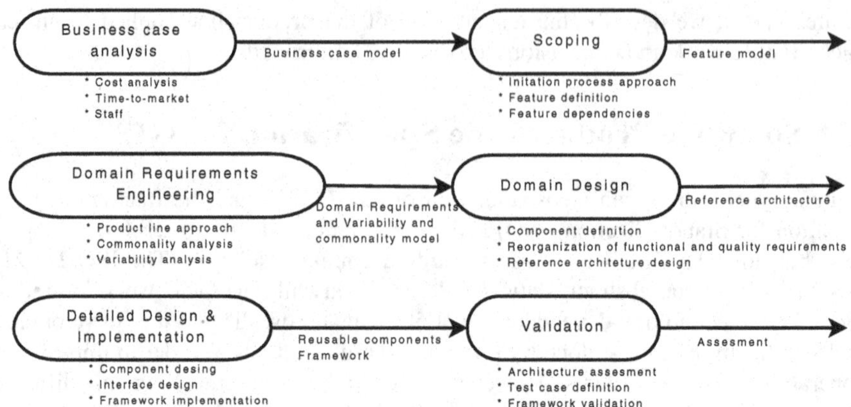

Fig. 1. Domain Engineering process

Following, we briefly describe how these tasks were applied to create the software product line for a GIS application within the marine ecological domain.

- *Business case analysis*: To perform this subprocess, the situation of the different organizations in Argentine working on the marine ecological domain was analyzed. In our case, few organizations had applications involving geographic information. They had used only office software tools in which almost all the tasks were made manually. Therefore, the costs and staff needed were analyzed by taking into account two main phases. In the first one, we analyzed the aspects needed to implement the product line and its supporting application framework. In the second phase, we analyzed what we needed to implement future products by instantiating the framework.
- *Scoping*: We applied an evolutionary approach as starting point for the development of the product line architecture. In this way, we started from a set of existing software products. However, by considering the aspects analyzed in the previous subprocess, we could not take the organizations' software products, which were incomplete and unreliable. Instead, we used a set of related geographic open source software tools for GIS, which provided features needed by our architecture. Then, we defined the features that were candidate for inclusion in the product line. In [1] *a feature is defined as logical unit of behaviour that is specified by a set of functional and quality requirements*. In our work, we firstly defined features by using the ISO 19119 standard as a starting point to define a set of specific features. Table 1[5] shows part of the resultant features. For brevity reasons we do not include here all of them.

  Then, we analyzed which services (shown in Table 1) are implemented by the geographic open source tools so we have a basis for implementing e-services

[5] In the table we can see that the term "feature" has a different meaning. In the standard a "feature" is defined as an abstraction of real world phenomena. We refer this term as "geographic feature" in order to differentiate it from the term "feature" defined by the domain engineering process.

into a particular platform. Seven tools were classified into three categories: *thin web clients, geographic databases, and map servers.* In the first category we analyzed four thin web clients (Mapfish[6], p.mapper[7], Ka-Map[8], and Map-Bender[9]) which implement the features S1, S2, S5 and S8, and partially implement the features S6 and S7. In the second category we analyzed databases which include geographic analysis. In this case, both MySQL GIS[10] and Postgis[11] databases can implement the features S3 and S6. In the third category, the map servers UMN MapServer[12] and GeoServer[13] were analyzed to implement the feature S4 allowing the access to geographic maps.

- *Domain requirements engineering*: We used a minimalist approach in which only the features used in all products are part of the product line. In our case, this approach allowed us to fully implement only common features and let the

Table 1. Part of geographic services required by our architecture

Categories	Service	Specific Features
Geographic human interaction	S1. Geographic viewer	S1.1) Show and query data of geographic features. S1.2) Show/hide layers. S1.3) Zoom tool. S1.4) Panning tool. S1.5) Scale. S1.6) Navigation buttons (previous/next)
	S2. Geographic feature editor	S2.1) See, query and edit geographic features graphically. S2.2) Add new geographic features by using the graphic interface
Geographic model/information management services	S3. Feature access service	S3.1) Perform queries to a geographic feature repository. S3.2) Manage data of the geographic features
	S4. Map access service	S4.1) Access to geographic maps
Spatial processing services	S5. Proximity analysis service	S5.1) Obtain all geographic features within a specific area
Temporal processing services	S6. Temporal proximity analysis service	S6.1) Obtain all geographic features within a specified time
Metadata processing services	S7. Statistical calculation service	S7.1) Generate statistics with data of geographic features
	S8. Geographic annotation services	S8.1) Add additional information to a geographic features. S8.2) Add additional information to a map

6 http://mapfish.org/
7 http://www.pmapper.net/
8 http://ka-map.maptools.org
9 http://www.mapbender.org/
10 http://dev.mysql.com/tech-resources/articles/4.1/gis-with-mysql.html
11 http://postgis.refractions.net/
12 http://mapserver.org
13 http://geoserver.org/

Table 2. Features that are part of the product-line and specific-product features

Products/Features	S1	S2	S3	S4	S5	S6	S7	S8	S9	S10	S11
Product-line	X	X	X	X	X		X	X			
Product 1						X					
Product 2									X		
Product 3										X	
Product 4											X

product-specific features be implemented by each different organization. Thus, our software product line is seen as a *platform* [4]. Table 2 shows the subset of features that are part of the product-line and the subset of features that are product-specific features.

As we can observe, features S1-S5 and S7-S8 are part of the product-line. S6 is a product-specific feature that will be implemented only by Product 1. Similarly, features S9, S10 and S11 are part only of each Product 2, 3 and 4, respectively. Feature S9 is a catalogue viewer service within the geographic human interaction category. It allows to locate, browse, and manage meta-data about geographic data or geographic services in a catalogue. Features S10 and S11 belong to the spatial processing services category. The first one, named *coordinate conversion service*, allows to change coordinates of a feature from one coordinate system to another one. Finally, feature S11, named *positioning service*, is provided by a position-providing device (like a GPS) to use, obtain and unambiguously interpret position information. In addition, within each feature we determined the commonality and variability models. Figure 2[14] shows the variability model associated to the feature S7.1 of the product-line. In this model we can see that statistics can be represented by using two variants – histograms or tables.

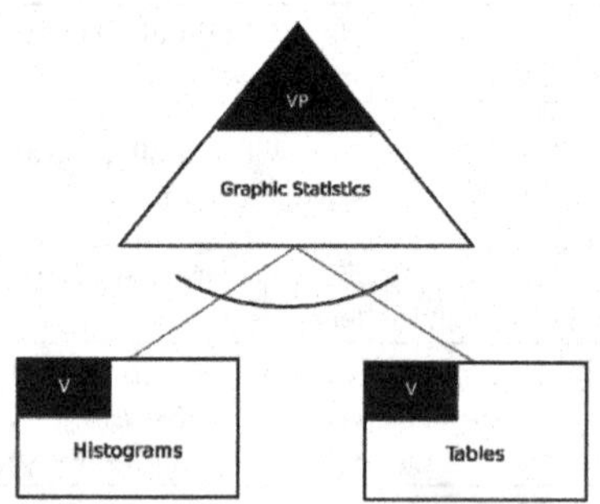

Fig. 2. Variability model of feature S7.1

- *Domain design*: Now, it is time to build the reference architecture based on the features defined in the previous subprocesses. We reorganized the features into two sets of requirements to separate functional from non-functional (quality) needs. These sets were the basis to define our architecture's components. We

[14] We use the graphical notation for variability models defined in [5].

chose a layered architectural style to facilitate dealing with modifiability and scalability requirements. The reference architecture is composed of three main layers: *geographic model, geographic processing, and user interface*. In the first layer we implemented the geographic model that allows the access to a geographic database. The second layer defines features involving processing (features S3-S8 described in Table 1); and the third layer defines the S1 and S2 features in which graphical aspects are involved. Special components in these layers are responsible for performing the operations that must be taken into account to publish, find and bind e-services. The next layers implement services as e-services provided to users or other systems.

- *Detailed design and Implementation*: In addition to define the architecture of the product line, we created an application framework to be used as a platform for each product of the product line. The framework covers the behaviour that is common for all products and allow developers to add product- specific features.
- *Validation*: There are several aspects to analyze within this subprocess.Firstly, some test cases were defined in order to test the framework and the specification of the product line. Secondly, we tested the instantiation of the product line by creating new GIS products (as the one we will describe in the next section).

3 Instantiating the Product Line: A Case Study

In this case, we build the Product 1 (Table 2) containing features of the product line plus a set of product-specific ones (S6). The other products in the software line (Products 2–4) will belong to other organizations within the marine ecological domain (Instituto Argentino de Oceanografía[15] , Centro Nacional Patagonico[16], and Laboratorio de Moluscos y Crustáceos belonging to the University of Mar del Plata).

Product 1 emerged from a project between GIISCO research group[17] and the Instituto de Biología Marina y Pesquera "Almirante Storni"[18] (IBMPAS). IBMPAS is responsible for analyzing and storing information about sea surveys in the San Matías Gulf, Patagonia Argentina. Each survey, perfomed once a year (when it is possible), collects information about the population of specific species living in this area. This information is then used for spatial processesing in order to obtain information about spatial distribution of data, population variation patterns in different scales, etc.

Table 3 shows the features of Table 1 redefined according to the requirements of the product. For example, the feature S1.1 is redefined as a set of new features (a-c) to show different geographic features of the sources; and the feature S1.2 allows the user to show and hide layers. In this product we implement several layers including sea zones[19], stations [20], and abundance and density of species[21] . For brevity reasons, we

[15] `http://iado.criba.edu.ar/web/`

[16] `http://www.cenpat.edu.ar/`

[17] `http://giisco.uncoma.edu.ar/`

[18] `http://ibmpas.org/`

[19] A zone is a maritime area bounded and defined with a specific name in the gulf.

[20] A station is a geographic point located within one of the defined zones. In this location the measures of population of species are obtained.

[21] The abundance of a species indicates the number of them in a specific location (in a zone or station, according to the geographical scale chosen). The density displays the number of individuals per m2.

only include here a subset of the layers and of the instantiated features within each feature category.

Following, the variability models must be also instantiated. In order to illustrate this, Figure 3 shows the instantiation in which the feature S7.1 (presented in Figure 2) is implemented by using histograms (not by using a table). The figure shows the component that implements this service (S7.1) and an arrow from the variant point (histogram) indicating that the component uses this variation.

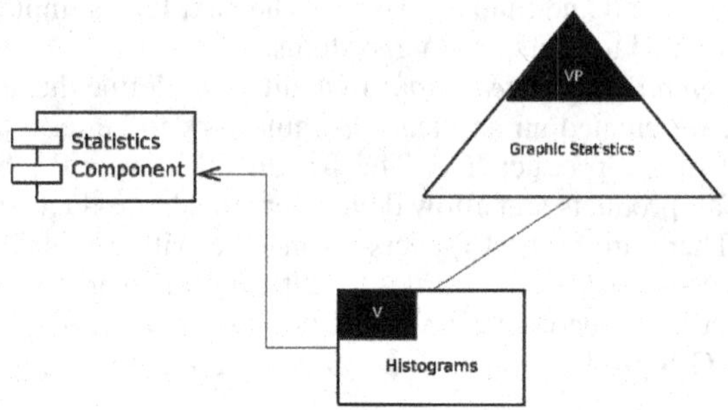

Fig. 3. Instantiated variability model of feature S7.1

Table 3. Instantiated features required in Product 1

Categories	Service	Specific Features
Geographic human interaction	S1. Geographic viewer	S1.1) a) Show zones. b) Show stations within a zone. c) ... S1.2) a) Show/hide the zone layer. b) Show/hide the density layer. c) ...
	S2. Geographic feature editor	S2.1) a) Show a map with the location of zones. b) Show a map with the abundance of species. c) Show a map with the density of a specific species. d)... S2.2) a) Add a station within a specific zone. b) Add the density of species within a specific station. c) ...
Geographic model/information management services	S3. Feature access service	S3.1) a) Query zones of density of species. b) Query zones in which the population of species are higher than a specific value. c) ... S3.2) a) Modify thematic attributes of a zone. b) ...
	S4. Map access service	S4.1) a) Allow to create an image showing the density of species in several zones. b) ...
Spatial processing services	S5. Proximity analysis service	S5.1) a) Obtain the location of stations within a specific zone. b) Obtain the number of species in a specific zone. c) Obtain the density of a determined species in a specific zone. d) ...
Temporal processing services	S6. Temporal proximity analysis service	S6.1) a) Obtain the number of specimens of specific species in a zone at different times. b) ...
Metadata processing services	S7. Statistical calculation service	S7.1) a) Generate a histogram with the density of species. b) ...

Finally, we have to create the architecture based on the reference architecture defined in the last section. The architecture of Product 1 is used to provide a set of different e-services to users of IBMPAS. As an example, we describe here two of them – *density of a specific species* and *length frequency of a specific species* services. The first one returns information about the number of specimens per *m*2 of a species in a specific location. The input of the service is an area of interest defined by the user, which may be a particular geographical zone or area that covers the entire gulf. Depending on the chosen scale, the service shows the number of this species in one zone or all zones in the gulf. The output of the service is a combination of three layers: *the zone* layer, *the station* layer (which are located within zones), and a layer showing *the density of species* at each station. Thus, it is possible to query the population of specific species found in different years and compare the generated maps to detect possible migrations of specimens of a species. In addition, it is possible to analyze different reasons of these migration movements. Figure 4 shows the output map when a user runs the *density of a specific species* service. In this case, data are displayed in all zones of the gulf. As we can see, each point indicates the density of the *Ostrea puelchana* species in a given station. The darker color indicates a greater concentration of the number of specimens per *m*2 of the species at that station. The polygons define the covered area by each zone.

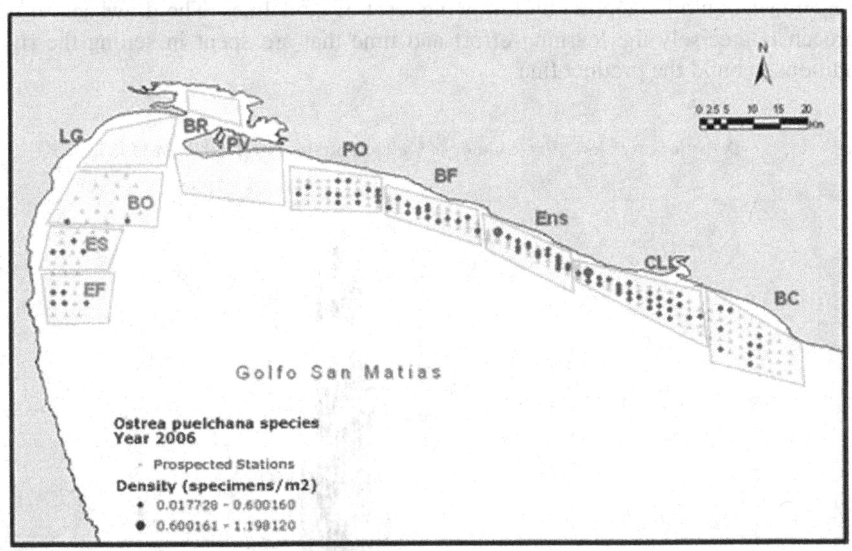

Fig. 4. A map representing the *density of a specific species* service

The other service, *length frequency of a specific species*, generates statistics data based on the stored information. In this case, from measures of each specimen found for a specific species, the service shows the frequency of occurrence of each size. Figure 5 displays a histogram of the length frequency of a species named *Vieyra Tehuelche*, in the Northwest zone of the San Matias Gulf.

Each of these two services uses several of the features defined in Table 3. For instance, the *density of a specific species* service uses the features S2.1)a) and c), S3.1)a), S4.1)a) and S5.1)c). Moreover, the *length frequency of a specific species* service uses the feature S7 that is implemented by using histograms.

3.1 Lessons Learned

We tried to ensure validity by using multiple sources of data to build the product line, i.e. interviews, document analysis, and validation sessions. We aimed to show that software product family practices can be applied in several different geographic contexts. Based on the results of the case study (Section 3), we identify the following lessons:

Software product family engineering can be applied to small ecological organizations. Our approach has successfully developed its products in a software product family. The benefits of this model of development have not been directly measured, but one indicator of the success is that the development cost and time-to-market were drastically reduced. Product 1 was available in the short time and the needed staff was fewer than the one needed for the creation of the product line. Of course, benefits would be better quantified whether the organizations follow a defined process, but this was not the case. However, although their processes were ad-hoc in most cases, our approach could be applied by following a set of guidelines. The drawback of our approach is precisely the learning effort and time that are spent in setting the right conditions to build the product line.

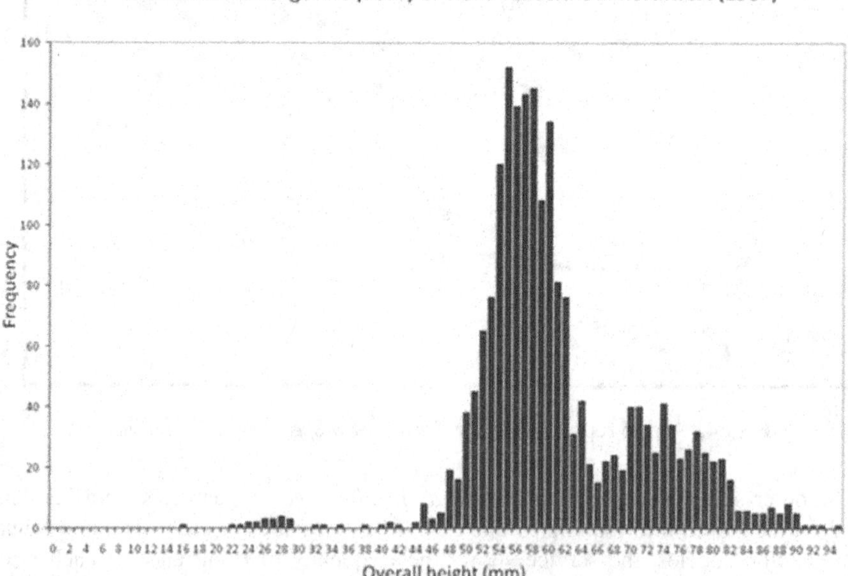

Fig. 5. A histogram representing the *length frequency of a specific species* service

A software product family development can cross organization borders. Geographic information development is shared among distributed ecological organizations. In fact, the challenge lies in specifying the required variability for each case of software. Extending existing variation points with new variants is easier than creating new variation points from scratch. It is not necessary to specify all possible variants, but it is essential to ensure that the new software implements some mechanisms for all variation points. To address this issue, we are currently analyzing the application of verification configurations models.

Building reusable assets requires variability mechanisms. A software product family requires effective ways of realising and implementing variability mechanisms. From our case, effective variability implementation is as much as important than effective variability management. Both aspects should be considered and we are extending the approach to explicitly include management guidelines. For instance, before we were able to implement the variability model of the product family, we had to externalize the variability information from the product family artifacts and the experts. During this externalization process, engineers and experts found many (previously unknown) conflicts in their own artifacts.

These conflicts were solved following a set of recommendations that should be institutionalized.

4 Conclusion and Future Work

In this work we have introduced a framework for building geographic information systems from a software product line, and we have illustrated the process through a case study. Our work emerges as a solution to different organizations within the marine ecological domain. The main goal is to reduce the development effort involved in the creation of this type of systems. In this way, two main requirements of every GIS software within the ecological domain might be fulfilled. On one hand, *flexibility* might be improved because new products can easily perform changes in the requirements by means of instantiating variable aspects of services. On the other hand, *reusability* might be reached because components of the architecture are created for that purpose.

As future work, the methodology and the framework need more validation by analyzing the process of building new products of the line. However, we are aware that developing management guidelines is also crucial for sucessfully applying the approach.

References

1. Bosch, J.: Design and use of software architectures: adopting and evolving a product- line approach. ACM Press/Addison-Wesley Publishing Co., New York (2000)
2. Parmas, D.: On the design and development of program families. IEEE Transactions on Software Engineering SE-2(1), 1–9 (1976)
3. Clements, P., Northrop, L.: Software Product Lines: Practices and Patterns. Addison-Wesley Professional, Reading (August 2001)

4. Van Der Linden, F., Schmid, K., Rommes, E.: Software Product Lines in Action: The Best Industrial Practice in Product Line Engineering. Springer, New York (2007)
5. Pohl, K., Böckle, G., van der Linden, F.: Software Product Line Engineering: Foundations, Principles and Techniques. Springer, Heidelberg (September 2005)
6. Matinlassi, M.: Comparison of software product line architecture design methods: Copa, fast, form, kobra and qada. In: Proceedings of the ICSE 2004: 26th International Conference on Software Engineering, Washington, DC, USA, pp. 127–136. IEEE Computer Society, Los Alamitos (2004)
7. Weiss, D., Lai, C.T.R.: Software product-line engineering: a family-based software development process. Addison-Wesley Longman Publishing Co., Inc., Boston (1999)

Ontology-Based Process for Recommending Health WebSites

Edelweis Rohrer[1], Regina Motz[1], and Alicia Díaz[2]

[1] Instituto de Computación, Facultad de Ingeniería,Universidad de la República, Uruguay
{erohrer,rmotz}@fing.edu.uy
[2] LIFIA, Facultad de Informática,Universidad Nacional de La Plata, Argentina
alicia.diaz@lifia.info.unlp.edu.ar

Abstract. Website content quality is particularly relevant in the health domain. A common user needs to retrieve health information that is precise, reliable and relevant to his/her profile. Website recommendation systems are an aid to get high quality health-related web sites according to the user's needs. However, in practice, it is not always evident how to describe recommendation criteria for health website. The goal of this paper is to describe, by an ontology network, the criteria used by a health website recommendation process. This ontology network conceptualizes the different domains that are involved in the *Salus* Recommendation Project as a set of interrelated ontologies[1].

Keywords: web site, recommendation system, ontology network.

1 Introduction

The use of the web by common people as a repository of information, especially in the health area, increases drastically day by day. This is a very worrying reality because many of health web sites do not contain data according to user´s necessities. For example, a technical content may not be a good quality reference for a person which is not able to understand technical vocabulary. On the other hand, the alternative medicine products that are offered on the Internet, the lack of quality controls (editorial boards) at the stage of production of the web site and the "lack of context", lead to information does not necessarily have to be false to harm [1]. Furthermore, the fact that the web is a very dynamic medium, once a person has obtained misinformation, then, it is very unlikely to be reversed by health professionals. In this sense, a decentralized, ontology-based recommender system can automatically give an evaluation about the quality of the sources according to the consumer's needs.

Quality in websites is determined by several diverse factors, some of which are general, and therefore, considered for any type of sites and for any domain. Such features include, for example, navigational aspects, user interface aspects, legibility

[1] This work was partially funded by: the SALUS/CYTED and PROSUL projects which are sponsored by the CnPq, Brasil and the CyTED, Spain. It is also supported by the PAE 37279-PICT 02203 which is sponsored by the ANPCyT, Argentina.

W. Cellary and E. Estevez (Eds.): I3E 2010, IFIP AICT 341, pp. 205–214, 2010.

(size of letter, colors, images), performance aspects (time it takes to access to the site content), the correct functioning of the site, its conformity with standards of language use or of accessibility like those described in normative such as the Web Content Accessibility Guidelines of the W3C[2]. Some quality models that take these features into consideration are WebQual [2] and WebQEM [3].

On the other hand, in this work we focus on the quality that arises of the information value that the site provides and its adequacy for the consumer's context. The consumer´s context contains two domains: the user profile and the query goal. The first is described by properties as gender, age, employment among others. The second relates to the purpose for which information is needed, it can be, for example, buy a drug, selecting a doctor or write a school paper.

Our approach is to consider, in an integrated way, the specific health domain of interest (i.e. diagnosis, treatment, etc.), the dimensions of quality factors, the user's context and the criteria to assure that some information is in accordance to the goal of "fitness for use" for a consumer [4]. With this aim, we specify a process driven by an ontology network that leads to give a recommendation of suitability of web contents to a particular user who makes a specific query. The ontology network describes how to set up the quality factors and the recommendation criteria considering the specific domain, properties of websites and consumer goals.

This paper is organized as follows. Section 2 describes issues about quality assurance and recommender systems. Section 3 presents the *Salus* ontology network. In section 4 we discuss the process for web sites recommendation based on the *Salus* ontology network. Finally, we discuss conclusions and future perspectives.

2 Background on Recommender Systems and Data Quality

Recommender systems could be defined as systems that produce individualized recommendations as output or has the effect of guiding the user in a personalized way to interesting or useful objects in a large space of possible options [9]. Within the broad range of existent works, we will mention some of the more recent ones.

The approach presented by Porcel et al. in [11] consists of a recommendation model based on vectors that represent the resource scope and users interests, and then to match them. There were distinguished four different classes of recommendation techniques: (1) *content-based systems*, based on the terms used about resources (2) *collaborative systems* that consider the user preferences, (3) *Demographic systems* that represent the different user profiles and (4) *knowledge-based systems*, based on inferences about resources that satisfy the users. These authors proposed a hybrid approach that combines content-based and collaborative techniques. In [10], Oufaida and Nouali present a multi view recommender system that includes collaborative, social and semantic views of the user's profile, related to a set of resources semantically annotated. Recently, in [12], it is presented the construction of a recommender system which is described as an iterative process; where at each iteration a model representing the preferential characteristics for the recommendation is obtained. The

[2] http://www.w3.org/WAI/GL/

system is an ontology-based recommendation process that produces recommendations by applying content-based, context-aware and collaborative criteria.

Unlike the mentioned works, our proposal of recommendation process is strongly based on the quality assessment of the web contents. However, there exist some common aspects with them. Considering the classification of recommendation techniques given by [11], our proposal also matches user profiles and resources, although we rather combine content-based (web content properties) and demographic (user profiles) approaches. Furthermore, some aspects faced by [12], as considering context issues (i.e. the query situation at the moment the user makes a query) and the exploitation of ontological structures that underlie the recommendation process, are also considered in our proposal. In the next section we present the quality assurance onto-logy and how it is related in the ontology network in order to specify a recommendation process.

There are, basically, two ways of defining data quality: the first one uses a scientific approach and defines data quality dimensions rigorously, classifying them as dimensions that are or are not intrinsic to an information system [4]. The second one is a pragmatic approach aimed at defining data quality in an operational fashion [5]. Wang et al. [4] identified four data quality dimensions: (1) intrinsic data quality; (2) contextual data quality, which defines the quality of the information within the context of the task; (3) data quality for data representation, which determines if the system presents the information in a concise, consistent, understandable way; (4) data quality regarding data access, which defines quality in terms of the role of the information system in the provision of the data.

Within each dimension it is possible to identify several factors, including: for *intrinsic data quality dimension*: believability, accuracy, objectivity and for *context dimension*: value-added, relevancy, timeliness, completeness, among others. The domain expert is the one who decides which of these factors are relevant for a specific domain and she/he is who defines the appropriate metrics to measure these factors. Regarding Believability, two definitions are introduced in [6]: *Believability,* which is *the extent to which data is regarded as true and credible* and *Reputation,* which is *the extent to which data is highly regarded in terms of its source or content.* About this factor in health domain, it is important to take into account the existence of sites with certified quality labels, such as HON (http://www.hon.ch/), WIS (http://www.portalesmedicos.com/) and WMA (http://wma.comb.es/). For the readability factor, in [7], it is introduced different readability metrics that were created for different domains and user profiles. It sets the following definition: *Readability is what makes some texts easier to read than others.* There are a lot of readability formulas created for different authors, like FOG[3] and SMOG[4] grade levels. Here also, the decision on which formula to use, FoG or SMOG, must be taken by a domain expert. The first step is to specify a formal model that represents the factors involved in the acquisition of the quality of web data as well as the different metrics that can be applied. The main intention of measuring the data quality is to provide a quantitative meaning of quality dimensions. Metrics are these quantitative or categorical representations of one or more attributes [15].

[3] FOG grade level = 0.4 (average sentence length + hard words).

[4] SMOG grade level = 3 + ?polysyllable count.

Our approach to face this challenge is the design of an ontological model inspired in our previous work [8] on web data warehouse quality, by modelling a generic ontology for quality factors, independent from the specific domain and the different types of web data sources. It is easily tailored to different user domains and different types of web data through its connection in the proposed ontology-network. In the next section we present the quality ontology in the context of an ontology network.

3 Salus Ontology Network

The *Salus* ontology network helps to obtain a reading recommendation of health-related web contents for a particular user. Specifically, it conceptualizes the different knowledge domains that are involved in a recommendation system in a shape of an ontology network. An ontology network is a collection of ontologies related together through a variety of different relationships such as mapping, modularization, and versioning, among others [13]. Accordingly, a networked ontology is an ontology included in such a network, sharing relationships with other ontologies. Intuitively, this implies to define the ontologies' content, but also to define metadata information about the networked ontologies. Ontology metadata refers to the information which is attached to the ontology itself, not to its content. This ontology metadata would cover ontology provenance, purpose and the relations with other ontologies and semantic resources. They are critical because they describe an ontology network as a whole.

Salus ontology network conceptualizes the following domains: specific health, web site, quality assurance, user context and recommendation. Each domain is represented by one or more interrelated ontologies.

- *Health domain* ontologies conceptualize the health domain. The core ontology may be an already existing ontology like UMLS[5] which models for example the impact, treatment, risk factors, diagnostic, effects, and phases of a disease. This ontology can be refined in terms of a specific disease i.e Alzheimer, and thus can be modelled the concept "Alzheimer treatment". *Salus* ontology network is specific to the health field, but it could be adapted to other domains just by changing the health ontology by other domain ontology.
- *Web Site domain ontologies* conceptualize the domain of webpages and particularly describe the web resources that will be considered to participate in a quality assessment. The main concepts of this ontology are *web resource* and *web resource property. A web resource* is any resource which is identified by a URL; for instance, it can be instantiated as a webpage which has attached content. *Web resource property* models the properties that can be attached to a *web resource*. For instance, possible properties of *web resources* could be the “author”, the “amount of words”, etc. Among these properties there is a particular one, the “hasTopic” property that relates concepts (web resources) from the *Web Site* ontology with concepts in the *Specific Health* ontology. The “hasTopic” property describes what a *web resource* is talking about. These kind of properties should be retrieved through a specific information retrieval mechanism, as it will be detailed below.

[5] http://www.nlm.nih.gov/research/umls/

- *Quality Assurance domain ontologies* conceptualize metrics, quality assurance specifications and quality assessments. *Metrics* are formula defined base on *web resource properties*. A *quality assurance specification* describes the different *quality dimensions*; for instance readability, precision, believability, completeness, timeliness, etc. The *quality assurance specification* associates to each quality dimension the suitable metric calculus. A *quality assessment* models the assessment of a particular web resource (i.e. a web document) for a particular quality dimension through a specific metric. It also models the obtained quality level.
- *Context domain ontologies* describe user profiles and query resources. The user profile conceptualizes user properties such as user age range, role, academic level, health domain expertise. among others. The query resource represents the context of the query. The main concept of the query resource is the query goal.
- *Recommendation domain ontologies* describe the different criteria of recommendation for a particular context (user and query situation) and quality dimensions and the obtained recommendation level.

Salus networked ontologies are interrelated (see in the upper of figure 1) by three different relationships: *uses*, *extends* and *describes* relationships:

- The *uses* relationship relates two ontologies by the import primitive. For example, this relationship occurs between the *Web Site* ontology and the *Specific Domain* ontology because of a *webpage topic* can be any concept at the specific domain ontology. In the *Salus* ontology network, *webpage topics* could be treatment, diagnostic, etc. Thus, "Alzheimer Treatment" is a topic of "Alzheimer Webpage".
- The *extends* relationship describes a more specific ontology which is the specialization of a more general one. The clearer example is the *Alzheimer* ontology, which is a specialization of the *Health* ontology. For example, at the *Health* ontology conceptualizes: diagnostic, treatment, risk factors, etc; then these concepts are specialized in the *Alzheimer* ontology.
- The *describes* relationship defines the relations between a model and its metamodel. For instance, the *Web Site* ontology is an instantiation of the Web Site Specification ontology. The later is a meta-ontology for the former. Webpages are typical concepts at the *Web Site* ontology and are modelled by the *webpage* class. This class is an instance of *Web Resource* class which is defined at the *Web Site Specification* ontology. Another example is the property "has Author" that is defined at the *Web Site* ontology as an instance of the *Web Resource Property* class, which is also defined at the *Web Site Specification* ontology.

On the bottom part of the Figure 1 is shown an example of the resulting knowledge base where the content of the "Alzheimer webpage" was assessed to be recommended to the user "Paul". The content associated to the "Alzheimer webpage" has "Alzheimer Treatment" and "Alzheimer Diagnostic" as topics. In this example the recommendation assessment took into account the "Believability" quality dimension, assessed by "provenance" metric, which uses the "has Author" property of the webpage. The recommendation assessment also considers the fact the user Paul is a teenager and the goal of his query is "looksFor". Later, in the section 4 more detail about the networked ontologies will be given.

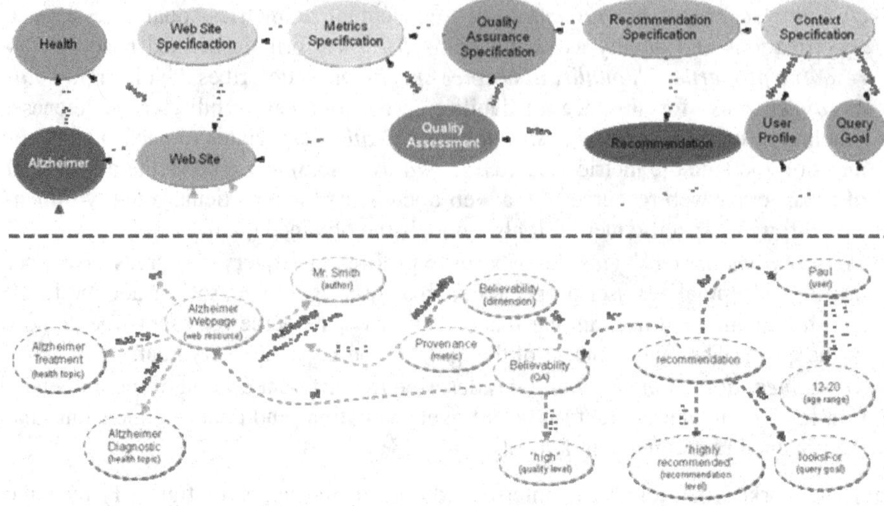

Fig. 1. An example of the *Salus* ontology network

4 *Salus* Recommendation Process

The *Salus* recommendation process covers the different tasks which have to be performed in order to recommend a set of web sites to a particular user. These tasks are organized in three different phases, namely, the start up of the recommendation system, the quality assessment of a set web pages and the execution of recommendation assessments. This process is characterized as an ontology-based process. Specifically, it is based-on the *Salus* ontology network described in previous section. During the execution of the *Salus* process, the *Salus* networked ontologies plays different roles: in some cases it helps to discovering knowledge domain units in the web pages (i.e. based on the specific health ontology), while in other cases, it helps to supporting quality or recommendation assessments. In the last cases, the *Salus* ontology network can be used to both: assist in the modelling and specification of a recommendation system and check the correctness of the resulting system specification. Particularly, this section will go in deep explaining the *Salus* ontology network during the recommendation start-up phase explanation.

4.1 Recommendation Start-Up Phase

The *recommendation system start-up phase* is in charge of preparing the information needed in order to recommend web pages. This phase consists of the tasks: web resource definition, quality criteria definition, recommendation criteria definition and context resource definition, schematized in Figure 2. Next, we will detailed them and show where, when and how the *Salus* ontology network is used.

Web Resource definition. It refers to the population of the Web site ontology according to a given set of webpages and their indexation based on the specific domain ontology. The *Web site* ontology is populated with *webpages* instances (one for each given webpages) and with properties that are involved in the newly defined instances; for example the "url" property is specified between a webpage and a URL. Then, these webpages are indexed according to the *Specific Domain* ontology; in *Salus*, it corresponds to the *Alzheimer* ontology. In this task the "hasTopic" property is specified between "Alzheimer webpage" and Alzheimer concepts, as it is shown in the figure 1. Then, in next task more properties will be discovered.

Quality criteria defnition. It refers to the definition of quality dimensions and metrics that will be supported by the recommender system. First of all, it have to be specified the repertoire of factors involved in the quality dimensions. Based on it, the definition consists on specifying which metric assets each quality factor and which are the possible obtained quality levels. Metrics are specified based on *web resource properties* (concepts of the Web site ontology). For example, when the "provenance" factor is instantiated, the "basedOn" property will be also instantiated in order to link the "provenance" factor with the "has Author" property. The "has Author" property has to be now specified as an instance of *web resource property* and it may be specified the metric used to capture this value. Then, the *Quality Specification* ontology has to be populated. Quality dimension concepts have to be instantiated. These quality dimensions are those supported by the recommender system. Each quality dimension concept at least has once defined the *assesedBy* property to link a quality factor to the metrics that enable its assessment. Quality dimension concepts also have defined the *assesTo* property to link a quality dimension to its possible quality levels. For instance, the dimension "Believability" has defined the *assesedBy* property which takes values in the "provenance" factor and the *assesTo* property to the set of strings: "high", "medium" and "low".

Recommendation criteria definition. It refers to the definition of recommendation criteria. Based on the quality criteria definition, a *recommendation definition* indicates which quality dimensions will be assessed and which *context resources* will be considered for a recommendation. *Context resources* are mainly *user properties* and *query resources*. The output of this task is a set of *recommendation rules* which specify the *recommendation level* for each assessed web page. These rules are like:

if recommendation definition(thisWebPage)
then thisWebPage **is** recommendationLevel(thisWebPage)

where *thisWebPage* is the currently processed webpage and the *recommendation definition(thisWebPage)* is described in terms of quality assurances and context. The recommendation level for a webpage is one of the scale values of the scales of recommendation levels of the recommender system (for example, "highly recommended", "strongly recommended"). Regarding, the example we have been followed along the paper, the rule below might be defined as follow:

if BelievabilityQA(AlzheimerWebpage) **assesTo** "high" **and** Paul **belongsTo** 12-20 age range **and** query goal **is** looksFor
then *AlzheimerWebpage* **is** *highly recommended*

Context resource definition. It is in charge of defining those *context resources* that have to be taken into account to make a recommendation. These *context resources*

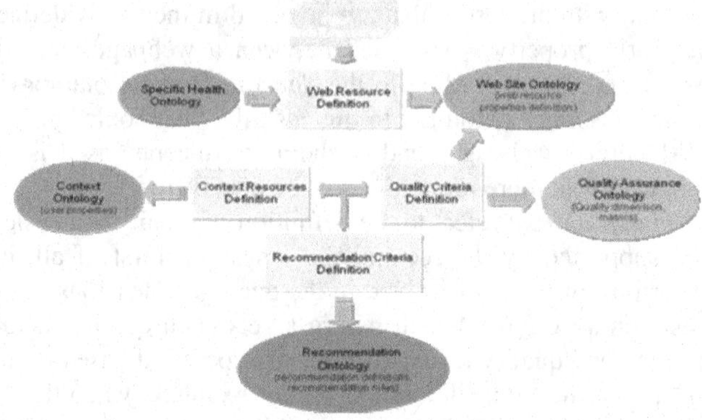

Fig. 2. Salus recommender start-up

will be identified in the recommendation criteria definition. Mainly, they are: the *user properties* and the *query resources*. The *user properties* are those that were already relieved at the recommendation criteria definition task and will be populated at the moment of registering a user at the recommender system: For instance, if at the recommendation criteria definition was specified the user property *belongs*, when she is registered to the system, this property is instanciated between *Paul* and *12-20 range*. The query resources refers to *query attributes* like *query goal*.

4.2 Web Page Quality Assessment Phase

After the recommendation start-up phase, the quality assessment of a set of web resources can be done. First of all, the web resources will be pre-processed to determine their properties and populate the web site ontology. The metrics over factors involved in a quality definition, determine the values of the web resource to be considered in the criteria of recommendation for this dimension of quality. For example, in the definition of the dimension "Believability" is used the "provenance" factor which refers to the author of the webpage, i.e. the "Alzheimer webpage" should have associated the "hasAuthor" property. Therefore, it have to be determined which information retrieval process have to be performed in order to discover these new web resource properties. The retrieved information will be used to complete the population of the Web site ontology. Thus, the *hasAuthor* property can be defined between the "Alzheimer webpage" and "Mr. Smith". In this phase, a set of specific domain web resources (webpages) will be assessed in order to determine their quality level. The quality assessment execution involves calculating the quality level of each web resource for each quality dimension. For that, the corresponding metric is executed and thus, it is determined the quality level of a web resource. In this phase, the quality assurance ontology is populated, mainly, by adding instances of the quality assessment and linking them with the web resource and the quality level. At this moment, the concept "BelievabilityQA" is instantiated as an individual of the *Quality Assessment* class and the *obtains* property is defined between "BelievabilityQA" and the "high" quality level.

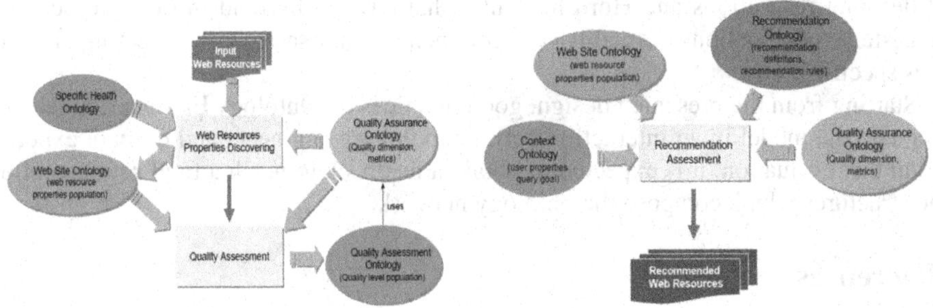

Fig. 3. Salus Quality Assessment

Fig. 4. Salus Recommendation Assessment

4.3 Recommendation Assessment Phase

A user query is the trigger of this *recommendation assessment phase*. When a logged on user makes a query, the recommendation system evaluates the *recommendation rules* in order to determine the recommendation level. All those web resources, which assets to an appropriated level for the considered user, will be recommended.

The evaluation of the recommendation rules is based on the user profile, the quality level of the considered web resources and the query resources. Both, the user profile and the web resource quality level, have been calculated in the previous two phases. Query resources have to be discovered at this moment. The output of this phase is a set of recommended web resources to a particular user query. The figure 4 summarizes the recommendation assessment phase.

5 Conclusions and Future Work

In this paper we have introduced a novel approach which uses an ontology network to assist the modelling and execution of a website recommendation system. It is a quality-based approach to get the more adequate websites for a consumer and context.

We have described *Salus* ontology network that models the different domains related to a recommendation system. Moreover, we showed how this ontology network can be tailored, to specific health domains and user points of views. The main aim of this design was to obtain a flexible model that was not dependent on any particular mechanism of websites content evaluation, such as a specific quality metric or health domain. Whenever it is required to assess a different quality dimension or to consider another health domain, new extensions of web site, quality and recommendation ontologies might be added, keeping up the core model intact.

In addition, a valuable feature of driving the recommendation process by ontologies is the property of checking the consistency among concepts and relationships that allows one to detect inconsistencies at the design phase. Based on the intrinsic properties of ontologies, the model provides a high level abstraction that allows specifying in simple way relations between dimension and metrics for defining quality assurance. Besides, it worth to mention that having an ontology-based recommendation system implemented using OWL language and SWRL rules, is helpful to validate the resulting configuration of the recommender system. These tools offers the possibility of defining restrictions and Horn-like rules that have to be hold in order to achieve consistent specifications of quality or recommendation assessments, detecting anomalous specifications.

Starting from the presented design, good practices on Ontology Engineering lead to evaluate the model in an interaction between ontology engineers and domain experts. From this evaluation, it is expected to obtain a feedback to reach a final refinement of the structures which compose the ontology network.

References

1. Gunther Eysenbach, T.L.D.: Towards quality management of medical information on the internet: evaluation, labelling and filtering of information. BMJ 317, 1496–1502 (1998)
2. Barnes, S., Vidgen, R.: Webqual: An exploration of web-site quality. In: Proceedings of the Eighth European Conference on Information Systems, Vienna, July 3 (2000)
3. Mich, L., Franch, M., Inverardi, P.N., Marzani, P.: Choosing the "rightweight" model for web site quality evaluation. In: Cueva Lovelle, J.M., Rodríguez, B.M.G., Gayo, J.E.L., Ruiz, M.d.P.P., Aguilar, L.J. (eds.) ICWE 2003. LNCS, vol. 2722, pp. 334–337. Springer, Heidelberg (2003)
4. Wang, R.Y., Strong, D.M.: Beyond accuracy: what data quality means to data consumers. J. Manage. Inf. Syst. 12(4), 5–33 (1996)
5. Wand, Y., Wang, R.Y.: Anchoring data quality dimensions in ontological foundations. ACM Commun. 39(11), 86–95 (1996)
6. Pipino, L.L., Lee, Y.W., Wang, R.Y.: Data quality assessment. ACM Commun. 45(4), 211–218 (2002)
7. Dubay, W.H.: The principles of readability. Impact Information, Costa Mesa (2004)
8. Llambías, G., Motz, R., Toledo, F., de Uvarow, S.: Learning to get the value of quality from web data. In: Meersman, R., Tari, Z., Herrero, P. (eds.) OTM-WS 2008. LNCS, vol. 5333, pp. 1018–1025. Springer, Heidelberg (2008)
9. Burke, R.: Hybrid recommender systems. User Modeling and User-Adapted Interaction 12(4), 331–370 (2002)
10. Oufaida, H., Nouali, O.: Exploiting Semantic Web Technologies for Recommender Systems. In: A Multi View Recommendation Engine. Proc. of the ITWP 2009, Pasadena, California, USA, July 11-17 (2009)
11. Porcel, C., Moreno, J., Herrera-Viedma, E.: A multi-disciplinar recommender system to advice research resources in University Digital Libraries. Expert Systems with Applications 36(10), 12520–12528 (2009)
12. Bellogín, A., Cantador, I., Castells, P., Ortigosa, A.: Discerning Relevant Model Features in a Content-based Collaborative Recommender System. In: Fürnkrans, J., Hüllermeier, E. (eds.) Preference Learning. Springer, Heidelberg (2010)
13. Suárez-Figueroa, M.C., Dellschaft, K., Montiel-Ponsoda, E., Villazon-Terrazas, B., Yufei, Z., de Cea, G.A., García, A., Fernandez-Lopez, M., Gomez-Perez, A., Espinoza, M., Sabou, M.: Neon deliverable d5.4.1. Neon methodology for building contextualized ontology networks. Technical report, NeOn Project (2008)
14. Olson, J.: Data Quality: the Accuracy Dimension. Morgan Kaufmann, San Francisco (2003)
15. Caro, A., Calero, C., Caballero, I., Piattini, M.: A proposal for a set of attributes relevant for Web portal data quality. Software Quality Journal 16(4), 513–542 (2008)

A Morphological Box for Handling Temporal Data in B2C Systems

Gerhard F. Knolmayer and Alessandro Borean

University of Bern, Institute of Information Systems, Engehaldenstrasse 8, CH-3012 Bern, Switzerland
{gerhard.knolmayer,alessandro.borean}@iwi.unibe.ch

Abstract. User interfaces are key properties of Business-to-Consumer (B2C) systems, and Web-based reservation systems are an important class of B2C systems. In this paper we show that these systems use a surprisingly broad spectrum of different approaches to handling temporal data in their Web interfaces. Based on these observations and on a literature analysis we develop a Morphological Box to present the main options for handling temporal data and give examples. The results indicate that the present state of developing and maintaining B2C systems has not been much influenced by modern Web Engineering concepts and that there is considerable potential for improvement.

Keywords: B2C Systems, Reservation Systems, Usability, Temporal Data, Morphological Analysis.

1 Introduction

Business-to-Consumer (B2C) transactions involve a large number of users who are not willing to undergo site-specific learning processes and who should be able to use the system intuitively. Therefore, user interfaces are a key feature of B2C systems. Web-based reservation systems have become a highly relevant distribution channel in the travel industry [1]. Handling temporal data (HTD) in Web interfaces has a high relevance in these reservation systems, because each reservation is time related. Fabre and Howard [2] argue that "good practices" for HTD should find their way into style guides, screen design guidelines, and repositories of reusable interface designs.

In this paper we show that temporal data is handled by Web-based reservation systems very differently, sometimes in user-unfriendly ways and in contradiction to usability guidelines, and in some cases even erroneously. The remainder of this paper is organized as follows: In Section 2 we refer to previous work on usability issues of B2C systems and on handling time in information systems. In Section 3 we describe procedures used for HTD in airline and hotel reservation systems in a Morphological Box and discuss the characteristics of the features. Section 4 provides a summary and considers opportunities for further research.

2 Previous Research

Many publications report usability problems of B2C sites [3-8], and in particular of Web-based travel and reservation systems [9-14].

W. Cellary and E. Estevez (Eds.): I3E 2010, IFIP AICT 341, pp. 215–225, 2010.

ISO 9241-110 specifies seven principles for designing dialogues between humans and information systems, which include self-descriptiveness, conformity with user expectations, and error tolerance [15]. Of special relevance in our context are 23 usability guidelines on data entry, recommending that data formats should be clearly indicated for inputs, text entry fields should indicate the format of data to be entered, dropdown menus should be used in preference to text entry fields, and forms should be validated before submission [16].

There is a huge body of time-related research. At least 13 bibliographies on HTD in information systems have been compiled [17-18], focusing on temporal databases and artificial intelligence topics. HTD gained broad public interest in connection with solving the Year 2000 (Y2K) problem; in early January 2000 some Websites displayed seriously wrong date representations [19].

Temporal aspects are often neglected in usability research [2]. In their comparison, among many other matters, Law et al. [20-21] consider whether such features as "Free entry of check-in/out date," "Date/time available for booking," and "Warning of incorrect date/time entry" are supported. Detailed recommendations for system developers are given by Bainbridge [22]. However, approaches to improving usability differ remarkably between academia and practice [23].

Information engineering concepts such as patterns and services can also be useful for HTD. Temporal patterns are discussed, e.g., in [24]; several temporal services are compiled in [25].

3 A Morphological Analysis of Handling Temporal Data

The perceived usability of a B2C site is often seen as an indicator of the quality of the product or service offered by the company. In this paper we focus on HTD and, thus, consider a single element of the user interface in more depth than previous analyses. Needless to say, HTD is only one aspect to be considered in the evaluation of a user interface. However, this feature seems to carry considerable potential for errors and demotivation if designed in a user-unfriendly way, and may result in higher transactions costs, loss of revenues, and lost customers.

Below we discuss reservations made on the sole basis of online information and directly by travelers via the Web and exclude communications via contact forms or e-mails. We consider interval-related dates for reservations; the scope of the paper does not extend to sequences of more than two dates (occurring, e.g., when multiple destinations are booked) or to intraday temporal data.

3.1 Methodology

A morphological analysis is characterized as an ordered way of looking at things [26-27]. The Morphological Box can be applied to provide a systematic overview of elementary courses of action and how they are combined in existing products and services. We develop a Morphological Box (Table 1) in which we show the elementary options for HTD in reservation systems. Each of the 10 rows describes a main feature of HTD in reservation systems and the corresponding table entries show the elementary

Table 1. Morphological Box for Handling Temporal Data

<table>
<tr><th>Sect.</th><th>Feature</th><th colspan="12">Characteristics</th></tr>
<tr><td>3.2.1</td><td>Definition of the Booking Interval</td><td colspan="3">t_s, t_e</td><td colspan="3">t_s, d</td><td colspan="3">d, t_e</td><td colspan="3">t_s, d, t_e</td></tr>
<tr><td>3.2.2</td><td>Display of Calendars</td><td colspan="3">No calendar</td><td colspan="3">After clicking in date entry field</td><td colspan="3">After clicking on calendar icon</td><td colspan="3">Without user action</td></tr>
<tr><td>3.2.3</td><td>Entry and Changes of Temporal Data</td><td colspan="4">Keyboard</td><td colspan="4">Click in dropdowns</td><td colspan="4">Click in calendar</td></tr>
<tr><td>3.2.4</td><td>Display of Date Format</td><td colspan="3">Not indicated</td><td colspan="3">Abstractly (e.g., mm/dd/yyyy)</td><td colspan="3">Numerically (e.g., 11/03/2010)</td><td colspan="3">With months shown as text</td></tr>
<tr><td>3.2.5</td><td>Representation of and Access to Temporal Data</td><td colspan="4">No calendar</td><td colspan="4">Rectangle with sequential access to months</td><td colspan="4">Rectangle with direct access to months</td></tr>
<tr><td>3.2.6</td><td>Default Values</td><td colspan="4">No default values</td><td colspan="4">Default values set with warning</td><td colspan="4">Default values set without warning</td></tr>
<tr><td>3.2.7</td><td>Temporal Integrity Constraints</td><td colspan="4">Not supported</td><td colspan="4">Check t_s and t_e (and, if applicable, d) only individually</td><td colspan="4">Check t_s and t_e (and, if applicable, d) individually and also their relationship(s)</td></tr>
<tr><td>3.2.8</td><td>Error Messages</td><td colspan="4">Avoided by setting default values</td><td colspan="4">Immediate at data entry</td><td colspan="4">Delayed until subsequent user action (e.g., Search)</td></tr>
<tr><td>3.2.9</td><td>Temporal Flexibility on Entry Page</td><td colspan="3">No flexibility offered</td><td colspan="3">Flexibility interval(s) >0, but undefined</td><td colspan="3">Flexibility with preset interval(s) (e.g., ± 3 days)</td><td colspan="3">Flexibility with user-defined interval(s)</td></tr>
<tr><td>3.2.10</td><td>Temporal Data after “Major Changes”</td><td colspan="6">Temporal data is lost</td><td colspan="6">Temporal data is kept</td></tr>
</table>

Legend:
t_s … Start of reservation interval; d … Duration; t_e … End of reservation interval

options available for this feature. All reservation systems can be characterized by one marking in each row and a profile line which connects these markings. Multiplying the number of elementary options per feature results in almost 125,000 combinations; however, some of them are not feasible.

The following section is structured according to the Morphological Box (Table 1). We describe the main features of HTD and add comments and examples where necessary. The features were found by literature analysis and by a critical review of many reservation systems. In this phase of research we did not perform a quantitative analysis of a well-defined set of systems, because we first wanted to build a framework of approaches for HTD. Our examples primarily describe inadequate or user-unfriendly solutions to show the potential benefit of applying information engineering methods and tools for Web Engineering more rigidly in the future.

3.2 Ten Features in Handling Temporal Data

3.2.1 Definition of the Booking Interval

For a reservation the user has to define the corresponding time interval, which can be described by its starting day t_s, its duration d, and/or its end t_e. Two of these elements suffice to define the interval. Most systems expect the entry of t_s and t_e. In a few cases t_s and d have to be entered and we are not aware of any system that expects the entry of d and t_e.

In rare cases interfaces allow entry of all three values (t_s, d, and t_e). At first glance, this looks user-friendly and the third element can be determined automatically as soon as the user entered two elements. However, if the user is changing one of the three date elements after his original entry, the system does not know which of the remaining two date elements should be modified. The resulting temporal integrity problems are discussed in more detail in [28].

3.2.2 Display of Calendars

We define a calendar as a rectangular structure displaying the days of a month; columns represent the weekdays and rows stand for weeks. Calendars can be displayed without user action or after the user requests it, e.g., as a calendar popup after a calendar icon or a date entry field has been clicked [22]. Some calendars already show whether a reservation is possible or not.

3.2.3 Entry and Changes of Temporal Data

Temporal data is typically entered via the keyboard or with a pointing device ("date picker"). The pointing device may be used to click in a dropdown element or in a calendar. Keyboard, dropdown, and calendar date entry can be combined; therefore one could also show all seven combinations in the Morphological Box. Some systems impede changes via the keyboard by positioning a pop-up calendar above the field that displays the date. Surprisingly, the behavior of some systems depends on how the date has been entered [28].

If only a single component of the date information (in particular days) is shown, it is mostly displayed linearly in a dropdown, which may show either numbers only or, more conveniently, the numbers together with (maybe abbreviated) names of days. Often only a subset of all days is displayed, and the user may have to scroll to other days. For a given Browser the subset may be static (e.g., days 1-20 are shown initially) or context specific (e.g., as a "rolling dropdown" [22], starting with the current day). The length of the month should be taken into account if the user has already entered his preferred month for travelling; for example, a dropdown for selection of the day should not offer the value 31 for November. However, many systems miss these requirements [28].

Shneiderman and Plaisant [29] argue that providing a "graphical calendar" will reduce the number of errors, and UserFocus [16] suggests avoiding text entry fields if possible. If calendars are used, the options presented can be restricted to feasible values. For instance, days that are already past or lie beyond the booking horizon should be suppressed, faded out, crossed out, or grayed out.

After a date has been entered via a pointing device, it can often be corrected via the keyboard. Such changes may result in errors, because temporal integrity checks are often missing in this case [28].

Displaying the (full or abbreviated) name of the weekday and month in or close to the date field may reduce errors [3, 22].

3.2.4 Display of Date Format

With respect to keyboard entry it must be borne in mind that dates are represented in different cultures in diverse formats and that this nasty problem without good solutions is a source of misunderstandings, confusion, and errors [29-31]. Although ISO 8601 defines YYYY-MM-DD as the standard representation of days, this standard is not widely accepted by the general public. W3C [32] discusses three possible solutions to this problem; other design guides for date display have also been proposed, primarily in a healthcare context [33-34].

Nonetheless, Web-based reservation systems use an astonishing variety of date representations; among the 37 (!) variants we detected for displaying, e.g., the day 2010-11-03 we found such displays as

10-11-3,
3. November 2010,
some with no reference to year, such as Nov 3,
Nov-03-2010,

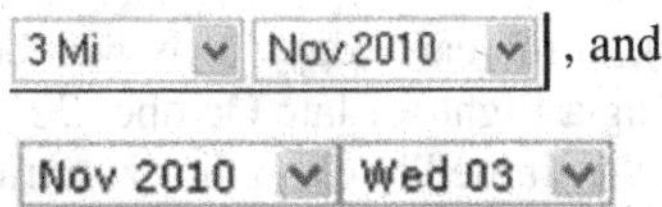

, and .

In particular if keyboard entry of dates is allowed, the user should be informed which date format is used by the system. This could be done in abstract form (e.g., MM/DD/YYYY) or with a numerical example, often displaying a default value in the entry field. However, if the example uses day numbers ≤ 12, the display will be ambiguous with respect whether the format is MM/DD or DD/MM. Although some reservation systems ask where the user is located, the date format used is typically not adjusted to this information.

3.2.5 Representation of and Access to Temporal Data

Many reservation systems provide some type of calendar information, usually with names or verbal abbreviations of months and a numerical representation of days. Information about and links to many calendar implementations are compiled in [25]. Typically no week numbers are displayed when showing calendars.

The user may see one or more (mostly <4) months on the same screen. Months that are not displayed can be selected either directly, by clicking on an element of a list or of a rectangular representation of months (cf. Figure 1), or via browsing the calendars by moving forward or backward one month at a time until the relevant month appears; in rare cases the moves jump several months forward or backward with a single click.

In different cultures weeks are assumed to start with either Sunday or Monday. This means it is essential that the user is paying attention, and although some reservation systems ask where the user is located, the representation of weeks typically is not adjusted to this information.

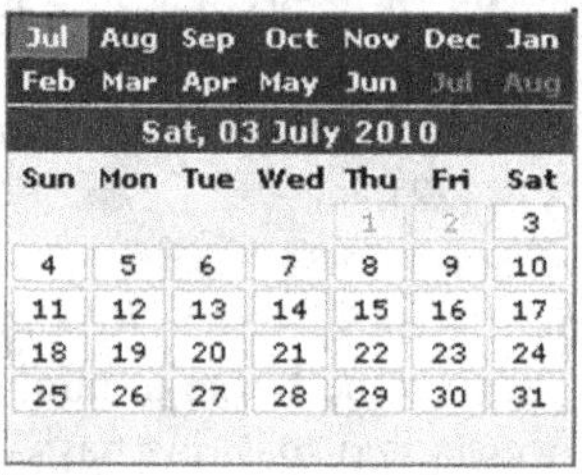

Jul	Aug	Sep	Oct	Nov	Dec	Jan
Feb	Mar	Apr	May	Jun	Jul	Aug
Sat, 03 July 2010						
Sun	Mon	Tue	Wed	Thu	Fri	Sat
				1	2	3
4	5	6	7	8	9	10
11	12	13	14	15	16	17
18	19	20	21	22	23	24
25	26	27	28	29	30	31

Fig. 1. Direct access to months via a 2x7 rectangle (http://www.qantas.com.au/travel/airlines/home/au/en)

3.2.6 Default Values

Many reservation systems assume default values for t_s, d, or t_e. When a user enters a site, the system often shows default values for t_s and t_e. Popular default values for hotel reservations are t_s = today and $t_e = t_s + 1$. One reason for showing default values may be that the systems want to show the date formats applied (cf. Section 3.2.4).

Some systems provide or adjust a default value for t_e as soon as t_s is entered. If default values are inserted, a distracted user may not recognize that the value has been set by the system. Therefore, setting default values could be accompanied by a warning message; however, we found very few warnings.

Owing to a limited booking horizon (cf. Table 2), in the early days of November 2010 many systems will not offer the option of booking a flight for late October 2011, as an example; however, if a user who is unaware of the limited booking horizon tries to book for December 2011, many systems will automatically switch to December 2010. This is a potential source of error, particularly if the system does not show the year of the reservation.

Some reservation systems avoid infeasible travelling dates $t_s > t_e$ by heuristically adjusting t_s according to t_e, or vice versa. Problems of such adjustments and their sometimes strange results are discussed in the following section, and in more detail in [28].

In general, it is doubtful whether default date values inserted by reservation systems benefit the users, and we assume that they are a major source of error, which could be avoided by nullifying instead of defaulting inconsistent date entries.

3.2.7 Temporal Integrity Constraints

Several types of temporal integrity constraints have to be considered for defining valid reservation intervals. They check t_s and/or t_e and/or d individually, or also the relationship(s) between these values. Of course no days that are already past and no inexistent days should be suggested to the user or accepted by the system. However, many systems offer, for instance, the day 31 also when the user already defined a month with less than 31 days.

The constraint today $\leq t_s \leq t_e$ looks highly plausible, but in some situations checking it becomes quite challenging and is not sufficient [28]: Systems should consider the local time at the departure location for checking this constraint. For instance, a user staying in Sydney could want to make a reservation shortly after midnight for a traveler staying in Rio de Janeiro. In this case, the constraint may be violated if the system compares t_s with the date in Sydney.

Minimal periods from today to t_s and maximal time periods up to t_e may have to be considered. Most systems do not make the booking horizon explicit. For booking flights, the horizon often lies between 320 and 365 days. Table 2 gives examples and shows the update behavior after 1 week and 1 month.

Table 2. Maximum intervals between booking day and day of service [YYYY-MM-DD]

Reservation system	**Address**	**Number of days bookable at**		
		2009-11-16	**2009-11-23**	**2009-12-15**
Ebookers	www.ebookers.ch	330	330	330
Japan Airlines	www.ch.jal.com/en	330	330	330
Priceline	www.priceline.com	330	330	330
Singapore Airlines	www.singaporeair.com/saa/en_UK	350	350	350
Air Canada	www.aircanada.com/en	353	353	353
Lufthansa	www.lufthansa.com	361	361	361
SAS	www.flysas.com/en/us	361	361	361
SideStep.com	www.sidestep.com	365	365	365
Southwest Airlines	www.southwest.com	*172*	*165*	*143*
American Airlines	www.aa.com	*329*	*329*	*330*
SWISS	www.swiss.com	*344*	*339*	*339*
Austrian Airlines	www.aua.com	*349*	*342*	*361*
Northwest Airlines	www.nwa.com	*352*	*331*	*331*
Hertz	www.hertz.ch	*379*	*372*	*381*
Avis	avis.ch	*380*	*380*	*381*

Often, the last bookable day is adjusted on a daily basis ("moving windows" of different lengths; cf. the upper part of Table 2). Southwest Airlines (www.southwest.com) fixed the last bookable day during our research period. No regular update behavior could be found at other Websites (cf. lower part of Table 2). Some systems show calendars relating to long periods but allow bookings only within a comparatively short horizon. For instance, Aban Air (www.abanair.com) offers year entries between 1910 and 2020. It is user-unfriendly if a system offers an option for clicking and rejects in a later step the entry of a date that has been offered.

If an intermediary admits a long booking horizon, there will be very few reservation systems of the final service providers (e.g., hotels) that also support this horizon. The user may be surprised to find that the number of options offered diminishes with increasing time from the day of the booking request. This behavior can be found, e.g., at http://www.hotel.de/Search.aspx?lng=EN.

In addition, many hotels restrict the length of a reservation to a maximum number of days [28].

If a user plans a reservation in September for a trip starting in November, the calendars for September and October should be suppressed when the calendar to be used for determination of t_e is shown. More generally, no options for entering $t_e < t_s$ should be offered, and if the user entered t_e first, the system should hide all $t_s > t_e$. Conformity expectations are violated if, for example, the SAS reservation system (www.flysas.com/en/ch) suppresses infeasible return days after entry of the outward day but does not suppress infeasible outward days after entry of the return date [28].

Special integrity issues arise when the user changes previously entered data. Many systems try to keep integrity by default adjustments if the user prepones t_e; however, not all of them react analogously if t_s is postponed. This again infringes conformity expectations of users.

3.2.8 Error Messages

Temporal integrity can be checked either when the user enters the date in the form (Stage 1: "immediate method") or when he submits the form and starts a request, which may be named as search, go, etc. (Stage 2: "delayed method") [22, 35]. If the immediate method is applied, a user who wants to modify both t_s and t_e could receive an error message after the first change; however, this problem is typically avoided by a heuristic adjustment of the other date. Some systems ask for additional information in stage 2 even if the dates are infeasible because a check of temporal integrity constraints is postponed until the user provided additional, probably obsolete, entries.

Several Websites show bizarre and misleading error messages [29]. Examples of informative and misleading error messages in the case of violated temporal integrity constraints are given in [28]. Some systems avoid error messages generally by setting default values; however, this is an error-prone procedure (cf. Section 3.2.6).

3.2.9 Temporal Flexibility on Entry Page

Before deciding about a reservation, the user may consider several variants of destinations and temporal intervals. Some reservation systems allow temporal flexibility for t_s and t_e on the entry page. Intervals for temporal flexibility are typically preset by the systems; American Airlines used to allow a user-defined flexibility interval, which, however, seems to have disappeared in the meantime. Some systems show travel options for different days on the result page after executing the search, even without user request. This may be regarded as valuable information by some users and as information overload by others.

Options with respect to intraday flexibility may also exist. On some sites the user may enter favored hours for departure, while other systems use (sometimes imprecise) verbal paraphrases. For example, Continental Airlines (www.continental.com/web/en-US) offers the user a choice of such fuzzy data as "early morning," "morning," and "late morning."

3.2.10 Temporal Data after "Major Changes"

If a user alters his potential destination, switches from a one-way or a multicity flight to a roundtrip, or clicks on the Browser's "Return" button, we call his action a "major change." Below we focus on destination changes and their impact on previously entered temporal data. On his way to a reservation decision, the user may tentatively want to receive information on traveling to another destination than the one originally considered. However, the time interval may be identical to the previous query, e.g., because of fixed holidays. In this situation it is inconvenient if the system forces the user to enter the temporal data again and again; the dates defined in the previous search could be used as temporal default values. Many systems save temporal data in case of major changes. Among the systems that lose temporal information when the user clicks the return button are those of United Airlines and Continental Airlines (www.united.com; www.continental.com/web/en-US for users applying the Firefox Browser).

4 Discussion and Outlook

This paper shows that reservation systems handle temporal data in surprisingly different and sometimes inadequate ways. Therefore, we developed a Morphological Box that presents the main features needed for handling temporal data and their characteristics in a systematic way.

System developers seem to reinvent the wheel over and over again, often without following guidelines and without using patterns or services. The ambiguity of today's implementations shows that many Web-based systems are still developed individually without (re)using existing services even for a basic functionality such as handling temporal data. From a Web Engineering viewpoint this finding is disappointing: Contrary to the broad consensus about the benefits of methodological approaches, the adherence of guidelines, the development and use of temporal patterns as a basis for implementations, and the reusability of services seem to be still in their infancy. Also Web sites of major travel intermediaries, which reduce the relevance of the reservation systems of the final service providers, handle temporal data not without flaws.

The Morphological Box presented in Table 1 and the issues discussed in Section 3 will be used in further work to evaluate B2C systems. We plan to have the features and characteristics defined in the Morphological Box evaluated by usability experts. The results will allow to weight the relevance of the features and to distinguish between more or less favorable characteristics. This allows to restructure the Morphological Box for an easier comparison of different profile lines. The empirical results will allow to develop a maturity model for handling temporal data and to assign existing reservation systems to maturity classes.

Another stream of research could evaluate the options described in the Morphological Box from the perspectives of users with disabilities or of elderly citizens.

References

1. Marcussen, C.H.: Trends in European Internet Distribution - of Travel and Tourism Services (2009), http://www.crt.dk/uk/staff/chm/trends.htm
2. Fabre, J., Howard, S.: Introduction to the Special Issue on Temporal Aspects of Usability. Interacting with Computers 11, 1–7 (1998)
3. Nielsen, J.: Designing Web Usability: The Practice of Simplicity. New Riders, Indianapolis (2000)
4. Green, D., Pearson, J.M.: Development of a Web site usability instrument based on ISO 9241-11. Journal of Computer Information Systems 47, 66–72 (2006)
5. Cappel, J.J., Huang, Z.: A Usability Analysis of Company Websites. Journal of Computer Information Systems 48, 117–123 (2007)
6. Hu, H.-J., Yen, J., Guan, S.-S.: A Study on the Interface Usability of B2C Hypermarket E-commerce Website. In: The 3rd IEEE Asia-Pacific Services Computing Conference, pp. 1202–1207. IEEE Computing Society, Los Alamitos (2008)
7. Lituchy, T.R., Barra, R.A.: International issues of the design and usage of websites for e-commerce: Hotel and airline examples. Journal of Engineering and Technology Management 25, 93–111 (2008)
8. Tucker, S.-P.: E-commerce standard user interface: an E-menu system. Industrial Management & Data Systems 108, 1009–1028 (2008)
9. Selvidge, P.: How Usable are the Airline Websites? Usability News 1 (1999), http://www.surl.org/usabilitynews/11/Usability_airline.asp
10. Crichton, E., Frew, A.J.: Usability of Information and Reservations Systems: Theory or Practice? In: Fesenmaier, D.R., Klein, S., Buhalis, D. (eds.) Information and Communication Technologies in Tourism 2000, pp. 408–417. Springer, Wien (2000)
11. Chariton, C., Choi, M.-H.: Enhancing Usability of Flight and Fare Search Functions for Air-line and Travel Web Sites. In: Proceedings of the International Conference on Information Technology: Coding and Computing (ITCC 2004), pp. 320–325. IEEE Computer Society, Los Alamitos (2004)
12. Malizia, A.: Adding flexibility to B2C booking systems using a virtual intermediate travel agent. In: Proceedings of the 2005 IEEE Symposium on Visual Languages and Human-Centric Computing, pp. 337–338. IEEE Computer Society, Los Alamitos (2005)
13. Zhou, Q., DeSantis, R.: Usability Issues in City Tourism Website Design: A Content Analysis. In: Proceedings of 2005 IEEE International Professional Communication Conference, pp. 789–796. IEEE Press, Piscataway (2005)
14. Essawy, M.: Testing the Usability of Hotel Websites: The Springboard for Customer Relationship Building. Information Technology & Tourism 8, 47–70 (2006)
15. ISO 9241-110, Ergonomics of human-system interaction - Part 110: Dialogue principles (2006), http://www.iso.org/iso/catalogue_detail.htm?csnumber=38009
16. Userfocus: 23 forms and data entry usability guidelines (2009), http://www.userfocus.co.uk/resources/formschecklist.html
17. Grandi, F.: An Annotated Bibliography on Temporal and Evolution Aspects in the World Wide Web, TimeCenter Technical Report TR-75 (2003), http://timecenter.cs.aau.dk/TimeCenterPublications/TR-75.pdf

18. Grandi, F.: Introducing an Annotated Bibliography on Temporal and Evolution Aspects in the World Wide Web. SIGMOD Record 33, 84–86 (2004)
19. Knolmayer, G.: Endzeitstimmungen in einer hochtechnisierten Gesellschaft: Das Jahr 2000-Problem, seine Wahrnehmung und mögliche Konsequenzen. In: Moser, R., Zwahlen, S.M. (eds.) Endzeiten – Wendezeiten, Lang, Bern, pp. 13–26 (2004)
20. Law, R., Leung, R.: A Study of Airlines' Online Reservation Services on the Internet. Journal of Travel Research 39, 202–211 (2000)
21. Law, R., Leung, K., Au, N.: Evaluating Reservation Facilities for Hotels: A Study of Asian Based and North American Based Travel Web Sites. In: Wöber, K.W., Frew, A.J., Hitz, M. (eds.) Information and Communication Technologies in Tourism, pp. 303–310. Springer, Wien (2002)
22. Bainbridge, A.: Hotel Date Entry: Design & Usability Report. Travel UCD (2002), http://www.tourcms.com/company/research/pdf/date_entry_hotel_july2002.pdf
23. Furniss, D., Blandford, A., Curzon, P.: Usability Work in Professional Web Site Design: Insights from Practitioners' Perspectives. In: Law, E.L.-C., Hvannberg, E.T., Cockton, G. (eds.) Maturing Usability: Quality in Software, Interaction and Value. Human-Computer Interaction Series, pp. 144–167. Springer, London (2008)
24. Fowler, M.: Temporal Patterns (2005), http://www.martinfowler.com/eaaDev/timeNarrative.html
25. Lennartz, S.: Online Calendars and Date Pickers. Smashing Magazine (2007), http://www.smashingmagazine.com/2007/10/23/online-calendars-and-date-pickers/
26. Zwicky, F.: Morphological Astronomy. The Observatory 68, 121–143 (1948)
27. Zwicky, F.: Discovery, Invention, Research Through the Morphological Approach. Macmillan, Toronto (1969)
28. Knolmayer, G.F., Helfenstein, L.E.: Usability Aspects of Ensuring Temporal Integrity Constraints: A Critical Appraisal. In: Proceedings of the Fifth International Conference on Human-Computer Interaction, Lahaina 2010 (2010)
29. Shneiderman, B., Plaisant, C.: Designing the User Interface: Strategies for Effective Human-Computer Interaction, 5th edn. Addison-Wesley, Upper Saddle River (2010)
30. Nielsen, J.: Usability Engineering. Morgan Kaufmann, San Francisco (1993)
31. Hanna, J.: Date & Time Formats on the Web, http://www.hackcraft.net/web/datetime/
32. W3C: Date formats (2007), http://www.w3.org/International/questions/qa-date-format
33. NHS: CUI CAPS Development Lifecycle (2008), http://www.isb.nhs.uk/docs/cui-1/cui-draft/SubCUI.pdf
34. Microsoft: Design Guidance - Date Display, Version 3.0.0.0 (2010), http://www.mscui.net/DesignGuide/Pdfs/DesignGuidance-DateDisplay.pdf
35. Greene, S.L., et al.: Entry-based versus Selection-based Interaction Methods. In: Proceedings of the Human Factors Society - 32nd Annual Meeting, pp. 284–287. Human Factors and Ergonomics Society, Santa Monica (1988)

Trust and Privacy Enabled Service Composition Using Social Experience

Shahab Mokarizadeh[1], Nima Dokoohaki[1], Mihhail Matskin[1,2], and Peep Küngas[3]

[1] ICT School, Royal Institute Of Technology (KTH), Stockholm Sweden
[2] Norwegian University of Science and Technology (NTNU), Trondheim, Norway
[3] University of Tartu, Tartu, Estonia
{shahabm,nimad,misha}@kth.se, peep.kungas@ut.ee

Abstract. In this paper, we present a framework for automatic selection and composition of services which exploits trustworthiness of services as a metric for measuring the quality of service composition. Trustworthiness is defined in terms of service reputation extracted from user profiles. The profiles are, in particular, extracted and inferred from a social network which accumulates users past experience with corresponding services. Using our privacy inference model we, first, prune social network to hide privacy sensitive contents and, then, utilize a trust inference based algorithm to measure reputation score of each individual service, and subsequently trustworthiness of their composition.

Keywords: Social Network; Privacy; Trust; Web-service; Web-service Composition.

1 Introduction

Emergence of Internet of Services (IoS)[3] as convergence of Web 2.0 and SOA, has promoted the role of human users in IT supported business models. The aim of IoS is to empower (non professional) human users with ability to discover and utilize resources (e.g. services) through supporting them with flexible, human centric Web 2.0 features which provide tagging resources (to indicate their evaluation) or mashing up resources according to their requirements [9].

In the open and redundant service environment of IoS, service consumers will face a problem of selecting the most appropriate services among bunch of services providing similar functionality. In fact, recent studies [14] have shown high degree of functional equivalence in available services. In this light, Quality of Service (QoS) features has been leveraged as a reasonable metric for evaluation of services. As the current Web service technology does not support enough QoS or other non functional aspects of Web services, service selection mechanisms have been dependant on QoS information advertised by service providers, or on collected data on service consumers' side. The problem in this case is that reliability of the information advertised by service suppliers cannot be verified and collected experience on the consumer side is quite limited. This is why exploiting WEB 2.0 for capturing end-user experience and learning the quality of services from collective user experience are promising solutions [4][16]. User's experience can be aggregated through ratings, tags or even

W. Cellary and E. Estevez (Eds.): I3E 2010, IFIP AICT 341, pp. 226–236, 2010.

textual reviews on different aspects of utilized resources (e.g. services). Because user feedback is vulnerable to malicious user's manipulation, only experience which is provided by trusted users should be taken into account. Social Networks, as a Web 2.0 trend, are repositories of resources capable of documenting and revealing trust relationships among other nodes on the network. The ultimate goal here is finding highly trusted atomic or composite services based on reputation of users. Although this approach may support Web service discovery and composition, currently, it is mainly focused on clarifying some specific steps in trustworthy service selection and composition rather than on proposing generic yet comprehensive architecture accommodating Web 2.0 components with SOA requirements. In addition, the increasingly important aspects of privacy of user information in Social Networks need to be taken into account for practical solutions.

In this paper, we present our ongoing work in Web 2.0 enabled Web service composition framework. A goal of this work is providing an ordinary service consumer with tools allowing finding the most appropriate composition of services based on his/her past experience as well as on experience of other trusted users. The distinguishing feature of this work is our privacy inference model which protects visibility of user profile information from low trusted users. Notion of service trustworthiness [1] is employed to measure the quality of service composition. Trustworthiness of services is defined in terms of service reputation from service consumers' perspective which is extracted from user profiles. A semantic Web enabled structure is proposed to aggregate personal user information and its past experience.

The rest of the paper is organized as follows. Section 2 gives an outline of our approach to computing trustworthiness of services including population of profiles, trust and privacy inference models and social network pruning algorithms. The architecture of trustworthy service composition framework is presented in Section 3. Section 4 reviews some important relevant work. Finally, concluding remarks and directions for future work are presented in Section 5.

2 Solution Outline

Our solution targets IoS and combines Web 2.0 trends with SOA paradigm by pursuing reputation based approach for service selection. We consider Web 2.0 as a platform for a trustworthy service selection and composition framework. The solution relies on user feedback, profiling and information extracted from social network as the major resources for computing reputation of Web services. We extend Kuter and Golbeck's formalism [1] for computing Web service trustworthiness by taking into account privacy of users in a social network.

The cycle of service selection, composition, rating and profiling in our solution is initiated by the end-user through submitting the request for service(s) which might not be implemented yet. Due to the fact that we are underlining service composition issue in this work, we refer to the end-user as a "composer user". The composer user's request is decomposed into a bunch of candidate services which should potentially satisfy the request. Next, a set of alternative composite services, which comply with the request, is generated. The composite services, in this set, need to be ranked to allow execution of only highly ranked services. In order to do that we delve into a (social) network of users who already exploited the candidate services. During the social network exploration process the privacy concerns of users and trustworthiness of users are taken into account. Based on the information from the network, reputation of each individual service constituting composite services is computed according to the given user ratings, trust and privacy measures. Having in hand reputation of each individual service, trustworthiness of their composition is measured and the most trusted composite service is selected. After invocation (consuming) the service, the composer user may provide his/her experience with the composite service (and, possibly, with each component service) as a rating which may be published in the social network for future utilization.

We consider a scenario where a third party application provides recommendations for selecting appropriate services (e.g. hotel, flight or trip online booking services). This selection is made amongst a set of alternatives by exploiting the past experience of inter-related trusted users while preserving their privacy concerns over their profiles. As the third party applications do not have direct access to profile contents, they are obliged to obey inferred privacy assertions of profiles, which are computed by the system which is handling the profiles (e.g. the online social networking website). Issues related to technical application or legal enforcement of such privacy policies remains outside of the scope of this work. In the next sections we describe the approach in details and provide algorithms for collecting the required information and computing metrics in different steps of the aforementioned process. We also would like to underline that in this paper we are focusing on models and algorithms proposed and developed in the framework while leaving the experimental results for the future work.

2.1 User Profiles

Profiling of users' personal information and capturing users' past experience have shown to be reliable approaches for predicting user models [6][13] .We specifically emphasize active involvement of user in the process of enriching its experience through supplying explicit feedback. User profile consists of two segments: 1) Basic personal information including pieces revealing connections to social network(s) and 2) User past experiences with services.

The first segment is grounded to well known FOAF (Friend Of A Friend) ontology [5] which is extended to capture trust relationships and privacy concerns [6]. Both *Trust* and *Privacy* assertions take values ranging from 0 to 1. In case of *Trust* assertions, 0 implies complete distrust and 1 implies absolute trust towards the individuals for whom the assertion has been issued. *Privacy* assertion, unlike *Trust* assertion, takes discrete values where value 0 makes profile content visible for everyone and, in contrary, no one will be able to access the content if its *Privacy* value is set to 1. Tuning *Privacy* level of profile with values in range [0, 1] allows more control on the visibility of profile content by vast number of loosely defined acquaintances. We consider a single *Privacy* assertion over second segment of the profile (past experiences).

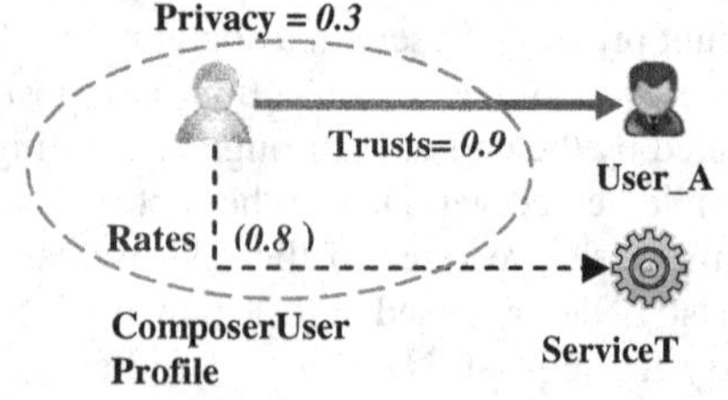

Fig. 1. Structure and Content of User Profile

The second segment accumulates user experience with services (i.e. ratings). Ratings reflect user's overall satisfaction over the utilized services. For the sake of simplicity we only consider numerical ratings in range [0, 1]. Fig.1 presents sample profile content for *ComposerUser*, where *User_A* is a highly trusted friend of *ComposerUser* (trust value = 0.9). *ComposerUser* had utilized *ServiceT* and was satisfied by assigning it high (0.8) rating value. Finally, *ComposerUser* is willing to expose her profile content to certain individuals due to low privacy value (0.3) assigned to profile content.

2.2 Populating User Profile Content

Basically, there are two scenarios to populate the user profile content which differ due to the availability of resources:

1) In the first scenario, we are employing a social network application (e.g. a *Facebook*[23] *Application*) which allows us to exploit certain user profile information, specifically friend list, quality of friendship (e.g. best friend , friend, acquaintance, etc), privacy values defined over profile items, and ratings provided over utilized services or applications. This all together provides ready to use ingredients for populating both segments of the user profiles. In a social network, the quality of a trust relationship between every two friends is not necessarily symmetric. For example, two friends may label each other in two different friend category lists (e.g."close friend" and "acquaintance"). This case raises the privacy concern over profile content, especially when the certain profile information is a subject to abuse by less trusted users.

2) In the second scenario, we do not have any social network available; hence we have to preliminary harvest user ratings (feedbacks, textual reviews, etc) from some resources; for example *Apple App. Store*, where such information is publicly available. Then we approximate trust relationship between users based on similarity measures over provided ratings. In fact, several researches have denoted a strong correlation between trust and overall similarity [13][20]. Based on calculated trust relationship, we can build a trust network between users. If we don't have any explicit privacy policy in the harvested user information, we assign a default privacy value to all constructed user profiles.

After populating the user profiles, they are mined in order to extract social network of composer user by exploring FOAF segment of profiles and chaining those profiles embodying past experiences about interested services.

2.3 Trust and Privacy Inference Models

As we follow reputation based approach, we make use of a centralized trust and privacy inference server to compute global trusts for all users in the system. Having some trust and privacy relations between neighbor users in the social network (see Section 2.3) we might need inference models for calculation of trust and privacy for users having indirect relations in the network. In this paper we propose usage of the following inference models.

Trust Inference Model: As there has been outstanding research on trust inference in Web based social networks, instead of proposing a new inference model, we exploit off-the shelf trust-inference algorithms. The only restriction we have is that the selected trust inference model should not be dependent on privacy value of the user profile because of our privacy inference model is computed based on the inferred trust value. If we presume availability of a social network, any trust-inference algorithms such as TidalTrust[7], Appleseed [8], or even probabilistic trust inference model [21] can be employed to compute trust between two individuals. While in the case of second scenario, we can recruit, for example, nuanced profile similarity approach [20] or T-Index method [13] to compute inferred trust. In both cases, we refer to the inferred trust value of user *s* towards user *u* by *trust(s,u)*. In particular, in our previous experiments T-index method was successfully used [13].

Privacy Inference Model: To the best of our knowledge, there is no privacy inference model in the context of social networks. As a matter of fact, we consider privacy as an inverse function of trust towards the individuals for whom privacy assertion is issued. In other words, decreasing confidence in someone leads to strength of privacy level towards him or her, as presented in following formula:

$$\begin{cases} privacy \propto (1 - trust) \\ trust \rightarrow [0,1], \quad privacy \rightarrow \{0, 0.1, \dots, 1\} \end{cases} \tag{1}$$

Unlike trust values, privacy level takes a discrete value from range of {0, 0.1... 0.9, 1}. The reason for utilization of such coarse grained privacy values is that privacy can be associated to different visibility level of information in the profile. The idea behind formula (1) intuitively makes sense: people consider more relaxed privacy concerns for their highly trusted friends, while they are not willing to expose so much (if any) information to less trusted friends or strangers. As an evidence supporting this observation, we point out to the fuzzy approaches proposed by [12] to compute privacy values from user trust values. Based on this observation, we justify our privacy inference model. Let's presume availability of two nodes (individuals) *s* and *u* in our target social network and consider p_s as given privacy value to profile of individual *s*. Thus, inferred privacy rating of node *s* from perspective of node *u* can be computed by formula (2).

$$privacy(s,u) = \begin{cases} \alpha(1 - trust(s,u)) + \beta\, p_s & ,if\ trust(s,u) \geq Min_{trust} \\ \gamma(1 - trust(s,u)) + p_s & ,else \end{cases} \tag{2}$$
$$0 < \gamma < 1,\ 0 \leq \alpha, \beta < 1,\ \alpha + \beta = 1,$$

where Min_{trust} denotes the trust threshold for considering user *u* as trusted individual and *trust(s,u)* represents inferred trust value from node *s* to node *u* to be computed using any of the algorithms pointed out in the previous section. According to formula (2), less trusted nodes are always ignored by shrinking their visibility (i.e. higher privacy level). In fact, the amount of ignorance is partially tuned by parameter γ .This is quite compatible with aforementioned observations for increasing privacy level for non-trusted neighbors. If the result is higher than maximum privacy level then the maximum privacy value (equal to 1) will be considered. In contrast, formula (2) can be generous towards highly trusted nodes by enforcing $\alpha \gg \beta$ as a constraint on the weights. In this case, highly trusted nodes are rewarded by decreasing the privacy level they face to access the content. The granted visibility volume is tuned through weights assigned to initial privacy and inferred trust.

2.4 Social Network Pruning Algorithm

Before moving to utilization of ratings provided by the composer user's social network, privacy concerns of content owners need to be preserved. In other words, we need to identify those individuals who are not willing to expose their past experience to the composer user and then mark them as empty nodes (a node with empty profile which is preserved only for the sake of network connectivity). Fig. 2.a shows the outline of our network pruning algorithm. The input to the procedure consists of: *src* referring to the composer user node, *network* presenting the network to be pruned, Min_{trust} denoting the trust threshold and $Max_{privacy}$ which is the maximum tolerable privacy value to make content of a profile accessible. The algorithm computes inferred privacy of every node in the network from perspective of node *src*. For every node *sink* in the network, first, the inferred trust towards *src* is computed using *TrustInference* procedure which could implement any of the aforementioned trust inference models. Then the respective inferred privacy of node sink towards *src* is measured by *PrivacyInference* procedure that implements the privacy model presented in formula (2). If the inferred privacy value is greater than maximum tolerable privacy threshold, then the profile content is not visible and the node will be marked as intermediate node.

As an illustrative example we consider a fragment of social network showing the network's trust relationship towards *ComposerUser* presented in Fig. 2.b. The edges show trust relationships between users and labels over directed edges denote the trust values. Let us assume the following simple probabilistic interpretation of trust [21] where two trust links (e.g. (*D* ,*B*) and (*B*, *ComposerUser*) in the graph in Fig. 2.b) correspond to two independent trust measures; the trust that *D* has for *ComposerUser* corresponds to the intersection of those two events:

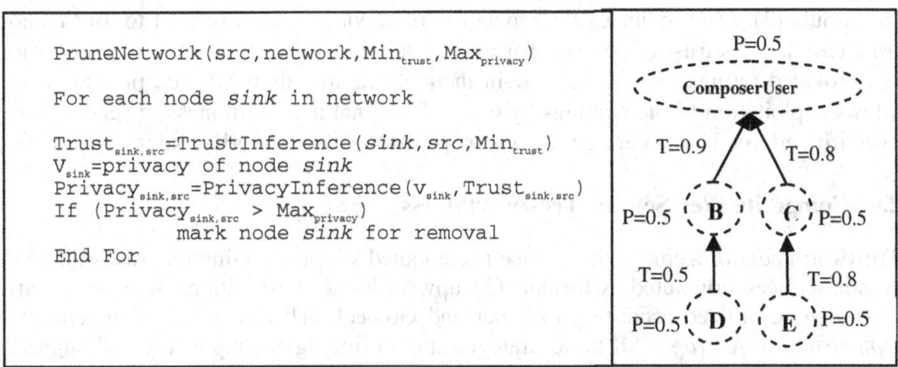

Fig. 2. (a) Left; Social Network Prunning Algorithm (b) Right; Sample Social Network showing Network's Trust towards ComposerUser

trust(D, ComposerUser) = trust (D, B). trust(B, ComposerUser)

Accordingly, we will have the following inferred trust values: *t(D)=0.45, t(E)=0.64.* Having the trust values, observed privacy level of nodes by *ComposerUser* can be calculated using formula (2). Inferred privacy values, for $\alpha = 0.15$, $\beta=0.85, \gamma= 0.15, Treshold_{trust} = 0.5$, are as follows: *p(D)=0.5825, p(E)=0.479, p(C)=0.455 ,p(B)=0.44*

Applying network pruning algorithm leads us to removal of node *D* because of its inferred privacy level exceeds the maximum threshold ($Max_{privacy}$=0.55) assumed to make the content (i.e. profile) of a node visible to *ComposerUser*, despite to the fact that its (not inferred) privacy level *(0.5)* meets the designated threshold. This simple example shows how the inferred privacy value can be personalized (the privacy may decrease or increase) to each individual user in a social network by taking into account the inferred trust value. The optimal values for respective parameters in formula (2), i.e. α, β, γ, $Max_{privacy}$, and Min_{trust}, will be determined after we perform extensive experiments with real world datasets (these experiments are in progress now).

2.5 Web-Service Trustworthiness

We adopt Kuter and Golbeck's[1] formalism for Web service trustworthiness in our work. Web service trustworthiness is defined as a function of user ratings over QoS characteristics of Web services. As the ingredients for computing trustworthiness can be harvested from user profiles and the respective social network, we continue with formalism and computation steps. If *w* represents a Web service then rating of composer user *u* over service *w* is denoted by $\rho_u(w)$. Let us U be a set of all individuals in the social network who rated service *w*. Consequently, the reputation of service *w* from the user *c* perspective can be computed as follows:

$$t_c(w) = \frac{\sum_{u \in U} \rho_u(w)\, trust(c,u)}{|U|} \tag{3}$$

In formula (3), $t_c(w)$ indicates the reputation of service *w* with respect to user *c* and *trust(c,u)* denotes trust of composer user *c* to individual user *u* in set *U* of users who has provided ratings over service *w* in their profile and their inferred privacy level allows exploitation of their ratings by user *c*. The final trustworthiness of service *w* is considered as the average of its reputation across all users in set *U*.

2.6 Composite Web Service Trustworthiness

Trustworthiness of a composite service is computed via propagating the trust values of atomic services, computed by formula (3), upward in the composition. Here three strategies can be utilized according to Kuter and Golbeck [1]: *Overly-Cautious, Overly-Optimistic* and *Average*. All these strategies aim in finding a composition with highest trust value. The goal of the first strategy is maximizing the minimum expected trust value that the composer user has in atomic services of the composite service. In other words, it assumes that if something bad could happen it would definitely happen, thus it avoids incorporating low trusted services. In contrast to the first strategy, *Overly Optimistic* strategy promotes the influence of highly trusted atomic services into trust of the composite service because of it believes that nothing bad happens if low trusted services are taken into account for composition. The last strategy is an intermediate approach looking for compositions with maximum average trust.

3 Service Composition Architecture

Taking into account the above-mentioned methods and algorithms we develop a framework for trust and privacy enabled service composition. The proposed framework is an extension of our previous work [2] by incorporating components dealing with trustworthiness of services and profiling of user experience with service. The architecture of the framework is depicted in Fig.3. For newly introduced layers, we point out relevant sections in this paper while for some other layers references to our previous works are provided: *A)* **Requirement Expansion Layer**: It expands user requirement statement, specified in terms of available input and expected output parameters of services, with relevant concepts in order to increase service discovery efficiency. We obtain these terms and concepts from our pre-populated knowledge base which is built based on our ontology learning methodology [22]. The requirement expansion is performed according to the method proposed by Kungas and Dumas [11]. ***B)* Problem Decomposition Layer:** The objective of this layer is discovery of potential services in the problem domain that could realize end-user expanded requirement [2]. ***C)* Service Composition Engine Layer:** The goal of this layer is generation of a plan (plans) to fulfill the user requirement through composition of discovered services [2]. ***D)* Trust & Privacy Inference Engine:** It accommodates the trust and privacy inference algorithms and implements network pruning algorithm to compute the trustworthiness of a service from a specific user's perspective (Sections 2.3, and 2.4). ***E)* Composition Trust Designator Layer:** This layer receives the inferred trust for each individual service in the generated compositions and utilizes any of the three strategies mentioned in section 2.5 to compute trustworthiness of each

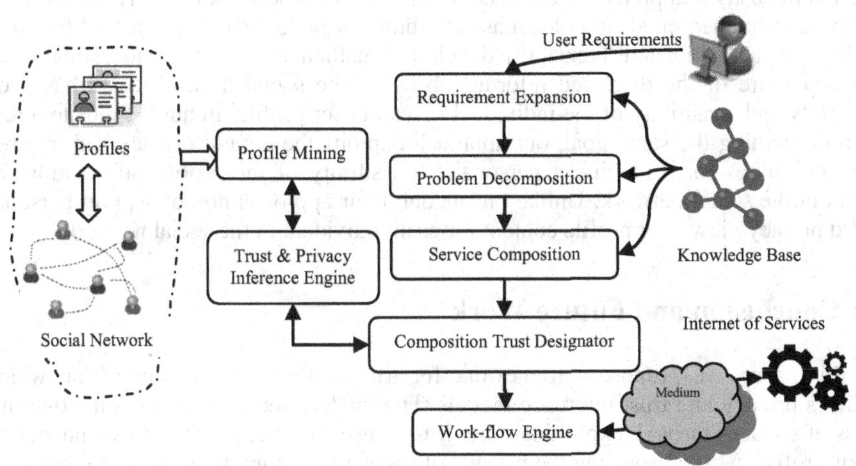

Fig. 3. Trustworthy Service Composition Architecture

alternative composition. The highest trusted composition is delivered to Work-flow engine for execution. ***F) Work-flow Engine Layer:*** This layer provides components for orchestration and execution of atomic services in composite services [2]. It manages the control flow, performs data mediation and invokes the services. ***G) Profile Mining Layer:*** The profiler component manages a profile repository and implements mechanisms for collecting and archiving user experience and also mining the content of user profiles to build a social network of users (Section 2.2). While the individual layers of the framework are developed their integration and experiments with real data at the time of writing the paper are under construction.

4 Related Works

Pursuing a feedback based service selection approach (see [4][16]) exploited user feedback to measure Web service trustworthiness and social trust to receive feedback only from trusted users. This work is similar to our solution in the sense that we both are employing Web 2.0 social and technology trends. However, unlike our approach which aims to find highly trusted service composition, this solution solely tackled only the service selection issue.

Trust aware approaches for Web service composition have been investigated widely in the literature [1][10][15][17]. While Galizia et al. [10] presented a policy based approach (WSTO) for selection of WSMO semantic Web services, Kuter and Golbeck [1] targeted OWL-S upper ontology and followed a reputation based approach for selecting highly trusted composite web service. Paradesi et al. [15] adopted a multi-agent based reputation model to define trustworthiness of services. Moreover, they developed a trust framework to derive trust for a composite service from trust model of component services. Nepal et al. [17] tackled the problem of fair reputation propagation of a composite service into its component services. Unlike our work, none of the aforementioned trust aware approaches considered privacy of users when they infer trust relationships or exploit their profile content.

Banks and Wu [18] proposed a hypothesis on possible relationship between interaction intensity and privacy preference for online social network users. However, their proposal remained on abstract level as they didn't provide the detailed model for computing privacy. Liu and Trezi [19] developed mathematical models to estimate the privacy score of the disclosed information by online social network users based on visibility and sensitivity of the individual items in user profile. In quite opposite direction but aiming the same goal, our approach exploits the default privacy and inferred privacy values for providing a personalized visibility of the profile information for users in the social network. Unlike our model, their approach do not support personalized privacy view over profile content for each individual in the social network.

5 Conclusion and Future Work

In this paper, we propose a framework for trustworthy service composition which utilizes privacy and trust inference models. The models permit measuring trustworthiness of services through exploiting other trusted users past experience (accumulated in their profile) while respecting the privacy of users. Our future work includes analyzing the efficiency of the proposed privacy model using real world dataset and the effect of privacy on quality of composition. Results will reveal appropriate values to be assigned to each privacy inference parameters. Finally we need to develop a fair algorithm for propagation of composite service rating into the ratings of component web services.

Acknowledgement. This work was partially supported by the Grant 621-2007-6565 from the Swedish Research Council.

References

[1] Kuter, U., Golbeck, J.: Semantic Web Service Composition in Social Environments. In: Proceedings of the 8th International Semantic Web Conference (2009)

[2] Mokarizadeh, S., Grosso, A., Matskin, M., Kungas, P., Haseeb, A.: Applying Semantic Web Service Composition for Action Planning in Multi-robot Systems. In: Proc. of Fourth International Conference on Internet and Web Applications and Services, pp. 370–376. IEEE Computer Society, Los Alamitos (2009)

[3] Schroth, C., Janner, T.: Web 2.0 and SOA: Converging Concepts Enabling the Internet of Services. IT Professional 9(3), 36–41 (2007)

[4] Leitner, P., Michlmayr, A., Rosenberg, F., Dustdar, S.: Selecting Web Services Based on Past User Experiences. In: Proc. of 4th IEEE Asia-Pacific Services Computing Conference (2009)

[5] http://www.foaf-project.org

[6] Dokoohaki, N., Matskin, M.: Personalizing human interaction through hybrid ontological profiling: Cultural heritage case study. In: Ronchetti, M. (ed.) 1st Workshop on Semantic Web Applications and Human Aspects, In Conjunction with Asian Semantic Web Conference (2008)

[7] Katz, Y., Golbeck, J.: Social network-based trust in prioritized default logic. In: Proceedings of the 21st National Conference on Artificial intelligence, vol. 2, pp. 1345–1350 (2006)

[8] Ziegler, C., Lausen, G.: Spreading Activation Models for Trust Propagation. In: Proceedings of the 2004 IEEE International Conference on E-Technology, E-Commerce and E-Service, pp. 83–97 (2004)

[9] O'reilly, T.: What is Web 2.0: Design Patterns and Business Models for the Next Generation of Software. Communications & Strategies 1, 17 (2007)

[10] Galizia, S., Gugliotta, A., Domingue, J.: A Trust Based Methodology for Web Service Selection. In: Proc. of the international Conference on Semantic Computing, pp. 193–200 (2007)

[11] Kungas, P., Dumas, M.: Cost-Effective Semantic Annotation of XML Schemas and Web Service Interfaces. In: Proceedings of the 2009 IEEE International Conference on Services Computing Symposium on Compiler Construction, pp. 372–379. IEEE Computer Society, Los Alamitos (2009)

[12] Zhang, Q., Qi, Y., Zhao, J., Hou, D., Niu, Y.: Fuzzy Privacy Decision for Context-Aware Access personal Information. University Journal of Natural Sciences 12(5), 941–945 (2007)

[13] Zarghami, A., Fazeli, S., Dokoohaki, N., Matskin, M.: Social Trust-Aware Recommendation System: A T-Index Approach. In: Proceedings of the 2009 IEEE /WIC /ACM International Joint Conference on Web Intelligence and Intelligent Agent Technology, vol. 3, pp. 85–90. IEEE Computer Society, Los Alamitos (2009)

[14] Kahan, D.R., Nowlan, M.F., Blake, M.B.: Taming Web Services in the Wild. In: Proceedings of the IEEE International Conference on Web Services, ICWS, pp. 957–958. IEEE Computer Society, Los Alamitos (2006)
[15] Paradesi, S., Doshi, P., Swaika, S.: Integrating Behavioral Trust in Web Service Compositions. In: Proceedings of the 2009 IEEE International Conference on Web Services, pp. I453–I460 (2009)
[16] Cai, S., Zou, Y., Xie, B., Shao, W.: Mining the Web of Trust for Web Services Selection. In: Proc. of 2008 IEEE International Conference on Web Services, pp. 809–810. IEEE Computer Society, Los Alamitos (2008)
[17] Nepal, S., Malik, Z., Bouguettaya, A.: Reputation Propagation in Composite Services. In: Proc. of the 2009 IEEE International Conference on Web Services, pp. 295–302. IEEE Computer Society, Los Alamitos (2009)
[18] Banks, L., Wu, S.F.: All Friends Are Not Created Equal: An Interaction Intensity Based Approach to Privacy in Online Social Networks. In: International Conference on Computational Science and Engineering, vol. 4, pp. 970–974 (2009)
[19] Liu, K., Terzi, E.: A Framework for Computing the Privacy Scores of Users in Online Social Networks. In: Proc. of 9th IEEE International Conference on Data Mining, pp. 288–297 (2009)
[20] Golbeck, J.: Trust and nuanced profile similarity in online social networks. ACM Trans. Web 3(4), 1–33 (2009)
[21] Bonnati, P.A., et al.: Rule-based Policy Specification: State of the Art and Future Work. Reasoning on the Web with Rules and Semantics, 61–62 (2004), `http://rewerse.net/deliverables/i2-d1.pdf`
[22] Mokarizadeh, S., Kungas, P., Matskin, M.: Ontology Learning for Cost-Effective Large-scale Semantic Annotation of XML Schemas and Web Service Interfaces. In: Proc. of 17th Int. Conf. on Knowledge Engineering and Knowledge Management, EKAW 2010 (to appear 2010)
[23] `http://www.facebook.com`

Trust and Compliance Management Models in Emerging Outsourcing Environments

Aljosa Pasic, Juan Bareño, Beatriz Gallego-Nicasio, Rubén Torres, and Daniel Fernandez

Atos Origin sae, Albarracin 25, Madrid, 28037, Spain
Tel.: +34 91 2148663; Fax: + 34 91 7543252
aljosa.pasic@atosorigin.com

Abstract. Businesses today have more than ever a sharp focus on reducing capital and operational expenses. Business Process Outsourcing (BPO), Knowledge Process Outsourcing (KPO) and adoption of shared service models have all increased on a global scale. This results in an emerging complexity and volatility of business relationships. As the future internet of services evolves towards dynamic "service marketplaces", where shared services are discovered, negotiated and choreographed at run-time, the new approaches to the compliance management in complex environments are needed. We argue that one of the key issues to address is trust. This paper describes the compliance management models in emerging outsourcing environments that include use of shared services such as cloud computing services. In this context, we briefly present MASTER project that, among other things, integrates several mechanisms to increase the trust levels among stakeholders. Finally, we present a solution for the automated evidence collection at the service provider site and discuss related trust issues.

Keywords: Compliance, Internal Control, Trust, Cost Reduction, Outsourcing.

1 Introduction

Businesses today have more than ever a sharp focus on reducing capital and operational expenses. Market push and cost saving is driving the convergence of different sources of value in souring options: outsourcing specialized in knowledge or resources are now being mixed with those specialised in convenience and scale.

The advent of cloud service providers, for example, may now allow specialized business process outsourcing (BPO) providers to focus on knowledge and still provide compelling scale in the infrastructure by using shared services online. In a "classic" business process outsourcing context the outsourcing partner not only takes over the ICT but also takes responsibility for the compliance related tasks such as evidence collection. Business Process (BP) execution is assisted by often software tools that should be able to collect compliance-specific evidence and to generate respective execution events. Although business process outsourcing involves a re-allocation of responsibility for performing all or part of a business process, the regulatory

W. Cellary and E. Estevez (Eds.): I3E 2010, IFIP AICT 341, pp. 237–248, 2010.

compliance responsibility and obligations remains with the process owner, which puts a lot of emphasis on trust relationships.

In this paper we start with an analysis of emerging trends and shifts in outsourcing models and partner relationships. Then we cover compliance management (CM) in general and CM in specific outsourcing contexts where a change in trust relationship is directly related to reallocation of evidence collection responsibility.

Implementing business process compliance requires means of compliance engineering, control tasks, assessment etc as well as some level of automation for some of these tasks. Full or partial automation of CM tasks is another trend covered in this paper and we will present how our approach, developed in MASTER project [1], facilitates CM task automation and flexibility. MASTER project is a collaborative project funded under the EU 7th Research Framework Programme and is currently developing a framework that will help, in particular, to reduce the compliance risk in externalization scenarios and will ensure an effective control as if business processes were running in a trusted administrative domain. Finally, this paper concludes with the trust assessment for different CM models and outsourcing settings.

2 Trends and Shifts in Outsourcing

Sourcing is a wide concept that entails various approaches. The choices range from insourcing, i.e. in-house operations, to complete outsourcing. Information Technology (IT) Outsourcing, for example, suggest externalisation of variety of IT services, ranging from Data Entry Jobs, through Software Development to Website Designing. While various kinds of partial outsourcing options as well as joinsourcing options exist, another approach, derived from the evolution of IT services markets is emerging. Traditional low value human resource-driven (HRD) outsourcing e.g. call centre, desktop and helpdesk support or maintenance of mainframe computers are now complemented by shared service based (SSB) IT services market such as on-demand or cloud computing. The value shift is towards scale, usability etc. In parallel, existing Expertise and knowledge-driven (EKD) outsourcing, such as legal assistance or third party assessments (TPA), is becoming the mainstream trend in the IT markets.

For a long time, IT outsourcing has been perceived as a technology issue, but actually it has less to do with technology than with the business itself or its costs. The existence of different outsourcing models and possibilities is therefore stimulated by cost analysis as much or even more than capabilities or value proposition of service provider. Historical experience says that company can save a minimum of 20% reduction in costs [2] by outsourcing. We argue that, besides cost and the additional value for the business, trust relationships are going to play an increasingly important role in this analysis of outsourcing options and we will illustrate this with examples considered in MASTER project. In principle, trust is already considered in some outsourcing approaches. In joinsourcing (co-sourcing), for example, a customer and its IT providers form an alliance in which operations are not fully outsourced and the customer keeps IT under its own control. Service level and value agreements are common in this form of outsourcing, but the main advantage for customer is close monitoring of these agreements and increased perception of trust. Another form of sourcing is the solution partnership that typically supports a specialised business line or product. Centre of excellence [4] idea was presented in 2004 with several advantages within the "hybrid" or "global sourcing" frameworks. Atos Origin, the second largest BPO provider in Western Europe [3], launched another outsourcing model in 2009, so called "agile outsourcing" that spans over three lines of our business: Managed Operations, Infrastructure Solutions (including utility services) and Application Management.

The most dynamic outsourcing model, however, is yet to come. It should combine many of the above mentioned elements, including transformation partnership or expertise and knowledge-driven (EKD) services as well as ad-hoc composition of shared services for ICT support. For this theoretic model, that will be enabled by the existence of "dynamic service markets" in the future internet, hybrid value proposition and relationship driven coalitions will be the main drivers. We introduce term "combo-sourcing" to refer to this model. Service Oriented Architectures (SOA) provides a common platform that allows integrating services and components across organisational domains, reusing them in different business settings, and building applications through orchestrating services following the business needs. SOA not only allows the IT infrastructure to keep pace with the increased complexity and scale of modern business networks, but its flexibility and adaptability turns out to be a necessary precondition to execute business within these networks. These architectures, however, are characterized by an inherently distributed security administration and a number of unsolved security issues [5]. The move towards services also increases the emphasis on relationships, negotiations, and agreements. This brings particular challenges for the area management and measurement of security. Rather than being predefined and fixed over long periods of time, as in conventional computing, the architecture of shared service is defined in terms of the requirements specified for the service functionality and the discovery, selection, choreography or adaptation processes applied across all relevant services. These processes, hence the architecture, may also be governed by models, patterns, and policies. We argue that in the current state of the art, issues such as compliance may limit ad-hoc changes in service compositions compliance while patterns may constrain entire architectures that have been proven to work well in specific contexts.

3 Compliance Management

Compliance is a term generally used to refer to the conformance to a set of laws, regulations, policies, or best practices. While compliance is a final goal, process designed to help the organization accomplish it is called internal control process [6]. As a matter of fact, compliance or business objective setting is a precondition to implement an internal control framework. Compliance management, as defined in [7] is the term referring to the definition of means to avoid policy violations where policies are derived from compliance requirements. Compliance management (CM) also refers to standards, frameworks, and software used to ensure the monitoring and control of this policy enforcement.

Compliance Management consists of many tasks roughly grouped around three main phases:

- Compliance engineering: Compliance engineering consist in the translation of non-trivial regulatory compliance requirements, business goals or organizational policy aspects, that are often expressed in natural language, into technical controls that can be deployed in operational infrastructure and can generate evidences which, at a later stage, enables compliance risk assessment and eventual audit certification. Set of operation policies is used as an interface to operational compliance infrastructure and internal control process.

- Operational compliance infrastructure: indicators that are tailored to measure levels of compliance are used in combination with software components and different types of internal controls that enable evidence collection as well as some kind of corrective/compensating actions. Parts of this infrastructure include signaling, monitoring and enforcement components.
- Assessment of compliance: in ideal situation, companies should have ability to continuously assess compliance levels not only for processes running on ICT systems at their premises, but also for those processes that run on external IT systems. Evidence aggregation, correlation, analysis, control refinement, risk re-assessment, etc., are some of tasks related to this phase of compliance management. Internal audits, sometimes called first party audits, are conducted by, or on behalf of, the organization itself for internal purposes. The internal or external auditors assess whether the controls are properly designed, implemented and working effectively, and make recommendations on how to improve internal control

Currently, compliance management is relying heavily on manual, error-prone, sample-based procedures undertaken by either internal or external auditors. Automation can be achieved by means of software tools [8], although there is still a way to go. Many software vendors moved to Governance, Risk and Compliance (GRC) market with previously existing tools and without sound CM framework that could actually remediate governance gaps which are especially relevant in outsourcing environments. Choice of security controls, for example, which is often based on static risk assessment driven by regulatory compliance requirements, is a typical top-down process which is not sufficient to assure compliance in environments with complex governance such as outsourcing environment. Actually, there are a multitude of reasons for which deviations from an expected business process might happen (e.g., human factors, service downtimes). The accuracy and coverage of these security controls could be increased through automated evidence collection, tools that provide feedback based on operational indicators or tools such as event correlation analysis. However, the information from these tools used in compliance management detection and assessment phase should be used not only for upper level reporting, but also for real time corrective actions. In addition, this information could be used to improve trust management (e.g. through event tagging, reputation mechanisms etc) in complex outsourcing environments. MASTER framework for integrated compliance management is one of the first attempts to provide coherent coverage of these issues.

4 Modeling Compliance Management in MASTER

In the emerging outsourcing environment, the BPO or service provider may not be able to offer all the required information or compliance evidences to the customer, the business process owner. Customers might believe that events or related evidences provided by service providers are not authentic. Service provider may not want to reveal all contents of events emitted by the outsourced business process or shared services, since this may expose sensitive information about the service provider unnecessarily. In addition, customers can constrain information flow of sensitive information or can impose security objectives for each type of data. Consequently, the whole trust framework for Compliance Management requires some re-assessment for these environments with multiple trust levels (we will use shorter term multi-trust environment).

One possibility in the complex outsourcing scenario is to move the responsibility for the fulfilment of the control objective to the outsourcing-provider together with the outsourced business process. To establish an agreement between parties, key assurance indicator (KAI) can be used. The basic idea behind the indicators originally introduced in [22] is that they give a meaningful evaluation of compliance of the process (Key Assurance Indicator, KAI) and measure how well the control process is implemented (Key Security Indicators, KSIs). More formally speaking, KAI defines how good is the process P is with respect to the ideal process P (ideal), e.g. if all the traces of this process are 100% compliant. Alternatively, service provider might expose the controls in place which implement the required control objective (KSI in this case). The intuitive meaning of Key Security Indicator for Correct Operation of Controls (KSIcorrect) is that it defines how good is a given control process (CP) applied to business process (BP) with respect to CPideal applied to BP. In the KSIcorrect definition we also use an evaluation function that compares a result of applying CP to BP and result of CP(BP) that is also produced by CPideal(BP). Intuitively speaking, in this way we define how good is the CP with respect to CPideal for our BP. Another indicator is Key Security Indicator for Control Coverage that, for a given observation period O and evaluation function Eval, defines the coverage of our BP by the given CP (full definitions can be found in [22]).

The advantage of approach that uses KSI is that the providers can make their own choice on how to implement the control (as long as it is complies with the abstract specification of the control process or as long as it guarantees satisfaction of the outsourced control objective) and thus keep the control over the business process. However, the service provider might not be able to implement the specified control process or might not want to be responsible for the violation of the control objective. In this case the implementation of the control objective and responsibility for its fulfilment is kept external from the party which implements business process Thus, the service provider doesn't have to worry about the enforcement of the control objective, but must provide sufficient visibility and control to the party responsible for the control objective fulfilment to enable monitoring and enforcement of this control objective. The advantage of this approach is that the providers do not have to implement any controls and thus the provider selection is more flexible (assuming enough evidence and control are provided). However, service providers might not want any external influence on their business processes due to the possibility of violation their internal regulations, and might not want to provide information the process uses internally due to the information disclosure. Thus, the outsourcing-client (or service requester) and outsourcing-provider (or service provider) need to agree on how much control and visibility are provided on the one hand and how much responsibility the provider holds on the other hand. The challenge in this case is an appropriate disaggregation of the control objective and the corresponding control process (implementation of the control objective) – parts of it will be ensured on the provider side and other parts on the requester side. In case where parts of the control objective are outsourced, they specify high-level requirements the provider must fulfil (outsourcing on the specification level, defining "what" must hold). In case control process fragments are outsourced, they define abstract operational semantic the provider must comply to (outsourcing on the implementation level, specify "how" to do it). To enable outsourcing on the specification and implementation levels, service providers must describe available functionalities to execute outsourced parts, such as monitoring and enforcement capabilities.

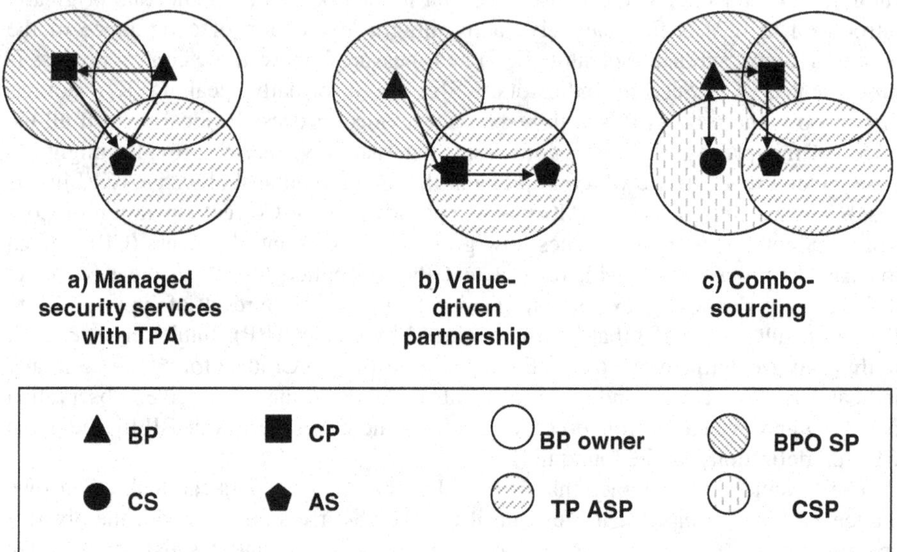

Fig. 1. Illustration of different outsourcing settings and flows for CM

In practice, control processes and a CM component placement is constrained by organizational governance models as well as a mapping between equivalent or complementary aspects of organisations that are involved in trust-driven exchange of information. The following roles are defined:

- Customer (owner of business process)
- Service providers (SP), here regarded as business process outsourcer (BPO) and Cloud Service Providers (CSP) that offer consumption and delivery model for shared IT services
- Third-party (TP) that offers services, such as assessment or auditing. Both SP and customer might want to use these third-party services (ASP is Audit Service Provider)

Compliance related events could be later automatically delivered either to the customer or to the TP that has compliance assessment knowledge and capabilities, as well as necessary event correlation or intelligence tools. Automated evidence gathering for compliance purpose, however, becomes a significant challenge in the case of processes outsourced to the BPO that also uses another outsourcer or CSP services such as storage or computing. An additional challenge is when service running at CSP is shared by several customers and CSP can not provide segregation of events so that the right information goes to the right customer. The following figure presents a number of combinations between business process (BP), control process (CP) and cloud services (CS). All of these might be requested to provide events or evidences to the TP services such as assessment services (AS) or external auditors. As we will see, the operational effectiveness of these controls depends strongly on trust between these stakeholders.

In all depicted settings there should be an agreement, corresponding to each data flow that spans two different "trust zones" and that includes constraints from both points of view. MASTER assumes the existence of a shared vocabulary between organisations (possibly negotiated offline), which is then used to label organisations, processes, and data. Once this labeling is in place, policies such as "don't send data labelled X to organisations labelled Y" can be stated.

Another situation occurs when the service provider may not be able to offer all the required evidences to the customer, such as the case of event generation at CSP. The typical public cloud service provider offers generic services (with some configuration options) to many clients. While each client requires being perfectly isolated from all other clients, the service provider has different ways of achieving this requirement. Basically, the service provider has to decide at which layer it wants to enforce the isolation. For example, if all applications share the same operating system, which may run on a massive compute cluster, multiple instances of MASTER can be deployed on the operating system so that each client application has its own MASTER instance and there is no chance that client accidentally sees events from other clients (see also [15] and [21]). However, operating system level controls may not be efficient as they can no longer be configured to meet the requirements of all clients. For instance, when a single application instance at CSP accommodates multiple clients, it becomes very difficult to tell which client generated the events.

5 Mechanisms to Manage Trust in MASTER

If we look at today's TP audit services, wherein traditional audits are conducted for "after-the-fact" detection, often through manual checks by expensive consultants, we will see that implicit trust is already contemplated in this model. TP auditor usually physically visits the company and controls whether the company has correctly interpreted the existing regulations, whether control activities adequately covered the risks in the audit scope and have been correctly implemented, or whether business processes have been executed according to the policies. Although required interventions or authorisation are stipulated in contracts or depend on business affiliation, in practice there is always also a subjective component. Business relationships are based not only on business affiliation between parties, but also on the past history of working together, disposition toward each other's expected behaviours, collaborative membership in common circles, and so on. Therefore, there are elements of business relationship that are uncertainty (the degree to which one party can predict the actions of another) and vulnerability (the level of consequence that occurs as a result of relating). The expectations of the behaviour of a party are also subject to change in time and the perception of the quality of the performance depends on these expectations. In this sense, trust level can also be seen as a local value based on local context and reputation.

Evaluation of trust mechanisms was done during the implementation of the first prototype for the financial sector scenario within the MASTER project. The prototype comprises two different parts: the simulation of the business flow and the conceptualization of the several entities which are part of the financial field. The evaluation contained trust-related information for all involved parties although it is focused on the architectural design and the software implementation taking into account the project's test-bed and the nature of the solution MASTER is intended to provide. The scenario involves users interested in the financial status of companies –ie. a bank that needs to decide whether to grant a loan. These users can initiate the simulation of the scenario by performing services such as a Debtor Identification followed by a Risk Classification Request. Identification of the debtor company is done by its tax code or name. In the latter case, it may result in a number of companies from which the user directly selects one. The debtor information is displayed to the user, which inputs the risk information –requested amount, payment deadline, etc. The external expert is queried for risk information about that particular debtor company following an automated decision tree. We evaluated several possibilities to increase trust, namely adjustable automation, delegation mechanisms and compensation actions.

Our conclusion was that the level of automation should be adjustable for the control of flow that goes back and forth between the human supervisor and the Control Infrastructure. This level may include also manual controls that could be monitored from the Control Cockpit. However, the input for manual controls would not be the event traces but would be from the human operator. The decision on automation level will depend both on component placement in outsourcing settings and trust between involved event producers and consumers. This means that we will likely have to add administrative delegation in the next prototype version. The trust level could be then increased by applying more complex monitoring rules, which execute additional checks on the middleware or even hardware event level. These rules take advantage of SOA and the possibility to decouple the components responsible for signaling and monitoring of events (evidence collection part of CM) and components responsible for correlation and assessment. SP can delegate access control to a third party with a higher reputation if this results in the overall trust level increase. The administrative delegation mechanism offers ways to apply fine grained distributed access control to monitoring and configuration rules in MASTER. Internal control process owner may delegate or specify who can have access to which MASTER infrastructure components.

6 Related Work

A rather recent approach in CM is to provide some level of automation through automated detection. The majority of existing software solutions for compliance follows this approach. The proposed solutions hook into variety of event generating components and prepare data that supports auditing against hard-coded checks performed on the requisite system. These solutions often specialize in certain class of checks, for example the widely supported checks that relate to Segregation of Duty violations in role management systems. However, this approach still resides in the space of "after-the-fact" detection and there is limited applicability to outsourcing environments. In situations where complexity of the situation is conditioned by the presence of dynamically changing processes with services sometimes shared with other organisations, the complexity of compliance management requirements yields for a highly systematic and well grounded approach and we believe that MASTER is the right step in that direction.

There has been ongoing work on semantic compliance management, as shown in [11] and [12], where an approach for semantic compliance management for BPM is presented. However, the approach used concentrates on implementing internal controls based on static risk assessment. In a dynamic environment, such as the one that we address, risks are only partially known at the moment of compliance engineering.

Another approach is presented in [13] where the authors introduce the modelling of internal control objectives in business processes as a mean to integrate compliance requirements in business process design. Policies are meant to be more generic and do not depend on the previous definition of risks in processes. Like in our approach, policies are meant to be directly extracted from regulatory requirements which allows exchange of policies between stakeholders or discovering of policy conflicts.

There are also other approaches [14] that use deontic logic to model obligations and permissions, which can then be used in the design phase of a business process to verify the compliance of the process. There is also already a lot of work on trust and compliance, including trust calculi. In regard to CM business environment modelling, a related approach is for example Service Networks (SN), a graph-based approach to model a business environment as a set of business partners and their relations. The refinement from SNs to executable processes and software services has been motivated in [9] and first steps towards mapping of SNs to service choreographies are described in [10]. Similar to MASTER, the value calculations are based on a set of Key Performance Indicators (KPI) for measuring the performance of underlying business processes of the SN. The main difference, however, is that our focus is on Compliance Management and KPI are used to compare the compliant event traces (i.e., traces that have been made by running an ideal process) to all traces that have been made by a process within an observation period. Indicators are based on evidence, which in the context of MASTER is also provided by event traces. Therefore we can easily related policy violation to key performance indicators.

Clearly, trust management, contract management and autonomic security mechanisms are important aspects and these topics have been already extensively investigated. Trust management was firstly defined in [23] as "A component of security in network services. Trust management problem include formulating security policies and security credentials, determining whether particular sets of credentials satisfy the relevant policies and deferring trust to third parties". The pioneers of trust management have been tools such as PolicyMaker [24] and KeyNote [25]. Another very well known tool is Simple Public Key Infrastructure/Simple Distributed Security Infrastructure [26] that merged two previous approaches SPKI and SDSI, which combines binding names to public keys with authorization services. Few ideas of trust management are reflected in Cassandra [27], which is a role based trust management system ,Trust Policy Language (TPL) [28], and Query Certificate Manager (QCM) [29]. The topic of trust also incorporates issues such as trust establishment and trust negotiation. The existing research work and tools are exploiting different properties of trust, such as its relativity to a given context (not absolute), its directionality (from a relying party to a trusted party), its quantifiability, its existence and evolution in time and its transferability (potentially in absence of relational transitivity). Trust is modelled differently based on the reference application and nature of the established relationships between interacting entities. However, as we show in MASTER complex outsourcing scenarios, the challenge is to enable trust management with more modular that combined with distributed Compliance Management Infrastructure, could support the different phases and evolving models of outsourcing life-cycle.

7 Conclusions

As organizations are continuously exposed to an endless number of newly appearing and / or changing threats and as emerging outsourcing models affect its operation or the fulfillment of its objectives, the risk baseline is on a continuous shift. In addition, cost-driven changes in outsourcing settings, such as the use of shared services, might be in conflict with coherent compliance management and governance alignment. Here we have presented a compliance model framework that should fit a wide variety of needs as well as business models.

Compliance Management and related tools are attracting attention of both software vendors and customers that own business processes that are subject to regulatory compliance. An increasing number of organisations are moving towards the automated evidence data collection through deployment of tools while more advanced organisations use also automation of control checks and process (CCM/A, Continuous Control Monitoring or Auditing through tools such as GRC (governance, risk, compliance) software). This is obviously bringing many benefits, such as for example alignment of governance levels or executive dashboard implementation, where different risk or compliance views are presented to different governance levels. Although GRC tools can help management and internal auditors in the monitoring,and auditing of business processes, they will need to trust these tools,. Therefore, external auditors will first need to perform general computer controls reviews on these tools to get reasonable assurance that are operated and maintained securely. The other issues that influence dynamicity of trust in described environments include, for example, trust in inputs of monitoring tools (e.g. integrity of events produced at service provider or event traces aggregated by some software component) that have been monitored). In this paper we present approach based on adjustment of automated compliance evidence collection, flexibility in CM component placing, administrative delegation mechanisms and fine-grained compliance monitoring policies. These CM innovations would potentially bring changes in future business models that include third party assessment and external auditing.

References

1. `http://www.master-fp7.eu/`
2. Maximizing Business Potential Through Outsourcing, Atos Origin White Paper
3. Gartner The Market trends: Business process outsourcing, Western Europe (2003-2008)

4. Can you do more with less?, Atos Origin White Paper, José Barato, Juan Carlos Gracia, Ricard Manias, Alejandro Elíces (July 2004)
5. Pasic, A., Serrano, D., Soria, P., Clarke, J., Carvalho, P., Maña, A.: Security and Dependability in the Evolving Service-Centric Architectures. Published in the Book "At Your service". MIT Press, Cambridge (2009)
6. `http://www.coso.org/`
7. Kharbili, M.E., Stein, S., Markovic, I., Pulvermüller, E.: Towards a Framework for Semantic Business Process Compliance Management. In: Proceedings of GRCIS 2008 (2008)
8. Henry, T.: Products for Managing Governance, Risk and Compliance: Market Fluff or Relevant Stuff?, Burton Group In-Depth Research Report (March 18, 2008)
9. Bitsaki, M., Danylevych, O., Van den Heuvel, W.J., Koutras, G., Leymann, F., Mancioppi, M., Nikolaou, C., Papazoglou, M.: An Architecture for Managing the Lifecycle of Business Goals for Partners in a Service Network. In: Mähönen, P., Pohl, K., Priol, T. (eds.) ServiceWave 2008. LNCS, vol. 5377, pp. 196–207. Springer, Heidelberg (2008)
10. Bitsaki, M., Danylevych, O., Van den Heuvel, W.J., Koutras, G., Leymann, F., Mancioppi, M., Nikolaou, C., Papazoglou, M.: Model Transformations to Leverage Service Networks. In: Proceedings of the 4th International Workshop on Engineering Service-Oriented Applications (WESOA 2008). Springer, Heidelberg (2008)
11. Namiri, K., Stojanovic., N.: Towards Business Level Verification of Cross-Organizational Business Processes. In: Workshop on Semantics for Business Process Management (SBPM 2007), Budva, Montenegro (2006)
12. Namiri, K., Stojanovic., N.: A Formal Approach for Internal Controls Compliance in Business Processes. In: 8th Workshop on Business Process Modeling, Development and Support (BPMDS 2007), Trondheim, Norway (2007)
13. Sadiq, S., Governatori, G., Namiri, K.: Modeling Control Objectives for Business Process Compliance. In: Alonso, G., Dadam, P., Rosemann, M. (eds.) BPM 2007. LNCS, vol. 4714, pp. 149–164. Springer, Heidelberg (2007)
14. Kharbili, M.E., Stein, S., Markovic, I., Pulvermuller, E.: Towards a Framework for Semantic Business Process Compliance Management. In: GRCIS 2008 (June 2008)
15. Anstett, T., Monakova, G., Schleicher, D., Strauch, S., Mietzner, R., Karastoyanova, D., Leymann, F.: MC-Cube: Mastering Customizable Compliance in the Cloud
16. Olivier, W.: The Economic Institutions of Capitalism. The Free Press, New York (1985)
17. Pasic, A., Soria-Rodriguez, P., Gallego-Nicasio, B., Calvo, J., Llarena, R., Bastos, C.: Towards a Real-Time Risk Assessment for Compliance Enforcement. In: eChallenges 2009, Istambul (October 21-23, 2009)
18. MASTER Technical Architecture, D2.3.2, `http://www.master-fp7.eu/`
19. Refsdal, A., Stølen, K.: Employing key indicators to provide a dynamic risk picture with a notion of confidence. In: Proceedings of the 3rd IFIP International Conference on Trust Management, IFIPTM 2009 (2009)
20. Perez, M.G., Lopez, G., Skarmeta, A.F.G., Pasic, A.: Advanced Policies for the Administrative Delegation in Federated Environments. In: DEPEND 2010 Conference (submitted 2010)
21. Schleicher, D., Anstett, T., Leymann, F., Mietzner, R.: Maintaining Compliance in Customizable Process Models
22. Di Giacomo, V., Julisch, K., Burri, S., Karjoth, G., Martin, T., Miseldine, P., Bielova, N., Crispo, B., Massacci, F., Neuhaus, S., Rassadko, N., Pretschner, A., Refsdal, A.: Protection and Assessment Model for Single Trust Domain. Public Deliverable of EU Research Project D2.1.1, MASTER - Managing Assurance, Security and Trust for sERvices, Report (2009), http://www.master-fp7.eu

23. Blaze, M., Feigenbaum, J., Lacy, J.: Decentralized Trust Management. In: IEEE Symposium on Security and Privacy, Oakland CA (1996)
24. Blaze, M., Feigenbaum, J., Lacy, J.: Decentralized Trust Management. In: Proc. 17th IEEE Symposium on Security and Privacy, pp. 164–173. IEEE Computer Society Press, Los Alamitos (May 1996)
25. Blaze, M., Feigenbaum, J., Ioannidis, J., Keromytis, A.: The KeyNote Trust-Management System, Version 2. IETF RFC 2704 (September 1999)
26. Clarke, D., Elien, J.E., Ellison, C., Fredette, M., Morcos, A., Rivest, R.L.: Certificate Chain Discovery in SPKI/SDSI. Journal of Computer Security 9(4), 285–322 (2001)
27. Becker, M.Y., Sewell, P.: Cassandra: Distributed Access Control Policies with Tunable Expressiveness. In: Proc. 5th IEEE International Workshop on Policies for Distributed Systems and Networks (POLICY 2004), pp. 159–168. IEEE Computer Society Press, Los Alamitos (2004)
28. Herzberg, A., Mass, Y., Michaeli, J., Ravid, Y., Naor, D.: Access Control Meets Public Key Infrastructure, Or: Assigning Roles to Strangers. In: Proc. IEEE Symposium on Security and Privacy, pp. 2–14. IEEE Computer Society Press, Los Alamitos (2000)
29. Gunter, C., Jim, T.: Policy-directed Certificate Retrieval. Software: Practice & Experience 30(15), 1609–1640 (2000)

Security Architecture of Smart Metering Systems

Natasa Zivic and Christoph Ruland

University of Siegen, Institute for Data Communications Systems,
Hoelderlinstrasse 3, 57076 Siegen, Germany
{Natasa.Zivic,Christoph.Ruland}@uni-siegen.de

Abstract. The main goals of smart metering are the reduction of costs, energy and CO_2 by the provision of actual metering information to the providers and the customer. They allow for flexible possibilities to influence the customers' energy consumption behavior and to adapt dynamically the power generation and distribution to the requested energy by smart grids. Metering devices are under control of governmental organizations, which are responsible for the permanent correct delivery of metering data. The governmental organizations accept online metering, administration and even software download of regulated software only, if strong, lawful security requirements are fulfilled. This paper describes such a security system. It considers not only the security mechanisms of the metering devices, but also of the complete system hierarchy, which is planned for the communication system of smart metering. It supports also new use cases, which are caused by the liberalization of the energy and metering services markets.

Keywords: Smart Metering, Smart Grids, Liberalization of Energy and Metering Market, Power Line Communication, Security Requirements, Security Protocols, Public Key Infrastructure, Asymmetric and Symmetric Cryptography.

1 Introduction

The liberalization of the telecommunication market in the last decade of the last century was followed by the liberalization of the energy market, which led to the liberalization of the metering market (in some countries). It meant the separation of generation, transport, distribution, selling and metering of energy, and the consumer mutated from a subscriber to a customer. Everyone is allowed to buy and to sell energy or to offer related services. The customer can choose the manufacturer of energy, the provider of energy, of the meters and of the metering services. The customer can even choose more than one provider, for example depending on the load profile, day and night. The customer is able to switch from one provider to another one as he wants. By this way, at one hand, the liberalization should strengthen the competition and save money. Online metering is a prerequisite for such possibilities.

At the other hand, the energy manufacturers and energy providers are interested to get actual information about the energy situation, so they can react instantly on the situation, how much energy of what source is consumed by the customers. Load profiles are required in industrial scenarios. That needs also a frequent online access to

W. Cellary and E. Estevez (Eds.): I3E 2010, IFIP AICT 341, pp. 249–259, 2010.

the metering devices. Additionally, the behavior of the consumers should be influenced in such a way, that energy is saved. The consumer should have the permanent possibility to monitor the consumption. The politics want to strengthen the energy awareness of the society. At the end, the governmental department, which is responsible for the correctness of metering, wishes to have access to the meters to check the correctness of hard- and software. Under strong restrictions they allow software download of metrological software [1].

Many national laws have to be respected, when online metering is planned, which cover data protection and privacy, security, regulation of energy and telecommunication, as well as teleservices.

Other rules and guidelines have to be considered, which cover the metrological aspect. On the highest international level it is OIML, which issues the software requirements for Software Controlled Measuring Instruments [2], there exist the WELMEC group with software requirements [3] and software guides [4] for metering, and the (binding) European Metering Instruments Directive [6]. Last, but by far not least, laws and regulations on the national level have to be fulfilled, which are applied for the approval process of metering devices.

The structure of the paper is as follows: in chapter 2 the communication system structure of smart metering is explained, the type of exchanged information is characterized and the security requirements are derived. Chapter 3 presents the architecture of the security solutions, before the key management is described in Chapter 4. Chapter 5 handles use cases of the operation of the security system and chapter 6 concludes the paper.

2 Communication System of Smart Metering Devices

2.1 Structure of the Communication System

The source of metering data and the destination of commands regarding metering are the metering devices. New generations of meter devices are equipped with electronics, for example embedded systems, which allow them to store, process and to exchange information over networks. The communication module supports one of the older interfaces like IEC 1107 over RS 485, or Power Line Communication, LAN or GSM/GPRS. Electricity meters are mostly better equipped with electronic power, so they can work additionally as a master for water meters or gas meters using RS 485 interfaces or the M-Bus (optional wireless). Of course, it is also possible to run a water or gas meter independently on a electricity meter. Online metering itself and secure online metering is usually for a couple of years [7], but new communication concepts and new requirements have been developed recently.

The configuration of an electricity, gas and water meter is a typical scenario in a residential family house.

In apartment houses or office buildings there are clusters from 1 to hundreds of electricity, gas and water meters. For such larger scenarios the concept of a MUC has been specified [8]. MUC (Multi Utility Communication) acts as a concentrator in a building and supports communication to external entities, but also to the customers. The customer gains direct access from the apartment to the meters to get information about the history and actual consumption of energy. The interface used for this access may be a LAN or via a PLC adapter (LAN-Interface/Power Line Communication). Additionally, consumption displays may be located in the rooms of the apartment to strengthen the awareness of power consumption and power saving.

Remark. The customer has also access to its metering information (combined with the billing data) stored in the database of the metering service provider, but this access is out of the scope of the smart metering communication system.

Power Line communication plays an important role in metering communication, because electricity meters are connected always physically by power lines and meters are located very often in basements, where no wireless communication is available. Power line communication is the cheapest method to connect electricity meters, and the other meters are mostly closed by.

Some MUCs (of one big building or more buildings in a street) are connected via Power Line Communication to a concentrator (CN), which could be located in the next transformer station. This concentrator supports wireless communication or DSL, for example, to the outside world: to the metering provider, to the data collection provider, to the power provider, to the metrological institute, etc. All of them have specific access rights to exchange information with the system components.

TCP/IP or IP Telemetry Protocol is used between MUCs, concentrators and providers, but the metering devices communicate to the MUC by specific protocols, which are introduced in the metering device industry, for example, DLMS, IEC 1107, M-Bus (wireless).

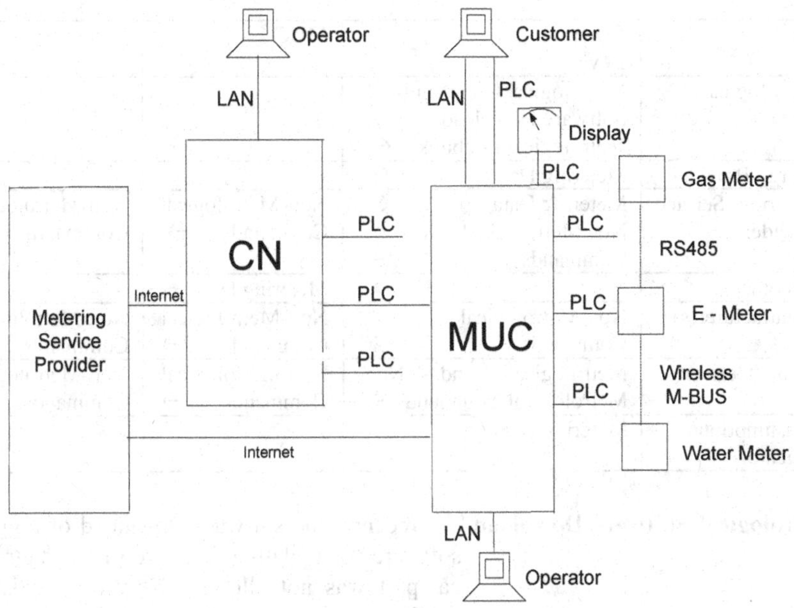

Fig. 1. Communication Architecture

2.2 Data Traffic

The context of data, which is exchanged between the components of the metering communication system, has to be analyzed, before their security requirements can be specified.

Metering Data Data of the meter of the consumption of energy, extended by timestamps, tariff information. They can contain single records, or a bulk of metering data over a certain time, load profiles, etc.

Metrological Parameters Parameters with impact on the metrological part of the metering device may be set or modified by an entity, which is authorized by the governmental metrological institute, which is responsible for approval, calibration and examination of metering devices. Such parameters are: set of date and time, metering parameters, calibration, etc

Metrological Logbook Each write access to or trial to modify (alert!) the metrological part is recorded in the metrological logbook, which can be read and reset only if authorized by the governmental metrological institute.

Table 1. Exchanged information (sent to/read from the device: →/←)

	Metering Device	MUC	Concentrator
Metrological Institute	Metrological Commands Software Download → Metrological Logbook ←		
Energy Provider	Metering Data ←		
Metering Service Provider	Metering Data ← Non Metrological Commands →	Non-Metrological Commands →	Non-Metrological Commands →
Customer		Metering Data ←	
Manufacturer(s)	Non-Metrological Commands →	Non-Metrological Commands →	Non-Metrological Commands →
Local Operator(s)	Metrological and Non-Metrological Commands →	Non-Metrological Commands →	Non-Metrological Commands →
Consumption Indicator	Metering Data ←		

Metrological Software Download Till recently the software Download of regulated software for updating software of the metrological part was not allowed. Now rules exist and conditions are specified, how this is possible in the future [1].

Non Metrological Parameters, Logbook, Software Download Metering Devices are separated into a metrological and a non metrological part, which is under the responsibility of the manufacturer, provider, etc. The security requirements of the non metrological part (hard- and software) are specified by the manufacturer, not by the government.

2.3 Security Requirements

For the types of data listed in table 1 are following security requirements mandatory.

Authentication of Data Origin and long term Non-Repudiation of Origin are necessary for:

- Metering data
- Metrological Logbook
- Metrological commands
- Software Download into the metrological part of a metering device

The information needed for support of non repudiation of origin (Non Repudiation of Origin Token, for example specified in ISO 13888-2) has to be stored together with the information itself. It should be possible anytime for the authorized entities to verify the proof of origin. The non repudiation of origin is needed by the legal meaning of the metering information.

Authentication of Data Origin
has to be provided for the access to the metering information and to the non-metrological part of metering devices, to MUCs and concentrators and mutually for the exchange of information.

Confidentiality
is not required by metrological laws, but by the data protection law – as soon as the privacy of the people is concerned. Metering data themselves are considered as "pseudonymous", as long as they don´t allow a direct relation to a person, but very often a relation to a person or family can be established, so confidentiality of metering data is needed by privacy reasons.

Other reasons to use confidentiality for the data traffic are manufacturer´s product specific administrative information including the software download.

Access Control
As seen in chap. 2.1., there are many roles requesting access to metering devices and the components of the metering system:

It is necessary to execute access control for each function or action, which can be activated. For each function it has to be specified, which role is allowed to send a command. The access control has to be based on strong authentication.

3 Security Mechanisms and Protocols

In chap. 2 the communication scenario of smart metering under security aspects has been described. In this chapter a security solution is presented. The security mechanisms and protocols are chosen, which support the security requirements.

Non-Repudiation of Origin
Digital signatures are used together with a regulated (trusted, under law control) infrastructure similar to the requirements specified for qualified digital signatures of the Digital Signature Law. The private key has to be physically protected against reading and modification. The digital signature is generated at the source in a protected hardware environment and coded together with the (metering) information, which has to be sealed. The digital signature will stay together with the information for the lifetime of the information. The root of the PKI is based on the governmental metrological institute.

SML signatures are used for the integration of digital signatures into the data format used for end-to-end data exchange. SML signatures are very similar to XML signatures. SML (Smart Metering Language) is a special type of XML adapted for the needs of metering.

Authentication of Data Origin of Commands
Digital signatures are used based on a Certification Authority (Trusted Third Party) as anchor of the PKI. The security properties of storage and usage are specified by the metering service provider.

SML signatures are used for the integration of digital signatures into the data format used for end-to-end data exchange.

Confidentiality
Transport-oriented authentication of origin and confidentiality are provided by TSL/SSL on all communication channels, which use TCP/IP. A Certification Authority (Trusted Third Party) is used as anchor of the PKI.

Some connections don´t use TCP/IP because of the protocol overhead, so on Power Line Communication between the apartment (customer or the consumption display) and the MUC, or on the wireless M-Bus. Both communication technologies (PLC and wireless M-Bus) support symmetric cryptographic algorithms (AES), which are used for confidentiality.

Access Control
Access Control is given by access control tables for all of the commands. These include not only the execution of functions but also changes of access rights. The need of change of access rights are caused by the liberalization to change or sell the providers.

4 Key Management

4.1 Public Key Infrastructure

Energy Metering Device
Each Energy Meter (EM) generates its own asymmetric key system during the calibration process, the public key PK_{EM} is read out, certified by the calibration authority, $CERT_{EM}$ written into the metering device and published, for example in a LDAP server. The private key SK_{EM} is stored internally. These key systems are used for digital signatures providing long term non-repudiation (SML signatures, SML_{SIG}).

Concentrator and MUC

Each concentrator (CN) and MUC generates its own asymmetric key system, the public key PK_{CN}, rsp. PK_{MUC} is read out and certified by the manufacturer and published as $CERT_{CN}$, rsp. $CERT_{MUC}$. The private key SK_{CN}, rsp. SK_{MUC} is stored internally. These key systems and certificates are used for SSL/TSL communication.

Manufacturers

Each manufacturer (MFC) of MUC, concentrator and energy meter has an asyrmmetric key system. The public key PK_{MFC} is certified ($CERT_{MFC}$) by a Certification Authority (CA) and published. The private key SK_{MUC} is stored internally. These keys systems and certificates are used for SSL/TSL communication. CA owns also a public key system PK_{CA}, SK_{CA}, using the private key SK_{CA} to issue the certificates.

The manufacturer writes its own public key into the metering device, concentrator or MUC during production.

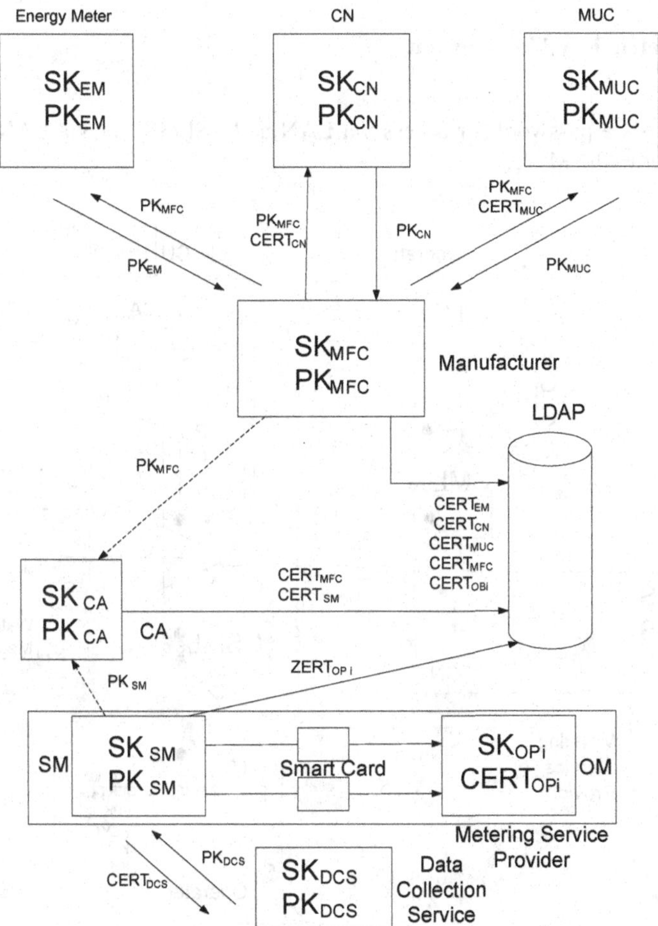

Fig. 2. Public Key Infrastructure

Provider of Metering Services

The provider of metering services should be divided in two departments: security management (SM) and operational management (OM).

The security management owns a public key system. The public key PK_{SM} is certified by CA and published ($CERT_{SM}$). The private key SK_{SM} is stored internally.

The security management generates public key systems (SK_{OPi}, PK_{OPi}) and issues certificates extended by role oriented access rights to the members of the operational management. These certificates $CERT_{OPi}$ are published and enable local and remote maintenance.

The private key of SM is also used for digital signatures of security relevant commands to the components.

Optionally the provider of metering devices can delegate the data collection service (DCS) to a third party. In this case DCS generates its own public key system (PK_{DCS} , SK_{DCS}) and will receive a certificate $CERT_{DCS}$ from the security management of the metering devices provider including the attribute of the right for data collection.

4.2 Symmetric Key Management

User

The user needs a password for access via LAN and TSL/SSL or via LAN/PLC by a PLC-Adapter to the MUC.

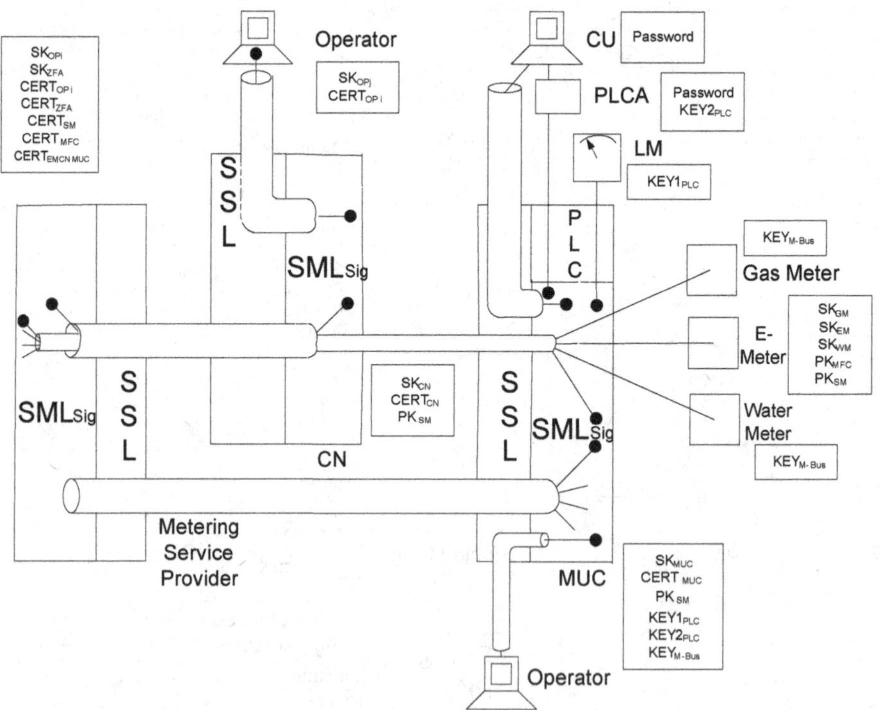

Fig. 3. Distributed Keys after Initialization without negotiated SSL/TSL keys

PLC-Adapter and MUC
A symmetric key is needed for PLC encryption ($KEY2_{PLC}$)

Wireless M-Bus
If metering devices, e.g. gas and water meters are connected by wireless M-Bus, they need symmetric keys for wireless M-Bus encryption and data integrity ($KEY_{M\text{-}Bus}$). The peer entity, e.g. the electricity meter or MUC, needs the same key as well.

Energy Consumption Display
The adapter of the energy consumption display (ECD) holds a symmetric key for PLC encryption ($KEY1_{PLC}$) as well as the MUC.

4.3 Initialization

During initialization the components get all the certificates, which they need for verification of authentication to perform access control and for SSL/TSL online from the Authentication Directory, for example a LDAP Server.
The symmetric keys have to be installed locally.

If the Initialization is finished and operation is in process, the components have those keys and credentials, which are presented in Fig. 3.

5 Use Cases

- Reading of metering data
  Reading is done using Pull method. The reading command is signed by the entity and verified by the MUC including checking the authorization. The metering (SML) data are digitally signed by the meter inside the meter using the private key. The MUC transmits the data via SSL/TSL and TCP/IP to a concentrator or the Metering Service Provider.
  If the metering device is not able to generate digital signatures, the metering data are transmitted from the metering device to the MUC using symmetric encryption, and the digital signature is generated by the MUC.
- Maintenance
  An operator establishes a SSL/TLS connection to MUC or CN using an asymmetric key system with exchange of certificates. If commands should be executed on the metering device, they have to be signed digitally by the operator. The certificate is sent to the metering device. For verification of the certificate the metering device uses the public key of the Metering Service Provider, which has been loaded after installation. The Metering Service provider issues the certificates of the maintenance operators.
- Replacement/Repair of metering instruments devices
  If a metering device has to be replaced, the memory is completely erased internally, and a new installation is performed as described in chap. 4.1 and 4.3.

The liberalization of the energy and metering service market enables the participants of the market to choose and to change their contract partners. Therefore there are new use cases, which have to be supported:

- Change of Metering Service Provider
  If a Metering Service Provider surrenders metering devices to another Metering Service Provider, the operator of the first metering service provider sends the certificate of the second metering service provider to the MUCs. The new public key overwrites the old one. New addresses are set in the components by using maintenance commands.
  If the first metering service provider hesitates to admit access to the new metering service provider, the manufacturer is also able to delete the public key and access rights of the former metering service provider. Therefore the metering devices know the public key of the manufacturer since production time.

- Download of Metrological Software
  There are different digital signatures, which have to be verified before new metrological software is accepted and executed by a metering device. The manufacturer sends new software to the metrological institute, which checks the correctness and approves the software. The object code of the new software is signed by the metrological institute and returned to the manufacturer. The manufacturer signs the software additionally and distributes it to the metering service provider for distribution to the metering devices. The metering devices verify the authorization of the metering service provider by checking the digital signature of the maintenance command, then the digital signature of the manufacturer is verified and, finally, the digital signature of the metrological institute. A powerful software version management has to be used. If the new software can´t be executed successfully, a mechanism restarts the preceding version. Therefore the metering devices must be able to store two or three software images and require an operating system. The metering service provider, manufacturer and metrological institutes are always permitted to check the version and correctness of the running software. The metering device can calculate a checksum of the software, sign this checksum and send it to the requesting entity. The security mechanism for the download of metrological software requires higher security levels than other transactions.

If the functionality of the Metering Service Provider is divided in different parts, and some of them are delegated to other providers, for example Metering Data Collection, additional use cases will happen and have to be supported.

6 Summary

The liberalization of the energy and metering services markets need new communication systems for smart metering devices and a security architecture, which satisfies all legal requirements and the requirements of the providers and customers. The communications system has been described, the exchanged information has been analyzed for their security needs, and a security architecture has been proposed, which covers all use cases. The focus was on the key management, which supports the security mechanisms and protocols. A special requirement of the key management is the possible change of the stakeholders caused by the liberalization of the markets.

References

1. Hick, S., Ruland, C.: Security Aspects for Secure Download of Regulated Software. In: Lambrinoudakis, C., Pernul, G., Tjoa, A.M. (eds.) TrustBus 2007. LNCS, vol. 4657, pp. 219–227. Springer, Heidelberg (2007)
2. International Organization of Legal Metrology: General Requirements for Software Controlled Measuring Instruments, OIML TC 5 / SC 2 – Committee Draft OIML CD 1 (May 2007), http://www.oiml.org
3. WELMEC 7.1 (issue 2): Development of Software Requirements (May 2005), http://www.welmec.org/publications/7-1.pdf
4. WELMEC 7.2 (issue 1): Software Guide (Measuring Instruments Directive 2004/22/EC (May 2005), http://www.welmec.org/publications/7-2en.pdf
5. http://eur-lex.europa.eu/LexUriServ/LexUriServ.do?uri=OJ:L:2004:135:0001:0080:EN:PDF
6. MID-Software: Software Requirements and Validation Guide, Version 1., European Growth Network, http://www.lne.fr/fr/metrologie_legale/documents/MIDSW_1.00.pdf
7. Lo Iacono, L., Ruland, C., Zisky, N.: Secure Transfer of Measurement Data in Open Systems. Computer Standards & Interfaces 28, 311–326
8. Multi Utility Communication (MUC), Version 1.0, 8/2009, VDE, http://www.vde.de/de/fnn/arbeitsgebiete/messwesen/documents/FNN_LH-MUC_1-0_2009-08-05.pdf

IT Alignment in the 3PL Industry: A Comparative Study

Kwok Hung Lau

School of Business IT and Logistics, RMIT University
Level 17, 239 Bourke Street, Melbourne 3000, Australia
charles.lau@rmit.edu.au

Abstract. This research article reports the findings of a survey-based comparative study on current IT utilization by 3PL firms in the United States (US) and the People's Republic of China (PRC). The findings reveal that in general the level of IT utilization and IT focus of 3PL firms in the PRC are lower than that of their counterparts in the US. This may result in a bigger gap between customer expectations and experiences relating to IT capabilities of 3PL firms as observed in the Annual 3PL Studies. The gap may due to a misalignment in IT strategy and infrastructure between the 3PL firms and their customers. The contribution of this study is that, through the comparative analysis, it reveals the possible causes of the continuing IT capability expectation/performance gap as disclosed by the annual global 3PL studies and points to a potential solution to narrow the gap.

Keywords: IT utilization, IT focus, IT alignment model, Supply chain management, Outsourcing, Third-party logistics industry.

1 Introduction

Efficiency and responsiveness can be regarded as the primary goals in supply chain management [7]. To achieve these two objectives, effective communication and real-time information sharing are the keys. Information technology (IT) therefore plays a vital role in managing modern-day complex supply chains. It permits effective coordination of day-to-day replenishment and distribution activities hence minimizes delay and waste. It also provides visibility to enable tracing and tracking of inventory items thereby allows better control and greater flexibility in matching supply and demand. In addition, the technology enables internal as well as external integration. It helps promote collaboration among business partners through collective decision making using real-time data and information stored and shared on a common platform. Together with automation employing data captured via technologies such as barcode, global positioning, and radio frequency identification, IT can significantly reduce labour, errors, and response time across the entire supply chain. This will not only lower total supply chain costs (i.e., higher efficiency) but also enhance overall customer service (i.e., improved responsiveness). In fact, the significance and benefits of IT in the logistics industry has long been recognized in many studies [4, 5].

W. Cellary and E. Estevez (Eds.): I3E 2010, IFIP AICT 341, pp. 260–271, 2010.

1.1 IT for the Third-Party Logistics Industry

Globalization and outsourcing have impacted significantly on modern-day supply chain management. The former has resulted in extended supply chains with global configurations and multiple entry and exit points. The latter has given rise to the prosperity of integrated logistics service providers who look after all the logistics activities in a supply chain for various customers. IT plays a significant role in these changes. It is used to link up business partners in a supply chain to facilitate communication, coordination and collaboration. For example, fast expansion of the Internet and rapid advancement of Web technologies in the last couple of decades have extended the use of Electronic Data Interchange (EDI) from large corporations to small and medium-sized enterprises (SMEs). Similarly, instead of relying on costly Enterprise Resource Planning (ERP) systems for integration, SMEs can now employ newer and less expensive technologies such as Web Services to integrate with business partners that operate with different internal systems [26, 29]. Radio Frequency IDentification (RFID) technology, which permits real-time tracking and automation, enables efficient order assortment of fast moving products and achieves seamless integration between supply chain stages [9].

With more and more organizations outsourcing their logistics activities to third-party logistics (3PL) firms, IT has become an important asset to 3PL firms to integrate their systems with those of their clients in order to take over the logistics function effectively. As a bridge connecting clients and other members in the supply chain, IT in 3PL firms plays a critical role in synchronizing and coordinating complex supply chain activities across logistics users and their customers [19]. However, the high investment cost of some sophisticated IT systems, such as ERP, and the lack of IT expertise have dampened the utilization of IT by 3PL firms [25]. This is particularly so for small logistics firms which are usually limited in resources.

1.2 Objectives of the Study

Comparative studies on IT utilization by 3PL firms in developed and developing countries are relatively limited. While there are studies on the use of IT in logistics and supply chain management, many of them looked at general benefits [4, 15], strategy formulation [6, 17], applications [8, 28], and impacts on competitive advantage and firm performance [19, 29]. To fill the gap in the literature, this study attempts to compare IT utilization in the 3PL industry using the US and the PRC as examples. Effort is also made to investigate the possible reasons for the IT expectation/performance gap identified in annual global 3PL studies. The findings may shed light on how the expectation/performance gap can be narrowed. Through a questionnaire survey, answers to the following research questions are sought:

- RQ1 – What are the current levels of IT utilization in the 3PL industry of the US and the PRC?
- RQ2 – What are the competitive advantages obtained from IT utilization as perceived by the 3PL firms?
- RQ3 – What are the possible reasons for the expectation/performance gap in IT utilization?

2 Literature Review

Third-party logistics is a booming industry. The latest findings from the 2009 14th Annual 3PL Study [20] show that expenditures on outsourcing as percentages of total logistics expenditures in the four regions under study, namely North America, Latin America, Asia-Pacific, and Europe, range from 47% to 66% in 2009 and are projected to increase to 54% to 74% by 2014 (p. 11). Many multinational corporations (MNC) seeking integrated logistics services tend to form alliances with large 3PL firms to simplify management and improve service quality [21]. In order to provide efficient and responsive service to clients, 3PL firms are investing in IT to improve communication, enhance visibility, and integrate with clients' information systems. Study has shown that "information technology is viewed as central to the overall performance and effectiveness of 3PL-customer relationship" [20] (p. 13). The advantages of using IT in supply chain management are many. At the operational level, it helps reduce costs and errors through enhanced visibility, improved coordination, and data-driven automation. The reduction in lead time and waste translates into cost savings and other values in terms of greater efficiency and better responsiveness. At a strategic level, IT permits real-time information sharing among business partners to enable collaborative planning and collective decision making. This fosters alliances and partnerships and increases competitiveness of the whole supply chain in the long run.

2.1 IT Capability Expectation/Performance Gap

While there continues to be significant opportunities for outsourcing IT-based services, the Annual 3PL Study from 2002 to 2009 also consistently find a gap of 45% on average between shipper expectations of 3PL IT-based services and their actual experiences with these services [20] (p. 14). In the 2009 Study (p. 25), the biggest recurring issue as reported by the 3PL users is the lack of integration among internal 3PL systems (55% of respondents reported such an issue). This can mean a lack of global visibility of orders and shipment with the 3PL managed network leading to unnecessary costly errors and delays. Other issues include inadequate performance reports (42%), lack of sufficient project management processes or trained personnel (38%), inability to provide sufficient order/shipment/inventory visibility (38%), and data not available in a timely fashion (30%), etc. They are all related to the lack of integration among the 3PL internal systems or with the customer's systems to obtain and share accurate real-time information. The persisting expectation/performance gap not only suggests an urgency for 3PL firms to further invest in IT in order to meet the needs of their clients but also a need to understand why such a gap exists and how it can be narrowed in the long run.

2.2 Resource-Based View and Network Theory

The resource-based view [2, 27], which sees a firm as a bundle of resources and assets and emphasizes the use of rare, valuable, in-imitable and un-substitutable resources to gain sustainable competitive advantage, can serve as the underpinning theory for IT utilization by firms in general. Wu et al. [29] (p. 494) contend that "IT can facilitate the development of higher-order organizational capabilities, namely supply chain capabilities, which are firm specific and hard to duplicate across organizations". It is the information advantage achieved through the adoption of sophisticated technologies and the synergistic benefits achieved through an integrated system that provide a firm with sustainable competitive advantage [3]. On the other hand, the network theory (NT), which contends that performance of a firm depends not only on how efficiently it cooperates with its direct partners but also how well these partners cooperate with their own business partners through exchange and mutual adaptation processes [11, 16], can be used to account for the significance of IT utilization by the 3PL firms. Study by Posey and Bari [24] suggests that the degree to which supply chain members' information systems are compatible with each other plays a significant role in information-processing capabilities. As an integrated service provider to many supply chain members, IT capability of the 3PL firm can determine the overall competitiveness and success or failure of a supply chain.

2.3 A Proposed IT Alignment Model

According to Wu et al. [29], supply chain capabilities encompass four dimensions: information exchange (which refers to a firm's ability to share knowledge with its supply chain partners), coordination (which refers to a firm's ability to coordinate transaction-related activities with supply chain partners), inter-firm activity integration (which refers to the extent to which a firm coordinates its strategic channel activities such as planning and forecasting with its supply chain partners), and supply chain responsiveness (which refers to the extent to which channel members respond cooperatively to environmental changes). Without investing in the appropriate IT, a 3PL firm will not be able to acquire these capabilities in order to operate and manage the logistics and supply chain activities of its clients effectively. Wu et al. [29] also propose that adoption of IT should focus on proper advancement and alignment. IT advancement refers to the extent to which a firm adopts the most sophisticated technology. For a 3PL service provider, proactive adoption and implementation of advanced IT to find solutions for customers ahead of competitors is crucial in gaining a competitive edge. IT alignment refers to the extent a firm's IT is compatible with that of its channel partners. For a 3PL firm, it is important that the IT systems it uses can integrate with those of its clients and their supply chain partners to enable information sharing and coordination. The IT capability gap as revealed in the Annual 3PL Study clearly reinforces the significance of these two considerations. To facilitate analysis, this study uses a framework adapted from the strategic alignment model developed by Henderson and Venkatraman [12]. Figure 1 depicts how IT advancement and alignment, both internal and external, can be achieved through strategic fit and functional integration. For example, if a 3PL firm decides to adopt a blue ocean strategy [18] to develop new markets to enjoy greater first-mover benefits, it would have to invest continuously in latest IT technologies and use them to provide more efficient and value-added services to its clients. Also, it would collaborate closely with its clients using IT to form long-term business partners to share risks and rewards. This would lead to mutual alignment of their respective IT systems in the long run to facilitate effective communication and information sharing for synchronization and optimization of various logistics processes [17]. While the capability building process as advocated in the RBV theory accounts for the internal IT advancement, external IT

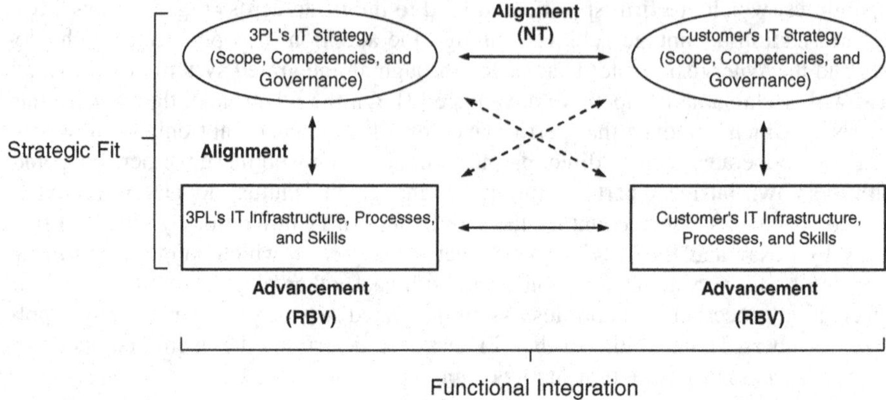

NOTE: The RBV theory accounts for internal IT advancement as a capability building process.
The NT accounts for external alignment through exchange and mutual adaptation processes.

Source: Adapted from Henderson and Venkartraman [12]

Fig. 1. IT advancement and alignment between 3PL firm and its customer

alignment is made possible through the exchange and mutual adaptation processes as emphasized in the NT.

3 Methodology

This research used a self-administered questionnaire survey approach to collect data for analysis. A list of 3PL firms operating in the Yangtze Delta Region (YDR) of the PRC was compiled using the information obtained from the Ministry of Communications (MOS) of China. The choice of the YDR as a study area, which includes major cities such as Shanghai, Wuxi, Hangzhou, Suzhou, Kunshan, and Ningbo, is that it is the most fast developing economic region in China in recent years attracting a significant amount of foreign investment. YDR has now become one of the major manufacturing centres in China with a booming 3PL industry. 300 companies were randomly selected from the list for survey. For comparison, 300 3PL firms in the US were also randomly selected for survey from the member list of the Council of Supply Chain Management Professionals (CSCMP). Questionnaires were sent by e-mail to the selected companies obtained from the company websites. Follow-up telephone calls were made to solicit response and assist in the completion of the questionnaire where necessary. The survey was conducted and completed in May of 2009. A total of 75 valid responses, 36 from the US firms and 39 from the Chinese firms, were gathered with an overall response rate of 12.5% which is quite typical for self-administered questionnaire survey.

To facilitate response, close-ended questions are asked in the questionnaire. The questions are set on the basis of the literature review with reference to the Annual 3PL Studies in design. To encourage response, a relatively short questionnaire is employed. There are a total of 30 questions investigating the current level of IT utilization in the firm, the IT focus, and the competitive advantages brought to the company because of the use of IT. The first section (with 2 questions) collects background information of the company as to the size (in terms of number of employees) and years of operation in the industry. The second section (with 11 questions) investigates the current level of IT utilization. The areas of investigation are similar to those explored in the Annual 3PL Studies. Respondents were requested to use a 5-point Likert scale ranging from 1 (Very Low) to 5 (Very High) to measure the level of utilization. The third section (with 7 questions) investigates the current level of IT focus in the surveyed firm. The last section (with 10 questions) investigates the perceived competitive advantages that IT has brought to the firm. For questions in the last two sections, a 7-point Likert scale ranging from 1 (None) to 7 (All) is used to gauge the views. The self-evaluation approach has been adopted in many studies on supply chain and logistics performance [22, 23]. Although there might be possibilities of under- or over-assessment of performance on certain activities by individual respondents, the aggregate findings should reflect more or less the current situation. The emphasis on relative rather than absolute performance using ranks in a comparative study will further lessen the impact of any random assessment bias. As the data are collected in ordinal scale, non-parametric tests were used in analysing the data.

4 Findings and Discussion

4.1 Profile of the Companies Surveyed

Among the 75 3PL companies surveyed, 10 are small companies (with 50 or less employees), 43 are medium-sized (with 51 to 250 employees), and 22 large companies (with more than 250 employees). The classification follows the EU practice [10]. Most of the surveyed companies are not new establishments. While the majority (53%) has a history of establishment between 3 to 8 years, 44% of the companies have been in the business more than 8 years. The proportions of responding firms by firm size (in terms of number of employees) and years of operation in the two samples are not quite the same. Chi-square tests confirm that at $\alpha = 0.05$ the proportions in the

Table 1. Profile of the companies surveyed

	US	PRC	Total
Mailouts and Returns			
▪ Questionnaires sent	300	300	600
▪ Valid returns received	36	39	75
▪ Response rate	12.0%	13.0%	12.5%
Number of Employees			
▪ Less than 50	0	10	10
▪ 50 - 250	18	25	43
▪ More than 250	18	4	22
Years of Operation			
▪ Less than 3 years	0	2	2
▪ 3-8 years	15	25	40
▪ More than 8 years	21	12	33

two samples are different. The greater numbers of large and long established 3PL firms in the US sample may suggest that the development of the 3PL industry in the US is more mature.

4.2 Current Level of IT Utilization

Respondents were asked to gauge on a 5-point Likert scale their current level of IT utilization in 11 areas, which include visibility enhancement, Web-based communication, transport management, warehouse/DC management, etc. The results are summarized in Table 2. On the whole, the US 3PL firms are using IT to a greater extent in all areas when compared with their counterparts in the PRC. The Mann-Whitney *U* test results confirm that the median values of the two samples in all the 11 aspects are significantly different. Nevertheless, it seems that the use of visibility tools (VT), Web-based communication technologies such as Web-based EDI (WEDI), transport management system (TMS), and warehouse management system (WMS) is relatively common in both cases. For the US firms, the use of collaborative tools, Internet-based transportation logistics exchange, supplier relationship management system, and customer order management system are also relatively extensive suggesting that the 3PL firms are also investing in integration and collaboration with supply chain partners using IT. While VT, WEDI, TMS, WMS are essential to the provision of logistics services, integration and collaboration tools are important to integrated logistics providers to provide total supply chain solutions to customers. The heavier usage of these tools by the 3PL firms in the US suggests a greater awareness of the significance of IT alignment with their clients as shown in the proposed IT advancement and alignment framework (Figure 1). The alignment can help reduce the expectation/performance gap in the long run. The tighter integration and collaboration may also help to increase the overall efficiency and responsiveness of the whole supply chain as advocated in the network theory.

Table 2. Current level of IT utilization by the 3PL firms surveyed

	US (N_1=36) Median	PRC (N_2=39) Median	M-W *U* Test Calculated *Z*
IT Utilization			
▪ Visibility tools	4	3	-6.07
▪ Web-enabled communication	4	3	-6.58
▪ Transportation management	4	3	-6.64
▪ Warehouse/DC management	4	3	-6.08
▪ RFID	3	1*	-6.81
▪ Collaboration tools	4	3	-6.92
▪ Internet-based transportation logistics exchange	4	3	-6.94
▪ Supplier relationship management	4	3	-5.70
▪ Customer order management	4	3	-5.90
▪ Customer relationship management	3	2	-4.69
▪ Supply chain planning	3	3	-5.53

Scale: 1 = Very Low, 2 = Low, 3 = Mid-range, 4 = High, 5 = Very High

* N_2 = 33 as 6 respondents did not use RFID, α= .001, Critical Z = -3.09

Another interesting observation is that in comparison with their 3PL firms in the PRC, the US firms are more willing to invest in RFID which is still a more expensive technology than barcode. In this regard, the Chinese 3PL firms are lagging far behind with six out of 39 firms (all are small and medium-sized firms) not using RFID at all. Nevertheless, as RFID is likely to become a major technology in supply chain management in the near future, the earlier a 3PL firm to adopt the technology the greater a competitive edge it can enjoy over its competitors. This observation suggests that 3PL firms in the US may have a greater awareness of the importance of IT advancement as shown in the proposed IT advancement and alignment framework (Figure 1). It may corroborate the resource-based view theory that the 3PL firms in the US are using RFID as a unique capability to achieve sustainable competitive advantage.

4.3 Current Level of IT Focus

Respondents were asked to gauge their current focus on IT in terms of budget, infrastructure and equipment (i.e., hardware and software), and personnel using a 7-point Likert scale. They were also requested to indicate the level of involvement of their IT managers in company-wide strategic planning activities in comparison with other functional mangers again on a 7-point Likert scale. The results are summarized in Table 3. It can be seen that the US firms are putting more focus on IT than their Chinese counterparts in all the surveyed aspects particularly in budget. The Mann-Whitney *U* test results again confirm the difference. The findings suggest that 3PL firms in the US may have a greater awareness of the significance of IT for their business and are therefore more willing to invest. The greater involvement of their IT managers in strategy formulation for the company also suggest that a greater understanding of the significance of internal IT alignment and advancement as shown in the proposed framework (Figure 1). The same conclusion may apply to the 3PL firms in the PRC although, in comparison, their IT focus is not as strong as their counterparts in the US probably because of resource constraints and shorter history of establishment.

Table 3. Current level of IT focus of the 3PL firms surveyed

	US (N_1=36) Median	PRC (N_2=39) Median	M-W *U* Test Calculated Z
Resources Invested in IT			
▪ Budget	6	4	-6.14
▪ Infrastructure and equipment	5	4	-4.37
▪ Personnel	5	4	-5.93
Involvement in Company's Strategic Planning Activities			
▪ IT manager	6	5	-6.89
▪ Operation manager	5	4	-5.41
▪ Human resources manager	5	4	-3.82
▪ Finance manager	5	4	-5.08

Scale: 1 = None, 2 = Very little, 3 = Little, 4 = Average when compared with others, 5 = Much, 6 = Very much, 7 = All α= .001, Critical Z = -3.09

4.4 Perceived Competitive Advantages

To find out what competitive advantages IT has brought to the 3PL firms, all the surveyed companies were asked to gauge the different advantages they perceived on a 7-point Likert scale. 10 different advantages were investigated which can be grouped into three main categories in terms of cost, service variety, and service quality. As shown in Table 4, again the US firms are reporting greater perceived advantages than their Chinese counterparts in all aspects as confirmed by the results of the Mann-Whitney *U* tests. An interesting observation is that in comparison with the 3PL firms in the PRC, 3PL firms in the US tend to be more eager to pass the cost benefits brought by IT to their clients in terms of lower service charge – an example of mutual benefits through shared risks and rewards. This can lead to stronger alliance and closer relationship with clients suggesting that 3PL firms in the US may be focusing more on long-term benefits than short-term gains. The tighter integration and collaboration through IT alignment with customers may contribute to the cost advantage they enjoyed. This lends support to the use of the proposed IT advancement and alignment framework as a yardstick to measure the IT capability expectation/performance gap. The more extensive use of IT by the US firms obviously pays off in terms of greater service variety advantage they enjoyed over their Chinese counterparts. This is important to 3PL firms regardless of whether they are mere logistics service providers or total supply chain solution providers. As for service quality advantage, heavier investment in IT by the US firms definitely improves responsiveness, accuracy, and customer service level. This is particularly conspicuous in the speed of service delivery as information sharing and centralized processing using IT is vital to the

Table 4. Competitive advantages brought by IT utilization as perceived by the firms surveyed

	US (N_1=36) Median	PRC (N_2=39) Median	M-W *U* Test Calculated *Z*
Cost Advantage			
▪ Lower operating cost	6	5	-6.46
▪ Lower service charge to customers	6	4	-5.80
Service Variety Advantage			
▪ More services available to customers	6	4	-5.66
▪ Customized services to customers	5	4	-5.77
Service Quality Advantage			
▪ Faster delivery of service	6.5	5	-4.83
▪ More reliable delivery of service	6	5	-4.66
▪ More accurate order management and inventory control	6	5	-5.09
▪ Quicker response to customer requirement	6	5	-4.05
▪ Faster follow-up with customer claims and complaints	6	5	-3.76
▪ Smoother communication with customers	5	5	-5.50

Scale: 1 = None, 2 = Very little, 3 = Little, 4 = Average when compared with others, 5 = Much, 6 = Very much, 7 = All α = .001, Critical Z = -3.09

coordination, synchronization, and optimization of logistics activities which can help remove all the unnecessary delay in the process to achieve seamless operation. Again, these observations support the use of the RBV, the NT, and the proposed IT advancement and alignment framework to understand the causes of the IT capability expectation/performance gap and develop solutions to reduce the disparity.

5 Conclusions and Further Research

Through a sampled questionnaire survey, this study has investigated the current IT utilization, focus, and perceived competitive advantages in the 3PL industry of the US and the PRC. The findings reveals that IT is being extensively utilized in the industry of both countries but the US firms are obviously investing more in IT as having a stronger IT focus. The findings also suggest that the US firms are more aware of the significance of external IT alignment with their customers as well as internal IT advancement. The greater use of collaboration tools and automatic data capture technology such as RFID manifests this awareness. It is believed that the emphasized IT investment and focus by the US firms is a capability building process which can help them achieve long-term competitive advantages as advocated by the resource-based theory [2, 27]. Their external IT alignment can also be accounted for by the network theory [11, 16]. In contrast, 3PL firms in the PRC tend to use IT more for the provision of routine logistics services instead of total integrated supply chain solution. The relatively lower investment in integration and collaboration tools and RFID may be due to the lack of resources as well as the shorter history of establishment. As a result, external IT alignment with customers and internal IT advancement may be limited. The lower IT investment brings relatively lower cost, service variety and quality advantages to the Chinese firms in comparison with their US counterparts. This suggests that without building IT as a unique capability, 3PL firms in the PRC may not be able to achieve greater long-term competitive advantage as predicted by the resource-based theory. The slow progress in external IT alignment and internal IT advancement also means that the expectation/performance performance gap identified in the Annual 3PL Study would be likely to remain in the near future.

This study is a relatively simple survey using non-parametric statistical analysis to present a general picture of the current IT utilization in the 3PL industry of the US and the PRC for comparison purpose. Although it does have contributed to knowledge by providing a snapshot of the current situation as well as corroborating the theories with the findings, the relatively short questionnaire has prohibited the gathering of more in-depth information to explore the myriad factors affecting a firm's decision on IT investment. Also, the survey has focused only on the service providers. The perspective of the users has yet to be investigated particularly when measures to narrow the expectation/performance gap are to be explored. Future research may extend the survey to cover a larger sample and to include customers as well as other business partners in the supply chain so as to investigate the benefits of IT utilization across the whole supply chain. Another limitation is that cultural impact has not been duly controlled in this comparative study [13, 14]. Although this study follows the practice of major 3PL surveys such as the Annual 3PL Study [20] and the World Bank's study on global logistics performance index [1] in which cultural influence is not considered a major factor in the comparative analyses, it would be desirable to take the cultural elements into account in future investigation.

Acknowledgments. The author would like to thank the companies and their employees surveyed in this study for providing the information. His sincere thanks also go to the three anonymous reviewers for offering their valuable comments and suggestions on improving the paper.

References

1. Arvis, J.-F., Mustra, M.A., Panzer, J., Ojala, L., Naula, T.: Connecting to Compete – Trade Logsitics in the Global Economy: The Logistics Performance Index and Its Indicators. The World Bank (2007), `http://www.worldbank.org/lpi`
2. Barney, J.B.: Firm resources and sustained competitive advantage. Journal of Management 17, 99–120 (1991)
3. Bharadwaj, A.S.: A resource-based perspective on information technology capability and firm performance: an empirical investigation. MIS Quarterly 24, 169–196 (2000)
4. Bowersox, D.J., Daugherty, P.J.: Logistics paradigms: the impact of information technology. Journal of Business Logistics 16, 65–80 (1995)
5. Bowersox, D.J., Closs, D.J., Stank, T.P.: 21st century logistics: making supply chain integration a reality. Supply Chain Management Review 3, 17–28 (1999)
6. Carr, N.: IT doesn't matter. Harvard Business Review 81, 41–49 (2003)
7. Chopra, S., Meindl, P.: Supply Chain Management: Strategy, Planning, and Operations. Pearson Prentice-Hall, New York (2010)
8. Davenport, T., Brooks, J.: Enterprise systems and the supply chain. Journal of Information Management 17, 8–19 (2004)
9. Deloitte: Chips with Everything. Deloitte, London (2003), `http://www.rfid4u.nl/downloads/deloittechipwitheverything.pdf`
10. European Commission: Enterprise and Industry - Small and medium sized enterprises (SMEs). European Commission (2003), `http://ec.europa.eu/enterprise/policies/sme/facts-figures-analysis/sme-definition/index_en.htm`
11. Haakansson, H., Ford, D.: How companies interact in business networks? Journal of Business Research 55, 133–139 (2002)
12. Henderson, J.C., Venkatraman, N.: Understanding strategic alignment. Business Quarterly 55, 72–79 (1991)
13. Hofstede, G.: Culture's Consequences – Comparing Values, Behaviors, Institutions and Organizations Across Nations. Thousand Oaks, London (2001)
14. House, R.J., Wright, N.S., Aditya, R.N.: Cross-cultural research on organizational leadership: measurement of cultural dimensions. In: Earley, P.C., Erez, M. (eds.) New Perspectives on International Industrial/Organizational Psychology, pp. 571–581. New Lexington Press, San Francisco (1997)
15. Introna, L.D.: The impact of information technology on logistics. International Journal of Physical Distribution and Logistics Management 21, 32–37 (1991)
16. Johanson, J., Mattsson, L.G.: Inter-organizational relations in industrial systems: a network approach compared with the transaction cost approach. Inter-Organizational Studies of Management and Organization 17, 34–48 (1987)

17. Kim, C., Yang, K.H., Kim, J.: A strategy for third-party logistics systems: a case analysis using the blue ocean strategy. Omega 36, 522–534 (2008)
18. Kim, W.C., Mauborgne, R.: Blue ocean strategy: from theory to practice. California Management Review 47, 105–121 (2005)
19. Lai, F., Zhao, X., Wang, Q.: The impact of information technology on the competitive advantage of logistics firms in China. Industrial Management and Data Systems 106, 1249–1271 (2006)
20. Langley Jr., C.J., Albright, D., Morton, J., Wereldsma, D., Alf, M., Swaminathan, S., Smith, G., Murphy, J., Deakins, T.A., Hoemmken, S., Peters, K.: 2009 Third-Party Logistics: Results and Findings of the 14th Annual Study. Capgemini, Georgia Institute of Technology, Oracle (2009), http://www.3plstudy.com
21. Lau, K.H., Ma, W.L.: A supplementary framework for evaluation of integrated logistics provider. International Journal of Information Systems and Supply Chain Management 1, 49–69 (2008)
22. Lin, C.Y., Ho, Y.H.: RFID technology adoption and supply chain performance: an empirical study in China's logistics industry. Supply Chain Management: An International Journal 14, 369–378 (2009)
23. McCormack, K., Ladeira, M.B., de Oliveira, M.P.V.: Supply chain maturity and performance in Brazil. Supply Chain Management: An International Journal 13, 272–282 (2008)
24. Posey, C., Bari, A.: Information sharing and supply chain performance: understanding complexity, compatibility, and processing. International Journal of Information Systems & Supply Chain Management 2, 67–76 (2009)
25. Sum, C.C., Teo, C.B., Ng, K.K.: Strategic logistics management in Singapore. International Journal of Operations and Production Management 21, 1239–1260 (2001)
26. Vidgen, R., France, D., Powell, P., Woerndl, M.: Web service business transformation: collaborative commerce opportunities in SMEs. Journal of Enterprise Information Management 17, 372–381 (2004)
27. Wernerfelt, B.: A resource-based view of the firm. Strategic Management Journal 5, 171–180 (1984)
28. White, A., Daniel, E.M., Mohdzain, M.: The role of emergent information technologies and systems in enabling supply chain agility. International Journal of Information Management 25, 396–410 (2005)
29. Wu, F., Yeniyurt, S., Kim, D., Cavusgil, T.: The impact of information technology on supply chain capabilities and firm performance: a resource-based view. Industrial Marketing Management 35, 1317–1323 (2006)

Against All Odds - A Story of a Successful Mobile System Acceptance among a Tough Crowd

Jonna Järveläinen[1] and Annukka Vahtera[2]

[1] Turku School of Economics, University of Turku, Information Systems Science, Rehtorinpellonkatu 3, 20520 Turku, Finland
[2] Turku Centre for Computer Science (TUCS) and
Turku School of Economics , University of Turku, Information Systems Science, Joukahaisenkatu 3-5, FI-20520 Turku, Finland
{Jonna.Jarvelainen,Annukka.Vahtera}@utu.fi

Abstract. Two public organizations in early childhood education adopted a simple mobile system with female employees in their 50's to replace an internal paper based data collection system in order to improve information quality and accelerate the billing and payroll process. The workers of this sector emphasize the human-to-human interaction with children and parents, and perceive ICT as time consuming nuisance leaving less time for actual child caring. The objective of this paper is to explore why the mobile system was accepted, although the odds were against it. The system acceptance and incentives seem to have a connection to information timeliness and quality in this context.

Keywords: mobile system, attitude toward technology, technology acceptance.

1 Introduction

Governments and municipalities are continuously creating new ways to utilize ICT in their activities. In the recent years, e-government has become everyday reality to many citizens. E-government refers to the use of information and communication technology in the public decision making and in the delivery of public services [1]. The aim of e-government is to improve productivity, effectiveness and citizens' well-being, by rethinking missions, re-engineering processes and implementing information technology solutions [2].

Finland is often been ranked as one of the leading countries in e-government ratings (see e.g. [3], [4]), but it has lost its peak position in the most recent studies (see e.g. [5]). Therefore the Finnish government has launched a new e-government program to regain country's leading position. The Finnish e-government is now being lead by the 'National Knowledge Society Strategy 2007-2015', which emphasizes the use of technology to improve the quality of life. Particular importance in the strategy is given to measures aimed at promoting the reform of the service sector, citizens' well-being and the nation's and companies' competitiveness. The aim of the Finnish e-government is for public administration to provide secure and user-friendly online services, such as saving trouble and expense for its customers and empowering the

W. Cellary and E. Estevez (Eds.): I3E 2010, IFIP AICT 341, pp. 272–281, 2010.

citizen [6]. One of the many actors in Finnish public sector is early childhood education (ECE), which has recently also begun to streamline its processes with the use of ICT. Traditionally ECE has not adopted many technologies or information systems for other functions than administration. The workers of this sector emphasize the human-to-human interaction with children and parents, and perceive ICT as time consuming nuisance leaving less time for actual child caring.

In this paper we study the acceptance of a mobile system in early childhood education settings in Finland. Two public organizations adopted a simple mobile system with female employees in their 50's to replace a paper based data collection system in order to improve information quality and accelerate the process. Although the directors of early childhood education were eager to re-engineer the process, the actual users as well as some of their supervisors had their doubts whether the system would actually consume more of their time. With this kind of setting the odds were that the system would not be accepted although the system use was not voluntary. In fact, if a user did not want to use the system, she would have to quit her job (one or two actually did). After a few months of system use, a Unified Theory of Acceptance and Use of Technology and Technology Acceptance Model 3 based questionnaire was sent out to test whether the mobile system was accepted or not. It was discovered that the users used the system and managers of these users indicated that the system was well accepted.

The objective of this paper explore why the mobile system was accepted, although the odds were against it. The system acceptance and incentives seem to have a connection to information timeliness and quality in this context. Furthermore we test whether attitude toward technology use can be used as a dependent variable explaining system acceptance when behavioral intention or actual usage do not have to be explained.

2 Unified Theory of Acceptance and Use of Technology and TAM3

The evaluation of system acceptance is based on Unified Theory of Acceptance and Use of Technology (UTAUT), which was developed by integrating eight theoretical models related to user acceptance [7]. UTAUT argues that user's perception of performance expectancy, effort expectancy, social influence and facilitating conditions affect whether she accepts the technology and uses it. Performance expectancy means that if a user perceives that the technology increases her performance in her work somehow (e.g. is useful, allows her to work faster etc.) then she would use the technology [7]. Effort expectancy means the effortlessness of the technology, which is perception of ease-of-use, ability to use the technology, not fearing the technology [7]. Social influence has also an effect on acceptance, if a user feels that her supervisor and colleagues think that the technology should be used, then user is more likely to use it [7]. The existence of facilitating conditions such as a user manual or a helping colleague also affects system use [7].

Computer self-efficacy, computer anxiety and attitude towards technology use were found to not to have effect on behavioral intention [7]. Computer self-efficacy is defined as "judgment of one's ability to use a technology to accomplish a specific task"[8], where as computer anxiety means that a person is anxious or considers computers intimidating. Attitude (towards technology use) has been used as an independent variable in many studies, especially after Ajzen and Fishbein presented the theory of reasoned action in 1975 [9]. Several studies have found that attitude has a significant effect on behavioral intention (e.g. [10]). UTAUT has also been used in hundreds of academic articles, many of them concentrating on acceptance of mobile services [11], [12] and even of information kiosks [13].

However, a Technology acceptance model 3 was presented in 2009 [14]. It continued reorganizing of independent variables, namely subjective norm (social influence in UTAUT) was a determinant of perceived usefulness (performance expectancy in UTAUT) as well as emphasizing two variables excluded from UTAUT, namely computer self-efficacy and computer anxiety, as determinants of perceived ease-of-use (effort expectancy in UTAUT). TAM3 included also several other variables, which have been studied in connection to technology acceptance. However, there was no place for attitude towards technology use in the theory. Since TAM3 is such a novel development in the field of user acceptance, it has not been used in published papers.

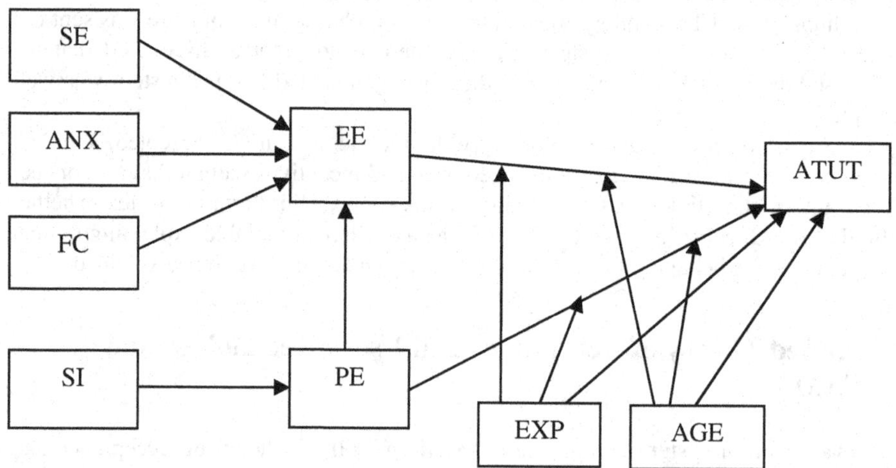

Fig. 1. The proposed model. PE= Performance expectancy, EE= Effort expectancy, ATUT= Attitude toward using technology, SI= Social Influence; FC=Facilitating conditions, SE= Computer self-Efficacy, ANX=Computer anxiety.

For the purposes of this paper it was decided to combine these two models. The simple UTAUT was the basis of the model, but social influence was expected to affect performance expectancy, as in TAM3, since it was known that representatives of the organization and supervisors of the users had participated in training sessions or even trained part of the users themselves. Furthermore, since the crowd of users was quite tough – females in their 50's, some of them very inexperienced with technology – it was proposed that computer self-efficacy and computer anxiety affected effort expectancy as in TAM3. Facilitating conditions variable was not included in TAM3, but it was used in UTAUT. Since users used peer support as well as short manuals to gain control over system, it was proposed that facilitating conditions could affect also effort expectancy.

The major modification was to include attitude toward using technology as an independent variable, since it was known that the users used the mobile system, and intended to do so also in the future. Moderators in the model are experience (referring to system usage experience) and age of the user. However, we could not test for the moderating effect of gender or voluntariness, since all users were female and the system use was obligatory. The proposed model is shown in Figure 1.

3 Research Context

E-government may be understood broadly as the use of information and communication technologies in governmental processes and services, and there are many different actors in governmental level, such as national, state or local [1]; the last one being the context of this paper. If Layne & Lee [15] stage model is considered, the mobile system studied here can be positioned into transactional stage; the system is designed to ease the internal transactions that are required by payroll and billing systems. The system automates the former paper based data gathering system and redesigns the process by excluding a few phases. The current study may also be positioned in eGovRTD2020 framework [16] as an information quality study, focusing on generating incentives to create higher information quality in a timely manner.

The mobile system was adopted in the context of early childhood education (ECE), which refers to the care of children under compulsory school age (ages 0–6). In Finland, every child has a statutory subjective right to receive public day care and municipalities have the obligation to organize day care according to the demand. Public day care is mostly organized in day care centers (approx. 70 % of the children) and family childcare, which offer full day, full year service for children whose parents are either working or studying. The main goal in day care is to promote children's healthy growth, development and learning skills. Day care should also support parents raising their children [17], [18]. Early childhood education in Finland is a well-developed system and much appreciated by parents. Early childhood education is assured by public investments, and quality regulations are clear and strictly enforced. Charges for municipal day care are based on family size and income level. [19] The charge for a municipal day care place cannot exceed 233 € a month (in 2010).

In the focus of this study are the family day care workers. In 2008, there were approximately 160 000 children in day care and 46 000 of them attended family day care [20]. In 2007, family day care employed 16 000 family day care workers [21]. According to the same statistic, in 2007 the Finnish social care employed 177 600 employees of which 34% employed in early childhood education. The average age of family day care workers is relatively high: 47,1 years and it is calculated that 36% of them will retire during the next ten years; therefore the family day care workers are the oldest occupational group in the Finnish social and health sector [21].

In recent years ICT has found its way also to early childhood education. ICT enables for example new working practices in day care, more effective communication between different early childhood education actors and better quality education. The pressure also comes from parents' side: the use of Internet and different e-services has also increased the demand for ICT solutions and e-services in day care. [22]

In this case a paper-based data collection system for calculating salaries for family day care workers and bills for children was considered to be too laborious, slow and including many possibilities for entry errors which would weaken the information quality. The paper based system was substituted with a mobile system in two small towns in South-West Finland. Earlier every family day care worker filled manually a form with arrival and departure times of each child (usually four children per a worker) she took care of during the day. These forms were signed by parents monthly and sent to administrative clerk who manually transferred the times to the payroll and billing system. The data entry phase took one to two weeks for one clerk's working time each month.

This time-consuming process was identified by directors of early childhood education to be a bottleneck process. Municipality's IT directors decided that the process could be redesigned, although emphasizing that the independent users, most of them having a doubtful or even negative attitude towards any information technology, might not welcome the system. Another obstacle was that not all of the users had a mobile phone, and those who had one, did not have a "smart phone", which was a system requirement.

Purchasing "smart phones" for the users was realized to be an incentive which potentially could have a crucial role in system acceptance. A work mobile phone was perceived as a status symbol, since normally only white collar workers with a managerial position had one, and family day care workers did not identify themselves as part of this group. Therefore in order to accelerate the data gathering and improve the service level and information quality it was decided that a "smart phone" would be purchased to each family day care worker and they would be trained to use the new interface.

The interface of the mobile system was not difficult to use, but it was different from basic SMS and call functionalities which the users were familiar with. First the name of the child had to be sought from the list downloaded to their work mobile phone, and either press "ok" to accept the present time as an arrival or departure time, or enter another time by themselves. The process was to be repeated with each child after their arrival and departure. There were some teething troubles during the first few months of system usage; for instance going into summer (daylight saving) time confused the system and users. The times were directly imported to the payroll and billing system, thus eliminating the data entry phase and allowing the administrative clerk to do other administrative tasks.

4 Data Collection

After the mobile system had been implemented and been in use for 4-5 months, a questionnaire to test attitude towards using technology was sent to 74 family day-care workers (29 from Town A, 45 from Town B) - that is the whole population - and 44 were returned, response rate being therefore 59,5%.

The questionnaire used items from [7] with few modifications. Some questions were inappropriate for the context, so they were replaced with more suitable questions which were found or based on items used as root scales for UTAUT. 5-point Likert scale was used for all items.[1]

---

[1] The questionnaire may be acquired via e-mail from the first author.

Table 1. The descriptives of respondents

	Town A	Town B
Respondents	19	25
Age (mean)	53,75	53,42
Female	100%	100%
Experience with mobile system (mean)	4,4 months	5 months
Experience as family day-care worker (mean)	More than 10 years	More than 10 years
Experience with mobile phone (mean)	6-10 years	6-10 years
Experience with SMS (mean)	3-5 years	3-5 years
Experience with computer (mean)	3-5 years	3-5 years
Experience with the Internet (mean)	1-2 years	3-5 years

The descriptives of respondents are presented in table 1. To summarize, the users were mature women, with some or no experience in ICT. The age range of the respondents was from 34 to 64, but only three were under 45 years and 30 respondents were 50 or older. Their experience in family day-care was great, but ICT experience was more limited. At least 4 persons did not have any experience with mobile phones before this project and 14 respondents had no experience with computers or Internet. However, the majority of respondents had 6-10 years of experience with mobile phones, and many over 10 years which is quite normal in Finland.

5 Results

The analysis was done with partial least squares software, SmartPLS 2.0 [23]. The results indicate that the mobile system adopted was welcomed well. All relationships were discovered to be significant, except for the moderating effects of experience to effort expectancy as well as age to either effort expectancy or performance expectancy. The reason for the insignificancy might be that there were no great differences in respondents' ages and system experience.

Computer self-efficacy and computer anxiety as well as facilitating conditions were able to explain almost 70% of the variance of effort expectancy, which indicates that user's fears towards the system and their need for assistance in using the system affect the perception of ease-of-use of the system, although these constructs were omitted from the UTAUT [7]. Effort expectancy and social influence had also significant relationships with pèrformance expectancy and explained more than a third of the variance. These results are consistent with TAM3 results [14] confirming that perception of ease-of-use and supporting social environment affect the perception of usefulness. As expected, performance expectancy, effort expectancy, system experience and age had a significant relationship with attitude toward using technology, and explained over 70% of the variables variance. The perception of usefulness had a greater effect on attitude than perception of ease-of-use, which is similar than other acceptance studies, where perceived usefulness has had a bigger effect on behavioral intention than perceived ease-of-use, indicating that the usefulness is more important than the ease-of-use when accepting a technology. Furthermore system experience had a moderating effect to performance expectancy.

Convergent validity of the model is appropriate since all t-values of the significant relationships are over 1.96, most of them actually are over 2.576, as can be seen from Figure 2. In table 2, composite reliabilities are all over 0.8 and AVE of each construct is above 0.5. In table 3, the square root of AVE is greater than any correlation with the construct. In addition the cross loadings were small between items. Therefore the discriminant validity is also good.

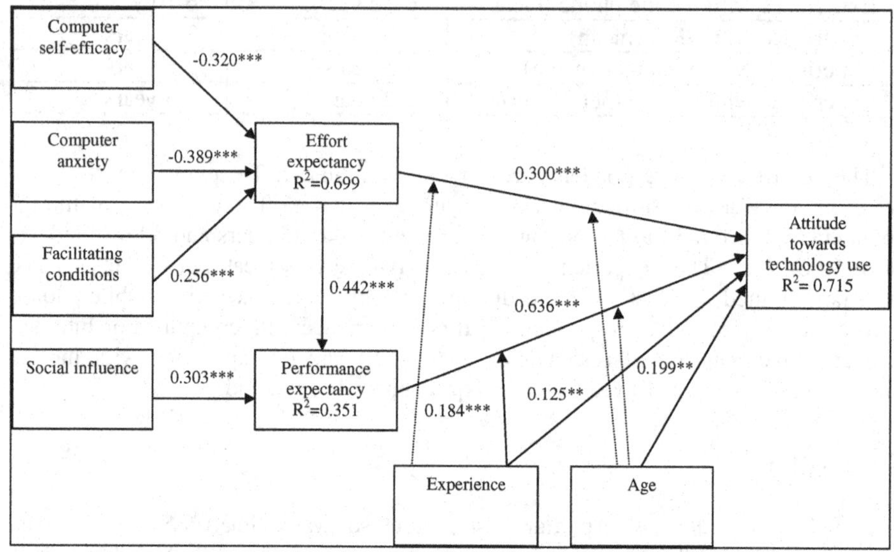

Fig. 2. Tested model. ** t > 1.960, *** t > 2.576.

Table 2. Composite reliablities (C.R.) average variance extracted (AVE) values, communalities and redundancies for constructs (PE= Performance expectancy, EE= Effort expectancy, ATUT= Attitude toward using technology, SI= Social Influence; FC=Facilitating conditions, SE= Computer self-efficacy, ANX=Computer anxiety)

Variable	C.R.	AVE	Communality	Redundancy
AGE	1.0000	1.0000	1.0000	
ANX	0.9688	0.8860	0.9571	
ATUT	0.9510	0.8292	0.9310	-0.0097
EE	0.9355	0.7841	0.9081	0.3482
EXP	1.0000	1.0000	1.0000	
FC	0.9617	0.9263	0.9225	
PE	0.9324	0.7754	0.9041	0.1944
PE*EXP	0.9444	0.8109	0.9225	
SE	0.8491	0.5850	0.7807	
SI	0.8427	0.5742	0.7564	

Table 3. Latent variable correlations between constructs. Diagonal elements are the square root of AVE of each construct (PE= Performance expectancy, EE= Effort expectancy, ATUT= Attitude toward using technology, SI= Social Influence; FC=Facilitating conditions, SE= Computer self-efficacy, ANX=Computer anxiety).

	AGE	ANX	ATUT	EE	EXP	FC	PE	PE*EXP	SE	SI
ANX	-.239	.941								
ATUT	.071	-.522	.911							
EE	.132	-.767	.603	.885						
EXP	-.184	.438	-.062	-.338	1.000					
FC	.265	-.562	.427	.640	-.233	.962				
PE	-.140	-.351	.768	.516	-.139	.233	.880			
PE * EXP	-.302	.075	.216	-.048	-.212	-.070	.126	.900		
SE	-.142	.732	-.567	-.737	.372	-.516	-.472	.001	.765	
SI	-.251	-.101	.380	.290	-.025	.090	.428	-.011	-.049	.758

6 Discussion

The paper reports the results of a successful mobile system acceptance among a difficult user population in e-government context. The average user was appr. 53 year old female who preferred human-human interaction to ICT, and these facts proposed problems in system acceptance. However, many studies have discovered that this kind of user usually prefers an easy-to-use system rather than useful one (e.g. [24],[7]) and this study supports that finding.

Theoretically we argue that attitude toward using technology could be used as a relevant variable in technology acceptance studies. Some respondents may consider questions such as "I intend to use the system in the next <n> months.", "I predict I would use the system in the next <n> months." and "I plan to use the system in the next <n> months." Humiliating and foolish, and refuse to answer these kinds of questions, especially when they do not have choice but to use the system, and this may affect the response rate. Many studies have found that attitude is in fact relevant variable when explaining intentions and intentions significantly affect actual behavior (e.g. [10]). Therefore, we should not drop out attitude from acceptance studies, but continue investigating its role.

As regards the contributions to practice, this paper provides some insights on the successful implementation of a mobile system to the developers in early childhood education and in social sector more widely. The paper also pursues to inspire directors and developers of social sector to consider implementing ICT into their working environment despite the fact that the field is traditionally seen as "laggard" in ICT usage. When implementing ICT into a crowd who is new to technology and do not consider it necessary in their working practices, much attention is to be paid to the training and usefulness of the applications: when users have incentives to use the system and they are trained well, even the most improbable adopters might accept new technology. In this case, the system acceptance improved the timeliness and quality of the information, which then improved e-government service quality in billing the parents.

The study has some limitations. All the results cannot be explained by the model used in this study. We recognize several other variables to be significant in the positive outcome of the above described system implementation. For example, the family day care workers attended training sessions where they learned to use the system. Family day care workers also considered receiving a mobile phone from their employee as an indication of a trust and it boosted their work confidence. The municipality was also one of the first municipalities to implement the system, so the software company was easily reached in case of an occurred problem. The successful implementation can perhaps also be explained by some extent by the fact that the old manual system was utterly poor and time consuming, so any enhancement in the process would be accepted with pleasure.

Due to its limitations, this study leaves room for future research. Future research should examine other factors that affect implementation success. The study should contain the above mentioned factors, such as the impact of training, peer support and social environment. In fact, we have already started this sort of study, and the results will be published in the near future.

References

Gil-Garcia, J.R., Martinez-Moyano, I.J.: Understanding the evolution of e-government: The influence of systems of rules on public sector dynamics. Government Information Quarterly 24(2), 266–290 (2007)

Kamal, M.M.: IT innovation adoption in the government sector: identifying the critical success factors. Journal of Enterprise Information Management 19(2), 192–222 (2006)

Accenture, Leadership in Customer Service: Delivering on the Promise, Accenture (2007)

OECD, E-Government in Finland: An Assessment, OECD, Geneve (2003)

UN, UN e-government survey 2008 - From e-Government to Connected Governance, United Nations, New York (2008)

The National Knowledge Society Strategy 2007–2015 - A renewing, human-centric and competitive Finland. Government Policy Programmes, Information Society. Information Society Programme, Prime Minister's Office (2006)

Venkatesh, V., Morris, M.G., Davis, G.B., Davis, F.D.: User acceptance of information technology: Toward a unified view. MISQ 27(3), 425–478 (2003)

Compeau, D.R., Higgins, C.A.: Computer self-efficacy: Development of a measure and initial test. MISQ 19(2), 189–211 (1995)

Fishbein, M., Befief, A.I.: Attitude, Intention and Behavior: An Introduction to Theory and Research. Addison-Wesley, Reading (1975)

Sheppard, B.H., Hartwick, J., Warshaw, P.R.: The Theory of Reasoned Action: A Meta-Analysis of Past Research with Recommendations for Modifications and Future Research. The Journal of Consumer Research 15(3), 325–343 (1988)

Carlsson, C., Carlsson, J., Hyvönen, K., Puhakainen, J., Walden, P.: Adoption of Mobile Devices/Services – Searching for Answers with the UTAUT. In: 39th Hawaii International Conference on System Sciences (2006), http://www.virtual-community.org/images/7/7e/250760132a.pdf

Park, J., Yang, S., Lehto, X.: Adoption of Mobile Technologies for Chinese Consumers. Journal of Electronic Commerce Research 8(3), 196–206 (2007)

Wang, Y.-S., Shih, Y.-W.: Why do people use information kiosks? A validation of the Unified Theory of Acceptance and Use of Technology. Government Information Quarterly 26(1), 158–165 (2009)

Venkatesh, V., Bala, H.: Technology Acceptance Model 3 and a Research Agenda on Interventions. Decision Sciences 39(2), 273–315 (2008)

Layne, K., Lee, J.W.: Developing fully functional e-government: A four stage model. Government Information Quarterly 18(2), 122–136 (2001)

Wimmer, M., Codagnone, C., Janssen, M.: Future e-Government Research: 13 Research Themes Identified in the eGovRTD2020 Project. In: 41st Annual Hawaii International Conference on System Sciences (2008)

Day care Act, in: 36/1973, Day care Act 36/1973

Ministry of Social Affairs and Health, Decision in Principle of the Council of State Concerning the National Policy Definition on Early Childhood Education and Care, Ministry of Social Affairs and Health, Helsinki (2002)

OECD, Starting Strong II. Early Childhood Education and Care. OECD Publishing (2006)

Sotkanet, Statistics service of National Institute for Health and Welfare (2010), `http://uusi.sotkanet.fi`

Ailasmaa, R.: Sosiaali- ja terveyspalvelujen henkilöstö 2007 (Personnel in social and healthcare services, in Finnish). Statistical report, National Institute for Health and Welfare (2010), `http://www.stakes.fi/tilastot/tilastotiedotteet/2010/Tr07_10.pdf`

Järveläinen, J., Koskivaara, E., Pihlaja, P., Salmela, H., Tähkäpää, J., Kestilä, T., Kinos, J.: Value-creating e-government business models for early childhood education in Finland. International Journal of Electronic Government Research 3(3), 72–86 (2007)

Ringle, C.M., Wende, S., Will, A.: SmartPLS 2.0, beta (2005), `http://www.smartpls.de`

Venkatesh, V., Morris, M.G.: Why don't men ever stop to ask for directions? Gender, social influence, and their role in technology acceptance and usage behavior. MISQ 24(1), 115–139 (2000)

Critical Success Factors of Open Markets on the Internet in Terms of Buyers

Sung Ho Ha and Luo Tao Liu

School of Business Administration, Kyungpook National University, Sangyeok-dong, Buk-gu, 702-701 Daegu, Korea
hsh@mail.knu.ac.kr

Abstract. Online shopping in open markets becomes increasingly popular with the development of the Internet. The purpose of this study is to formulate and evaluate critical success factors in the open market from the perspective of buyers. Based on an extended technology acceptance model, this study assumes that the success of open markets are influenced by several factors, including perceived website quality, perceived usefulness, third party recognition, satisfaction, and trust. An empirical survey is conducted and questionnaires are collected from the respondents who had experience in using the open markets. The hypotheses are verified by using the structural equation modeling. Testing results are summarized and managerial implications are discussed.

Keywords: Open market, e-commerce, extended technology acceptance model, purchase intention.

1 Introduction

Open markets provides consumer-to-consumer (C2C) electronic commerce on the Internet. They use online auctions, web forums, chat rooms, and third party listing. They are one of the applications that come close to emulating the success of the other two main e-commerce models, business-to-business (B2B) and business-to-consumer (B2C) [1]. Although there have been many researchers discussing the issues of transaction intention in B2C e-commerce, a few studies have attempted to explain the factors influencing the adoption of C2C e-commerce [2], and there has been a few research on the critical factors influencing C2C purchase intention in the open market. Therefore, it is necessary to conduct an analysis of which factors influence people's intention to take part in online transactions and a study on how to encourage consumers to accept C2C shopping in the open market.

The transactions in C2C e-commerce are conducted between two consumers, so it is difficult to build trust between them. A third party then plays an important role in C2C e-commerce. Under the third party's control, more users are willing to trust open markets. However, there are still many barriers, which deter users from participating in C2C e-commerce. Security of payment, trust, and privacy policies are the reasons that users are reluctant to shop online. Previous research has found differences between C2C and B2C e-commerce, pinpointing that B2C e-commerce methods have

W. Cellary and E. Estevez (Eds.): I3E 2010, IFIP AICT 341, pp. 282–291, 2010.

limitation to be utilized in C2C e-commerce [3]. Consumers' purchase intention in the open market has thus proven to be a distinct area of research, and its operation requires the use of new models.

Based on Davis' technology acceptance model (TAM) [4], this study investigates which factors may influence consumers' purchase intention in the open market. Previous studies have suggested that website quality that meets consumer needs could affect consumers' purchase behavior [5]. Therefore, this study modifies TAM and proposes that perceived website quality has an effect on consumer behavior. This study also focuses on the concept of trust. Both perceived website quality and third party recognition affect consumer's trust toward the vendor. Based on these hypotheses, this study investigates the acceptance of C2C e-commerce in the open market. The remainder of the paper is organized as follows: Section 2 addresses previous relevant research and formulates research hypotheses. Section 3 describes an analysis methodology and presents empirical results. Section 4 concludes this study.

2 Research Hypothesis and Related Literature

The model proposed in the paper presents purchase intention as being influenced by direct and indirect relationships with perceived website quality, perceived usefulness, third party recognition, satisfaction, and trust.

2.1 Perceived Web Site Quality (PWSQ) and Perceived Usefulness (PU)

As Szymanski and Hise observed [6], a few studies have examined the factors that affect whether online consumers are satisfied with their online experiences. Jeong and Lambert proposed that website quality consisted of six potential dimensions: information accuracy, completeness, relevancy, clarity, ease of use, and navigation quality [7]. According to these studies, website quality can be analyzed by using two major constructs, such as functionality and usability. Functionality relates to content of a website, while usability relates to issues of design. Functionality relates to the information richness of a website, whereas usability refers to the degree of ease with which users can use a website.

Researchers have indicated that the greatest threat to e-commerce is consumer awareness. An individual's perception of the environment would affect his risk and safety assessment [8]. Even if consumers have a positive buying experience, the early concern about the atmosphere could prevent further transactions. In addition, the quality of websites related to perceived usefulness and had an effect on the user's online purchase intention [9]. The website quality was an important driver of consumer perception about the future online activity [10]. Bai et al. [11] have confirmed the relationship between website quality and satisfaction in an e-commerce environment. In addition, Everard and Galletta showed that website quality affected consumer trust in an online store [12]. Jones and Leonard's study confirmed that website quality had an impact on trust in the C2C e-commerce [3].

In an open market, a website is a medium connecting vendors and buyers. This study thus assumes that perceived website quality (PWSQ) is associated with perceived usefulness (PU), satisfaction (SAT), and trust (TRU). The first three hypotheses are listed as follows:

H1: PWSQ of an open market positively influences PU.
H2: PWSQ of an open market positively influences SAT.
H3: PWSQ of an open market positively influences TRU.

TAM has been based on the theory of reasoned action, proposed by Fishbein and Ajzen [13]. TAM predicts information technology acceptance and usage in the workplace and makes IT adoption research more efficient [4]. Its effectiveness has been revealed by numerous empirical studies. Information system usage is regarded as an important success indicator of information systems in the TAM. User satisfaction has been widely used by researchers as an alternative success indicator of information systems and as an indicator of technology acceptance. TAM suggests that perceived usefulness has a direct and significant impact on users' attitudes. Previous research has shown that perceived usefulness has a significant effect on user satisfaction in technology adoption [14] and in electronic markets [15]. Therefore, this study hypothesizes that:

H4: PU positively influences SAT.

2.2 Third Party Recognition (TPR), Satisfaction (SAT) and Trust (TRU)

Lee and Turban presented the important relationships between consumer trust in e-commerce and three groups of antecedents: trustworthiness of the Internet merchant, trustworthiness of the Internet shopping medium, and infra-structural factors (effectiveness of third party functions, certification, and effectiveness of security) [16]. Sultan et al. demonstrated that website characteristics (navigation, brand, advice, no errors, presentation, order fulfillment, and community) and consumer characteristics (previous experiences with the Internet and with a particular website) significantly affect trust in a website [17]. Gefen et al. showed how trust and TAM were related to the purchase intention of low-risk goods from vendors [18].

In an e-commerce environment, consumers find it difficult to get comprehensive information. Especially in open markets, vendors deal with buyers as individuals, and most of the goods being traded is not expensive. Because the third party connects vendors and buyers, its recognition (reputation) is found to be a significant factor in an open market. A third party institution has been shown to reduce uncertainty the buyer feels and to increase his trust when making online transactions. McKnight et al. referred it as institution-based trust [19], which is considered as a fundamental requirement in open markets. Third party recognition affected trust in an online shopping environment [20]. In addition, third party recognition was found to be positively related to confidence of buyers and to be negatively related to purchase risk perception. Based on Jones and Leonard's study [3], perception of website quality and third party recognition influenced C2C e-commerce trust. Therefore, this study hypothesizes that:

H5: TPR positively influences TRU.

From Ajzen and Fishbein's research [21], behavior intention was found to be determined by the individual's attitude toward the behavior, and a person's attitude is affected by his beliefs. An empirical study has indicated that trust is strongly related to attitude [22]. In a buyer-seller relationship, buyer's evaluation of trust before a specific exchange is found to have a direct influence on their post-purchase satisfaction [23]. In an e-commerce situation, trust has been empirically found to be a strong predictor of satisfaction [24]. If buyers feel that vendors are trustworthy, they are more satisfied with the open market. Therefore, the following hypothesis is proposed:

H6: TRU positively influences SAT.

2.3 Purchase Intention (PI)

It is important to understand purchase intention of buyers, because their behavior can usually be predicted by their intention. Zeithaml and Parasuraman asserted that the purchase intention could be seen as a dimension of behavioural intention [25]. Purchase intention is correlated to actual behavior [21] and this relationship has been empirically tested in hospitality and tourism businesses [26]. In addition, customer satisfaction turns out to be an important factor of behavioural intention in an online business [7].

Satisfaction is a quasi-attitudinal construct and often considered as an attitude [27]. Davis suggested that users' attitudes could affect users' behavioral intention directly [4]. As a result, satisfaction has been investigated as an antecedent to the continuous intention of e-commerce services in technology acceptance [28]. Several researchers in marketing have empirically shown that satisfaction has a significant and positive effect on consumer purchase intention [29]. Information system researchers also have confirmed the relationship between satisfaction and continuous intention of e-commerce services [15]. Thus, this study advances:

H7: SAT positively influences PI.

TAM stated that perceived usefulness had a direct effect on the user's behavioral intention, because users are more willing to use technology if it can afford benefits. Perceived usefulness mediates the effect of perceived ease of use on behavioral intention. Most empirical studies have provided strong evidence that perceived usefulness directly influences users' intention of adopting new technology [30]. Several empirical studies have supported this 'perceived usefulness–user intention' connection in the open market, including He et al. [1], for example. The following hypothesis is thus proposed:

H8: PU positively influences PI.

Many researchers have indicated that trusting trading partners can sometimes increase efficiencies. The action of sharing confidential information creates a situation that may be convenient to one or both partners [31]. This suggests a need for trust. Trust plays a vital role in online business, and it is a critical antecedent of building a relationship between buyers and sellers [32]. McKnight et al. suggested that a willingness of purchase was determined by trust [19]. Gefen and Heart suggested that trust significantly influences consumers' purchase intention in an e-commerce [33]. Therefore, this study presents the last hypothesis as follows:

H9: TRU positively influences PI.

3 Analysis and Results

3.1 Characteristics of the Sample

Scales for perceived usefulness were adopted from studies of He et al. [1]. Measures for perceived website quality, satisfaction, and purchase intention were adopted from Bai et al. [11]. Measures for third party recognition and trust were adopted from Jones and Leonard [3]. All items were measured by 5-point Likert scale with anchors ranging from 'strongly disagree' (1) to 'strongly agree' (5).

The survey was conducted in Korea. Most online shopping users were between 20 and 40 years of age and more than half of them were buying on open markets (C2C websites). 177 samples were collected (81% return rate). 19 of these had no C2C experiences in the open markets, and 11 contained incomplete answers or obvious self-contradictions. As a result, 147 responses were used in continued analysis. The characteristics of the sample were as follows: Male and female responders showed even distribution. The respondents were relatively young, so that 87.1% were between 21 and 30 years old. Most of the samples (80.3%) were high school graduates, 10.2% were university graduates, and 9.5% had a higher education. 9.5% were employees. Most of the respondents (78.9%) bought goods in open markets once or twice a month and often bought goods from Gmarket.com (60.6%) and Auction.co.kr (38.8%).

3.2 Validation of Reliability and Validity

Structural Equation Modeling (SEM) was used to analyze survey data (AMOS 7.0). To assure the quality of research, reliability and validity are often considered as indicators of how good a piece of research is. While reliability is concerned with the accuracy of the actual measuring instrument or procedure, validity is concerned with the study's success at measuring what the researchers set out to measure. Cronbach's α was used for the reliability test, which is a measure of the squared correlation between observed and true scores. If α is greater than 0.7, it means that it has high reliability and if α is smaller than 0.3, then it implies that there is low reliability. All Cronbach's α values are displayed in Table 1. All values in the table are above 0.7, which means a good level of reliability. This study then performed a confirmatory factor analysis (CFA) to evaluate the convergent validity of the constructs. The results as well as the recommended values for the measures are also shown in Table 1.

Additionally, discriminant validity is shown to be good when the square root of each construct's average variance extracted (AVE) is larger than its correlations with other constructs. As shown in Table 2, the square root of the AVE (written in bold) is much larger than its correlations with other constructs.

Table 1. Reliability and convergent validity

Construct	Factor loadings	Cronbach's α (> 0.7)	AVE
PWSQ			
PWSQ1	0.917		
PWSQ2	0.943	0.860	0.881
PWSQ3	1.0		
PWSQ4	0.723		
PU			
PU3	0.708	0.785	0.660
PU4	1.0		
SAT			
SAT1	1.0	0.800	0.847
SAT3	0.788		
SAT4	0.925		
TPR			
TPR1	0.909	0.753	0.595
TPR2	1.0		
TRU			
TRU1	1.0	0.813	0.839
TRU2	0.913		
TRU3	0.760		
PI			
PI2	0.791	0.824	0.582
PI3	1.0		

Table 2. Inter-construct correlations and discriminant validity

	PWSQ	PU	SAT	TPR	TRU	PI
PWSQ	**0.939**					
PU	0.366	**0.812**				
SAT	0.329	0.578	**0.920**			
TPR	0.281	0.338	0.386	**0.772**		
TRU	0.303	0.262	0.369	0.383	**0.916**	
PI	0.415	0.465	0.633	0.380	0.409	**0.763**

3.3 Path Analysis and Hypothesis Testing

The model fit the observed data well. Several model fit indexes conformed to the recommended values. NFI was marginally acceptable at 0.890 and other fit indexes were within acceptable thresholds: GFI=0.912, AGFI=0.873, CFI=0.973, RMR=0.048, and RMSEA=0.044. Fig. 1 shows the standardized path coefficients.

All paths were significant except the path between perceived website quality and satisfaction (γ=0.672, t=0.786), and the path between perceived usefulness and purchase intention (γ=0.160, t=1.005), rejecting H2 and H8. The rejection of H2 is different from the findings of Bai et al. [11]. Perceived website quality has an indirect effect on consumer satisfaction through perceived usefulness. The rejection of H8 does not meet our initial expectations. Many other studies have shown that perceived

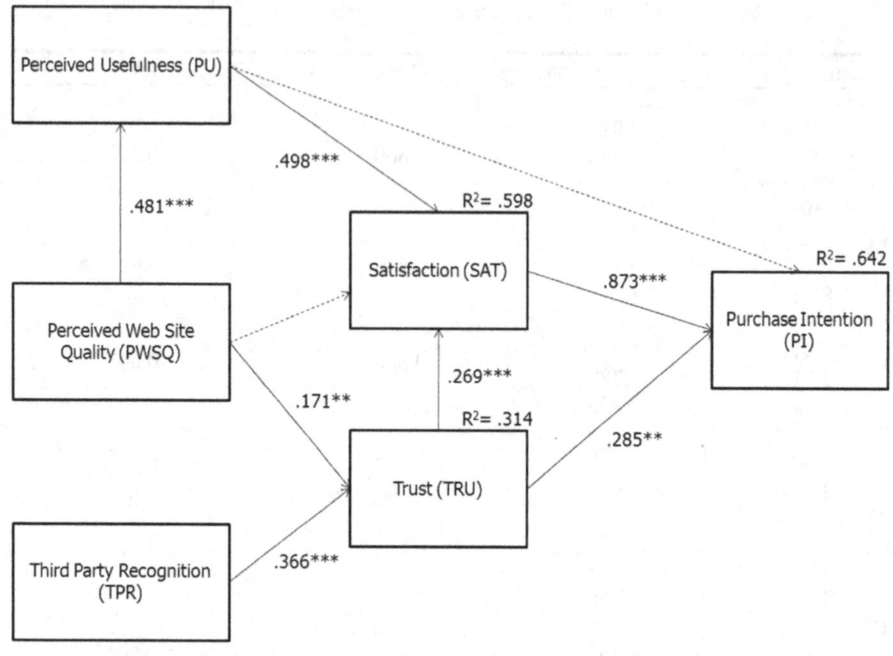

Fig. 1. Results of testing hypotheses (*: p<0.1, **: p<0.05, ***: p<0.01)

usefulness has a significant and direct impact on purchase intention [1]. In this study perceived usefulness can be found to have an indirect effect on purchase intention only through satisfaction.

The effect of perceived website quality on perceived usefulness (β=0.481, p<0.01) and trust (β=0.171, p<0.05) were significant, validating H1 and H3. The adoption of H1 is consistent with the findings of Liao et al. [10] who verified the significant relationship between perceived website quality and perceived usefulness from the perspective of consumers. The website quality (including color, language, goods information, and transaction system quality) can affect consumers' perceived usefulness. The better quality can make consumers feel that the website is useful to their shopping activity. There are several studies showing that perceived website quality has an effect on trust [3][10]. Website quality can enhance the confidence of buyers toward the vendor. When websites are easy to use and they are filled with quality, buyers would like to depend on the vendor to trust them.

Perceived usefulness was found to influence satisfaction (β=0.498, p<0.01), supporting H4. Previous studies indicated that perceived usefulness significantly influenced consumer satisfaction in online shopping [15]. When consumers feel using open markets can save their time and money, they certainly will be satisfied with C2C shopping. The effect of third party recognition on trust (β=0.366, p<0.01) was shown to be significant, validating H5. This is consistent with the findings of Jones and Leonard [3]. In open markets, third parties play an important role in dealing, so the third party's reputation seems to reduce uncertainty between buyers and vendors.

The effect of trust on satisfaction was also significant (β=0.269, $p<0.01$), validating H6. This result is consistent with the findings of Kim et al. [34], who presented trust had a significant and positive impact on consumer satisfaction. If consumers think a vendor is trustworthy and the information provided by the vendor is reliable, they will feel more satisfied with the open market. Satisfaction (β=0.873, $p<0.01$) was the strongest predictor of purchase intention, followed by trust (β=0.285, $p<0.05$), supporting H7, H9. The adoption of H7 confirms the findings of Bai et al. [11]. When consumers are satisfied with the open market and feel it is a good place to trade, they will be willing to participate in C2C transactions. The acceptance of H9 meets the findings of Gefen and Straub [35], which were based on the B2C environment.

4 Conclusions

This study has developed and empirically tested a theoretical model of C2C online shopping adoption in the open market. The results validated that C2C purchase intention was determined by perceived website quality, perceived usefulness, third party recognition, satisfaction, and trust. The results supported seven hypotheses.

The hypothesis-testing results showed perceived website quality significantly affected user perception of usefulness and trust. Therefore, online businesses that run open markets on the Internet should develop several capabilities including convenient transaction information search, easy transaction methods, and fast system access, to improve the perception of usefulness and trust. However, the results showed that perceived website quality did not significantly contribute to consumer satisfaction. A possible explanation is that satisfaction in the open market depends on transaction experiences, which are the most noticeable uncertainty related to trust, because users may overlook website quality.

The results also showed that perceived usefulness did not affect purchase intention. A possible explanation is that the responders in this study were consumers who have had several purchase experiences in open markets. Since they know that there are risks involved in C2C e-commerce, low price may be the only factor to influence new users' purchase intention. However, perceived usefulness was still an important issue related to purchase intention and the findings showed perceived usefulness influenced purchase intention indirectly through satisfaction. Third party recognition seems to have a significant effect on trust. This means that consumers in this study did care about third parties, their reputation, vendor evaluation system, and the number of successful transactions.

References

1. He, D.H., Lu, Y.B., Zhou, D.Y.: Empirical study of consumers' purchase intentions in C2C electronic commerce. Tsinghua Science and Technology 13, 287–292 (2008)
2. Vijayasarathy, L.R.: Predicting consumer intentions to use on-line shopping: the case for an augmented technology acceptance model. Information and Management 41, 747–762 (2004)

3. Jones, K., Leonard, L.N.K.: Trust in consumer-to-consumer electronic commerce. Information and Management 45, 88–95 (2008)
4. Davis, F.D.: Perceived usefulness, perceived ease of use, and user acceptance of information technology. MIS Quarterly 13, 319–340 (1989)
5. Poddar, A., Donthu, N., Wei, Y.J.: Web site customer orientations, Web site quality, and purchase intentions: the role of web site personality. Journal of Business Research 62, 441–450 (2009)
6. Szymanski, D.M., Hise, R.T.: e-Satisfaction: an initial examination. Journal of Retailing 76, 309–322 (2000)
7. Jeong, M., Lambert, C.: Adaptation of an information quality framework to measure customers' behavioral intentions to use lodging Web sites. International Journal of Hospitality Management 20, 129–146 (2001)
8. McKnight, D.H., Chervany, N.L.: What trust means in e-commerce customer relationships: an interdisciplinary conceptual typology. International Journal of Electronic Commerce 6, 35–59 (2002)
9. Schlosser, A.E., White, T.B., Lloyd, S.M.: Converting web site visitors into buyers: how web site investment increases consumer trusting beliefs and online purchase intentions. Journal of Marketing 70, 133–148 (2006)
10. Liao, C.C., Palvia, P., Lin, H.N.: The roles of habit and web site quality in e-commerce. International Journal of Information Management 26, 469–483 (2006)
11. Bai, B., Law, R., Wen, I.: The impact of website quality on customer satisfaction and purchase intentions: evidence from Chinese online visitors. International Journal of Hospitality Management 27, 391–402 (2008)
12. Everard, A., Galletta, D.F.: How presentation flaws affect perceived site quality, trust, and intention to purchase from an online store. Journal of Management Information Systems 22, 55–95 (2006)
13. Fishbein, M., Ajzen, I.: Belief, attitude, intention and behavior: an introduction to theory and research, Reading, MA (1975)
14. Adamson, I., Shine, J.: Extending the new technology acceptance model to measure the end user information systems satisfaction in a mandatory environment: a bank's treasury. Technology Analysis and Strategic Management 15, 441–455 (2003)
15. Lee, H.S., Choi, S.Y., Kang, Y.S.: Formation of e-satisfaction and repurchase intention: Moderating roles of computer self-efficacy and computer anxiety. Expert Systems with Application 36, 7848–7859 (2009)
16. Lee, M.K.O., Turban, E.: A trust model for consumer Internet shopping. International Journal of Electronic Commerce 6, 75–91 (2001)
17. Sultan, F., Venkatesh, S., Urban, G.L.: Online trust: A stakeholder perspective, concepts, implications and future directions. Journal of Strategic Information System 11, 325–344 (2002)
18. Gefen, D., Harris, L., Goode, M.: The four levels of loyalty and the pivotal role of trust: a study of online service dynamics. Journal of Retailing 80, 139–158 (2004)
19. McKnight, D.H., Choudhury, V., Kacmar, C.: Developing and validating trust measures for e-commerce: an integrative typology. Information Systems Research 13, 334–359 (2002)
20. Wakefield, R., Whitten, D.: Examining user perceptions of third-party organization credibility and trust in an e-retailer. Journal of Organizational and End User Computing 18, 1–19 (2006)
21. Ajzen, I., Fishbein, M.: Understanding attitudes and predicting social behavior. Prentice-Hall, Englewood Cliffs (1980)

22. Chow, S., Holden, R.: Toward an understanding of loyalty: the moderating role of trust. Journal of Managerial Issues 9, 275–299 (1997)
23. Singh, J., Sirdeshmukh, D.: Agency and trust mechanisms in consumer satisfaction and loyalty judgments. Journal of the Academy of Marketing Science 28, 150–167 (2000)
24. Jin, B., Park, J.Y.: The moderating effect of online purchase experience on the evaluation of online store attributes and the subsequent impact on market response outcomes. Advances in Consumer Research 33, 203–211 (2006)
25. Zeithaml, L.B., Parasuraman, A.: The behavioral consequences of service quality. Journal of Marketing 60, 31–46 (1996)
26. Ajzen, I., Driver, B.E.: Application of the theory of planned behavior to leisure choice. Journal of Leisure Research 24, 207–224 (1992)
27. Fournier, S., Mick, D.G.: Rediscovering satisfaction. Journal of Marketing 63, 5–23 (1999)
28. Thong, J.Y.L., Hong, S.J., Tam, K.Y.: The effects of post-adoption beliefs on the expectation-confirmation model for information technology continuance. International Journal of Human-Computer Studies 64, 799–810 (2006)
29. Yang, Z., Peterson, R.T.: Customer perceived value, satisfaction, and loyalty: the role of switching costs. Psychology and Marketing 21, 799–822 (2004)
30. Qiu, L.Y., Li, D.: Applying TAM in B2C e-commerce research: an extended model. Tsinghua Science and Technology 13, 265–272 (2008)
31. Williamson, O.E.: Markets and Hierarchies. Free Press, New York (1975)
32. Sirdeshmukh, D., Singh, J., Sabol, B.: Consumer trust, value, and loyalty in relational exchanges. Journal of Marketing 66, 15–37 (2002)
33. Gefen, D., Heart, T.: On the need to include national culture as a central issue in E-commerce trust beliefs. Journal of Global Information Management 14, 1–30 (2006)
34. Kim, J.Y., Jin, Y.H., Swinney, J.L.: The role of etail quality, e-satisfaction and e-trust in online loyalty development process. Journal of Retailing and Consumer Services 16, 239–247 (2009)
35. Gefen, D., Straub, D.W.: Consumer trust in B2C e-commerce and the importance of social presence: experiments in e-Products and e-Services. Omega 32, 407–424 (2004)

Service Oriented Approach for Autonomous Exception Management in Supply Chains

Armando Guarnaschelli, Omar Chiotti, and Enrique Salomone

INGAR-CONICET, Avellaneda 3657, S3002GJC
Santa Fe
{guarnaschelli,chiotti,salomone}@santafe-conicet.gov.ar

Abstract. Risk and uncertainty are inherent to Supply Chains; at the execution level unexpected events can disrupt the normal flow of supply processes creating a gap between planned operations and what is actually executed. These disruptions increment rescheduling frequency, generating reconfiguration costs and system's nervousness. This work proposes a web service based Business Process to support Autonomous Exception Management in Supply chains.

Keywords: Supply Chain, Exception, Rescheduling, Web Services.

1 Introduction

A supply chain is an event driven system and requires the task of execution control. Either done manually or through an Execution Control System this task includes the monitoring of events during the execution of an scheduled set of supply process orders, detecting unexpected events, and alerting of exceptions caused or likely to be caused by some of them. An exception can be defined as a deviation in the execution that prevents the fulfillment of one or more of these supply process orders. Within a supply chain an exception not only affects its epicenter but also propagates throughout and many times amplifying its effects as it goes farther away.

In presence of an unexpected event, the execution system has to identify its source and communicate it to all interested parties within the supply chain. If the execution schedule is robust enough the variation caused by the event can be absorbed, and execution continues, if not the execution schedule becomes invalid and consequently this triggers a rescheduling task. Current Supply Chain Management Systems lack of systematic approaches to exception/disruption management. This is a deficiency that needs to be addressed to preserve a supply chain competitive in the future landscape. As stated in [1] future supply chains will be more adaptive (able to react quickly and correctly to changes) and unexpected events will be managed and contained on site making rescheduling activities less frequent.

There are substantial benefits in repairing execution schedules rather than triggering full rescheduling activities. The methods found in the literature do not explicitly exploit the slack provided to resources in their execution schedule. If these slacks were systematically exploited, the ability to repair a disrupted schedule would be increased. Moreover most methods to repair schedules we have found in the literature [2-4] do not consider the distributed nature of supply chains.

W. Cellary and E. Estevez (Eds.): I3E 2010, IFIP AICT 341, pp. 292–303, 2010.

In this work we discuss a service oriented approach for supporting the business process of autonomous exception management in the context of supply chain execution control. We make an abstraction of the underlying monitoring and execution system and we adopt a service oriented approach to provide the functionality for handling exceptions and repairing disrupted supply processes, through standardized and self-contained descriptions that can be utilized by any sort of Supply Chain Execution System.

In particular, we present two essential components in the quest of building a service oriented solution to the mentioned problem. The first is an Exception Management Business Process, the second is a Feasibility Restoration Service.

These components are developed over the basis of a Reference Model for Supply Processes Exception Management, necessary to provide a general understanding of the problematic of execution control among supply chain business partners, previously described in [5]. This model has two main features: a) provides a self-contained description of any ongoing execution schedule of supply process orders with all the information required to assess its feasibility; b) it allows the automatic transformation into a constraint satisfaction program suitable for the autonomous search of local solutions for disrupted schedules.

These two features of the Reference model have been exploited to design an exception management business process, which autonomously supports the management of supply chain exceptions. In the context of this work the concept of exception management is addressed in a specific sense: automatically repairing a disrupted schedule with the advantages of: given an unexpected event, detecting future exceptions in advance across a whole supply chain, and everywhere possible avoiding the occurrence of exceptions making allowed local changes in execution schedules.

The business process relies on a service for feasibility restoration which uses instances of the reference model as the main business document to be exchanged with every partner's execution control process. The service encapsulates the functionality for translating this business document into a problem description suitable for automatic solution and return repaired schedules in the same form. We introduce the internal mechanism of this service which embeds a local repair algorithm for disrupted schedules. Finally an empirical validation of the proposed solution is given in form of a case study

2 Related Work

As Exception Management is a subject studied in many different areas we have identified two main areas closely related to our work, the generic area of complex software systems, and the specific area of Supply Chain Event Management (SCEM) Systems.

There is a parallelism between Exception Management in Supply Chains and exception handling in complex software systems such as Workflow Management Systems, Process Management Systems and Self-healing Systems. In the area of Workflow Management Systems the support for exception handling goes from the definition of exception handlers and methods for the specification of exceptional behavior to classification and forecasting of exceptions in workflows [6-8]. In Process

Management Systems the definition of exception handlers invoked under given conditions provide support for given types of exceptions [9-10]. And in the area of self-healing systems applied to service based applications and process management there are several approaches that diagnose faulty situations and to select and/or search for a recovery strategy [11-12]. While these approaches are useful frameworks for managing exceptions of general business processes, the nature of exceptions in the specific domain of supply chain processes can be exploited to build more powerful corrective actions to re-establish feasibility at the same time the exception is being handled.

In our work we intend to provide this additional feature by capturing, in a systematic way, the aspects of the supply process feasibility needed to automate a reparation mechanism.

Supply Chain Event Management is defined as the business process where significant events are timely recognized, reactive actions are quickly triggered, the material and information flows are adjusted and the key actors are immediately notified [13]. SCEM solutions according to [14] must implement the functions of: i) Monitor, providing on-going information about supply chain processes, workflows, and events, including the current status of inventories, orders, shipments, production, and supply. ii) Notification to relevant actors. iii) Simulation, supporting decision making by assessing what will happen if specific actions occur. iv) Control, letting a decision maker to introduce corrective actions, such as diverting a shipment or expediting an order. v) Measure, for assessing how well the supply chain performs.

Research in SCEM systems has mainly focused in addressing the monitoring, the capture and the communication of disruptive events. The ability to exert corrective control actions has been identified as an area barely explored [13, 15]. In our approach we allow the generation of a repaired execution plan that puts back on track the normal flows and also keeps alterations (actions needed to repair) to the original plan minimal (within planned slacks). The work of [16] gives a method to search for solutions to disruptions based on multi-agent negotiation. This approach do not consider the planned availability of resources versus resource utilization by orders), therefore the support of autonomic decisions is rather limited to give recommendations to a decision maker that will analyze them. Our work gives the basis for an autonomous exception management system automatically deriving repair actions (changes in a disrupted execution schedule) fully executable.

It is relevant to emphasize that the service oriented approach proposed in this work relies on the definition of an exception management business process that uses a Feasibility Restoration Service to generate the solution to the exception but does not require any specific architecture in the underlying SCEM system or execution control system in the supply chains that are affected by the exception.

3 An Exception Management Reference Model

3.1 Modeling Supply Processes

Whenever an exception occurs it is important to track its origin and delimit its propagation, to be able to attenuate its effects or even eliminating them. To do this we describe an on going execution schedule and the possible sources and propagation paths of an exception as a net of Resources and Supply Process Orders (SPOs) linking them. We adopt this representation not only because it can show the origin and propagation of an exception, but also allows monitoring and controlling events and exceptions at their origin, communication of the exceptions to the proper receptor (whoever has control of the resources and SPO involved) through the Supply Process Orders and eventually the evaluation of exception's effects propagation and impact.

In (Fig.1) we provide a UML Class Diagram Representation of a general Supply Process, linked Supply Processes conform a net of Resources and SPOs.

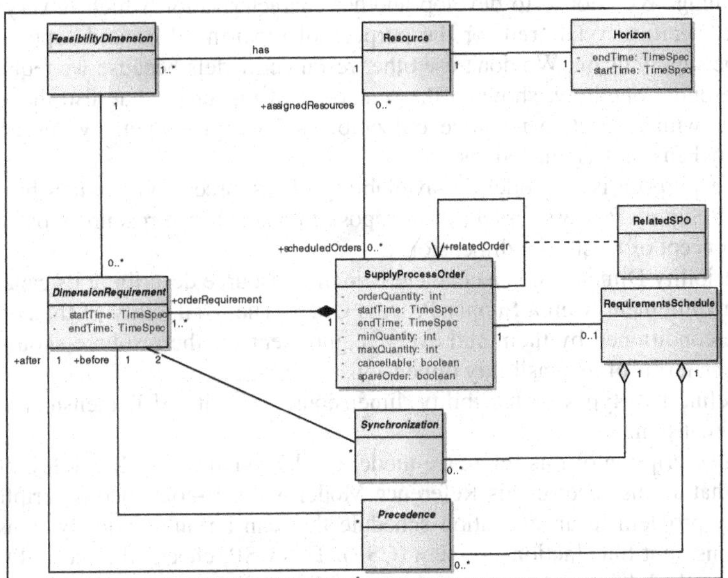

Fig. 1. Modeling Supply Processes

As stated in (Fig. 1) Class Diagram, a Supply Process is defined, through a SupplyProcessOrder (SPO), which is composed by a set of DimensionRequirements imposed to every FeasibilityDimension of the resources assigned for the execution of the SPO. When two SPOs belong to different business partners, their relation is captured by the association class RelatedSPO, which implies relationships between the two SPOs, such as same orderQuantity, same timing, etc.

Some SPOs, can be cancelled in favor of the feasibility of execution of other SPOs, and there can be special SPOs called spare, that are only executed in case of emergency, for example an SPO using a 3PL (third party logistics provider).

In a typical Supply Chain, an exception can cause different kind of losses, amongst them service level diminishment of the node causing the exception and in general for the whole supply chain. But the exception might not affect the totality of the on going execution schedule of the exception related nodes, but instead a set O of Supply Process Orders (SPO). Every SPO ε O is related to a set of resources required for its fulfillment belonging to any of the affected nodes. Whatever the exception, if the information required is on hand, it is possible to trace its origin to the unavailability of one of the related resources or to a change in one SPO.

3.2 Describing Resources by Feasibility Dimensions

In order to assess a resource's availability, the feasibility of its schedule and to evaluate the effects of events and exceptions, it is necessary to describe resources. A possible attempt is to classify resources by types as in [17], but this has the drawback that resources in a supply chain can be quite diverse, a more generic and extensible characterization is needed. There is a widely known resource characterization developed by [18] and is intended to use for the specification of scheduling model in constraint programming. We choose to develop another characterization which is very general also, but specifically tailored for the purpose of repairing disrupted supply process across the supply chain. We don't use other resource models because we require more than a resource ontology, showing the semantics of resources, but also the syntactic properties with respect to resource utilization and we give them by describing resources by Feasibility Dimensions.

As our purpose is to model the availability of resources and the feasibility of its scheduled Supply Process Orders, we propose to characterize resources by introducing the concept of feasibility dimensions.

A Feasibility Dimension is a characteristic of a resource describing its capability to fulfill a requirement from a Supply Process Order. The availability of the resource is therefore conditioned by them and every requirement for the resource should be expressible in terms of its feasibility dimensions.

We define two types of feasibility dimensions, Capacitated Dimension and State Based Dimension.

A full description of this reference model can be found in [5]. It is relevant to emphasize that an instance of this Reference Model is a self-contained description of a feasibility problem in an execution schedule that can be automatically transformed into a Constraint Satisfaction Problem (CSP). This CSP, checks the feasibility of the execution schedule, and also gives the possibility of identifying slacks in order to device a repair mechanism with minimum modifications, as the one presented here.

4 Exception Management Business Process Using a Web Service

The inter-organizational nature of Supply Chain Management requires coordination between different Supply Chain partners. Acknowledging this fact we rely the coordinated search for solutions given a disruption to a Specialized Compound Web Service called Feasibility Restoration Service (FRS). Autonomous Exception Management requires the existence of a Supply Chain Execution Control System, these Systems are usually specific and private for each Supply Chain partner. Therefore, a possible solution for this inter-organizational problem is using a third party FRS, that having the ability to understand Execution Schedules offers the functions of Exception Detection (evaluate the impact of an unexpected event) and automated repair of disrupted Supply Processes. This repair is done strictly using SPOs and resources explicitly scheduled slacks, and discovering implicit slacks, hidden in the interaction between SPOs and Resources.

The rationale of choosing a service oriented solution is that any effective business process to deal with exceptions in supply chains must be inter-organizational by nature. By adopting this type of architecture we can better address complex issues like the extent of information being shared among different parties, the control of the collaborative flows and the systems interoperability.

The FRS allows having a global view of the ramification of an exception across any number of business partners yet keeping the information of each partner isolated from the others.

4.1 Business Process Description

The EMBP begins when the Supply Chain Execution Control System (SCEC) identifies an unexpected event. Assuming previous service contract between SCEC and FRS, a *Request for Evaluation* is sent to the FRS. This request includes a business document which is an instance of the Exception Management Reference Mode, that is a Net of Supply Processes. This net might be the full Supply Chain Schedule, or just a portion where the event emerged.

To evaluate the event, the minimal information shared must contain, the origin of the event together with the associated resources if it was a SPO, or the associated SPOs, if the origin was a resource.

Then the FRS evaluates the unexpected event using the *Evaluate Unexpected Event* Service, if the event does not affect the Net of Supply Process, the EMBP finishes, as the scheduled slacks absorbed the effects of the unexpected event. If not, and the schedule results to be infeasible a notification is sent to the SCEC, and this must decide whether to rely on the FRS to search for a solution to this exception, or generate an alarm, using the FRS as a feasibility evaluation service.

If the SCEC decides to rely on the FRS to search for a solution another stage of the EMBP takes place, in it the FRS tries to find a local feasible solution to the disrupted schedule using the RepairNet service. The effort to search for this solution is based on the incremental sharing of Schedule information from the SCEC. This information is shared until a solution is found, and then the SCEC implements the new feasible schedule or until a solution was not found and the net cannot longer be expanded, or the SCEC is not willing to share more information. (Fig. 4) shows a BPMN [19] specification of the FRS. The aforementioned services Evaluate Unexpected Event and RepairNet are implemented using the CSP in [5]. In (Fig. 4) the relationship between the business document (an instance of the Exception Management Reference Model) and the FRS with these subservices is shown.

It is important to emphasize that an unexpected event may or may not cause an exception, monitoring resources, supply process orders and detecting deviations in their planned values is the way to detect unexpected events, the reference model intrinsically implies methods to detect unexpected events if there is a monitoring system of the status of resources (their availability) and the status of scheduled supply process orders (their specification) but this is not in the scope of this work in which the unexpected event is given. In fact as far as Supply Chain Execution Control concerns the only possible exceptions are caused by unexpected events that in an utopist Supply Chain can always be tracked to the unavailability of one resource, but in realistic terms resource descriptions when building execution schedules are incomplete and

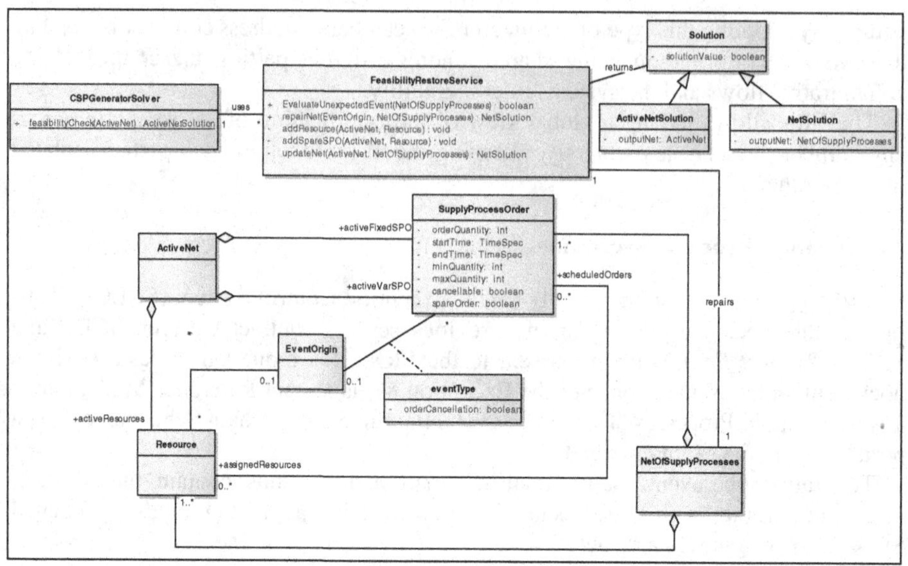

Fig. 2. Repair Service Class Diagram

whenever two different business partners interact they might have an incomplete view of each other's resources. So for these two latter cases, unexpected events are associated to supply process orders.

4.2 The Feasibility Restoration Service Internal Mechanism

The main functionality of the FRS is providing the functions of evaluating the effects of an unexpected event and repairing a disrupted schedule. Following we give a brief description of algorithm taking place when searching for a feasible solution.

Unexpected events are of two different types:

1. Events produced by unexpected changes in the availability of a controlled resource.
2. Events produced by unforeseen changes in the requirements of a Supply Process Order.

Events can also be produced by simultaneous changes in the availability of several resources and/or in the requirements of a several supply process orders. In this case, the initial reparation set will be composed of a set of resources and related orders.

An unexpected event may not cause an exception because planned resource and supply process orders slacks (in form of hedge capacity, inventory buffers, variable order sizes) might absorb automatically the variation caused by the event. Or in fact as the following mechanism proposes making small changes in resource utilization and supply process orders, reallocating these slacks can prevent the exception from taking place.

Suppose an event affected a Resource; the first stage of the mechanism checks the ability of the affected Resource to fulfill its scheduledOrders exactly as they were planned. Along the execution of this mechanism the set of SupplyProcessOrders which join it and keep their original specification is called activeFixedSPO.

If the event does not compromise the execution of any SupplyProcessOrder, which means that the CSP associated with the activeNet is feasible, then the event does not generate an exception and the outcome of the mechanism a feasibility confirmation. If a feasible solution to the activeNet's associated CSP was not found, the mechanism advances to the next stage, expanding the activeNet, and this stage is repeated until the stopping condition is fulfilled. This expansion consists in:

First: include in the set of activeVarSPO (the set of SupplyProcessOrders subject to modifications in the CSP), every spareOrder belonging to the set of scheduledOrders in the activeResources set (the set of resources in the activeNet). This also implies including the assignedResources of these recently included spareOrders, together with the scheduledOrders of these resources in the set of activeFixedOrders. If this new activeNet is feasible the Net of SupplyProcessOrders is updated with the operation updateNet, and the mechanism finishes, otherwise:

Second: Expand the net, making every SupplyProcessOrder in the activeFixedSPO set variable by including them in the activeVarSPO set and including all their assignedResources in the mechanism, together with their scheduledOrders in the set activeFixedSPO.

The stopping condition of the mechanism is fulfilled whenever a feasible solution to the CSP associated to the activeNet is found or there are no possibilities of expansion, that is the set of activeFixedSPO is empty.

The design of the Repair Mechanism was based in the concept of minimal impact on the current execution schedule, assuming that: modifications to SupplyProcessOrders and the use of resources is limited to their planned slacks, and that SupplyProcessOrders and Resources involved first are the nearest to the event origin, and expanding the involved elements only if necessary. This is a gradual radial expansion, as shown in (Fig. 3). In the figure, as the expansion takes place, the involved Resources and SupplyProcessOrders conform the ActiveNet (marked with V variable SPOs, and with F fixed SPOs) which is the subset of the Net under repair where feasibility is searched by means of the Constraint Satisfaction Model for Feasibility Check and Restoration.

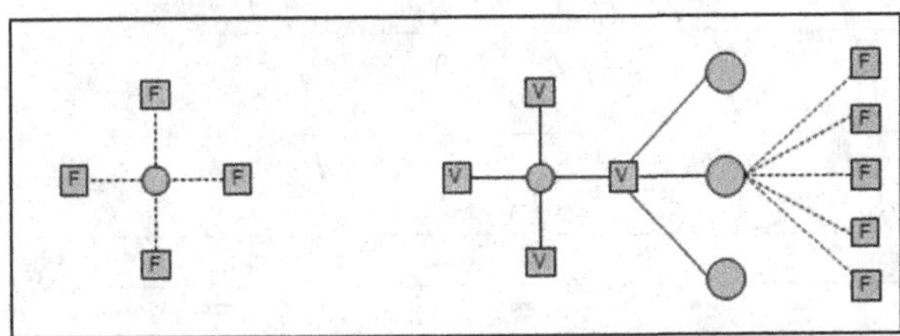

Fig. 3. Radial Expansion of the ActiveNet

Every expansion requires a request for Schedule information as stated in 3.1.

5 Urea Supply Chain Case Study for Empirical Validation

This Case Study assumes that within the supply chain exists an operative Supply Chain Execution Control System (with the functions of monitoring and requesting for the intervention of the Repair Service) where the control actions (monitor and detect exceptions) are generated using the reference model presented in section 2, therefore execution plans are described using the same reference model, and exception detection and repair actions are fulfilled using the Repair Mechanism.

In this Supply Chain Urea is produced, warehoused and distributed to three geographically distant Distribution Centers (DCs). The Factory Warehouse is located in Bahia Blanca (FWBahiaBlanca), Argentina, and DCs are: "Urea-DCSanLorenzo" at San Lorenzo, Argentina; "Urea-DCUruguay ", at Montevideo, Uruguay; "Urea-DCBrasil", at Rio Grande, Brasil.

A Distribution Resource Planning (DRP) System is used to generate a distribution schedule for a scheduling horizon of 33 days. In this schedule, product (Urea) availability in FWBahiaBlanca is considered to be infinite, this means that urea stock, demand and supply is managed for each Distribution Center attending constraints regarding to: Ships routes and availability, loading dock availability at factory warehouse, and inventory size and safety stocks constraints at each DC.

Two unexpected events were simulated the first consisted in the unavailability of a ship used to source "DC-Brasil" which was solved by using an alternative resource, provided by a 3PL (3rd party logistics provider). And the second consisted in a set of concurrent events that implied that 10 orders from DC-Uruguay augmented their size. This event was caused by absorbing the market share of a competitor who had an inventory stock-out. This would have caused an exception but the FRS found a solution and the possible exception and the solution can be seen in (Fig. 5). The solution consisted in checking the possibility of making an earlier second replenishment of Urea, this implied checking capacities and states of the ship, the loading dock, and the availability of Urea.

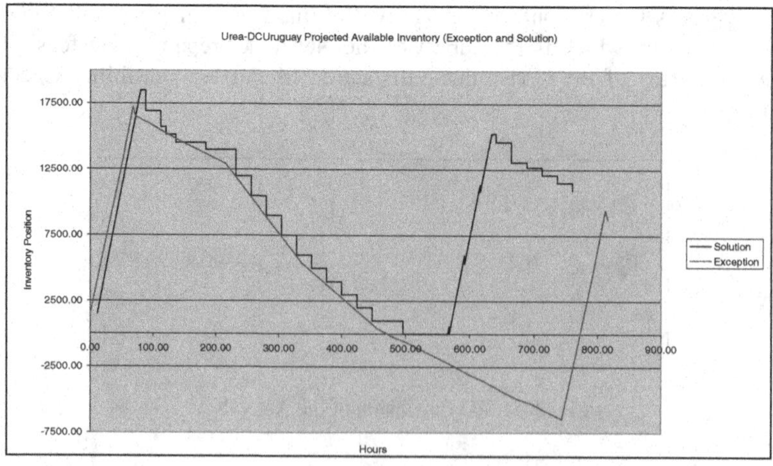

Fig. 4. Exception Solution given by the FRS

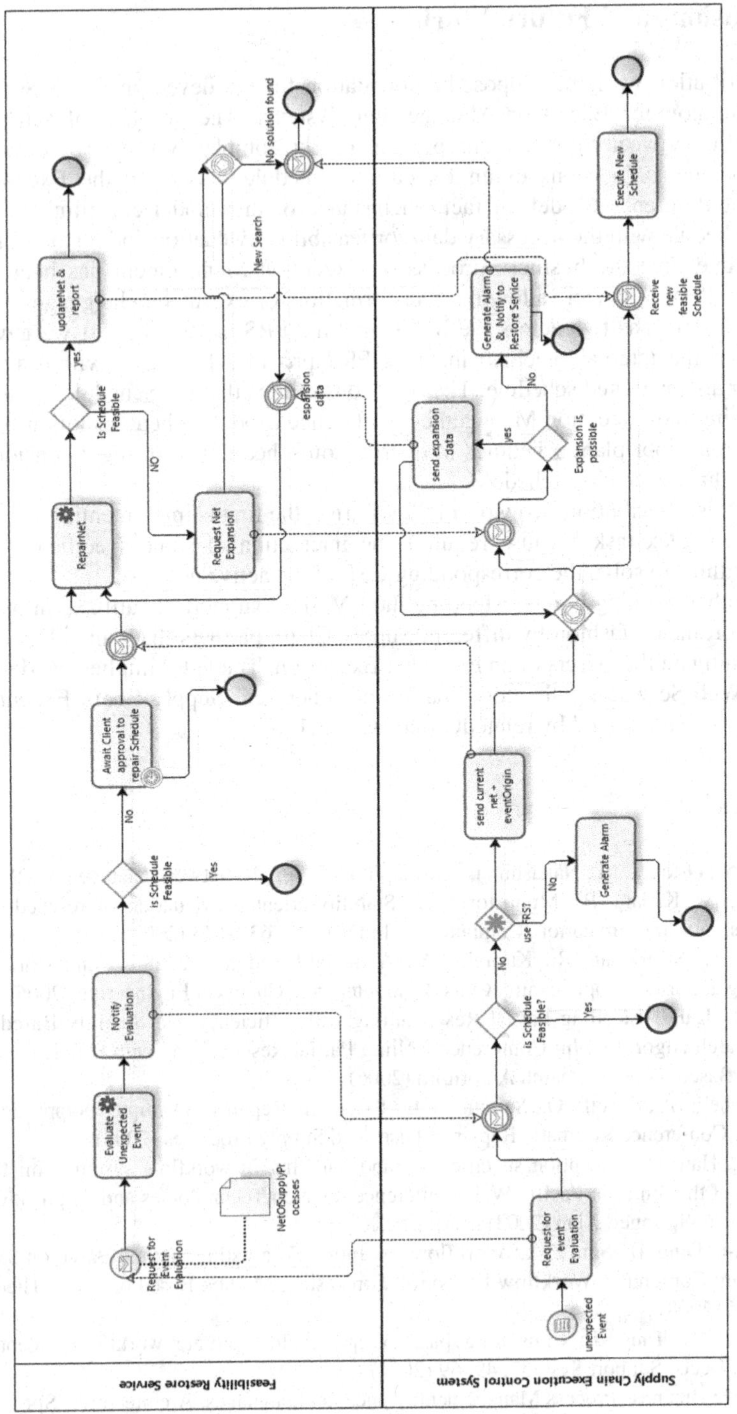

Fig. 5. Exception Management Business Process

6 Conclusions and Future Work

In this contribution we have proposed a foundation for the development of Service Oriented Autonomous Exception Management Systems. The problem of semantic interoperability between Supply Chain partners can be completely solved by defining business documents (portions of an Execution Schedule) based on the Exception Management Reference Model, in fact, an instance of this model constitutes a full execution schedule with the necessary data for feasibility evaluation and restoration.

At the same time the business process of Exception Management has been described as a BPMN model, allowing transformation to executable languages such BPEL. The EMBP has two actors the SCEC and the FRS, so for the last we gave a description of the internal mechanism. This FRS provides local and within slacks solutions for any disrupted schedule. The only constraint is that the Schedule has to be described using the Exception Management Reference Model. Schedules might be of any nature from floor plant schedules to distribution schedules, and might consider a full Supply Chain execution schedule.

Based in this contribution two working lines arise, the first is implementing a FRS, which is a complex task because requires the interaction of some specifically designed algorithms to solve the corresponding CSP of the active net.

And the other working line is extending the EMBP to support the utilization of the FRS in a coordinated fashion by different Supply Chain partners that can collaborate in order to mitigate the effects of an extended Exception. The latter implies the design of another Web Service for the coordination of concurrent Supply Chain Execution Schedules, which are linked by relatedOrders as in 3.1.

References

1. Radjou, N., Orlov, L.M., Nakashima, T.: Adapting To Supply Network Change (2002)
2. Pfeiffera, A., Kádára, B., Monostoria, L.: Stability-oriented evaluation of rescheduling strategies, by using simulation. Computers in Industry 58, 630–643 (2007)
3. Adhitya, A., Srinivasan, R., Karimi, I.A.: A model-based rescheduling framework for managing abnormal supply chain events. Computers and Chemical Engineering (2006)
4. Wang, B., Liu, T.: Rolling Partial Rescheduling with Efficiency and Stability Based on Local Search Algorithm. In: Conference Rolling Partial Rescheduling with Efficiency and Stability Based on Local Search Algorithm (2006)
5. Guarnaschelli, A., Chiotti, O., Salomone, E.: Sytematic Repair of Disrupted Supply Processes. In: Conference Sytematic Repair of Disrupted Supply Processes (2008)
6. Song, Y., Han, D.: Exception specification and handling in workflow systems. In: Proceedings of the 5th Asia-Pacific Web Conference on Web Technologies and Applications, pp. 495–506. Springer, Xian (2003)
7. Yuan, H.-t., Ding, B., Sun, Z.-x.: Workflow Exception Forecasting Method Based on SVM Theory. In: Conference Workflow Exception Forecasting Method Based on SVM Theory, pp. 81–86 (2008)
8. Hwang, S.-Y., Tang, J.: Consulting past exceptions to facilitate workflow exception handling. Decis. Support Syst. 37, 49–69 (2004)
9. Weske, M.: Business Process Management: Concepts, Languages, Architectures. Springer, New York (2007)

10. Hamadi, R., Benatallah, B., Medjahed, B.: Self-adapting recovery nets for policy-driven exception handling in business processes. Distributed and Parallel Databases 23, 1–44 (2008)
11. Griffith, R., Kaiser, G., Silva, L., Alonso, J.: 243, Multi-perspective evaluation of self-healing systems using simple probabilistic models. In: Proceedings of the 6th International Conference on Autonomic Computing, pp. 59–60. ACM, Barcelona (2009)
12. Friedrich, G., Fugini, M., Mussi, E., Pernici, B., Tagni, G.: Exception Handling for Repair in Service-Based Processes. IEEE Transactions on Software Engineering 36, 198–215 (2010)
13. Bearzotti, L., Salomone, E., Chiotti, O.: An autonomous multi-agent approach to supply chain event management. In: Conference An Autonomous Multi-Agent Approach to Supply Chain Event Management, pp. 524–529 (2008)
14. Montgomery, N., Waheed, R.: Supply Chain Event Management Enables Companies to Take Control of Extended Supply Chains (2001)
15. Zimmermann, R.: Agent-based Supply Network Event Management (2006)
16. Cauvin, A.C.A., Ferrarini, A.F.A., Tranvouez, E.T.E.: Disruption management in distributed enterprises: A multi-agent modelling and simulation of cooperative recovery behaviours. International Journal of Production Economics 122, 429–439 (2009)
17. Weiss, T.B., McGann, C., Ramakrishnan, S.: Formalizing Resources for Planning. In: Conference Formalizing Resources for Planning (2003)
18. Le Pape, C.: Implementation of Resource Constraints in ILOG Schedule: A Library for the Development of Constraint-Based Scheduling systems. Intelligent Systems Engineering 3, 55–66 (1994)
19. OMG: OMG/BPMN 1.2: OMG Specification (2009)

Author Index

Amandi, Analía 151

Baldo, Fabiano 161
Bareño, Juan 237
Belanche, Daniel 103
Borean, Alessandro 215
Buccella, Agustina 193

Campo, Marcelo 139
Casaló, Luis V. 103
Cechich, Alejandra 193
Chiotti, Omar 40, 51, 292
Chmielewski, Jacek 29
Crasso, Marco 139
Cresswell, Anthony 2

Díaz, Alicia 205
Díaz Redondo, Rebeca P. 118
Dokoohaki, Nima 226
Doldan, Maria del Socorro 193

Echizen, Isao 70
Ende, Bartholomäus 81

Fernandez, Daniel 237
Fernández, Erica 51
Fernández Vilas, Ana 118
Flavián, Carlos 103

Gallego-Nicasio, Beatriz 237
Ginige, Athula 61
Godoy, Daniela 151
Goeken, Matthias 93
Gomber, Peter 81
Grzech, Adam 17
Guarnaschelli, Armando 292
Guo, Jingzhi 127

Ha, Sung Ho 282
Hol, Ana 61

Ito, Masaki 5

Järveläinen, Jonna 272

Kamiyama, Komei 70
Khalifa, Mohamed 173
Kimura, Taisuke 5
Knolmayer, Gerhard F. 215
Küngas, Peep 226

Lamersdorf, Winfried 4
Lau, Kwok Hung 260
Liu, Luo Tao 282
Lutat, Marco 81

Matskin, Mihhail 226
Milicevic, Danijel 93
Mokarizadeh, Shahab 226
Morsan, Enrique 193
Motz, Regina 205

Ngoc, Tran Hong 70

Oya, Makoto 5

Pasic, Aljosa 237
Pazos Arias, Jose J. 118
Pernich, Patricia 193
Petrovic, Otto 182

Rabelo, Ricardo J. 161
Rodriguez, Juan Manuel 139
Rohrer, Edelweis 205
Ruland, Christoph 249
Rygielski, Piotr 17

Salomone, Enrique 51, 292
Shen, Kathy Ning 173
Suomi, Reima 112
Świątek, Paweł 17

Tello-Leal, Edgar 40
Torres, Rubén 237

Vahtera, Annukka 272
Van Grembergen, Wim 3
Villarreal, Pablo D. 40

Walczak, Krzysztof 29
Weber, Moritz C. 81
Wiza, Wojciech 29

Xiao, Guangyi 127

Yoshiura, Hiroshi 70

Zhang, Yanchun 1
Zivic, Natasa 249
Zunino, Alejandro 139